Lynda Weinman's | Hands-On Training

Includes CD-ROM with Exercise Files and Demo Movies

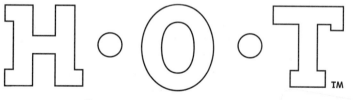

MACROMEDIA®
Dreamweaver® MX
H·O·T™
Hands-On Trair

D1316320

lynda.com/books

By **Garo Green**
and **Abigail Rudner**
developed by **Lynda Weinman**

Dreamweaver MX | H·O·T
Hands-On Training

By Garo Green and Abigail Rudner
developed with Lynda Weinman

lynda.com/books | Peachpit Press
1249 Eighth Street • Berkeley, CA • 94710
800.283.9444 • 510.524.2178 •
510.524.2221 (fax)
http://www.lynda.com/books
http://www.peachpit.com

lynda.com/books is published
in association with Peachpit Press,
a division of Pearson Education
Copyright ©2003 by lynda.com

ISBN: 0-321-11271-7

0 9 8 7 6 5 4

Printed and bound in the
United States of America

E. Ont.

H•O•T | Credits

Original Design: Ali Karp, Alink Newmedia *(alink@earthlink.net)*

lynda.com Director, Publications: Garo Green *(garo@lynda.com)*

Peachpit Project Manager: Suzie Lowey

Peachpit Copyeditor: Darren Meiss

Peachpit Proofreaders: Leslie Ayers, Darren Meiss

Peachpit Production: Myrna Vladic

Peachpit Compositors: Rick Gordon, Emerald Valley Graphics; Deborah Roberti, Espresso Graphics

Beta Testers: Steve Perry, Eleanor Culling

Cover Illustration: Bruce Heavin *(bruce@stink.com)*

Indexer: Emily Glossbrenner

H•O•T | Colophon

The original design for *Dreamweaver MX H•O•T* was sketched on paper. The layout was heavily influenced by online communication—merging a traditional book format with a modern Web aesthetic.

The text in *Dreamweaver MX H•O•T* was set in Akzidenz Grotesk from Adobe and Triplex from Emigré. The cover illustration was painted in Adobe Photoshop 6.0 and Adobe Illustrator 9.0.

This book was created using QuarkXPress 4.1, Adobe Photoshop 6.0, Microsoft Office XP, and Dreamweaver MX on a PC using Windows XP. It was printed on 50 lb. Utopia Book at Von Hoffman Graphics, Owensville, Missouri.

Dedications

For Jim Damm, a very special friend,
who took me under his wings and helped me
become the person I am today. I am so thankful for
your friendship, love, and support.

For Rosanna Yeung, my best friend,
who showed me how to be strong
in front of life's most difficult challenges.
I smile each time I think of you.

—Garo

For my father Michael M. Rudner,
who loves me, who gave me a great life,
taught me how to paint, write, and build,
to be open to the possibilities,
to see the beauty in the sublime,
to use a camera, and to love my work.

For my mother Ruth Rachel Binder Rudner
who held me like a precious treasure inside of her,
taught me to live a life like art,
to know the difference between honey and vinegar,
and who with my father taught me to play,
see, draw, paint, make pottery, build, grow, and love.

—Abigail

Dreamweaver MX | H•O•T _____ **Table of Contents**

Introduction

H•O•T
—————————————
Dreamweaver MX

A Note from Lynda Weinman

In my opinion, most people buy computer books in order to learn, yet it is amazing how few of these books are actually written by teachers. Garo Green and I take pride in the fact that this book was written by experienced teachers who are familiar with training students in this subject matter. In this book, you will find carefully developed lessons and exercises to help you learn Dreamweaver MX—one of the most well-respected HTML editors on the planet.

This book is targeted toward beginning- to intermediate-level Web developers who are looking for a great tool to speed up production, offer workflow flexibility, and create great code and results. The premise of the hands-on exercise approach is to get you up to speed quickly in Dreamweaver while actively working through the book's lessons. It's one thing to read about a product and another experience entirely to try the product and get measurable results. Our motto is, "read the book, follow the exercises, and you will know the product." We have received countless testimonials to this fact, and it is our goal to make sure it remains true for all of our hands-on training books.

Many exercise-based books take a paint-by-numbers approach to teaching. While this approach works, it's often difficult to figure out how to apply those lessons to a real-world situation, or to understand why or when you would use the technique again. What sets this book apart is that the lessons contain lots of background information and insights into each given subject, which are designed to help you understand the process as well as the exercise.

At times, pictures are worth a lot more than words. When necessary, we have also included short QuickTime movies to show any process that's difficult to explain with words. These files are located on the **H•O•T CD-ROM** inside a folder called **movies**. It's our style to approach teaching from many different angles, since we know that some people are visual learners, others like to read, and still others like to get out there and try things. This book combines a lot of teaching approaches so you can learn Dreamweaver MX as thoroughly as you want to.

This book didn't set out to cover every single aspect of Dreamweaver MX nor does it attempt to teach you the entire process of Web production. The manual, and many other reference books are great for that! What we saw missing from the bookshelves was a process-oriented tutorial that taught readers core principles, techniques, and tips in a hands-on training format.

We welcome your comments at dwmxfaq@lynda.com. Please visit our Web site at **http://www.lynda.com**. The support URL for this book is **http://www.lynda.com/products/books/dwmxhot/**.

It's Garo's and my hope that this book will raise your skills in Web design, HTML, JavaScript, and publishing. If it does, we will have accomplished the job we set out to do!

—Lynda Weinman

NOTE | About lynda.com/books and lynda.com

lynda.com/books is dedicated to helping designers and developers understand tools and design principles. **lynda.com** offers hands-on workshops, training seminars, conferences, on-site training, training videos, training CDs, and "expert tips" for design and development. To learn more about our training programs, books, and products, be sure to give our site a visit at **http://www.lynda.com**.

About Garo Green

Garo Green has been working with a wide range of computers since the tender age of 12. Those were the golden days of tape drives and 64K of RAM, when all you needed was a double-density floppy disk and a hole-puncher. ;-)

Garo has worked extensively in the development of custom curriculum and courseware for software training. He has over six years of teaching experience in both hardware and software applications. He is known worldwide for his enthusiastic, approachable, and humanistic teaching style.

Garo is the author of several Hands-On-Training books and Web design training CD-ROMs, including *Learning Dreamweaver MX, Learning Fireworks 3,* and *Learning Flash 5.* He has also been a featured speaker at the Web 99 and FlashForward2000 conferences.

In his spare time (he doesn't have much of that anymore, but that's OK), he has found that his passion for teaching and sharing what he knows is very fulfilling. He does sneak away, several times a day, to the local Starbucks for a double latte (to be honest it's usually a triple shot) with hazelnut. Of course, this might explain why he talks so fast!

About Abigail Rudner

Abigail Rudner is a dynamic designer and educator. She teaches Web design, Web graphics, illustration, and photo illustration courses with love and enthusiasm across the U.S.A. Using a synthesis of design methodology, visual thinking, and computer graphics tools and techniques, Abigail inspires and teaches students how to design and produce with purpose.

With a wealth of knowledge in marketing and psychology, as well as interactive media, Abigail and her team have produced and designed content for a wide range of Web and print projects since as early as 1991. Abigail's clients include: FAD and Publish magazines, Levi's, Wells Fargo, Dow Jones, America Online, Absolut Vodka, The SYDA Foundation, Amgen, Apple Computers, Microsoft, and Radius.

Abigail is a graduate of Parsons School of Design with a BFA in Communication Design and Photography. She is a certified trainer (via CompTIA International), a Macromedia Certified Expert in Flash, Fireworks, and Dreamweaver MX and an Adobe Certified Product Expert for PhotoShop 6.

Check out Abigail's web site at **http://www.rudner.com** or e-mail her at abigail@rudner.com.

Our Team

Lynda and Garo take a break from their busy schedules to smile at the camera.

When Garo isn't stuck behind a computer, you will find him at the nearest motocross track on his YZ125.

Abigail playing dress-up with Maya and Phoebe.

Sebastian, Garo's miniature schnauzer, getting a little too close to the camera.

Acknowledgments from Garo

This book, and every other book you read, could not have been possible without a strong team of dedicated, enthusiastic, and talented individuals. I was fortunate enough to work with the best.

My deepest thanks and appreciation to:

You, the reader. There is nothing I enjoy more than sharing what I know with others. I really like what I do, and it's my highest hope that you like it too! ;-)

My co-author Abigail Rudner. Your passion for teaching and hard work made working on this project so much fun. Good luck with your other book!

My dearest friend, Lynda Weinman; thank you for continued support and love. You have made Tuesdays a very special day of the week. ;-)

My friends at Peachpit, Nancy Ruenzel, Suzie Lowey, Nancy Davis, Cliff Colby, David Van Ness, Darren Meiss, Rebecca Pepper, Debbie Roberti, and Victor Gavenada, thank you for being there to make sure that I didn't cross my I's and dot my T's.

A special thanks to Debbie Roberti, thank you for your hard work and extra effort. Without you this project would have been impossible.

My beta testers, Steve Perry and Eleanor Culling. You guys did a great job of finding all the little mistakes. Of course, I left them there on purpose so that you would have something to do! Yeah right! ;-)

My friends at Macromedia, Dave Deming, Erik Larson, Diana Smedley, David Morris, and all of the Dreamweaver engineers. I am not sure how you did it, but Dreamweaver MX is the most amazing version of Dreamweaver yet. Keep up the good work!

The entire lynda.com staff. You guys make coming to work each day so much fun; what more could a person ask for?

Acknowledgments from Abigail

A very special thanks to all of the wonderful and loving people who have helped me, directly and indirectly with this book. Each contribution was unique, subtle, and important. Your support of me and my work is not taken for granted.

With great love, gratitude and respect, to:

My parents Michael and Ruth Rudner.

Aaron Rudner, my first best friend and number one member of our mutual admiration society!

Jennifer Michals, my best friend with benefits. Thank you for sharing your heart and your humor, for your strong support, for your patience, and for your vision.

Garo Green and of course Lynda Weinman. It has been a great honor working with you. I can't thank you enough for the opportunity to be part of creating this excellent volume and for caring as much as I do about sharing knowledge.

The Macromedia Dreamweaver MX team, for your brilliance and hard work creating a product that allows me to say I love my work!

To Diana Smedley for saying something good about me to the right person at the right time so that I eventually wound up here!

The folks at Peachpit Press. Thank you for the opportunity to learn, teach, and write about my passion in the form of this book. I will say another big thank you in advance, for all of what I do not know that will come from this work that is on the way!

Sally Smith of Connect Learning for empowering me to self-leadership, for inspiring me in so many ways, for countless amazing and wonderful hours of your time, and for believing in me.

The folks at Ciber training, Lesley Grizzell, Bill Ramirez, Amy Shen, and Jennifer Murray. Thank you for your support and encouragement and for believing in me.

My friends and associates, Steve McGuire, John Ulliman, Jennifer Gertz, Pippa Green, Kathy Klein, Fred Delisios, Carl Merchant, deAnna Harper, Lisa Kaplan, Dr. Lenny Cocco, and Patricia McDade.

My grandparents Abraham Binder and Golda Riva Goldstein Binder Klein, Hanna Garber Rudner, and Harry Rudner.

Dana Hope Margolis, for your support, coaching, guidance, and love, and for helping me to "be" in the best way possible.

My beloved Guru Mayi, Baba and Bagawan for your grace, compassion, guidance, and protection and for giving me the inner knowledge, vision, and experience of Muktananda and Chidvilasananda. I will never stop thanking your golden heart and laying my head at your lotus feet.

How to Use This Book

Please read this section—it contains important information that's going to help you as you use this book. The chart below outlines the information we cover:

Dreamweaver MX H•O•T
Information in this section:
The Formatting in This Book
HTML versus HTM
Macintosh and Windows Interface Screen Captures

Mac and Windows System Differences
  • "Open" for Mac and "Select" for Windows
  • "Open" in Mac System Is "Choose" in System 8.6

A Note to Windows Users
  • Making Exercise Files Editable on Windows Systems
  • Making File Extensions Visible on Windows Systems
  • Creating New Documents

Dreamweaver System Requirements
What's on the CD-ROM?

NOTE | The Formatting in This Book

This book has several components, including step-by-step exercises, commentary, notes, tips, warnings, and movies. Step-by-step exercises are numbered, and file names and command keys are shown in bold so they pop out more easily. Captions and commentary are in italicized text: *This is a caption.* File names/folders, command keys, and menu commands are bolded: **images** folder, **Ctrl+click,** and **File > Open.** Code is in a monospace font: **<html></html>.** And URLs are in bold: **http://www.lynda.com**.

HTML versus HTM

All of the HTML exercise files on the CD-ROM end with an .html extension. Windows users might be more used to naming files with an .htm extension. You can name your files either way, and a Web browser will be able to read them. The choice to name them with the four-letter extension represents a personal bias of ours. The shorter .htm suffix is a throwback to the old days of DOS when file names were limited to the eight-dot-three convention. That meant that file names could be no longer than eight characters and had to end with a dot and a three-letter extension. Those days are history since the advent of Windows 95/98/2000/XP, so we've named all the files with the more accurate four-letter extension. It does, after all, stand for HyperText Markup Language, not HyperText Markup! Now you know why we chose to name the files this way, but the bottom line here is that you can use either naming method and your HTML files will still work, as long as they have been referenced this way in the links. We simply made a choice to use the four-letter extension because that's what we prefer.

Macintosh and Windows Interface Screen Captures

Most of the screen captures in this book were taken on a PC using Windows XP. The only time we used Macintosh shots was when the interface differed from the PC under Windows XP. We made this decision because Garo does most of his writing on a PC. We also own and use Macintosh systems, so we noted important differences when they occurred and took screen captures accordingly.

Mac and Windows System Differences

Macromedia has done a great job of ensuring that Dreamweaver MX looks and works the same between the Macintosh and Windows operating systems. However, there are still some differences that should be noted. If you are using this book with one of the Windows operating systems, please be sure to read the following section, titled "*A Note to Windows Users*," carefully.

WARNING | "Choose" for Mac and "OK" for Windows

Throughout this book, you will be instructed to click the **Choose** button. This is the correct way to do it on the PC using Windows XP. On a Macintosh running OS X, you will instead see an **Open** button. The two buttons are interchangeable and do the same thing.

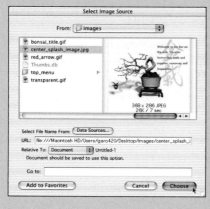

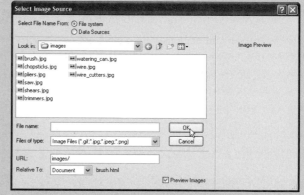

Click Choose on a Macintosh using OS X.

Click OK in Windows XP.

WARNING | "Open" in Mac System 9 Is "Choose" in System 8.6

Since some of you will be using System 8 and others System 9, it is necessary to be aware of the following difference. When you **Browse for Files**, System 8 displays a **Choose** button, whereas System 9 displays an **Open** button. Both buttons perform the same function, even though they have different names.

A Note to Windows Users

This section contains essential information about making your exercise folders editable, making file extensions visible, and creating new Dreamweaver documents from the document window versus the Site window.

Making Exercise Files Editable on Windows Systems

By default, when you copy files from a CD-ROM to your Windows 95/98/2000 hard drive, they are set to read-only (write protected). This will cause a problem with the exercise files, because you will need to write over some of them. When you define a site (you will learn to do this in Chapter 3, "*Site Control*"), you will notice that the files have a small lock next to them, which means they have been set to read-only. To remove this setting and make them editable, follow the short procedure below:

Note: *You do not need to follow these steps if you are using Windows NT, Windows XP Home Edition, or Windows XP Professional Edition.*

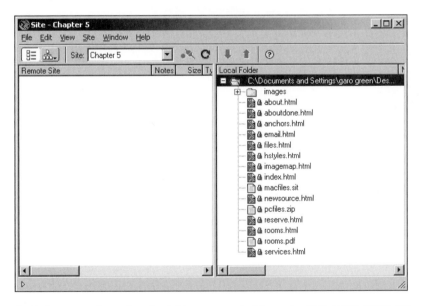

1. Define your site, using the folder you copied from the **H•O•T CD-ROM**. When the Site window opens, you will see little locks next to all of the files.

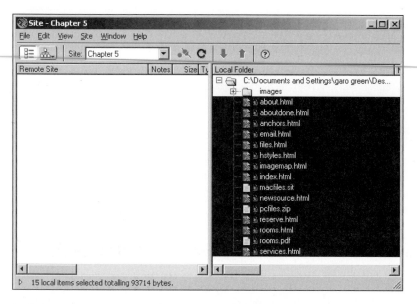

2. Ctrl+click on each of the files that has a lock next to it.

3. Once you have all of the files selected, select **File > Turn Off Read Only**.

Making File Extensions Visible on Windows Systems

In this section, you'll see three different examples of how to turn on file extensions for Windows 95, Windows 98, and Windows 2000. By default, Windows 95/98/2000 users cannot see file extensions, such as .gif, .jpg, or .html. Fortunately you can change this setting!

Windows 95 Users:

1. Double-click on the **My Computer** icon on your desktop. **Note:** If you (or someone else) have changed the name, it will not say **My Computer**.

2. Select **View > Options**. This opens the **Options** dialog box.

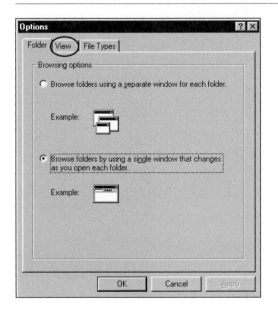 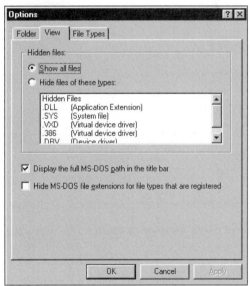

3. Click on the **View** tab at the top. This opens the **View** options screen so you can change the view settings for Windows 95.

4. Make sure there is no checkmark in the **Hide MS-DOS file extensions for file types that are registered** box. This ensures that the file extensions are visible, which will help you better understand the exercises in this book!

Windows 98 Users:

1. Double-click on the **My Computer** icon on your desktop. **Note:** If you (or someone else) have changed the name, it will not say **My Computer**.

2. Select **View > Folder Options**. This opens the **Folder Options** dialog box.

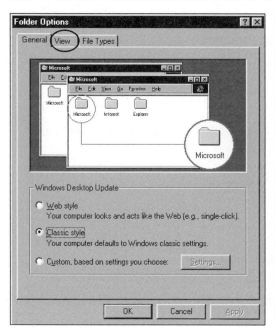 

3. Click on the **View** tab at the top. This opens the **View** options screen so you can change the view settings for Windows 98.

4. Uncheck the **Hide file extensions for known file types** checkbox. This makes all of the file extensions visible.

Windows 2000 Users:

1. Double-click on the **My Computer** icon on your desktop. **Note:** If you (or someone else) have changed the name, it will not say **My Computer**.

2. Select **Tools > Folder Options**. This opens the **Folder Options** dialog box.

3. Click on the **View** tab at the top. This opens the **View** options screen so you can change the view settings for Windows 2000.

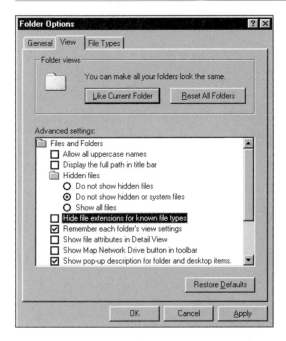

4. Make sure there is no checkmark next to the **Hide file extensions for known file types** option. This makes all of the file extensions visible.

Windows XP Users:

1. Double-click on the **My Computer** icon on your desktop. **Note:** If you (or someone else) have changed the name, it will not say **My Computer**.

2. Select **Tools > Folder Options**. This opens the **Folder Options** dialog box.

3. Click on the **View** tab at the top. This opens the **View** options screen so you can change the view settings for Windows XP.

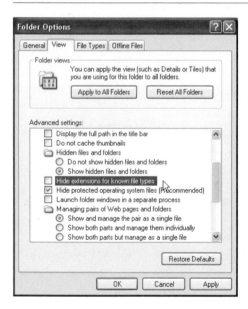

4. Make sure there is no checkmark next to the **Hide extensions for known file types** option. This makes all of the file extensions visible.

Creating New Documents

Creating a new document in the Windows version of Dreamweaver MX can vary a little, depending on whether you are in the document window or the Site panel.

• To create a new document with the document window open, select **File > New** or press **Ctrl+N**. This will open the New Document dialog box where you can choose a template to start your page.

• To create a new document that opens as a blank document window from the Site window, select **File > New File**. The document would appear only in the Site window, and not as a new untitled HTML document.

Dreamweaver MX System Requirements

This book requires that you use either a Macintosh operating system (Power Macintosh G3 running System 9.1 or later) or Windows 98, Windows 2000, or Windows NT 4.0, Windows ME, or Windows XP. You also will need a color monitor capable of 800 x 600 resolution and a CD-ROM drive. We suggest that you have at least 128 MB of RAM in your system, because that way you can open Dreamweaver and a Web browser at the same time. More RAM than that is even better, especially on Macintosh computers, which do not dynamically allocate RAM, as Windows does. Here's a little chart that cites Macromedia's RAM requirements, along with our recommendations:

Dreamweaver MX System Requirements		
	Dreamweaver Requires	We Recommend
Mac	96 MB	128 MB
Windows 95/98/NT	96 MB	128 MB

What's on the CD-ROM?

Exercise Files and the H•O•T CD-ROM

Your course files are located inside a folder called **exercise_files** on the **H•O•T CD-ROM**. These files are divided into chapter folders, and you will be instructed to copy the chapter folders to your hard drive during many of the exercises. Unfortunately, when files originate from a CD-ROM, under some Windows operating systems, it defaults to making them write-protected, meaning that you cannot alter them. You will need to alter them to follow the exercises, so please read the "Note to Windows Users" on pages xxiii and xxiv for instructions on how to convert them to read-and-write formatting.

Demo Files on the CD-ROM

In addition to the exercise files, the **H•O•T CD-ROM** also contains free 30-day trial versions of several software applications for the Mac or Windows. All software is located inside the **software** folder on the **H•O•T CD-ROM**. We have included trial versions of:
  • Macromedia Dreamweaver MX (trial version)
  • Macromedia Fireworks MX (trial version)
  • Netscape Navigator 3.0 • Netscape Navigator 4.7 • Netscape Navigator 7.0
  • Internet Explorer 3.0 • Internet Explorer 4.5 • Internet Explorer 6.0

We also have included several plug-ins on the **H•O•T CD-ROM**. If you don't have these plug-ins installed already, you should do that before working with any exercise in this book that calls for one of them. All of the plug-ins are located inside the **software** folder. We have included the following:
  • Flash 6.0 plug-in
  • Shockwave 8.5 plug-in
  • QuickTime 5.0 plug-in

I.

Background

What Is Dreamweaver MX?	Roundtrip HTML
Do You Need to Learn HTML?	What Does HTML Do?
A Look at HTML	HTML Deconstructed	What About XHTML?
A Look at XHTML	XHTML Deconstructed
DHTML?	JavaScript	Web Applications

No exercise files

Dreamweaver MX
H•O•T CD-ROM

We could start this book with lots of exercises, throwing you right into working with Dreamweaver MX without any preparation. But then you would be flying blind, without understanding basic Web-design fundamentals such as HTML, DHTML, XML, XHTML, and JavaScript. Instead, we are starting you off with some definitions, concepts, and guidelines to help with your hands-on Dreamweaver MX training. Feel free to scan this chapter for information if you already know some of what is here or you want the instant gratification of getting started.

What Is Dreamweaver MX?

At its roots, Macromedia Dreamweaver MX is a WYSIWYG (**W**hat **Y**ou **S**ee **I**s **W**hat **Y**ou **G**et) HTML generator. This means if you change something on the screen inside Dreamweaver MX, it will show you the results instantly. In contrast, if you were to code the HTML by hand, you would have to look at the code until you viewed the results from inside a Web browser. The instant feedback of a live design environment such as Dreamweaver MX speeds up your workflow tremendously because you can see whether you like the results while you are working. However, if you really look under the hood of Dreamweaver MX, you will see that it is also a complete Web application development tool, capable of developing advanced Web applications, e-commerce sites, dynamic data-driven sites, and much more.

Roundtrip HTML

Dreamweaver MX has gained a lot of great reviews and customer loyalty because of its invention of Roundtrip HTML. Roundtrip HTML means you can easily move between Dreamweaver MX and another HTML text editor, such as FrontPage, BBEdit, or HomeSite, with very little or no change to your code. Unless you are a programmer (and chances are you aren't if you are reading this book ;-)), this probably won't mean a whole lot to you right now. However, being able to move between different HTML development tools can be very important when you are working with a programmer or in a team environment where everyone might not be using Dreamweaver MX. It's nice to know that you can do this and not worry about Dreamweaver MX breaking your code by inserting unwanted changes. Don't you wish all programs were so respectful?

Programmers have looked at WYSIWYG HTML editors with dubious eyes because of their reputation for inflexibility and inclusion of nonstandard HTML code. Dreamweaver MX is one of the few WYSIWYG HTML editors to win the approval of programmers and designers alike. Programmers like the product because they don't have to worry about their code being changed by Dreamweaver MX. Designers like Dreamweaver MX because it writes clean code without inserting a lot of proprietary and self-serving tags, and because it allows them to do visual layout without understanding a line of code. Hard to believe there could be a tool that could please both of these divergent groups, but there is, and Dreamweaver MX is it!

Now, truth be told, by default Dreamweaver MX does make some minor changes to a page once it's opened. Because the few changes it makes are really aimed at cleaning up bad code, no one really frowns on these changes. There is no reason to get into those issues now; you'll learn about these changes and how to turn them off (if you even want to do so) in Chapter 12, "*HTML*."

Do You Need to Learn HTML to Use Dreamweaver MX?

Yes and no. If you use a WYSIWYG HTML editor, then technically you can create an entire Web page without writing a single line of code. However, there may come a time when you will have to edit the code manually to troubleshoot a problem, such as an incompatibility between browsers. For some of us, HTML is quite intimidating at first glance—your first reaction may be to avoid it at all costs. After all, when you design pages using Photoshop, QuarkXPress, or PageMaker, you don't need to look at raw PostScript code anymore. However, the early pioneers of desktop publishing had to know how to program in PostScript just to create a page layout! Most of the early Web developers were programmers, not artists, and they needed to write the raw code to create a Web page.

In the past, if you didn't know some HTML, you were at the mercy of a programmer who might have had more control over your design than you liked. Today, with Dreamweaver MX, you can get by without understanding or writing a single line of code. However, if you long to be a true professional Web designer or developer, we strongly recommend that you take the time to learn HTML. We have found that most people who don't learn a little HTML are at a disadvantage in the workplace, especially when they need to troubleshoot problems on their Web pages.

How do you learn HTML? You can take a class at school, take an online class, buy a training CD-ROM (we happen to know of a really good one!), or buy a book. There are endless ways to learn HTML; you should learn the way that works best for you. An easy way to learn HTML is to view the source code of pages that you like. In HTML the code is visible to everyone who uses a Web browser. To view the source code of a page, look under your browser's **Edit** menu and choose **View > Page Source** (Netscape) or **View > Source** (Explorer). This will show you the raw HTML, and once you get comfortable with some of the tags, you will likely be able to deconstruct how these pages were made. And if all else fails, you can hire the neighborhood 12-year-old, who learned it last weekend instead of mowing your lawn. ;-)

What Is XHTML?

HTML 4.01 is the most current version of HTML. As of October 4, 2001, the Web standards committee decided to discontinue HTML. Taking its place is **XHTML**, a language almost identical to HTML with the exception that it is written with different rules. Does this mean that if you learned HTML you wasted your time? Heck no. HTML will still be used, as well as XHTML, to create Web pages for a long time. In fact, knowing HTML will help you make the transition to XHTML, so don't worry. You'll find more details on XHTML later in this chapter in the "What About XHTML?" section.

HTML Resources

Many great resources are available, online and off, for learning HTML. Here are some online sites that are worth checking out.

World Wide Web Consortium
`http://www.w3.org/MarkUp/`

HTML: An Interactive Tutorial for Beginners
`http://www.davesite.com/webstation/html/`

Webmonkey: HTML Tutorial
`http://www.hotwired.lycos.com/webmonkey/teachingtool/index.html`

NCDesign: HTML Design Guide v5.0
`http://www.ncdesign.org/html/`

Index DOT HTML: The Advanced HTML Reference
`http://home.webmonster.net/mirrors/bloo-html/`

The HTML Writers Guild: A Resource List
`http://www.hwg.org/resources`

What Does HTML Do?

HTML stands for **H**yper**T**ext **M**arkup **L**anguage. It is a derivative of SGML (**S**tandard **G**eneralized **M**arkup **L**anguage), an international standard for representing text in an electronic form that can be used for exchanging documents in an independent manner.

Back in 1980, people had to use a form of markup in word processor documents. If you wanted something to have a bold face, for example, you had to tag it with the symbol **<B>** in order to create that formatting. You would never see the actual boldfaced text until the file was printed; back then, bold type could not even be displayed on the computer screen!

We've come a long way since then, and so has HTML. That's why programs such as Dreamweaver MX have become viable alternatives to writing all the tags by hand. With maturity and established standards, HTML in its raw form will likely become as hidden as the markup behind word processors is today.

At its heart, HTML allows for the markup of text and the inclusion of images, as well as the capability to link documents together. Hyperlinks, which are at the core of HTML's success, are what allow you to flip between pages in a site, or to view pages in outside sites. These hyperlinks are references that are contained within the markup. If the source of the link moves, or the reference to the link is misspelled, it won't work. One of the great attributes of Dreamweaver MX is that it has site-management capabilities, which will help you manage your internal links so they are automatically updated if the links are changed.

What Does HTML Look Like?

HTML uses a combination of tags, attributes, and values to generate its results. Here is a sample line of code that uses a **tag**, an **attribute**, and a **value**.

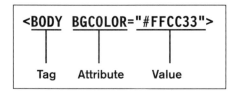

In this line of code, the tag is **<BODY>**, the attribute is **BGCOLOR**, and the value is **#FFCC33**. When put together, this collection of items within the brackets **< >** is called an **element**.

Many tags require **opening** and **closing containers**, as marked here for the **<BODY>** element.

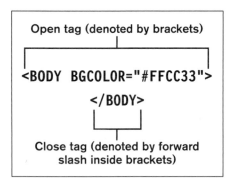

HTML Deconstructed

All HTML pages follow a basic structure. Each page must contain the **HTML**, **HEAD**, **TITLE**, and **BODY** tags. Whenever you open a new HTML document in Dreamweaver MX, this framework is already written. It is deconstructed for you below. Fortunately, you don't have to worry about getting this structure right. It is automatically built in to any page you create in Dreamweaver MX.

```
1. <HTML>
2. <HEAD>
3. <TITLE>Untitled Document</TITLE>
4. <META HTTP-EQUIV="Content-Type" CONTENT="text/html; charset=iso-8859-1">
5. </HEAD>
6. <BODY BGCOLOR="#FFFFFF">
7. </BODY>
8. </HTML>
```

1. Notice how the **<HTML>** tag is at the beginning of the document? It signifies that this is an HTML page. Without this tag, a browser cannot read the page. See line 8, the close **</HTML>** tag? This tag requires an open and a close tag. A closing tag is required for most HTML tags, but not all.

---

2. The **<HEAD>** element of the document contains the **HEAD** information, or the hidden information about your page. For example, the **TITLE** tag and the **META** tag are contained within the **HEAD**.

---

3. The **<TITLE>** is what appears at the top of the page inside a browser. If you leave the title **Untitled Document**, as in the previous code example, that is exactly what will appear! Dreamweaver MX has a setting for easily changing this title. You'll learn about this setting in Chapter 4, "*Basics*."

---

4. **META** tags are **HEAD** elements that are invisible when viewed in the browser, but contain information about the current page, such as the character encoding, author, copyright, and keywords. You can set many properties here, which you will learn about in Chapter 4, "*Basics*."

---

5. Here's the close tag for the **HEAD** element. Notice that the **TITLE** and **META** tags were nested within the **HEAD** tags.

---

6. The **BODY** tag is using the **BGCOLOR** attribute to specify that this page will be white, instead of the default gray. If you don't enter a **BGCOLOR** value here, the page will defer to browser defaults.

---

7. This is the close tag for **BODY**.

---

8. This is the close tag for **HTML**.

File-Naming Conventions

Working with HTML is much more restrictive than working with other types of computer media. The strictest part about HTML is its file-naming conventions.

Don't use spaces: It's best if you save your files using no spaces between the file name elements. For example, the file name **about lynda.html** would be considered illegal because of the space between the words **about** and **lynda.** Instead, you would write this file name as **about_lynda.html** or **aboutlynda.html**.

Avoid capital letters: It is best to avoid capitalization in your file names. Although **AboutLynda.html** will work as a file name, anytime you link to the file you will have to remember the correct capitalization because many UNIX servers are case-sensitive. It is far easier to simply use all lowercase letters.

Avoid illegal characters: The following chart contains a list of characters to avoid when naming files.

File-Naming Conventions	
Character	**Usage**
.	Periods are reserved for file name extensions or suffixes, for example, .gif and .jpg.
"	Quotes are reserved for HTML to indicate the value of tags and attributes.
/ or \	Forward slashes (/) indicate that the files are nested in folders. If you include a forward slash in your file name, HTML may lose your references, thinking you are specifying a folder. A backslash (\) isn't allowed on Windows servers.
:	Colons are used to separate certain script commands on Macs and Windows. Avoid them in your file names so as not to confuse a file name with a script command.
!	Exclamation marks are used in comment tags.

File Name Extensions

You may be curious about the many extensions used after the dot at the end of file names. The following chart lists the meaning of some extensions you'll commonly run across.

File Name Extensions	
Extension	**Usage**
.html, .htm	These two extensions are commonly used to denote an HTML file. The three-letter extension works just as well as the four-letter version. Older DOS systems didn't allow for four-letter extensions, which is why you sometimes see .html abbreviated as .htm. Dreamweaver MX defaults to using .htm.
.gif	GIF images
.jpg	JPEG images
.swf	Flash files
.mov	QuickTime movie files
.avi	AVI movie files
.aif	AIFF sound files

What About XHTML?

As you saw earlier, the current version of HTML is 4.01. There will not be a version 5 of HTML. Instead there will be XHTML 1.0. In fact, XHTML 1.0 already exists as a formal recommendation sanctioned by the World Wide Web Consortium (the standards committee of the Web). However, we are at a cross-road because XHTML is just now being accepted and supported by some software vendors, which means that HTML is still the prominent language used to create Web pages. The future of XHTML looks very promising, however, and we want you to be aware of its existence and intended purpose. The next version of XHTML, version 1.1, is already in development.

XHTML stands for e**X**tensible **H**yper**T**ext **M**arkup **L**anguage. How is XHTML different from its close companion HTML? The most visible difference between the two markup languages can be seen in their syntax, with all opening tags requiring a closing tag. Here are some of the key differences:

- All element and attribute names are in lowercase. For example, **<P>** would not be valid, but **<p>** would be a valid XHTML element.

- All attribute values must be contained within quotes, single or double. For example, in HTML you can write **<td nowrap>**, but in XHTML you have to write **<td nowrap="nowrap">**. Make sure you are consistent in the type of quotes you use; don't mix single quotes with double quotes, or vice versa.

- All nonempty elements must have a closing tag. For example, **<p>this is good text.</p>** is a valid XHTML element, whereas **<p>this is bad text.** would not be valid.

- All empty tags should be written with a space and a / symbol at the end of the tag. For example, **
** is a valid XHTML tag; **
** is not. This method of closing empty tags ensures that your pages are compatible with older browsers.

XHTML follows the XML rules and syntax guidelines. Because XML has very rigid requirements for writing code, XHTML is a more structured markup language than HTML. This more structured approach to markup languages will enable one document to be viewed on multiple devices (Web browsers, cell phones, PDAs, etc.) by simply creating different style sheets for each device. (You will learn about style sheets later in the book.) In a nutshell, XHTML is basically HTML 4.01 reformatted using the syntax of XML. You will be glad to know that Dreamweaver MX has full support for XHTML. In fact, Dreamweaver MX can even convert your existing HTML documents to XHTML. You will learn more about this in Chapter 12, "*HTML*." Sweet.

What Does XHTML Look Like?

If you have ever seen HTML code, you will find instant comfort in looking at XHTML code. Because XHTML is a reformatting of HTML, many things look the same or have only minor differences. Although some distinct and critical differences exist between XHTML and HTML, they are both markup languages and share many common traits. This is good news because it will lessen the learning curve for those of you familiar with HTML.

Here are some of the basic elements of an XHTML document written in correct syntax.

```
1.  <?xml version"1.0"?>
2.  <!DOCTYPE html public "-//W3C//DTD XHTML 1.0 Strict//
    EN"http://www.w3.org/TR/xhtml1/DTD/xhtml1-strict.dtd"
3.  <html xmlns="http://www.w3.org/1999/xhtml">
4.  <head>
5.  <title>
6.  </title>
7.  </head>
8.  <body>This is where the content of your page will be placed.
9.  </body>
10. </html>
```

XHTML Code Deconstructed

1. The **XML declaration**. This line identifies this document as an XHTML document.

---

2. The **Document Type Definition (DTD)**. This URL points to a file that outlines available elements, attributes, and their appropriate usage. Three XHTML DTDs are available:

- *XHTML Transitional:* This DTD lets you maintain backwards compatibility with older browsers while still providing access to HTML 4.01 elements.

- *XHTML Strict:* This DTD does not provide access to any of the HTML elements that were designed to control the appearance of a page. This is the truest form of XHTML elements.

- *XHTML Frameset:* This DTD gives you access to the HTML elements needed to create framesets.

3. The **XHTML Namespace**. This URL points to a file that gives detailed information about the particular XML vocabulary, which is XHTML in this case.

---

4. The **<head>** tag contains all of the header information.

---

5. The **<title>** tag defines the page title, which appears at the top of the browser window and in the bookmark lists.

6. All XHTML tags must be closed, so this is the closing **<title>** tag.

7. You guessed it! This is the closing **<head>** tag.

8. All of your visible content will be placed inside the **<body>** tag.

9. Yup, here is another closing tag. This is the closing **<body>** tag.

10. Last, but not least, is the closing **<html>** tag.

This example represents only a smidgen of the available XHTML tags, attributes, and values. But it shows the basics and is a great place to start your XHTML education. We cover more examples of XHTML in Chapter 12, "*HTML*."

What Is XML?

XML stands for e**X**tensible **M**arkup **L**anguage. XML is a set of guidelines for delimiting text through a system of tags so it can be read and processed by a device capable of reading a text file. You can think of it as a really customizable HTML that must follow a set of specific syntax rules. Because XML is a text format, you can imagine why so many developers like to work with XML data; you can do just about anything with a text file, regardless of what computer and operating system you are using. For this reason, XML is used to move data between different computers and different operating systems, which makes it perfect for e-commerce solutions and sending and retrieving data from a database.

Dreamweaver MX supports templates, covered in Chapter 17, "*Templates and Library Items*." One of the advanced features of Dreamweaver MX is the ability to export/import XML files through a template. Because XML is so complex and deep, and the use of databases is outside the scope of this book, we don't include any XML exercises in any of the chapters. Here are some places you can go to learn more about XML:

Macromedia Designer & Developer's XML Site
http://www.macromedia.com/desdev/topics/xml.html

World Wide Web Consortium
http://www.w3.org/xml/

Extending Dreamweaver MX

One of the neatest things about the Dreamweaver MX community is the way people share **objects**, **commands**, and **behaviors**, which are like plug-ins for Dreamweaver MX that let you add programming functionality without typing a single line of code. These prebuilt elements can be shared and distributed, much the way Photoshop plug-ins work. If you visit the Macromedia Dreamweaver MX Exchange (`http://exchange.macromedia.com/dreamweaver`) section of the Macromedia site, you'll find numerous ways to get more out of Dreamweaver MX without having to learn a complex programming language. In addition, you'll find a collection of third-party sites that can help you extend the capabilities of Dreamweaver MX. Here are a few of our favorites:

Project VII

`http://www.projectseven.com/`

This site has a great collection of Design Packs and Extension Kits that can help you get a lot more from Dreamweaver MX. Some of them must be purchased for a fee.

Dreamweaver Extensions Database

`http://www.idest.com/cgi-bin/database.cgi`

Features an extensive database, which includes all of the Dreamweaver MX extensions.

Yaromat

`http://www.yaromat.com/dw/index.php`

A personal home page that contains several very useful Dreamweaver MX extensions, including a great one for importing Fireworks-created rollovers.

Massimo's Corner of the Web

`http://www.massimocorner.com/`

A great resource for Dreamweaver MX extensions, objects, commands, and behaviors. It has an interesting DHTML interface, too!

Dreamweaver Designer & Developer Center

`http://macromedia.com/desdev/mx/dreamweaver/`

A new part of Macromedia's Web site that contains a large collection of articles, tips, and tutorials. If you are a Dreamweaver MX user, you should definitely visit this site.

What Is DHTML?

DHTML (**D**ynamic **HTML**) is a collection of different technologies. This can include any combination of HTML, JavaScript, CSS (**C**ascading **S**tyle **S**heets), and DOM (**D**ocument **O**bject **M**odel). By combining these technologies, you can author more dynamic content than what basic HTML affords.

Some of the things possible with DHTML include animation, drag-and-drop, and complicated rollovers (buttons that change when a mouse moves over them). Dreamweaver MX uses DHTML to enable you to create pages with buttons that change in more than one place on the screen at the same time.

Just like HTML, DHTML effects in Dreamweaver MX are coded behind the scenes. However, DHTML has some serious cross-platform issues, because it is supported quite differently by Netscape and Explorer (the two leading browsers). Fortunately, Dreamweaver MX lets you target specific browsers, as well as test the cross-browser compatibility of your DHTML effects.

DHTML uses a combination of HTML, JavaScript, CSS, and DOM. The following chart gives a short description of each.

DHTML Terms	
Technology	**Explanation**
HTML	(**H**yper**T**ext **M**arkup **L**anguage) The default markup for basic Web pages, and the root of DHTML.
JavaScript	A scripting language that extends the capabilities of HTML.
CSS	(**C**ascading **S**tyle **S**heets) A page-layout system supported by version 4.0 and later Web browsers, which allows for better control over the appearance and positioning of elements on a Web page.
DOM	(**D**ocument **O**bject **M**odel) A hook to outside scripting protocols, such as ActiveX, or external plug-ins, such as Shockwave or Flash. It allows scripts and programs to address and update documents.

What Is JavaScript?

JavaScript was developed by Netscape in 1996 and has become almost as popular as HTML. It actually has nothing to do with the Java programming language, but Netscape licensed the name from Sun Microsystems in hopes of increasing acceptance of the new scripting protocol. We're not sure if it was the name that did the trick, but JavaScript has become almost as widely adopted as HTML itself! The most common uses of JavaScript allow for rollovers, resizing of browser windows, and checking for browser compatibility.

Most of the JavaScript routines are accessed by the Dreamweaver MX Behaviors panel, which you will learn about in Chapter 10, "*Rollovers*," and Chapter 14, "*Behaviors*." This book covers many JavaScript techniques, including rollovers, browser-sniffing, and launching external browser windows.

You will not have to learn to write JavaScript by hand in order to use it within Dreamweaver MX. This is very fortunate for those of us who are not programmers because JavaScript programming is more complicated than HTML programming. For those of you who are JavaScript programmers, however, Dreamweaver MX offers a JavaScript Debugging feature. This feature is outside the scope of this book, but you will find documentation on it in the Dreamweaver MX manual or online Help system.

What Is a Web Application?

In broad terms, a Web application is a Web site that delivers dynamic data, such as Amazon.com and eBay.com, instead of static data that has to be updated manually. Web applications have also been referred to as data-driven, database-driven, and dynamic sites. In almost all cases, a Web application involves a database and server-side scripting, such as ASP, Cold Fusion, PHP, etc. Web applications aren't just one thing; they can take on many forms and serve many purposes. They can be used to handle e-commerce, inventory tracking, online auctions, and just about anything that uses a large amount of information. So what do Web applications have to do with learning Dreamweaver MX? Dreamweaver and UltraDev have been combined into one product, Dreamweaver MX. This means that Dreamweaver MX has the capability to create complete Web applications, in addition to static Web sites. Although creating Web applications is outside the scope of this book, you should know that you can use Dreamweaver MX to create them. As you advance your skills, you will find that you will not outgrow Dreamweaver MX, because the sky's the limit as far as its capabilities are concerned.

Now that you have a basic foundation in these key areas, you are ready to learn more about Dreamweaver MX itself. The next chapter introduces you to the Dreamweaver MX interface and prepares you for the many step-by-step exercises throughout this book.

2.

Interface

Setting Up Your Workspace	Welcome Panel
Interface Tour	Insert Bar	Insert Bar Tabs
Property Inspector	Launcher	Document Toolbar
Document Window	Document Views
Panels and Panel Groups	Preferences	Shortcuts

No exercise files

Dreamweaver MX
H•O•T CD-ROM

We have been big fans of the Dreamweaver MX interface for a long time. Other HTML editors we've used require that you open a lot of different-sized windows and panels in order to reach all of the features. Instead, Dreamweaver MX uses a system of panels and panel groups that change settings depending on the context of what you are doing. This saves screen real estate and makes learning the interface a lot easier. Although you might believe at this point that learning Dreamweaver MX represents a big learning curve, understanding the interface is probably one of the easier challenges ahead of you.

This chapter takes you through the basic concepts of the program's interface. In addition, we also share how to set up our favorite Dreamweaver MX Preferences settings and configurations.

You might be antsy to start in on some of the step-by-step exercises contained in later chapters, but you should review this chapter first to identify the toolbars, panels, and windows you'll be using.

Setting Up Your Workspace (Windows Only)

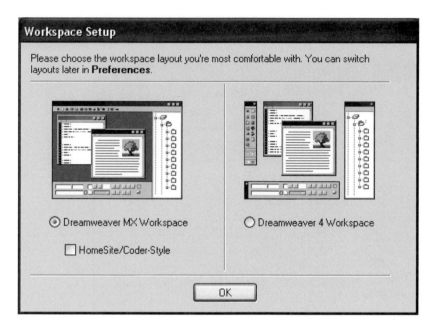

The first time you start Dreamweaver MX (Windows users only), you will be prompted to choose a **Workspace Layout**. This determines how the Dreamweaver MX interface is displayed and functions. You have three options:

- **Dreamweaver MX Workspace:** This option will set up your workspace as an integrated workspace where all the document windows and panels are contained within one larger window. This is the interface we prefer because it makes working with multiple documents and panels much easier than in the Dreamweaver 4 workspace.

- **HomeSite/Coder-Style:** This option is the same as the Dreamweaver MX workspace, except the panel groups are docked along the left side of the screen (this will look familiar to Macromedia HomeSite+ and ColdFusion users) and the document opens in Code view by default. This workspace is ideal for people who will be doing a lot of manual coding.

- **Dreamweaver 4 Workspace:** This option will set up your workspace in the vintage Dreamweaver 4 style, where all of the document windows and panels float around the screen. This option is really good for people who are familiar with the Dreamweaver 4 interface and don't want to change.

During the course of this book, we use the Dreamweaver MX Workspace, and we suggest that you choose the same workspace. However, when you are working on your own projects, be sure to choose the workspace you prefer. It's kind of like wearing your socks inside out; do whatever makes you most comfortable.

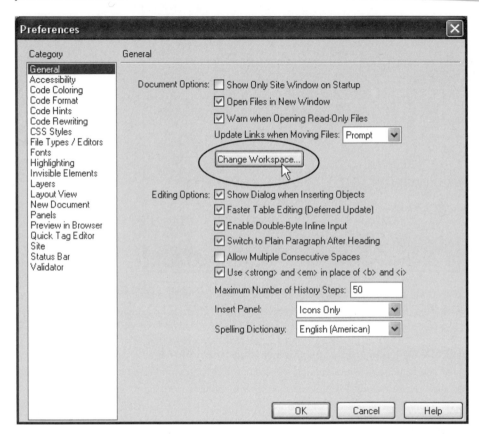

It can be a bit unnerving deciding what interface you want before you even have a chance to see the program. Don't worry, you can change your workspace at any time within the Dreamweaver MX Preferences by selecting **Edit > Preferences** and clicking **Change Workspace**. Phew.

The Welcome Panel

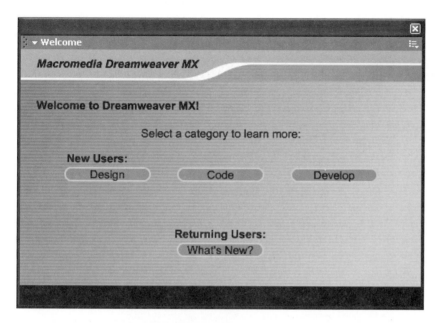

The first time you open Dreamweaver MX, you will see the **Welcome** panel. This panel contains four buttons that let you preview specific features of Dreamweaver MX. For example, if you are a designer and want to see the features that can help you, click **Design**. If you have used Dreamweaver before, you should click **What's New** to review just the new features in Dreamweaver MX. If you close this panel, you can reopen it by selecting **Help > Welcome**.

A Tour of the Interface

The Dreamweaver MX interface is an integrated workspace, which means the document window and all of the panels are contained within a larger window. This can make working with multiple documents and panels easier because the panels and document windows don't float all over the screen as separate objects. This integrated workspace is available to Windows users only. Because there are significant differences between the Windows and Macintosh versions of Dreamweaver MX, we cover both interfaces in this section. Regardless of your operating system, the interface has six main parts: the Insert bar, Document toolbar, Document window, Property Inspector, Panels, and Panel Groups.

Windows Interface

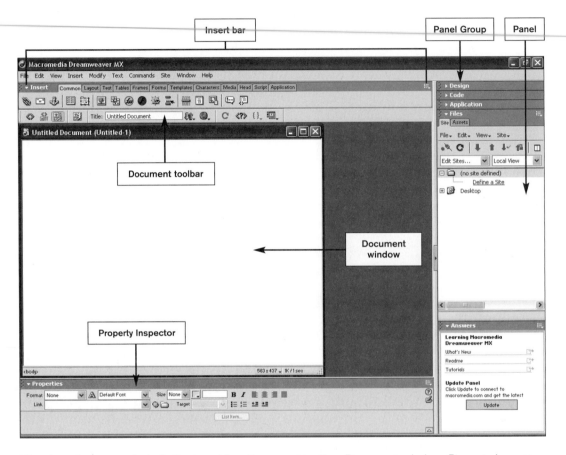

The six main features include the Insert bar, Document toolbar, Document window, Property Inspector, Panels, and Panel Groups. Whenever you open Dreamweaver MX, it defaults to opening a new blank Untitled Document, as shown here.

Macintosh Interface

The Dreamweaver MX interface in the Macintosh operating system resembles the Dreamweaver 4 interface, where the panels and document windows float around the screen independent of one another. However, Macintosh users have access to the same interface objects as Windows users: the Insert bar, Document toolbar, document window, Property Inspector, panels, and panel groups.

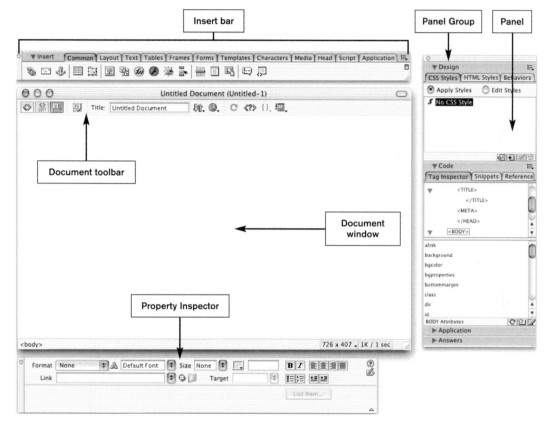

The Macintosh version of Dreamweaver MX has a floating interface where the panels and document windows are allowed to float around the screen independently of one another.

The Insert Bar

The **Insert bar** contains rows of object icons and is used as a one-click stop for many operations. If you move your mouse over the Insert bar and pause for a moment over each icon, you will see what each one of the icons stands for. You may alter the appearance of this panel in your Dreamweaver MX Preferences, if you want to see the object names in addition to, or instead of, their icons.

The Insert bar shown above is in its default mode (Icons Only).

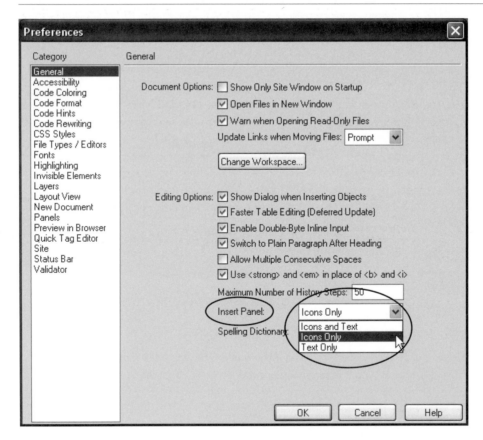

To change the appearance of the Insert bar, select Edit > Preferences > General > Insert Panel. You can change the Insert bar's setting to Icons and Text, Icons Only, or Text Only.

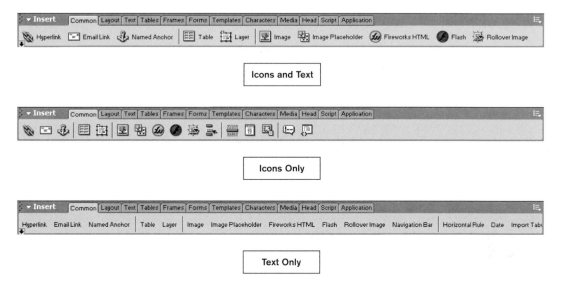

Icons and Text

Icons Only

Text Only

The three versions of the Insert bar shown above are the choices available in the Preferences. As you examine the Insert bar, you'll see that it allows you to access essential functions, such as inserting an image, a table, or a horizontal rule, which are otherwise known as "objects."

Many items that exist in the Insert bar also appear under the Insert menu in the top menu bar. The Insert bar provides a one-click alternative to using that menu bar. Some people are more comfortable clicking the icons, and others prefer the menu access. There is no right or wrong way to do this; it's just a matter of personal preference.

Types of Insert Panel Tabs

Like many of the toolbars in Dreamweaver MX, the **Insert panel** is context-sensitive. It defaults to showing what Dreamweaver MX calls the **Common objects**. You can change the Insert panel to show other categories of objects when you need them.

The Common tab contains the most frequently used objects in Dreamweaver MX, including Images, Tables, Layers, simple Rollovers, Insert Fireworks HTML, etc. You will use this panel a lot.

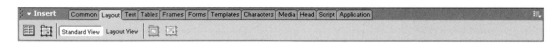

The Layout tab lets you insert tables and layers. You also switch between the Standard and Layout view using this tab. In Layout view, you can draw layout tables and layout cells. You will learn more about these in Chapter 8, "Layout View."

The Text tab lets you format text and insert a wide range of text formatting tags, such as b, em, p, hl, and ul.

The Tables tab lets you insert a complete table or specific tags, such as th, tr, and td. This tab is disabled in Layout view. You will learn more about these in Chapter 7, "Tables."

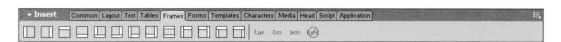

The Frames tab contains several preset framesets. With a click of the mouse, you can add any number of different framesets. You will learn more about these in Chapter 9, "Frames."

The Forms tab contains all of the objects essential for creating forms for your Web page. These objects include text boxes, buttons, menus, etc. You'll learn about these items in Chapter 13, "Forms."

The Templates tab lets you insert various regions in a template, such as editable, option, and repeating regions. You will learn more about templates in Chapter 17, "Templates and Library Items."

The Characters tab contains frequently used character entities, such as the ®, ©, and ™ symbols, so you no longer have to memorize tricky keyboard commands.

The Media tab lets you insert a wide range of media objects, such as Macromedia Flash buttons, Macromedia Flash text, Java applets, and more. You will learn more about these objects in Chapter 19, "Inserting Media."

The Head tab contains objects that are inserted in the HEAD tag of your Web page. These elements, although not visible on the page, can be an important part of your pages, because they include META tags, such as keywords and descriptions. Many of these tags are used for search operations.

The Script tab lets you insert scripts, such as JavaScript and VBScript. It also lets you insert the non-script tag and server-side includes. You will not be using this tab in this book.

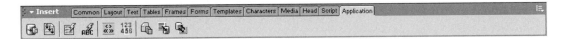

The Application tab is designed for inserting dynamic objects on your page. This is an important tab when you are creating a Web application. Because of its advanced purpose, you will not be using this tab in this book, so you can just ignore it.

The tab at the top of the Insert bar tells you what group of objects you are viewing. To access the other types of objects, click the various tabs to switch to another group of objects. Throughout the book, you'll get to learn how and when to use many of the objects in the Insert panel. For now, this is just a sneak peek to let you know they're there.

The Property Inspector

Like the Insert Panel, the **Property Inspector** is context-sensitive, meaning it constantly changes depending on what type of element is selected. The Property Inspector controls many settings, including those for text, tables, alignment, and images. Because Dreamweaver MX defaults to opening a blank page with the text-insertion symbol blinking, the Property Inspector defaults to displaying text properties, as shown here.

The Property Inspector changes depending on what is selected on screen. Because these elements change depending on context, future chapters cover the various properties on this bar in depth.

The Launcher

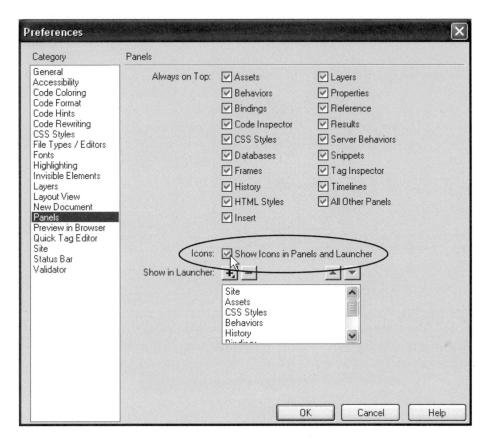

The **Launcher** is a part of the Dreamweaver MX interface that is not visible by default. The Launcher is a series of buttons that appear at the bottom of your document window. These buttons give you quick access to various panels. With a click of one of these buttons, you can open and close a panel. This can be a great way to keep your workspace free of extra panels. If you want to use this feature, you must modify the Preferences. If you select **Edit > Preferences** and select the **Panels** category, you can access the **Show Icons in Panels and Launcher** checkbox. Checking this box will make the Launcher visible at the bottom of each document window and place small icons in the panels. We have found that we use the Launcher less and less as we became more familiar with the Dreamweaver MX interface. There is no wrong or right way to work here; it's a matter of individual preference. We suggest you find a way that is comfortable for you and stick with it!

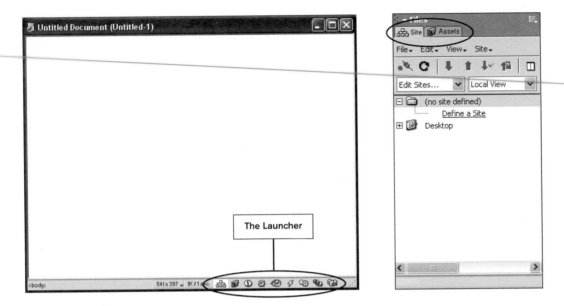

After you turn on the Launcher, you will see small icons in the panels and at the bottom of the document window.

The Launcher allows you to access several aspects of Dreamweaver MX with a single click. It basically "launches" the **Site**, **Assets**, **CSS Styles**, **Behaviors**, **History**, **Bindings**, **Server Behaviors**, **Components**, and **Databases** panels. Go ahead and try clicking each of the buttons to see what they do. You can't hurt anything, we promise! Click the button again, and the panel will close.

Launcher Features	
Feature	**Description**
Site	This opens the Site panel, where you will control Dreamweaver MX's powerful site-management features. This panel is covered in detail in Chapter 3, "*Site Control.*"
Assets	This panel lets you manage the assets for your site, such as images, colors, external links, movies, scripts, libraries, templates, etc. You can even organize your assets as "Favorites" so they can be renamed and accessed quicker.
CSS Styles	CSS Styles are an advanced feature of Dreamweaver MX. They allow you to automate the application of layout and text styles to multiple pages in your site. This feature is covered in Chapter 11, "*Cascading Style Sheets.*"
Behaviors	This feature allows you to add JavaScript to your pages, even if you are not a programmer. Some of the Behaviors features are covered a lot more in Chapter 14, "*Behaviors.*"
History	The History panel will list each step you have performed in the current document, up to a maximum number specified in the Preferences. You can then easily move forward and backward to undo and redo your actions. You can also save your steps as commands and replay them later in other documents.
Bindings	The Bindings panel enables you to define the source of dynamic content and place dynamic content on your pages. This panel is beyond the scope of this book and is not covered.
Server Behaviors	The Server Behaviors panel lets you add server behaviors to your page, edit server behaviors, and even create new server behaviors. This panel is beyond the scope of this book and is not covered.
Components	The Components panel enables you to create components and add them to your pages. This is an advanced feature of Dreamweaver MX and is not covered in this book.
Databases	The Databases panel lets you create connections to databases and insert the code needed to connect to the database in your pages. This is an advanced feature of Dreamweaver MX and is not covered in this book.

Customizing the Launcher

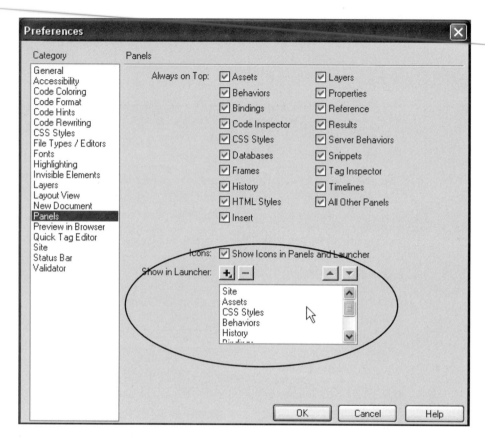

The Launcher contains default options. If you find that you aren't working with some of the choices, or crave different ones, you can change the options that appear in the Launcher by selecting **Edit > Preferences > Panels**. You can remove existing options by highlighting them and clicking on the minus sign (–). Clicking on the plus sign (+) will display a list of options you can add to the Launcher. You can easily reorder the selected options by highlighting an option and then clicking the up or down arrows.

Launcher Shortcuts

All of the Launcher features are available as items under the **Window** menu. In addition, the following function-key shortcuts are available for both Mac and Windows users.

If you memorize the F-keys for the Launcher items, you'll probably never need the large Launcher panel again. For example, we use the Site window and Code Inspector more often than the others, so we have memorized **F8** and **F10** as keyboard shortcuts. The following is a handy chart of the Launcher shortcuts.

Launcher Shortcuts			
Key	**Function**	**Key**	**Function**
F8	Site	**Ctrl+10**	Bindings
F11	Assets	**Ctrl+F9**	Server Behaviors
Shift+F11	CSS Styles	**Ctrl+F7**	Components
Shift+F3	Behaviors	**Ctrl+Shift+F10**	Databases
Shift+F10	History		

Note: Macintosh users will use the Command (Cmd) key instead of the Control (Ctrl) key

WARNING | Redundancy in the Interface

Truth be told, there is some redundancy in the Dreamweaver MX interface. For example, you can insert an image by clicking on the Insert bar or by choosing the Insert Image command from the Insert menu. You can often align objects using the Property Inspector or using a command on a menu. Though it's convenient at times to have different options, it can be confusing to learn a program that has two or three ways to accomplish the same task. Throughout the book, we cite our favorite ways to access features, but if you prefer an alternate method, don't let us stop you!

The Document Toolbar

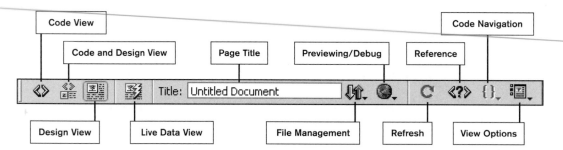

You can now access many of the options you need directly from the **Document toolbar**. The toolbar contains a series of buttons and drop-down menus that let you do things like change the document view, set the page title, preview the page in a browser, and access the Reference panel. The following chart gives you a more detailed explanation of each feature.

Document Toolbar Features	
Feature	**Description**
Code View	The Code view displays the code that creates your page. You can use this to edit the code directly and make changes without having to use a separate text editor, such as BBEdit or HomeSite. This Code view is helpful if you are comfortable coding your pages or need to create/modify custom code, such as JavaScript, ASP, etc. You'll have numerous opportunities throughout the book to work with the Code view.
Code and Design View	The Code and Design view splits your document in half, displaying both the code and the actual page layout. This view is helpful if you want to make some minor changes to the code and want to immediately see the visual effect they have on your page.
Design View	The Design view is the default view for your document window. This view will display your page in WYSIWYG (What You See Is What You Get) mode, which means you will see images, text, and other media as you add them to your page. This view is helpful if you aren't familiar with HTML or just don't want to take the time to type all of the code in yourself, plus it gives you a pretty accurate preview of what your page will look like in a browser as it's being designed. Cool.
Live Data View	The Live Data view lets you preview dynamic data. This is an advanced feature used when developing dynamic Web sites and is not covered in this book.
	continues on next page

Document Toolbar Features *continued*	
Feature	**Description**
Page Title	This text field lets you specify the Page Title for your page. This text will appear at the top of the browser window, and is used by some search engines to describe your site listing. It is also the name that identifies the page when you save it in a list as a bookmark or favorite in your browser. You can also set the title inside the Page Properties dialog box.
File Management	This drop-down menu lets you manage the files of your site by letting you upload/download files, unlock them, check them in or out, and work with design notes. It is great to have access to all of these options directly from the document window. You'll learn how to upload/download files in Chapter 20, "*Get It Online.*"
Preview/Debug	This drop-down menu lets you choose a browser to preview your page in a Browser or debug the JavaScript. You can also access the Define Browsers dialog box, which will let you define new browsers or change references to existing browsers that have already been defined. We don't get into debugging JavaScript in this book, but at least you know where to find it should the mood strike you!
Refresh Design View	This button lets you refresh the contents of the Design view. This can be helpful if you make changes to your page in the Code view and don't immediately see the changes.
Reference	This button lets you quickly access the Reference panel. This is especially helpful in the Code view; where you can highlight some code, click this button, and refer to the Reference panel for a complete explanation of the selected text. This is a great way to learn HTML, CSS, and even JavaScript. You'll learn more about this feature in Chapter 12, "*HTML.*"
Code Navigation	This option is for use in the Code view and lets you quickly select code for adding JavaScript functions. You probably won't use this feature unless you have a pretty good working knowledge of JavaScript.
View Options	This drop-down menu lets you control several options that modify the appearance of the Code view. You can set the Code view to word wrap, display line numbers, display syntax coloring, etc. You can also set the Design view to be on the top of the Code and Design view. You'll get to put this view into practice in Chapter 12, "*Code.*"

The Document Window

The **document window** is where all the action happens. This is where you assemble your page elements and design your pages. The document window is similar in appearance to the browser window when viewed from Netscape or Explorer. On both the Mac and Windows, Dreamweaver MX will create a blank Untitled Document each time you open the application. By default, the document window will be in the Design view.

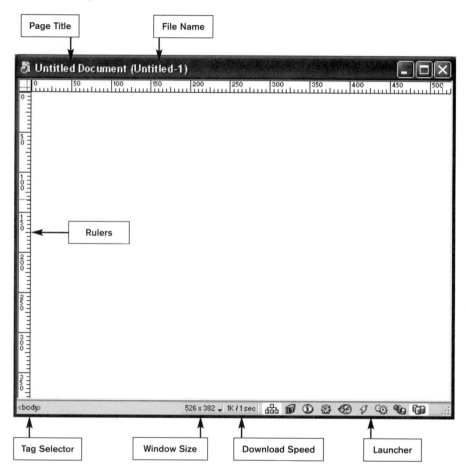

Document Window Features

Feature	Description
Page Title	This part of the document window displays the page title, which you can define in the Document toolbar and the Page Properties.
File Name	This part of the document window displays the actual file name.
Rulers	You can show or hide rulers by selecting View > Rulers and checking or unchecking Show.
Tag Selector	If you select visual elements on your screen, the Tag Selector highlights the corresponding HTML code. It's a fast and easy way to select different items on your page.
Window Size	This pop-up menu lets you resize your window to various preset or custom pixel dimensions.
Download Speed	This gives you the approximate size (kilobytes) and download time for the current page.
Launcher	The Launcher is a series of buttons that gives you quick access to various panels. You can customize these buttons to meet your individual needs.

WARNING | PC Users and Document Window

Dreamweaver MX is a bit different between the Mac and PC. If you are using Dreamweaver MX on a PC, you should know that you will be prompted to quit the program when you close the last open document window. This occurs only on the PC.

Document Window Views

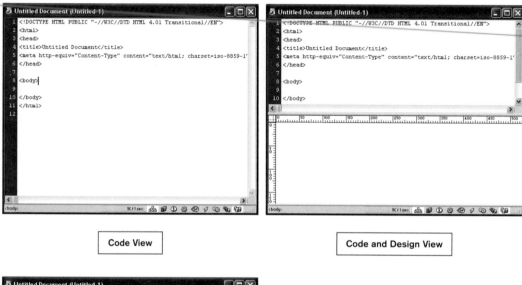

Code View

Code and Design View

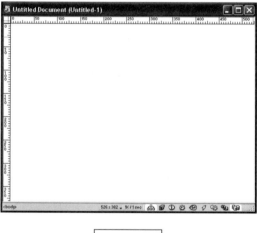

Design View

Dreamweaver MX gives you the added control and flexibility of viewing your pages in one of three different views, Code View, Code and Design View, and Design View. By default, all new documents open in the Design View. The three buttons in the left corner of the Document Toolbar let you change between the three different views.

Multiple Document Windows (Windows Only)

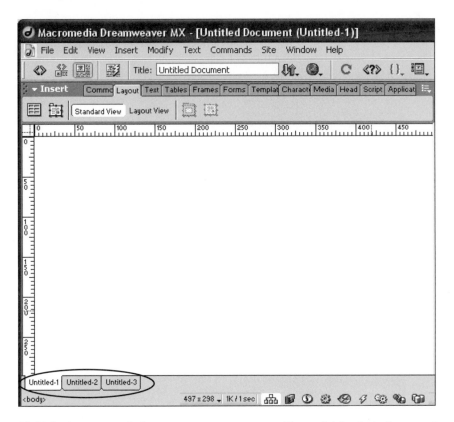

Multiple document windows are easy to manage with small tabs that allow you to move easily between documents.

Often you may want or need to work with several documents open at the same time. This can be a daunting task, even with a large monitor. Dreamweaver MX makes it easy to work with multiple document windows by placing a small tab at the bottom of each document window. You can jump from one page to another by clicking on a tab. **Note:** Your page must be maximized in order to see the tabs; otherwise the pages will float around as separate objects.

Panels and Panel Groups

Dreamweaver MX makes it easy to manage an otherwise complex interface through a system of Panels and Panel Groups. These two interface elements work together to help you customize your workspace so that you have open only the panels you need. Each Panel Group can contain several different panels, each identified by a tab. You can click each tab to quickly move between panels.

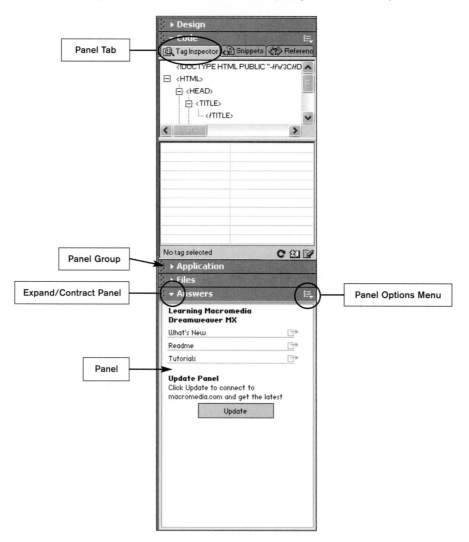

You can expand or contract panels by clicking on the small white arrow in the upper-left corner of the panel group's title bar. All of the panels are accessible from the Windows menu or by using a keyboard shortcut.

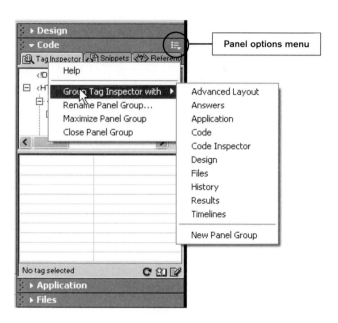

Some panels, such as the Answers panel, are in their own group. You can customize the panel groups by adding and removing panels in each panel group. If you **right-click** (Windows) or **Control+click** (Mac) on a panel tab or click the panel options menu button, you will get a menu that lets you group the selected panel with another panel group. You can even rename or make a new panel group by choosing that option from the panel options menu! This is a great way to customize the interface to meet your own needs. **Note:** You cannot click and drag the panels to add or remove them from other panel groups; you must use the contextual menu or the panel options menu.

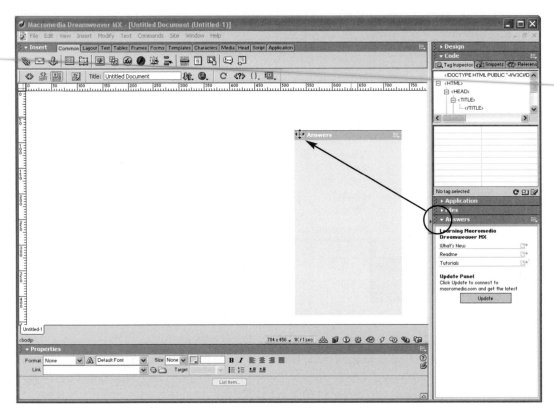

By default, all of the panel groups will be docked along the right side of the screen. You can undock a panel group by clicking on the small dots, referred to as the "gripper," in the upper-left corner of a panel group's title bar and dragging to a new position.

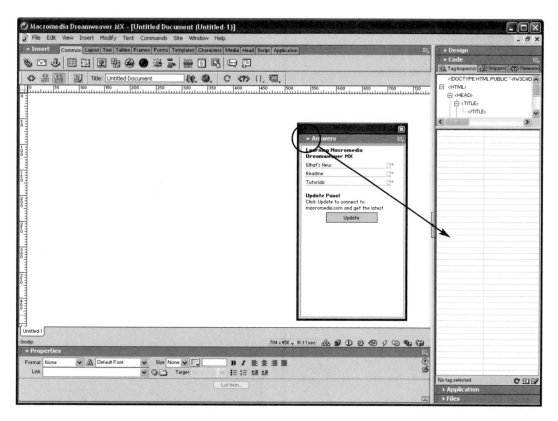

You can easily redock panel groups by clicking in the upper-left area again and dragging over any of the other panels. A dark line will appear between the panel groups, letting you know where the panel group will be placed when you release the mouse button.

Preferences

There are many different Preferences you can change to make Dreamweaver MX your very own custom HTML editor. You can change these settings at any time. To access the Preferences dialog box, select **Edit > Preferences**. Under the **General** category are settings that determine the appearance and operation of Dreamweaver MX as a whole. For example, you might consider changing the Insert panel appearance setting to **Icons and Text**, as described earlier in the chapter, until you become more familiar with the icons representing the various Dreamweaver MX objects. The next few pages explore Preferences you may set for external editors, preset window sizes, and browser choices.

External Editors

You can specify **External HTML Editors**. This means that you can specify another HTML editor, such as BBEdit or HomeSite, to edit the code that Dreamweaver MX generates. This book does not cover the use of external HTML editors, because they are mostly used by experienced programmers who want to more tightly control the code that Dreamweaver MX automatically generates. If you set your Preferences for an image editor, you can launch Fireworks or other image-editing applications from Dreamweaver MX by using the contextual menu or by selecting Edit in the Property Inspector.

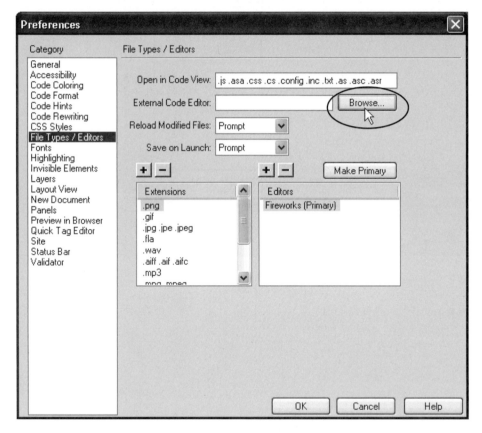

You can specify an external editor by choosing Edit > Preferences and clicking the File Types / Editors category. You can specify a separate editor for different types of files. For example, you can edit a GIF or JPG file in Fireworks or Photoshop, and you can open a MOV file in Adobe Premiere or Apple's QuickTime Player.

Preset Window Sizes

One of the pitfalls of Web design is that your page's look will change depending on the size of the monitor that displays it. Dreamweaver MX has a handy feature—the **Window Sizes** option—to help you design more accurately for a specific monitor size.

The Window Sizes menu offers a variety of preset sizes for the document window. For example, if you want to design for a **640 × 480** pixel screen, you can select this setting, and Dreamweaver MX will automatically resize the document window to reflect this size setting. This helps you visualize how your designs will look in browser windows of various sizes, but it doesn't physically change the browser window size for your end user. You will learn how to restrict the size of the HTML window for your end user, should you choose to do so, by using a behavior in Chapter 14, "*Behaviors*."

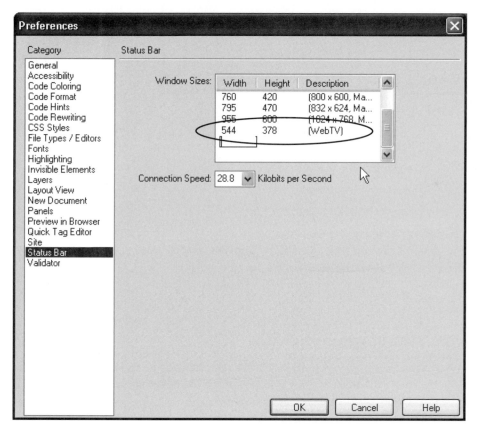

You can set your own window sizes settings by choosing Edit > Preferences and clicking the Status Bar category.

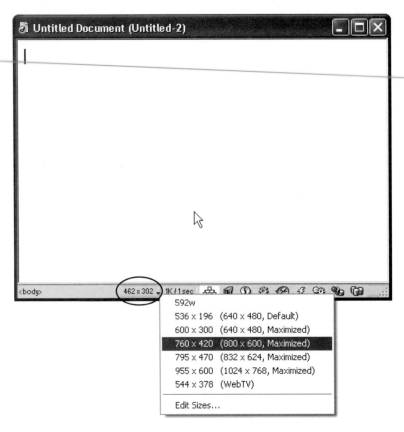

You can click the window sizes menu on the status bar to access the various default dimensions. If you choose Edit Sizes, you can add your own size presets. We suggest working with 760 × 420 or 795 × 470 because statistics show that most people are surfing the Web with a resolution of at least 800 × 600.

How to Define Your Browser of Choice

Internet Explorer 6.01 (Windows only) was used in all the screen captures for this book, and has been provided for you on the **H•O•T CD-ROM**. You are welcome to use the browser of your choice for the exercises in this book. **Warning:** A few exercise steps will not work in earlier browser versions. To set up your browser preference, follow these steps:

1. Choose **Edit > Preferences**.

2. Under **Category,** click on **Preview in Browser**.

3. Click the plus sign, minus sign, or **Edit** to add, remove, or change a browser from the list of choices. **Note:** The Primary Browser defines which browser will launch using the **F12** shortcut key. The Secondary Browser defines which browser will launch using **Ctrl+F12** (**Cmd+F12** on a Macintosh). Many designers like to preview in both Netscape and Explorer. Using a primary and secondary setting will allow you to do so easily.

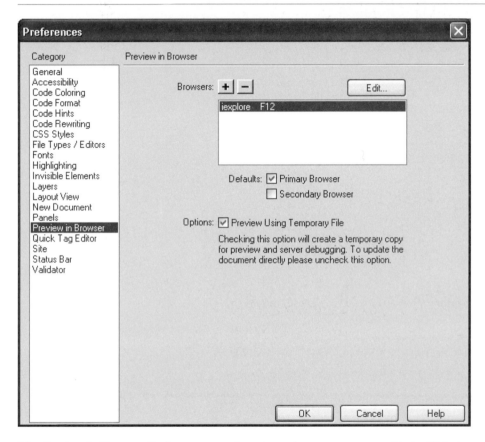

The Preview in Browser Preference sets the primary browser to open with the F12 shortcut key.

Shortcut Keys

Dreamweaver MX has lots and lots of shortcut keys, and all of them are listed in your manual. The following chart lists our favorites.

Shortcuts in Dreamweaver		
Command	**Mac**	**Windows**
New document	Cmd+N	Ctrl+N
Line break	Shift+Return	Shift+Enter
Page properties	Cmd+J	Ctrl+J
Select a word	Double-click	Double-click
Select a paragraph	Triple-click	Triple-click
Check spelling	Shift+F7	Shift+F7
Find and replace	Cmd+F	Ctrl+F
Layers	F2	F2
Objects	Cmd+F2	Ctrl+F2
Frames	Shift+F2	Shift+F2
Property Inspector	Cmd+F3	Ctrl+F3
Behaviors	Shift+F3	Shift+F3
Switch to Standard view	Cmd+Shift+F6	Ctrl+Shift+F6
Switch to Layout view	Cmd+F6	Ctrl+F6
Site window	F8	F8
Timelines	Option+F9	Alt+F9
Code Inspector	F10	F10
History	Shift+F10	Shift+F10
HTML styles	Cmd+F11	Ctrl+F11
CSS styles	Shift+F11	Shift+F11
Preview in primary browser	F12	F12
Preview in secondary browser	Cmd+F12	Ctrl+F12

TIP | Customized Keyboard Shortcuts

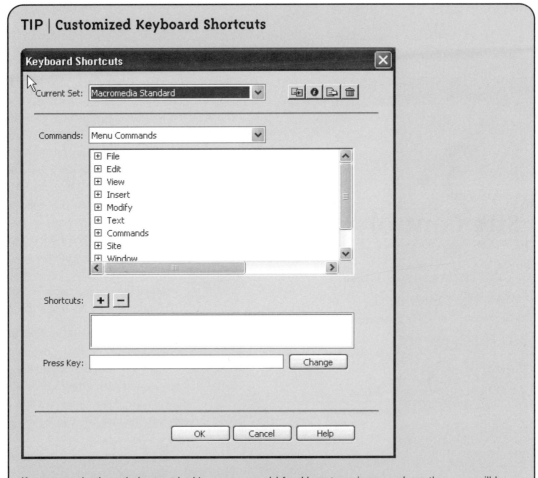

If you are a keyboard shortcut junkie, as we would frankly categorize ourselves, then you will be happy to know that Dreamweaver MX gives you the ability to easily create, save, and modify custom sets of keyboard shortcuts. There are even predefined sets of keyboard shortcuts set up for other programs you might already be familiar with, such as BBEdit, Macromedia HomeSite, and Dreamweaver 3. You can access this feature by selecting Edit > Keyboard Shortcuts.

Okay, enough about the interface. Besides, the best way to learn about the interface is to use it! The next chapter, "Site Control," will teach you some important lessons about site management, which is essential to building any Web site. It's time to move on to the step-by-step exercises. Woo-hoo!

3.

Site Control

| Defining a Site | Relative and Absolute Links |
| File and Folder Management |
| Understanding Paths | File Browser |
| Creating a Site Map |

chap_03

Dreamweaver MX
H•O•T CD-ROM

Those of you who have already built Web pages will likely agree that file management is one of the greatest challenges of this medium. So what is file management? File management is the organization, folder structure, and naming conventions of all the pages and graphics in your Web site. Few other disciplines require the creation of so many documents at once, because Web pages are usually comprised of numerous text and image files.

To compound the difficulty of managing numerous files, most people build Web sites from their hard drives, and when they're finished, they upload these files to a Web server so that the files can be viewed from the WWW. Let's say that you created a folder on your hard drive and called it **HTML** and created another folder called **graphics**. If you put your HTML and graphics files inside those two folders, you would have to replicate this exact folder hierarchy when you uploaded those files to your Web server, or your links to those files would break. In this chapter, you will learn how to avoid such misfortune, by building your Dreamweaver MX site management skills.

What Is a Local Root Folder?

Dreamweaver MX has a site management scheme that requires that you keep all your files within one main **local root folder**, so you can easily duplicate the folder hierarchy that's on your hard drive when you upload to a Web server. A local root folder is no different from any other kind of folder on your hard drive, except that you have specified to Dreamweaver MX that this is where all HTML and media files for your site reside.

If you think of the local root folder as the folder from which all other files stem, just like the roots of a tree, then you will understand its function. A local root folder can contain many subfolders, but Dreamweaver MX cannot keep track of elements unless they are stored inside the local root folder.

Taking the concept further, let's say that you decide midstream to change the folder hierarchy of your site by adding a folder or changing a folder name. If you were hand-coding the pages, making these changes would be a hassle. Dreamweaver MX makes this process painless, as long as you work within its site management structure.

By the time you are through with these exercises, you will have learned to define a site and a local root folder, create a site map, and reorganize files and folders. Not bad for a day's work!

> **WARNING | Site Management**
>
> You might think that site management in Dreamweaver MX is a neat but optional feature, and that you would rather skip it now to return later when you're in the mood. Don't do it! Site management is actually integral to Dreamweaver MX, and the program kicks up quite a fuss if you don't use it properly. This book asks that you define a site with each new chapter, because if you have files outside your defined area, you will be constantly plagued by warnings. If you choose to ignore this, you will not be using Dreamweaver MX properly and will run into problems.

NOTE | Mac and Windows Differences

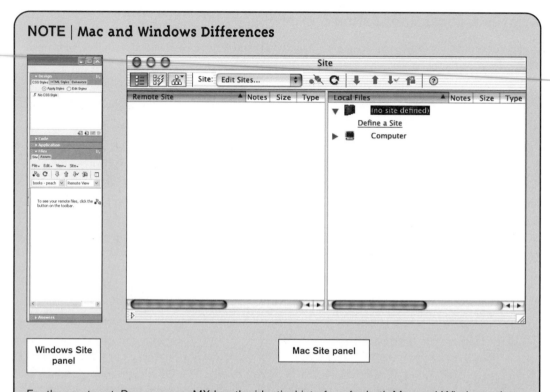

Windows Site panel

Mac Site panel

For the most part, Dreamweaver MX has the identical interface for both Mac and Windows platforms. One case where this is untrue is with Site panel. For this reason, this chapter sometimes contains different directives and screenshots for the Mac and the Windows users. Because the Site panel in Windows is docked along the right side of the screen, as part of the integrated workspace, it looks very different from the Site panel on the Mac. The screenshots above show what the different Site panels look like in their default state. **Note:** If you undock the Windows Site panel, it will look like the Site panel on the Mac.

I. _____Defining a Site

This exercise shows you how to define sites in Dreamweaver MX. You'll be working with a folder of HTML and image files from the **H•O•T CD-ROM** that you transfer to your hard drive. Once you've finished this exercise, Dreamweaver MX's site management feature will catalog all the files inside this folder by building a **site cache file**—a small file that holds information about the location and name of all the files and folders in your site.

This exercise teaches you how to define a site from an existing Web site. You would use this identical process if you wanted to use Dreamweaver MX on a site that you or someone else had already created outside of Dreamweaver MX. At the end of the chapter, you'll complete an exercise that will show you how to define a site from an empty folder, which will more likely simulate your approach when you are starting a new site from scratch.

1. Copy the **chap_03** folder from the **H•O•T CD-ROM** to your hard drive. For clarity, it's best if you leave this folder named **chap_03**.

The folder contains images and HTML files that are requested throughout this chapter. You will be asked to add and change files, which requires that you have all of the files on your hard drive.

2. Open Dreamweaver MX and press **F8** to bring up the **Site** panel, if it's not already open. Click the **Define a Site** link in the **Site** panel to open the **Site Definition** window. **Note:** If you've worked in Dreamweaver before, and have already defined other sites, you will need to choose **Site > New Site**.

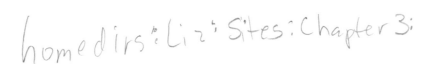

WARNING | Non-Windows XP Users

If you are working on a PC using any of the Windows operating systems, except Windows XP Home and Professional editions, make sure that after you have copied the files to your hard drive, you refer to the instructions in the beginning of the book. Some Windows operating systems will automatically lock the files that you copy from the CD-ROM, so you will have to manually unlock these files in order to work with them in this and other chapters. If you don't already know how to unlock files, the procedure is documented in the front of this book, and will walk you through the whole process.

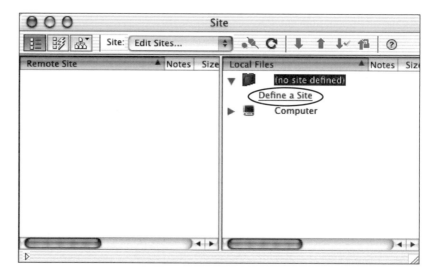

The Site panel will display a Define a Site link if you have not previously defined any sites. Once you define a site, this link will no longer appear.

3. Make sure the **Basic** tab is selected. This will display the basic mode of the Site Definition window, which will take you through the process of defining a site by having you answer a series of questions about your site. As you use Dreamweaver MX more and more, you will find yourself using the Advanced tab to define your sites.

---

4. Type **Chapter 3** in the **What would you like to name your site?** field. Click **Next**.

This is an internal naming convention, so you can use any kind of name you want without worrying about spaces or capitalization. Think of it as your own pet name for your project, just like you give a folder or hard drive a custom name.

5. The next screen asks if you want to use a server technology for your page. Make sure the **No, I do not want to use a server technology** radio button is selected. If you were creating a Web application or a site that connected to a database, you would select Yes to set up the proper options. A simple static Web site, like the one in this book, does not require any special server technology setup.

---

6. Click **Next**.

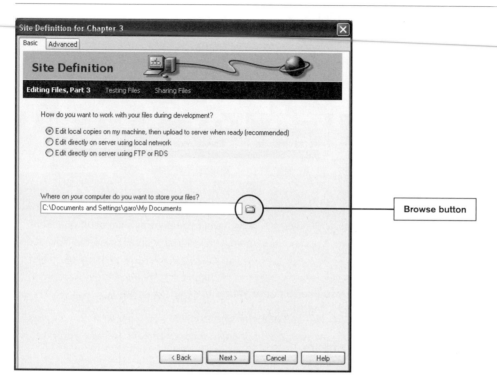

7. The next screen asks how you want to develop your pages. Make sure the **Edit local copies on my machine, then upload to server when ready (recommended)** radio button is selected. This lets Dreamweaver MX know that you will create and edit the Web pages on your computer and then upload them to the Web when you are ready. The other two radio buttons let you edit your pages over a network and directly on remote Web server.

8. Click the **Browse** button (small folder icon) and browse to the **chap_03** folder on your desktop.

- **Mac:** Highlight the **chap_03** folder and click **Choose**.

- **Windows:** Open the **chap_03** folder and click **Select**.

9. Click **Next**.

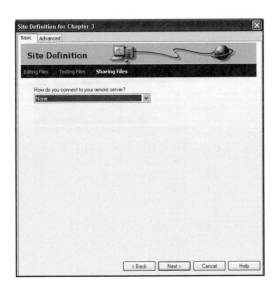

10. The next screen defines how you will connect to the remote Web server so you can upload your files. Skip this section for now because we cover it in detail in Chapter 20, "*Getting It Online*." Don't worry about coming back to this later; it's easy to change these settings, even long after you've created them. Make sure **None** is selected and then click **Next**.

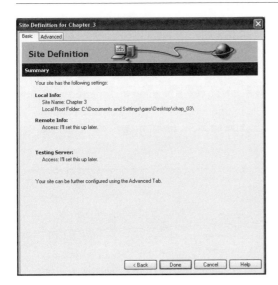

11. The next screen displays a summary of the settings you specified for your site. Take a moment to look over this screen to make sure you have everything set up properly. When you are ready, click **Done**.

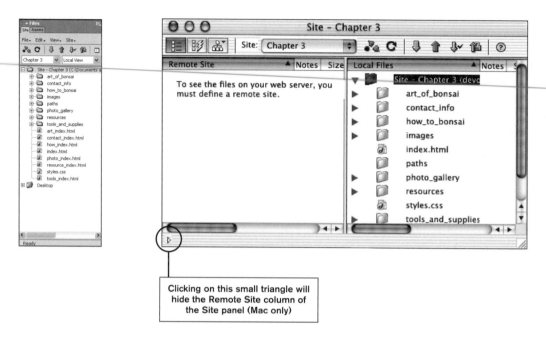

Clicking on this small triangle will hide the Remote Site column of the Site panel (Mac only)

The Windows Site panel and the Mac Site panel look slightly different. The Mac Site panel shows the Remote Site view, which displays the contents on the remote Web server.

The site is now defined as **Chapter 3**. The Site panel will display the contents of the **chap_03** folder on your desktop. This is the folder on your hard disk that contains all of your HTML files and images, also referred to as your local folder.

The left side of the Site panel displays the Remote Site view (Mac only). Nothing is displayed right now because you haven't gotten to that exercise yet. You will learn more about the Remote Site panel in Chapter 20, "*Getting It Online.*" **Windows Users Note:** If you see locks next to the file or folder icons, refer to the Introduction.

NOTE | Local Root Folder, Root Folder, Root

As you work through Dreamweaver MX, you will notice references to a local root folder, a root folder, and root. All these terms are interchangeable. Each refers to a folder on your hard drive that contains all of the HTML, images, etc. for your Web site. This can be any folder on your computer. It can be empty, or it can have an entirely completed Web site. Don't be confused by this slight difference in terminology.

---

on your Folder c:\dir

2. ————————Relative and Absolute Links

This exercise will help you understand two different types of links—those that are **relative** and those that are **absolute**. Relative links reference files that are part of your site. All the files that you see in the local root folder of your Site panel are internal files and can be referenced as relative links. If you want to link to an external file, such as someone else's site, you have to use an absolute link. If you don't understand the difference between these two types of links, read on.

Virtual HTTP.

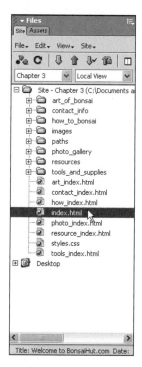

1. If your **Site** panel isn't still open, press **F8**. Locate the **index.html** file and double-click to open it. Alternately, you could choose **File > Open** and browse to the **chap_ 03** folder to locate **index.html**. But why make things more difficult?

We suggest that you train yourself to open HTML files from the Site panel instead of your hard drive. Doing so will ensure that you have successfully defined a site and that Dreamweaver MX's site management features are being enforced. Believe us, this will save you a lot of potential pain, because the alternative of not working within a defined site can cause your HTML code to produce broken links and images!

2. Click the **Art of Bonsai** (art_of_bonsai.gif) image at the top left of the screen to select it.

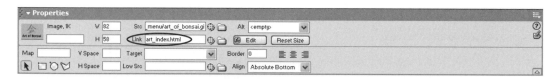

3. With the image selected, look at the **Property Inspector** and notice that this image links to **art_index.html**. **Tip:** If your Property Inspector doesn't show as many features as the one shown here, click the arrow at the bottom-right corner to expand it. The link **art_index.html** is a relative link. It does not have additional information in front of it, such as **http://www.bonsaihut.com/index.html**. The file does not need that information because the file name is relative to other internal files in the site.

4. Highlight the **treebay.com** text link at the bottom of the document window.

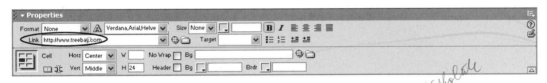

5. In the **Property Inspector**, notice that this image links to **http://www.treebay.com**. This is an external link to another site on the Internet. This type of link is referred to as an **absolute** link. It needs the additional information to specify its location because it is not relative to any internal documents, and it exists on its own server, separate from the **Bonsai Hut** site.

6. Close the **index.html** file. Do not save any changes if you are prompted.

NOTE | Absolute and Relative URLs

The term URL stands for Uniform Resource Locator. In plain English, URLs are the addresses you use when you go to a Web site. Some are simple, such as **http://www.lynda.com**, and others are very complicated and hard to remember, such as **http://www.lynda.com/dw4hot/lessons/chapterone**. Regardless of whether a URL is short or long, there are two different types: absolute and relative.

An absolute URL looks like this:

http://www.lynda.com/index.html

An absolute URL is a complete URL that specifies the exact location of the object on the Web, including the protocol that's being used (in this case, **http**), the host name (in this case, **www.lynda.com**), and the exact path to that location (in this case, **/index.html**). Absolute URLs are always used when you want to link to a site outside your own.

You can use absolute URLs within your own site, but it's not necessary, and most Web publishers opt to use relative URLs instead. If you use relative URLs for internal documents, it's easier to move them if you change your domain name.

A sample relative URL looks like this:

index.html

If we were linking from **pageone.html** of our site to **pagetwo.html** of our site, we wouldn't need to insert the entire **http://www.lynda.com** URL anymore.

3. ———————File and Folder Management

From within the Dreamweaver MX Site panel, you can create new folders and files, as well as move them around from one directory into another. When you do this, you're actually adding folders and files to your hard drive, as this exercise will demonstrate. Accessing your hard drive from within Dreamweaver MX is *essential* to site management practices because Dreamweaver MX can then keep track of where the files and folders have been moved, renamed, added, or deleted. This exercise will show you how to add folders and files to the Chapter 3 site.

1. Make sure the **Site** panel is open (**F8**).

2. Select the folder at the top of the **local folder** view.

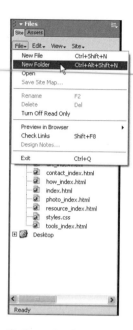

3. From the **Site** panel choose **File > New Folder** (Windows) or from the main menu choose **Site > Site Files View > New Folder** (Mac). This will add a new folder to the **chap_03** folder on your hard disk.

4. Type **html** for the folder name and press **Enter** (Windows) or **Return** (Mac).

5. Next, you'll learn to select files to move them into the folder you just created. Additionally, you'll learn how to select discontinuous files—files that are not adjacent to one another.

- **Mac:** Click **art_index.html**, then Cmd+click **contact_index.html**, **how_index.html**, **photo_index.html**, **resource_index.html**, and **tools_index.html**. (Make sure you hold down the **Cmd** key as you click the last five file names.)

- **Windows:** Click **art_index.html**, then Ctrl+click **contact_index.html**, **how_index.html**, **photo_index.html**, **resource_index.html**, and **tools_index.html**. (Make sure you hold down the **Ctrl** key as you click the last five file names.)

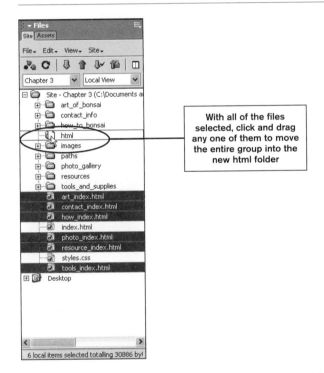

With all of the files selected, click and drag any one of them to move the entire group into the new html folder

6. Once you have all six files selected, drag them to the **html** folder that you just created. This will move all six files into this new folder. Woo-hoo! (If your html folder is in a slightly different location on the screen than ours is, that's OK.)

7. When you move files, Dreamweaver MX will prompt you to update their links. Click **Update**. Dreamweaver MX will list all the different files whose links were affected by the files you just moved. Once you click Update, these files will be rewritten automatically to reflect the change in file structure. Can you imagine how long it would take to do that manually?

WARNING | Use the Site Panel

If you want to add, modify, move, or delete files or folders in your Web site, do it inside Dreamweaver MX's Site panel, as shown in Exercise 3. If you make these folder changes on your hard drive without opening Dreamweaver MX, you'll have to go in and repair the links manually by relinking each page. If you make your changes inside the Site panel, Dreamweaver MX will keep track of them and automatically update your pages.

Understanding Path Structure

This next exercise shows how path structures are created and altered when you move files inside the local root folder. A path structure is how HTML represents the path to different files in your site, depending on where they are located. Relative and absolute URL paths can result in a variety of different path structures. In this exercise, you will move files around the local root folder in three distinct ways, each demonstrating a different type of path structure you might encounter. In this first example, you will simply insert a file that is within the same folder.

1. Make sure the **Site** panel is still open (**F8**).

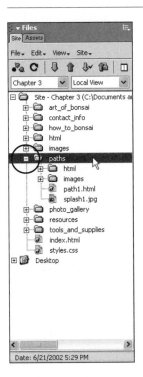

2. In the **Site** panel, click the **plus sign** (Windows) or **arrow** (Mac) next to the **paths** folder. This will expand the folder, and you'll see the contents of the **paths** folder.

3. Open **path1.html** by double-clicking it in the **Site** panel.

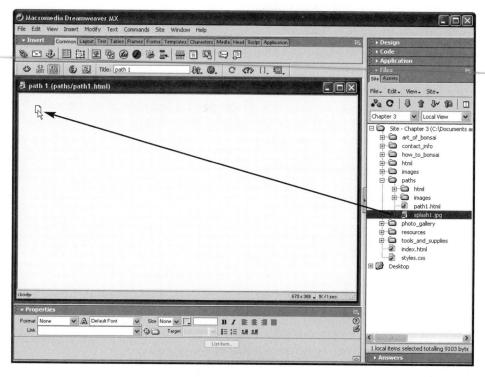

4. From the **Site** panel, click and drag the **splash1.jpg** onto the page. When you release the mouse button, the image will be inserted on the page.

5. Once you have inserted this image, make sure it's selected, and look at the **Property Inspector**. Notice that the **Src** is set to **splash1.gif**. As you become more experienced with building Web pages, you will begin to notice that a file name with no slash in front of it means that the file is in the same folder as the HTML that referenced it.

In this second example, you will insert an image that is inside another folder.

6. In the document window, delete the image that you just inserted by selecting it (clicking it once) and pressing **Delete**.

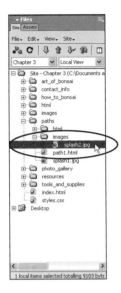

7. Click on the **plus sign** (Windows) or **arrow** (Mac) next to the **images** folder inside the **paths** folder. This folder contains one image, **splash2.jpg**.

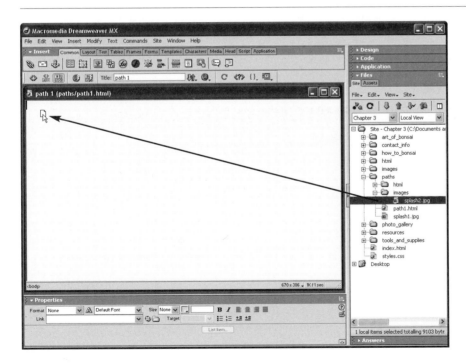

8. Click and drag **splash2.jpg** onto the page.

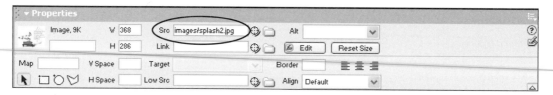

9. Once you have inserted this image, make sure it's selected, and look at the **Property Inspector** again. Notice that the **Src** is now set to **images/splash2.gif**. The slash means that the file is nested inside another folder.

10. Save your changes and close **path1.html**.

In this example, you will open an HTML document that is inside a folder and insert an image that is outside a folder.

11. From the **Site** panel, click on the **plus sign** (Windows) or **arrow** (Mac) next to the **html** folder nested within the **paths** folder. Double-click on the **path2.html** to open that file.

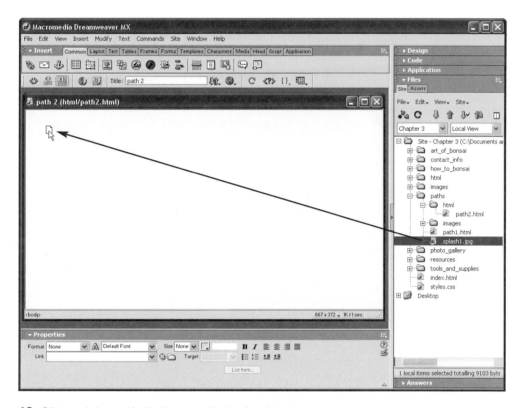

12. Click and drag **splash1.jpg** outside the **html** folder onto the page.

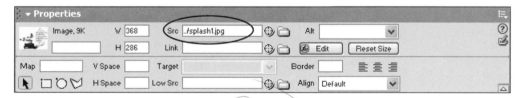

13. Once you have inserted this image, make sure it's selected, and look at the **Property Inspector** again. Notice that the **Src** is now set to **../splash1.jpg**. The two dots before the slash indicate that the image was one folder up from the HTML document that referenced it.

14. Save and close the **path2.html** file.

This point of this last exercise was simply to point out how different path structures are generated depending on how your files and folders are situated within the Site panel. Path structures are something you'll encounter as you build HTML pages in Dreamweaver MX, and this hopefully made them a bit less mysterious!

Different Path Notations

When you reference files in HTML, you must specify exactly where the document is. Dreamweaver MX writes the HTML for you, and it inserts different path structures depending on where the files are located. Below is a chart to reference how path structures are specified within HTML.

Path Notations in Dreamweaver MX	
Path Notation	**Description**
document.gif	No forward slash (/) or dots (..) indicates that the file is inside the same folder as the referring HTML file.
images/document.gif	The forward slash (/) indicates that the file is inside the images folder, or the file is located one level down from the referring HTML file.
../images/document.gif	The two dots (..) indicate that the folder is one level up from the referring HTML file.

5. _____Using the File Browser

As we stated earlier, it is important that all of the assets for your Web pages be inside your local root folder. This will ensure that the proper paths are created. However, sometimes you will need to work with an asset outside your local root folder. The **file browser**, within the Site panel, gives you direct access to all of the files and folders on your hard disk. You can use the file browser to easily move files into your local root folder. This is a convenient way to move files because you don't have to exit Dreamweaver MX. It also ensures that your files have the necessary path integrity. In this exercise, you will learn how to use the file browser to import a folder of images into your site.

1. Copy the **03_media** folder from the **H•O•T CD-ROM** to your desktop. This folder contains two images that need to be added to the site you defined earlier. Because this folder has been copied to your desktop, it is outside the local root folder you defined in Exercise 1.

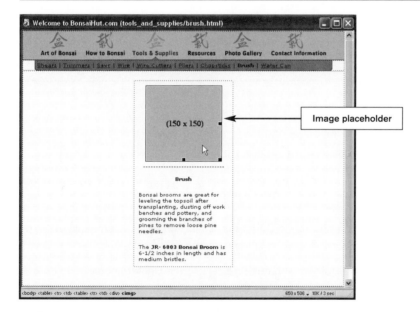

2. Open the **brush.html** file from the **tools_and_supplies** folder. This page contains an image placeholder, a visual element that specifies where images should be inserted onto the page. You will learn more about image placeholders later in the book.

For this page, we have inserted an image placeholder where we want the final image to be placed. In our layout design, we determined that the image should be 150 × 150 pixels. Unfortunately, the image you need to insert is not inside your local root folder. However, by using the file browser, you can very easily browse to any location on your hard drive and copy the image inside your local root folder so you can then insert it on the page.

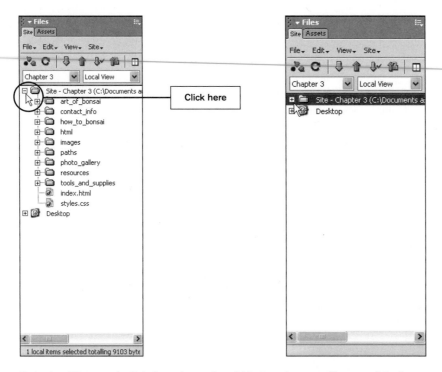

3. In the **Site** panel, click the **minus sign** (Windows) or **small arrow** (Mac) next to the local root folder. This will collapse and hide all of the contents in the local root folder.

4. The **Site** panel contains an integrated file browser that you can use to browse the contents of your hard drive:

- **Mac:** Click the **small arrow** next to the **Computer** icon. Then click the **small arrow** next to the **Desktop Folder** icon. This will display all of the contents on your desktop.

- **Windows:** In the **Site** panel, click the **minus sign** next to the **Desktop** icon. Then click the **minus sign** next to the **Desktop Items** folder. This will display all of the contents on your desktop.

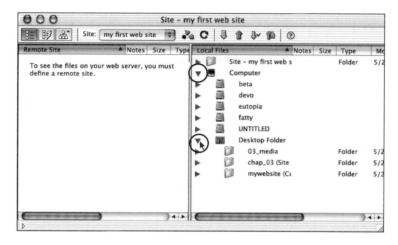

The Site panel displays green folders to show folders that are within your local root folders. Folders outside your local root folder are colored yellow (Windows) and blue (Mac).

5. Click and drag the **03_media** folder over the **local root folder** at the top of the **Site** panel, then release the mouse button. The **03_media** folder will be copied into the local root folder. Dreamweaver MX will always make copies of the files; it will not move the original files.

6. Once the folder has been copied into the local root folder, you can collapse the view of your hard drive contents:

- **Mac:** Click the **small arrow** next to the **Computer** icon. This will hide the file browser contents. Click the **small arrow** next to the **local root folder**.

- **Windows:** In the **Site** panel, click the **minus sign** next to the **Desktop** icon. This will hide the file browser contents. Click the **plus sign** next to the **local root folder**.

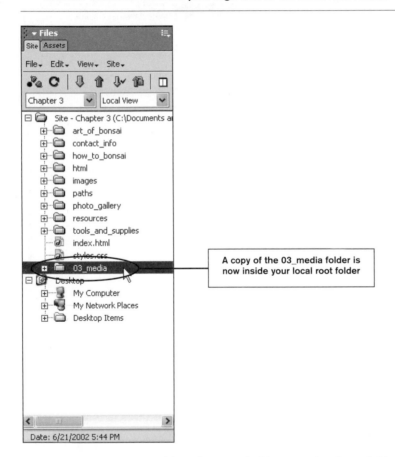

A copy of the 03_media folder is now inside your local root folder

Now that the files you need have been copied into your local root folder, you can replace the image placeholder with the correct image.

7. Click on the image placeholder to select it and press **Delete** to delete the image placeholder in the **brush.html** page. Now that you have the image you need, you no longer need the image placeholder.

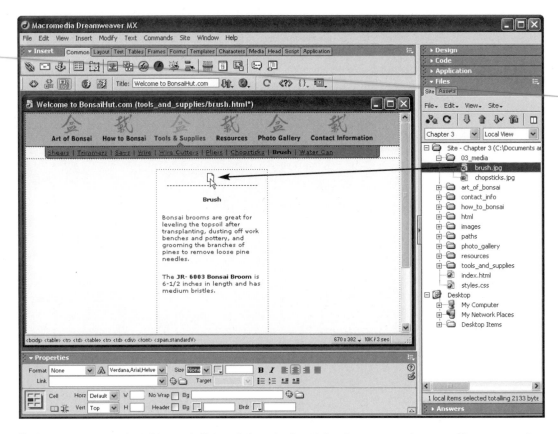

8. Open the **03_media** folder and click and drag the **brush.jpg** image onto the page. You want to drag it to the same location as the image placeholder.

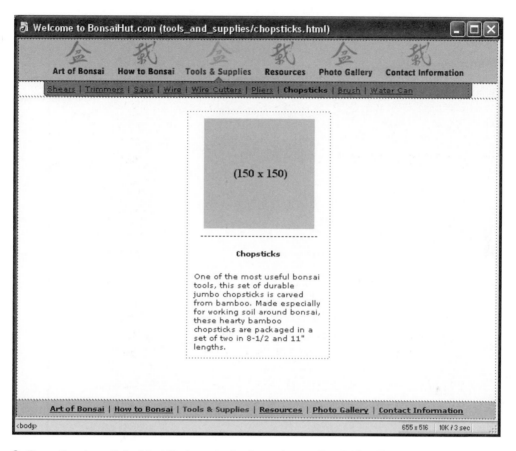

9. Open the **chopsticks.html** file from the **tools_and_supplies** folder. This page also contains an image placeholder. Click on the image placeholder to select it and press **Delete** to delete the image placeholder.

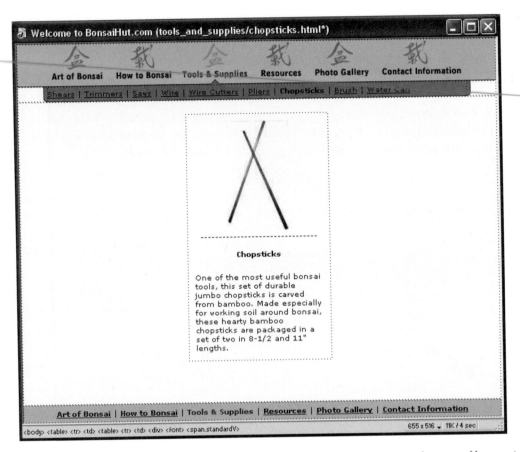

10. From the **03_media** folder, click and drag the **chopsticks.jpg** image onto the page. You want to drag it to the same location as the image placeholder. It will look like the window above when you're done.

11. Save and close all open files.

Now that the 03_media folder is inside your local root folder, for neatness sake you could move the brush.jpg *and* chopsticks.jpg *files into the images folder. Don't worry about the links breaking, Dreamweaver MX will update the links for you. This is yet another reason to use the Site panel and file browser to handle all of your file operations, such as creating, deleting, renaming, and moving your files and folders.*

6. Creating a Site Map

Creating a **site map** is a great way to examine the structure of your Web site because it allows you to see the different levels of your Web site and what is contained within those levels. Many people use site maps to show their client how the site looks from a structural viewpoint. It's handy that Dreamweaver MX can easily create site maps, and even render them as PICT or JPEG (Mac) or BMP or PNG (Windows) files. If you change the structure of the site, the site map will change as well. This exercise will show you how easy it is to create and save a site map.

1. If the **Site** panel is not already open, press **F8**.

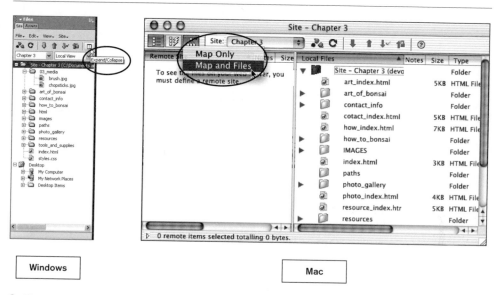

| Windows | Mac |

2. The process for viewing a site map is slightly different between the Mac and Windows versions of Dreamweaver MX:

- **Mac:** In the **Site** panel, click the **Site Map** button in the upper-left corner and choose **Map and Files** from the drop-down menu.

- **Windows:** In the **Site** panel, click the **Expand/Collapse** button in the upper-right corner. This will expand the Site panel so that it fills the entire screen. Click the **Site Map** button in the upper-left corner and choose **Map and Files** from the drop-down menu. Notice that you cannot see your document window or other panels when the Site panel is expanded.

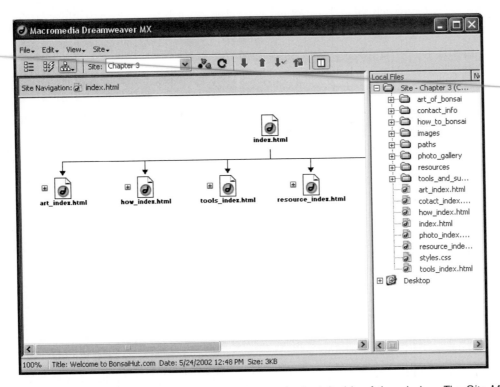

The Site Map view, set to Map and Files, will open in the left side of the window. The Site Map view is great if you want to see the overall structure of your Web site and how the different pages link to each other.

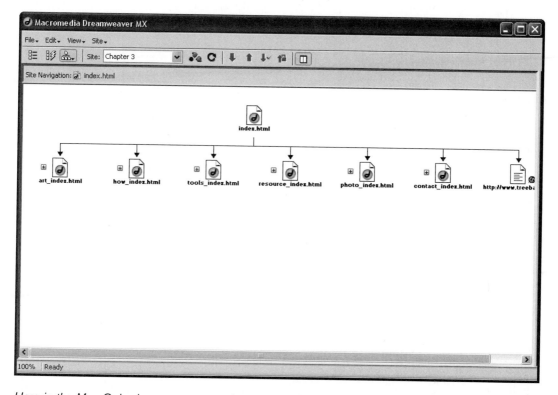

Here in the Map Only view, you can see the overall architecture of your Web site. If you click on any of the plus signs, you will see the pages linked to that page.

3. Saving the site map as an image, so you can view or print it later, is a bit different between the Windows and Mac systems:

- **Mac:** Select **Site > Site Map View > Save Site Map > Save Site Map as PICT**. You can name this file anything you want. **Note:** On the Mac, if you want to save this image in a compressed format, you could choose **Save Site Map as JPEG**.

- **Windows:** From the **Site** panel, select **File > Save Site Map**. A **Save As** dialog box will appear so you can name the map. You can name this file anything you want. You can save it as a BMP or PNG file.

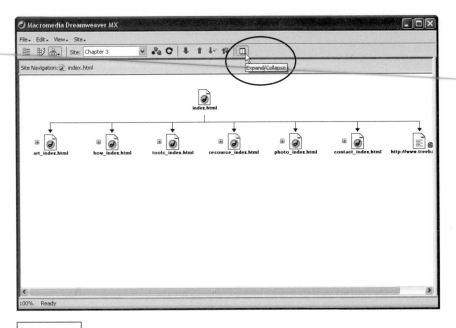

Windows

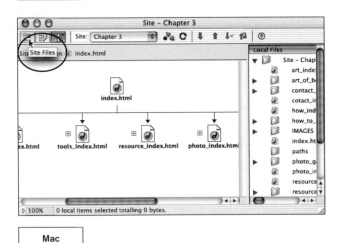

Mac

4. Return to the Site Files view:

> • **Mac:** At the top of the Site panel, click the **Site Files** button.

> • **Windows:** At the top of the Site panel, click the **Expand/Collapse** button.

5. You can leave the **Site** panel open for the next exercise.

7. ——————————Creating a Site from Nothing

So far, you've had a chance to work with the Dreamweaver MX site management window by defining a site based on folders and files from the **H•O•T CD-ROM**. What about when you finish this book and go to create your own Web site? You might know how to define a Web site that already exists, but not know how to go about creating a site from scratch. We wouldn't want that to happen to you, so this next exercise will walk you through the steps of defining a site before you have any content to put in it. This exercise will also introduce you to the **Advanced** tab of the Site Definition window.

1. Leave Dreamweaver MX open, but go to the desktop of your computer. Create a new empty folder on your desktop and name it **mywebsite**.

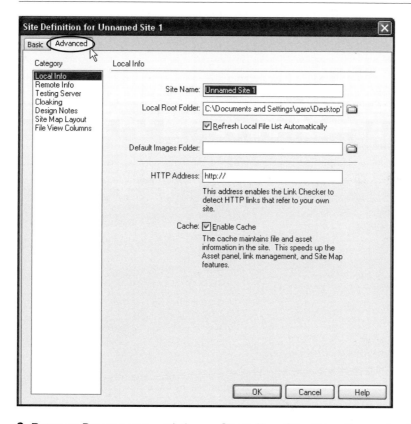

2. Return to Dreamweaver and choose **Site > New Site**. This will open the Site Definition window, where you can define a site using the Basic or Advanced tab. Make sure the **Advanced** tab is selected at the top.

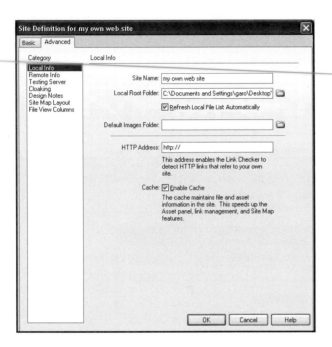

3. Fill in the **Site Name** (we chose **my own web site**, but you may name it what you want). For the **Local Root Folder**, click the folder icon and navigate to the empty folder you created on your desktop called **mywebsite**. Click **Open > Select** (Windows), or **Choose** (Mac), then click **OK**.

This is what your Site panel will look like now that you have created a new site based on an empty folder. Notice there's nothing in the Site panel. Dreamweaver MX is doing an accurate job of displaying the contents of an empty folder.

4. You can add files and folders directly from within the Site panel of Dreamweaver MX. This ensures that the files are automatically saved within the current local root folder (mywebsite), which is where they should be saved. To do so, make sure you highlight the local root folder at the top of the Site panel first, then:

- **Mac:** Choose **Site > Site Files View > New File**. The file will appear inside the Site panel as **untitled.html**. If the **New File** option is grayed out, make sure the local root folder is selected in the Site panel.

- **Windows:** From the Site panel, choose **File > New File**. The file will appear inside the Site panel as **untitled.htm**.

Note: You can name the file from the Site panel, just as you can rename an untitled document on your hard drive. Once a file has been created in the Site panel, its name will be highlighted and ready to be named. You can do it now, or later, by opening untitled.html (Mac) or untitled.htm (Windows) and selecting File > Save As.

---

5. Leave Dreamweaver MX open. Look on the desktop of your computer and open the **mywebsite** folder.

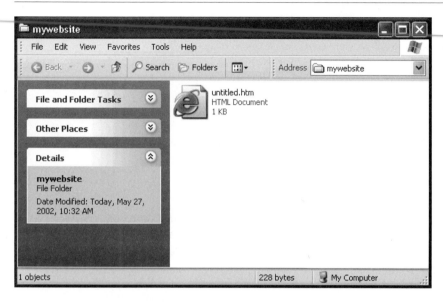

Lo and behold, there is an HTML document called untitled.html in there! The same HTML file that appeared in the Site panel is also on your hard drive.

6. Try creating some more files and saving them into this folder. When you return to Dreamweaver MX, these other files will appear in the Site panel. The Site panel is simply a mirror of what exists on your hard drive.

Importing Sites into Dreamweaver MX

There might be times when you need to work with an existing site in Dreamweaver MX, perhaps one that has been created in another program, such as FrontPage or GoLive. Dreamweaver MX doesn't have an "import Web site" command, but the process is pretty straightforward. Just create a new folder and copy all of the Web site assets (html, images, etc.) into that folder and then define that folder as a site in Dreamweaver MX. You will then have access to all of the Dreamweaver MX site management features. Yes, it is really that easy. ;-)

7. When you are finished, close all open files. It doesn't matter if you save your changes; you won't be using any of these files for the rest of the book.

Dreamweaver MX allows you to create files and folders directly from its Site panel. Some Web designers create a lot of images first and throw them into a folder and define that as a site inside Dreamweaver MX. Others might start with an empty folder and build empty HTML files first, then create and add images later. There is no right or wrong way to start a Web site, but Dreamweaver MX is flexible enough to work from scratch with an empty folder or to create a site around existing files.

4.
Basics

| Defining the Site | Creating a Document |
| Inserting and Centering Images and Text |
| Modifying Page Properties | Creating Links | META Tags |

chap_04

Dreamweaver MX
H•O•T CD-ROM

If you're the impatient type (as we would frankly characterize ourselves), this is the chapter you've been waiting for. The following exercises teach you how to define a site, create and save a page, insert and align images and text, link images and text, color text links, and insert META information (such as keywords and descriptions for search engines). Covering this much material may seem overwhelming, but fortunately Dreamweaver MX makes most of these operations as simple as accessing a menu or property bar.

By the time you are done with this chapter, your Dreamweaver MX feet will finally be wet, and you will be well on your way to understanding the program's interface for creating pages and sites. The exercises here will be your foundation for building more complex pages in future chapters.

I. ————————Defining the Site

In each new chapter, we request that you copy files from the **H•O•T CD-ROM** to a folder on your hard drive. In this exercise, you will revisit how to define a site based on the contents of the folder. Because each chapter of this book features different files, each chapter is defined as its own distinct site, so you will go through the process of this exercise many times. Normally, if you were working on a single site, you would most likely define your site once. If you switched projects, however, you would need to define a new site. Dreamweaver MX allows you to manage multiple sites, which is helpful if you have multiple clients or projects for which you plan to use the program.

1. Copy the **chap_04** folder from the **H•O•T CD-ROM** to your hard drive.

2. Make sure the **Site** panel is open. If it's not, press **F8**.

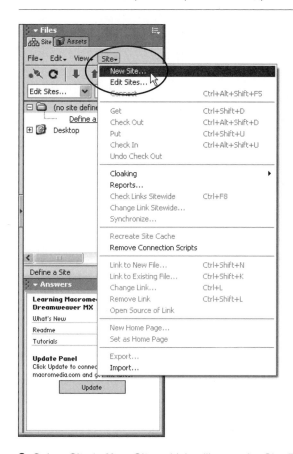

3. Select **Site > New Site**, which will open the Site Definition window.

4. Make sure the **Basic** tab, in the upper-left corner, is selected. In the **What would you like to name your site?** text field, type **Chapter 4**. This defines the name for your site. This name is an internal naming convention used by Dreamweaver MX. You can use any name you want, including special characters, such as spaces, dashes, etc. Click **Next**.

5. Make sure the **No, I do not want to use a server technology** radio button is selected. This tells Dreamweaver MX you are creating a static Web site and are not going to use a server technology, such as ASP, CFM, etc., with your site. A server technology is necessary if you were creating a Web site that connected to a database to generate dynamic data. Click **Next**.

Don't worry if you change your mind later. You can change all of the settings you define for your site at a later date. Phew!

6. Make sure the **Edit local copies on my machine, then upload to the server when ready (recommended)** radio button is selected. This tells Dreamweaver MX that you want to create the Web pages on your computer and upload them when you are ready. This is the most common way to create and publish Web pages.

7. Click the small yellow folder icon to open the browse dialog box. Locate the **chap_04** folder on your desktop:

- **Mac:** Highlight the **chap_04** folder and click **Choose**.

- **Windows:** Double-click the **chap_04** folder to open it. Click **Open**.

This specifies the folder you want to use as the local root folder for your site. In this case, you are using the **chap_04** folder as the local root folder. Each site you define in Dreamweaver MX must point to a folder that are using as the local root folder. Click **Next**.

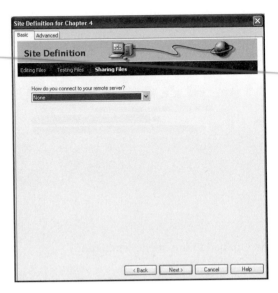

8. Make sure the **How do you connect to your remove server?** option is set to **None**. You will learn more about connecting to a remote Web server and how to upload files later in Chapter 20, "*Getting It Online*." Click **Next**.

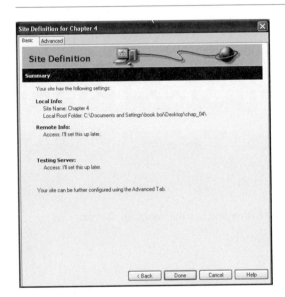

9. The next screen displays a summary of the settings you have specified for this site. Take a moment to review the information on this screen. If you have made a mistake, you can click **Back** to return to any of the previous screens to make any needed changes. Click **Done** if everything looks okay.

NOTE | Basic and Advanced Tabs

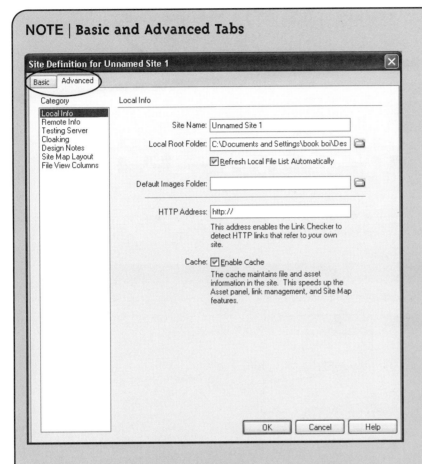

You might have noticed that the Site Definition window contains two tabs: Basic and Advanced. These tabs serve the same purpose: They both let you define a site. The Basic tab is more of a wizard approach, where you define a site by answering a series of questions. This is a great place to start if you are new to Dreamweaver MX. The Advanced tab is where more experienced Dreamweaver MX users will go to define a site. The Advanced tab gives you direct access to all the options necessary to define a site and work with other site features, such as Design Notes, modifying the Site Map Layout options, and changing the Site panel column options. As you become more experienced with Dreamweaver MX, you will find yourself using the Advanced tab to define your sites.

2. ———————————— Creating and Saving a New Document

This next exercise teaches you how to create and save a document in Dreamweaver MX. You will be saving this document as **index.html**, which has special significance in HTML, and almost always means that it is the beginning page of a site. Additionally, you will learn to set the title of this document to **The Bonsai Hut**.

1. If a blank document window is already open, close it and don't save any changes if you are prompted. Each time you open Dreamweaver MX, a new blank document window will open automatically. But, for this exercise, we want to show you how to create a new document from scratch.

2. Select **File > New**. This will open the New Document dialog box, which lets you choose a template for your new document.

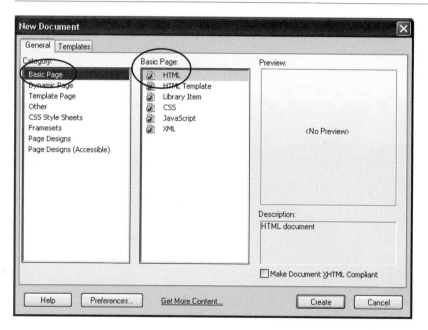

3. Make sure the **Basic Page** category is selected and then choose **HTML** under the Basic Page section. This tells Dreamweaver MX that you want to create an HTML page. Because you have selected HTML, Dreamweaver MX will create a new blank page with the basic HTML tags necessary to get started. Click **Create**.

NOTE | The New Document Dialog Box

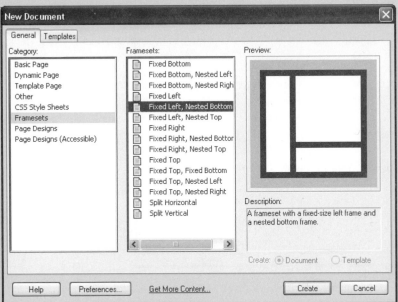

The New Document dialog box gives you access to many templates that you can use for creating new pages in Dreamweaver MX. These templates are designed to give you the necessary code to begin creating pages for specific purposes. Within each category are a number of different template options. For example, within the Framesets category are a number of different frameset designs. All of the templates are designed to save you time and get you started in the right direction. Some categories have a checkbox that will make sure the code is XHTML-compliant.

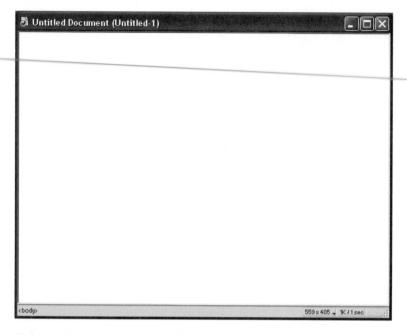

The New Document window will close, and a new blank HTML document window will open.

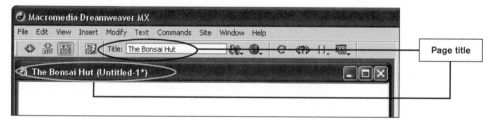

4. In the document panel's **Title** text field, type **The Bonsai Hut**. Press **Return/Enter**. This will define the page title for this page. The page title appears at the top of the browser when the page is being viewed and is the name used when a page is bookmarked. Right now the page is blank, but you're going to turn it into a cool and functional Web page in a jiffy.

Before you get started, it is very important that you save your file first. All of the site management benefits introduced in the last exercise depend on Dreamweaver MX knowing the name of your file. With this ability, the program constantly notifies you if you are working on an unsaved document. Besides, no one wants to unexpectedly lose work, and this practice is good insurance against system crashes and/or a power outage.

5. Save the file as **index.html** inside the **chap_04** folder on your hard disk. Leave this file open; you will be using it in the next exercise.

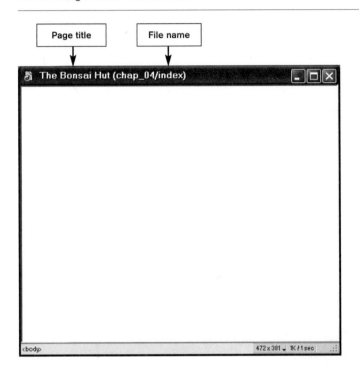

There are two names in the title bar of your document panel. The first is the title of the document (The Bonsai Hut). The second name is the file name (index.htm), which shows up to the right of the title. The title can be different from the file name, as in this example.

File Names versus Titles

As you create Web pages with Dreamweaver MX, you will need to specify various names for your files, folders, sites, etc. This might not seem tricky at first glance, but two different names are actually associated with HTML files: the file name and the title.

When you save a document, you will be assigning its file name. The file name must always end with the .htm or .html extension. The other name associated with the document is called the title. The file **index.html** here, for example, has the title **The Bonsai Hut**.

It is essential that file names do not contain spaces or special characters. Page titles, however, are much more flexible, and you should make them more descriptive than the file name. A title can contain spaces and special characters; file names should not. When the page is viewed from a Web browser, the title will be much more visible to your end user than the file name. Also, when end users bookmark this page, the title will appear in their bookmark list.

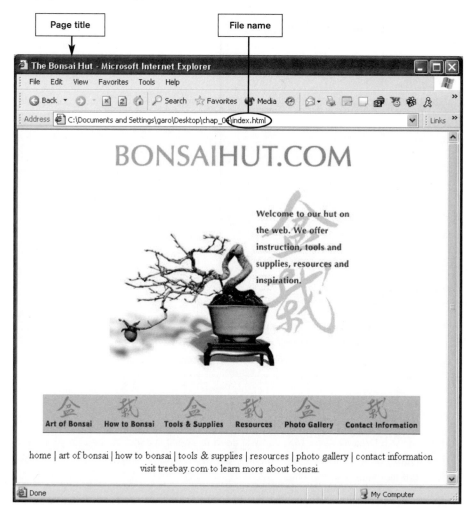

In this example (which you will build in this chapter), note that the title appears in the browser's title bar, and the file name appears in the URL. The file name is essential in that it allows the browser to understand that this is an HTML file, and to display the page properly. Titles are also important because they are sometimes used as the description for your site in search engines.

The Significance of index.html

You just created a document called **index.html**. What you may or may not appreciate is that this particular file name has special significance. Most Web servers recognize the index.htm (or index.html) as the default home page. You can use .htm and .html interchangeably; both will be recognized by the Web server as HTML pages. If you type the URL **http://www.lynda.com**, for example, what you will really see is **http://www.lynda.com/index.html**, even though you didn't type it that way. The Web server knows to open the index.html file automatically without requiring the full URL to be typed. Therefore, if you name the opening page of your Web site with the file name index.html, the Web server will know to automatically display this file first.

Taking this concept one step further, you can have an opening page for each section of your Web site, not just for your home page. This feature has definite advantages—among them, your users won't find themselves looking at a generic index like in the following example.

This is why the file name index.html is so significant. It's also the reason most professional Web developers use it as the **root file** name, although on some servers a different name is used, such as **default.html**. What you may not realize is that you are not limited to just one index.html on your site. You can have an index.html inside each folder that represents a category for your site, such as **Company**, **Services**, **Store**, and **Products**.

If you do not have an index.html file in your site, browsers will display a general list of your files, such as this example.

3. ———————————Inserting Images

In this exercise, you will continue working with the **index.htm** file and learn to insert images for your page's headline, logo, and navigation bar.

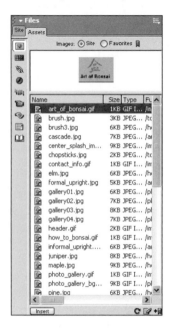

1. Make sure the **Assets** panel is open by choosing **Window > Assets** or by pressing **F11**. Inserting images from the Assets panel ensures that you are working only with images from within your local root folder. This is a good thing, because inserting images from outside your local root folder will cause problems when you try to upload your page to the Web server.

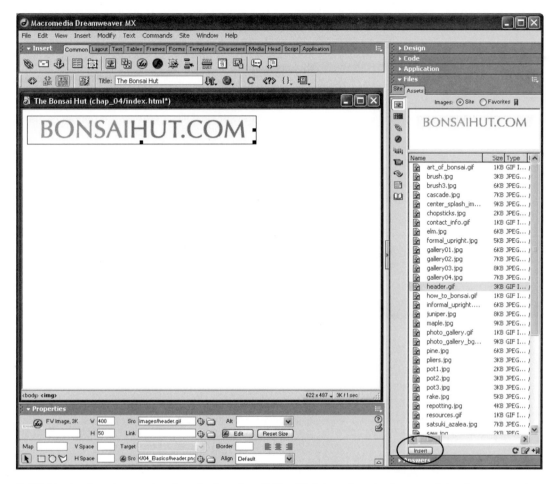

2. Within the **Assets** panel, select the **header.gif** file. Click **Insert** at the bottom of the Assets panel. This will insert the selected image onto your page.

3. In the **Document** window, click to the right of the header.gif image to deselect it, and press **Enter/Return** to create a paragraph break, causing a space to form between the headline graphic and the next image.

4. Within the **Assets** panel, select the **center_splash_image.gif** file. Click **Insert** at the bottom of the Assets panel. This will insert the selected image onto your page.

5. Click to the right of the image to deselect it, and then press **Enter/Return**. This inserts another paragraph break between this image and the next.

6. Within the **Assets** panel, select the **art_of_bonsai.gif** file. Click **Insert** at the bottom of the Assets panel.

7. Within the **Assets** panel, select the **how_to_bonsai.gif** file. Click **Insert** at the bottom of the Assets panel.

8. Within the **Assets** panel, select the **tools_and_supplies.gif** file. Click **Insert** at the bottom of the Assets panel.

9. Within the **Assets** panel, select the **resources.gif** file. Click **Insert** at the bottom of the Assets panel.

10. Within the **Assets** panel, select the **photo_gallery.gif** file. Click **Insert** at the bottom of the Assets panel.

11. Within the **Assets** panel, select the **contact_info.gif** file. Click **Insert** at the bottom of the Assets panel.

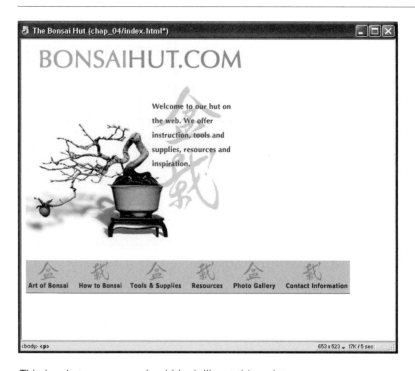

This is what your page should look like at this point.

12. Save your file and leave it open for the next exercise.

TIP | Other Ways to Insert Images

There are many ways to insert images in Dreamweaver MX. In this exercise, you learned how to use the Assets panel to insert images onto your page. We think this is not only the quickest way, but also the safest way to insert images onto your page. Why? First, only images within your local root folder are listed in the Assets panel. Second, by inserting images from within your local root folder you ensure that the proper paths will be created, so everything works when you upload your page to a remote Web server. But the Assets panel isn't the only way to insert images in Dreamweaver MX. Here are three other ways to insert images:

- Select Insert > Image

- Click the Insert Image button in the Insert panel.

- Press Ctrl+Alt+I (Windows) or Cmd+Option+I (Mac)

As you become more comfortable with Dreamweaver MX, you should use the method that feels most comfortable.

4. _____Inserting Text

Adding text to your Web page is simple in Dreamweaver MX. Just like your favorite word processor, you can simply start typing text on your page and the text will appear.

In this exercise, you will add some text at the bottom of your page as an alternate navigation system, which is useful to users who might have images turned off in their browser settings or be browsing in a nongraphical browser (such as those used by sight-impaired audiences).

1. Click to the right of the **contact_info.gif** file you inserted in the last exercise and press **Enter/Return** to create a paragraph break. Type **home**, press the **spacebar**, press **Shift+ backslash** to insert a small vertical line (|), or "pipe," and press the **spacebar** again.

2. Type **art of bonsai**, press the **spacebar**, press **Shift+backslash** to insert a pipe, and press the **spacebar** again.

3. Type **how to bonsai**, press the **spacebar**, press **Shift+backslash** to insert a pipe, and press the **spacebar** again.

4. Type **tools and supplies**, press the **spacebar**, press **Shift+backslash** to insert a pipe, and press the **spacebar** again.

5. Type **resources**, press the **spacebar**, press **Shift+backslash** to insert a pipe, and press the **spacebar** again.

6. Type **photo gallery**, press the **spacebar**, press **Shift+backslash** to insert a pipe, and press the **spacebar** again.

7. Type **contact information**.

8. Press **Shift+Enter/Return** to create a line break. This puts your type-insertion cursor on the next line without introducing a two-line paragraph return.

9. Type **visit treebay.com to learn more about bonsai.**

This is what your page should look like now.

10. **Save** your file.

NOTE | Paragraph versus Line Breaks

You may have noticed that each time you pressed the **Enter/Return** key, Dreamweaver MX skipped down the page two lines. Pressing this key inserts a single paragraph break. The HTML tag for a paragraph break is **\<p>**. This is useful when you want to increase the space between different paragraphs. However, there will be times when you just want to go to one line directly below the one you are working on without introducing extra space. Pressing **Shift+Return** (or **Shift+Enter**) inserts a line break instead. The HTML tag for a line break is **\
. Knowing the difference between a **\<p> and a **\
** will allow you to control the spacing between lines of text. **Note:** If your screen looks different from ours, that's because we changed a setting in the Code View panel called **Word Wrap**. You will learn to do this in Chapter 12, "*HTML*."

The paragraph tag **\<p>** *will enter an extra line between the closing paragraph tag* **\</p>** *and the next line of content. The line break tag* **\
** *will place content on the very next line. You can see both of these here.*

continues on next page

NOTE | **Paragraph Versus Line Breaks** *continued*

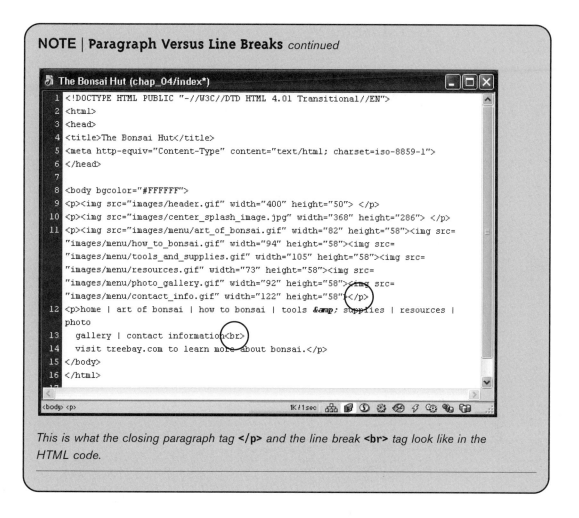

This is what the closing paragraph tag **</p>** *and the line break* **
** *tag look like in the HTML code.*

5. ————————Centering Images and Text

Now that you have added the images and text to your page, it's time to learn how to center them. This section shows you how to use centering procedures with text and images.

1. Select the **bonsaihut.com** logo image from the previous exercise (**header.gif**) at the top of the screen.

2. Click the **Align Center** button in the **Property Inspector**. This will snap the logo to the center of the screen.

3. Hold down the **Shift** key and click on the remaining images: the **tree image** (center_splash_image.gif), **Art of Bonsai** (art_of_bonsai.gif), **How to Bonsai** (how_to_bonsai.gif), **Tools & Supplies** (tools_and_supplies.gif), **Resources** (resources.gif), **Photo Gallery** (photo_gallery.gif), and **Contact Information** (contact_info.gif). Still holding down the **Shift** key, select the text at the bottom of the screen. Holding down the **Shift** key allows you to select multiple items at once.

4. Click the **Align Center** button in the **Property Inspector**.

Your page should look like this at the end of the exercise.

5. Save the file and leave it open for the next exercise.

6. —————————Modifying Page Properties

This exercise walks you through changing the colors of your page, using the **Page Properties** panel. The Page Properties feature controls many important attributes of your page, including the document title (which we looked at in Exercise 2), and the colors you set for your text and links.

1. Select **Modify > Page Properties** or use the shortcut—**Ctrl+J** (Windows) or **Cmd+J** (Mac)—to access Page Properties.

2. Move this panel to the side so you can see the Page Properties and your document at the same time.

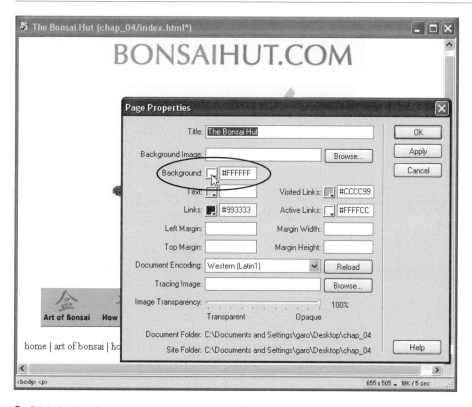

3. Click the small box to the right of the word **Background**. This will open the Dreamweaver MX color picker.

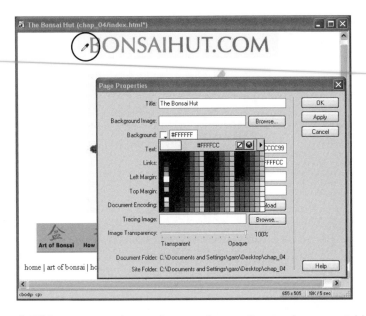

4. With your mouse button depressed, move the eye dropper outside of the Page Properties panel and release the mouse on the background of the **bonsaihut.com** image. This will set the background color of your page to match the edge of this image. To instantly see the results, click **Apply**. Don't click **OK** yet, because you still need to set more colors in the upcoming steps.

5. Click inside the text box next to the **Text** option. Type **#CCCC99**. Click **Apply**. You just colored all your text green in this document. The **Apply** button is actually accepting your changes; it is not merely a preview. Clicking it is the same as clicking **OK**, except that it does not close the panel.

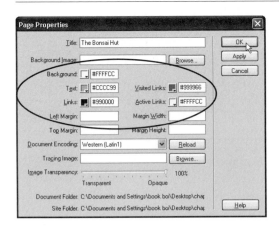

To set other colors, you can insert your own values.

6. Type **#990000** for the **Links** option, which will set the link text in this document to dark red. Type **#999966** for the **Visited Links** option, which will set visited link text to dark green, letting the user know that that link has already been viewed.

7. You could also choose a color by sight, instead of typing in a hexadecimal value. Click the box to the right of the words **Active Links** and the **color** picker will open. Move the eye dropper over the yellow background of the page and click. This will set the active link color to the same color as the background. The only time an active link color shows is when the mouse button is clicked on the link.

8. Click **OK**.

This is what the results of this exercise should look like.

9. Save the document and leave it open for the next exercise.

The Page Properties Panel

The Page Properties panel does more than just set the colors of the links and your document title. See the following chart for an explanation of all its features.

Page Properties	
Property	**Description**
Title	The title of your page is what will appear in the title bar of the Web browser and when your page is bookmarked. This name can contain as many characters as you want, including special characters, such as %(#*!.
Background Image	If you want a background image for your Web page, you would specify it here. A background image can be any GIF or JPEG file. If the image is smaller than the Web browser panel, it will repeat (tile).
Background	Sets the background color. The values can be in hexadecimal format or by name, for example red, white, etc.
Text	Sets the default text color. It can be overwritten for specific areas of text.
Links	Sets the color for links. This option can be overwritten for specific links.
Visited Links	A visited link color specifies how the link will appear after a visitor has clicked it.
Active Links	The active link color specifies how the link will appear while someone clicks it.
Document Encoding	Specifies the language for the characters and fonts used in the document.
Tracing Image	Tracing images are used as guides to set up the layout of your page. They can be any GIF, JPEG, or PNG file.
Transparency	Sets the transparency level of your tracing image.
Left Margin	Sets the left margin value in pixels. This attribute is supported only in Internet Explorer 4.0 or later.
Top Margin	Sets the top margin value in pixels. This attribute is supported only in Internet Explorer 4.0 or later.
Margin Width	Sets the margin width value in pixels. This attribute is supported only in Netscape Navigator 4.0 or later.
Margin Height	Sets the margin height value in pixels. This attribute is supported only in Netscape Navigator 4.0 or later.

The Dreamweaver Color Pickers

From the Page Properties dialog box, Dreamweaver MX gives you access to five different color pickers, from which you can select the colors for your pages. Two of the color pickers, Color Cubes and Continuous Tone, are browser-safe, and they're arranged in a manner that makes it easy to select pleasing color combinations. To understand each function of the color picker drop-down menu, see the color picker options chart.

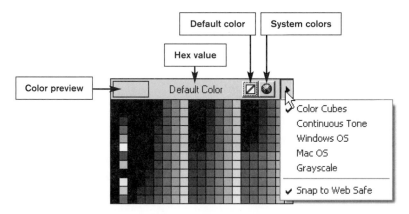

NOTE | What Is Browser-Safe Color?

Browser-safe colors are the 216 colors supported by browsers across platforms (Mac and Windows). If you use the browser-safe colors inside the Page Properties settings, you reduce the risk of having your colors shift when people view your Web pages.

Color Picker Options	
Option	**Description**
Color preview	Gives you a preview of the color that is currently selected or the color that the eye dropper is picking up.
Hex value	Displays the hexadecimal value of the current color or the color that the eyedropper is picking up.
Default color	Removes any colors you have selected. If you do not specify a color in the Page Properties, the user's browser will determine what colors are used for the different text options.
System colors	Opens the system color options for your computer—these options will vary between the Mac and Windows operating systems.
Color Options	This drop-down menu lets you choose from five different color arrangements. The Color Cubes and Continuous Tone options contain only Web-safe colors. The Windows and Mac options contain the system colors for the Windows and Mac operating systems. The Grayscale option contains grays ranging from black to white.
Snap to Web Safe	Automatically switches non–Web-safe colors to their nearest Web-safe value.

7. ———————Creating Links with Images and Text

The ability to link to pages and sites is what makes the Web dynamic. This exercise shows you how to set up links using the Dreamweaver MX Property Inspector.

1. Select the **art_of_bonsai.gif** (Art of Bonsai) image in the lower-left part of the screen.

2. Click the **Browse for File** icon, next to the **Link** option, in the **Property Inspector. Note:** If your Property Inspector panel is smaller than what is shown here, click the arrow in the lower-right corner to expand it.

3. Browse to **chap_04/art_of_bonsai/index.html** and click **OK** (Windows) or **Choose** (Macintosh). Congratulations, you have just created your first relative image link. Why is it relative? It is relative simply because it linked to a document within this site, not to an external Web site.

4. Highlight the **how_to_bonsai.gif** (How To Bonsai) image in the lower-left corner of the screen.

5. Click the **Browse for File** icon next to the Link option in the **Property Inspector**.

6. Browse to **chap_04/how_to_bonsai/index.html**. Click **OK**. This image is now linked to the **index.html** page inside the **how_to_bonsai** folder.

7. Repeat this process for the remaining navigation icons. Select the **tools_and_supplies.gif** (Tools & Supplies) image and link it to **chap_04/tools_and_supplies/index.html**. Click **OK**. Select the **resources.gif** (Resources) image and link it to **chap_04/resources/index.html**. Click **OK**. Select the **photo_gallery.gif** (Photo Gallery) image and link it to **chap_04/photo_gallery/index.html**. Click **OK**. Select the **contact_info.gif** (Contact Information) image and link it to **chap_04/contact_info/index.html**. Click **OK**.

You have just successfully added links to the images on this page! If you want to preview the links in a browser, press F12 and click any of the images. **Note:** *If a browser does not launch when you press F12, refer to Chapter 2, "Interface", to learn how to specify a browser to preview your pages.*

Next, you will create some links using text. The process is almost identical, except you will be selecting text instead of images.

8. Highlight the words **art of bonsai** in the lower-left corner of the page.

9. Click the **Browse for File** icon in the **Property Inspector**.

10. Browse to **chap_04/art_of_bonsai/index.html**. Click **OK**.

11. Repeat this process for each phrase in the text navigation bar at the bottom of the screen. Be sure to link the text at the bottom of the page to the same page as the corresponding images.

As you create the text links, you will notice the color of the text change. This happens because you set the Links color option in the Page Properties to red and Dreamweaver MX is previewing that setting for you.

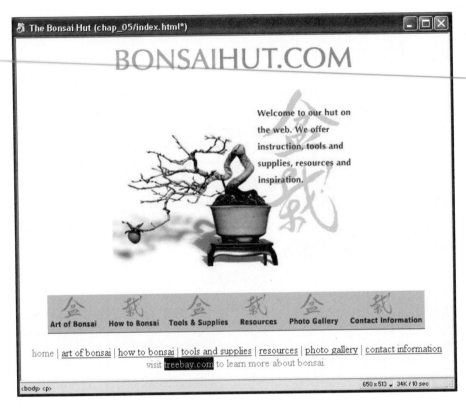

12. Highlight the word **treebay.com** at the bottom of the page.

13. Type **http://www.treebay.com** into the **Link** option in the Property Inspector and press **Return/ Enter**. Congratulations, you just created your first absolute link. It's an absolute link because it begins with an http header and includes the full address.

14. Save the file. You don't want to lose any of your work!

15. If you want to preview all of your links, press **F12** to launch a browser and try them out. **Note:** Only the links you created on the **index.html** page will be working. You will learn some effective and fancy ways to work with linking in Chapter 5, "*Linking*."

8. —————————META Tags

One of the big challenges (aside from building a Web site) is letting the search engines know that your site exists. There are two steps to getting your site listed: the first is to list it with all the various search engines out there, and the other is to insert **META** tags into your HTML so the search engines can find you on their own and correctly index your site. Many search engines send robots (also called spiders) out to search the Web for content. When you insert certain META tags into your document, you make it much easier for the search-engine robots to understand how to categorize your site. This exercise shows you how to enter META tags with specific attributes, so you can make your Web page more search-engine friendly.

1. In the **Insert** panel, click the **Head** tab. This panel contains several elements that are placed within the **HEAD** tag of a page, such as META elements.

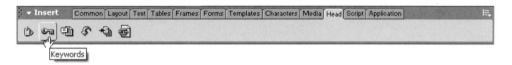

2. Click the **Keywords** icon. A dialog box will be displayed for you to enter in the keywords for your page.

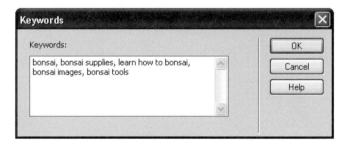

3. Type **bonsai, bonsai supplies, learn how to bonsai, bonsai images, bonsai tools**. Basically, you're listing words that someone might use in a search engine to bring up your site.

4. Click **OK**.

5. Click the **Description** button. A dialog box will appear in which you can enter the description of your Web page.

6. Type **A great place to learn more about bonsai. Learn how to bonsai and see a whole gallery of bonsai photos.**

7. Click **OK**.

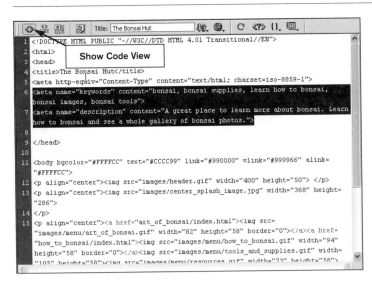

8. Click the **Show Code View** button to view the HTML in this document. See the META information inside the **HEAD** tag? Visitors to your site won't be able to see the META tag information because it's only visible inside your HTML. It's a part of authoring the page that has nothing to do with appearance—and everything to do with helping the search engines find your site.

9. Save and close this document.

WARNING | Keyword and Descriptions

Keywords are META tag values that specify certain words to help Internet search engines index your site. Many search engines limit the number of keywords you can use. Choose your words wisely and use no more than 10 to 15 keywords that best describe your site's contents.

Descriptions are META tag values that also help various search engines index your site. Some search engines will actually use in their directory the very descriptions you specify to describe your site. Again, some search engines limit the number of characters indexed, so keep it short and simple! If you would like more information about META tags, check out these URLs:

Web Developer: META Tag Resources
`http://www.webdeveloper.com/html/html_metatag_res.html`

Search Engine Watch
`http://searchenginewatch.com/webmasters/meta.html`

Onward ho! You just built a page, colored it, set links, and added META tags all in one chapter. Future chapters will reveal even more powers of Dreamweaver MX, so keep on reading!

5.

Linking

| Linking with Point to File |
| Linking to New Source Files |
| Browse for File and Link History | Email Links |
| Named Anchors | Image Maps | Linking to Files |

chap_o5

Dreamweaver MX
H•O•T CD-ROM

There are a few ways to create links that you haven't learned yet. In this chapter, you'll learn about **Point to File**, which allows you to point to a file inside your Site panel and create the link based on your selection. Another type of link is an **email link**. This special type of link launches your end user's email program and automatically enters a recipient address. You will also learn how to use the **Link History** to quickly replicate links across your site, which can save you time and effort. Another new type of link you'll work with here is called **named anchors**, which work in conjunction with links to allow you to jump to different sections of one page. Image maps are also covered in this chapter. Image maps are useful when you want a single image to contain multiple links. The final type of link that this chapter demonstrates is a **file link**. File links let you link to files, such as PDFs, SIT and ZIP archives, etc. If this all sounds abstract, dive into the chapter so you can get the hands-on experience that will make these new concepts understandable.

I. ——————Linking with Point to File

The Point to File feature is an alternate way to create links on your Web pages. This feature forces you to select files that are within your local root folder, which eliminates the unwanted possibility of linking to files located outside of your defined site. Here's how it's done.

1. Copy the **chap_05** folder from the **H•O•T CD-ROM** to your hard drive. Define your site for Chapter 5 using the **chap_05** folder as the local root folder. If you need a refresher on this process, visit Exercise 1 in Chapter 3, "*Site Control.*"

2. Open **index.html**. This file is complete except that it does not contain any links. You will create them using the Point to File feature.

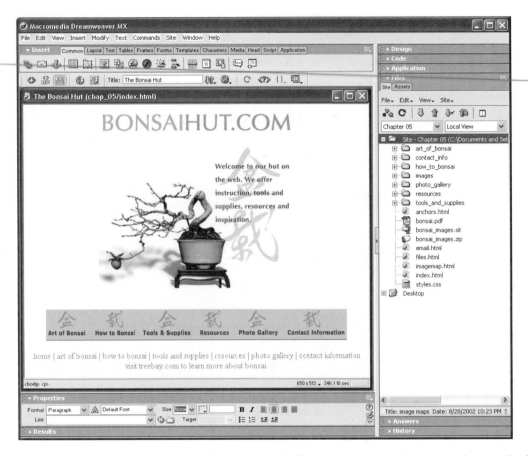

For the next step, if you are using a Mac or using the Dreamweaver 4 workspace, make sure the Site panel is open and visible. It does not have to be in the foreground, just open and visible in the background or side-by-side with your document on the screen.

3. Click the **art_of_bonsai.gif** (Art of Bonsai) image so that it is highlighted. Before you can create a link, you must first have the image or text selected.

4. In the **Property Inspector**, click and hold the **Point to File** icon next to the **Link** field. When you click on the icon and hold down the mouse button, the **Link** field will fill in with some text, telling you to point to a file to create a link.

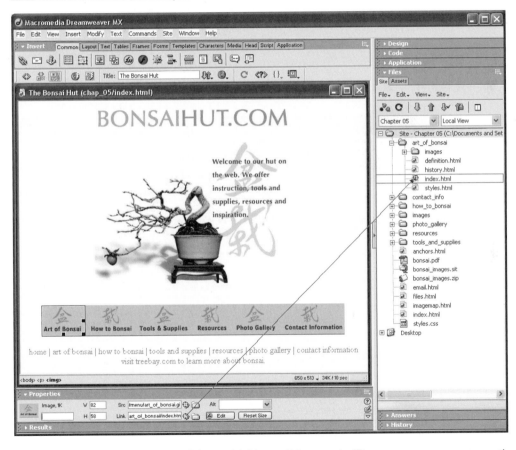

5. Move the cursor over the **art_of_bonsai** folder until it expands. Then move your cursor over the **index.html** so that it is highlighted, and release the mouse button. This will create a link to **index.html** inside the **art_of_bonsai** folder.

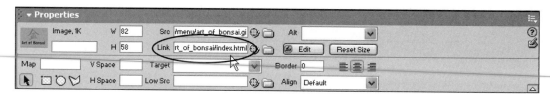

The Link field will display the file you are linking to. This is a good place to look if you forget what file you linked to. The great thing about using this technique is that there's no possible way to accidentally set the link to a misspelled or missing file name.

6. Click the **how_to_bonsai.gif** (How to Bonsai) image so that it is highlighted.

7. In the **Property Inspector**, click and hold the **Point to File** icon again. When you click and hold down the mouse button, the **Link** field will fill in with some text.

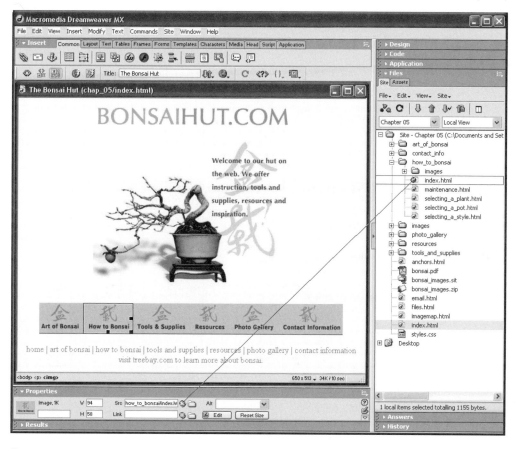

8. Move your cursor over the **how_to_bonsai** folder and hold it there until the folder expands. Then move your cursor over the **index.html** so that it is highlighted, and release the mouse button. This will create a link to **index.html** inside the **how_to_bonsai** folder.

9. Using the **Point to File** icon, create a link for the **tools_and_supplies.gif** (Tools & Supplies) image to **tools_and_supplies/index.html**; **resources.gif** (Resources) image to **resources/index.html**; **photo_gallery.gif** (Photo Gallery) image to **photo_gallery/index.html**; and a link for the **contact_info.gif** (Contact Information) image to **contact_info/index.html**.

10. Press **F12** to preview the page in a browser. Click any of the images you linked to see if they work. When you are finished, return to Dreamweaver MX.

11. Save the changes you've made, and close this file. You won't need it anymore.

2. ————————**Linking to New Source Files**

In the last exercise, you learned how to use the Point to File feature to create links on your pages. Although this is the most common use of this feature, you can also use it other ways. You can use the Point to File feature to quickly replace images or placeholders on your page. In this context, Point to File is an alternate method to using the Image object on the **Insert** panel, which you learned about in Chapter 4, "*Basics*." Sometimes there is more than one way to do the same thing in Dreamweaver MX. You'll find that you will develop your own preferences for which method to use as you gain experience in the program.

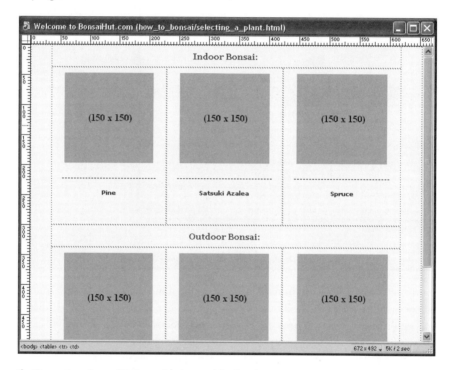

1. Open the **chap_05/how_to_bonsai/selecting_a_plant.html**. This HTML file contains a layout made with tables and several image placeholders.

NOTE | What Is a Placeholder?

A placeholder is an object that you can add to your page to represent where final content will be inserted. You can add a placeholder by clicking the **Image Placeholder** button in the Insert panel or by holding down the **Option** (Mac) or **Ctrl** (Windows) key while clicking the Insert Image object in the Insert panel. Then, you can resize the placeholder by selecting it first and then changing its height and width values in the Property Inspector. Placeholders are helpful in a workgroup where one person designs the page and another adds the content. You can resize the placeholder so that it matches the dimensions of the image that will replace it. This resizing will give you a more accurate preview of your page layout and positioning. You can quickly change the placeholder size by using the Width and Height options in the Property Inspector.

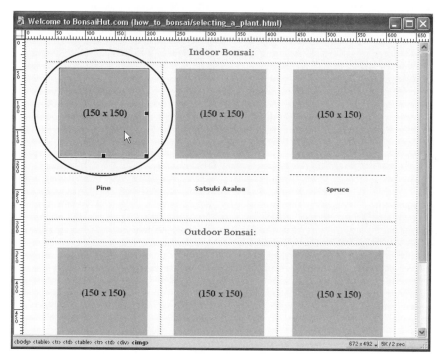

2. Click the image placeholder in the **upper-left corner** of the page to highlight it.

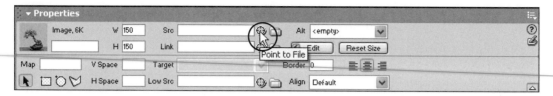

3. In the **Property Inspector**, click the **Point to File** icon next to the **Src** option and drag it over the Site panel. Hold your cursor over the **images** folder inside the **how_to_bonsai** folder. This will expand the images folder so you can select one of the images inside. Then move your cursor over the **indoor** folder until it expands, so you can access the images inside that folder.

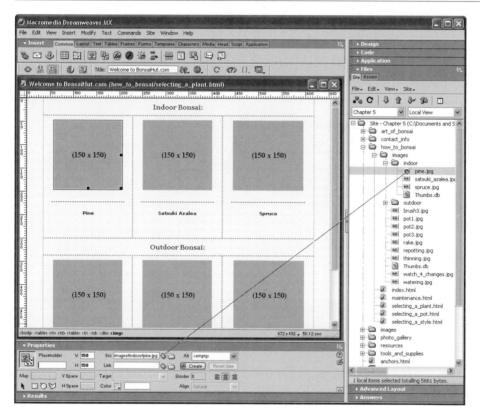

4. Move your cursor over the **pine.jpg** image and release the mouse button, which will select that image to replace the placeholder currently on your page.

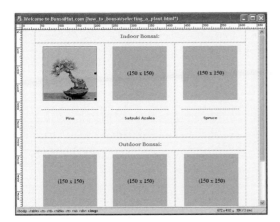

Notice that the placeholder has been replaced with the selected image.

5. Click to select the placeholder to the right of the image you just replaced.

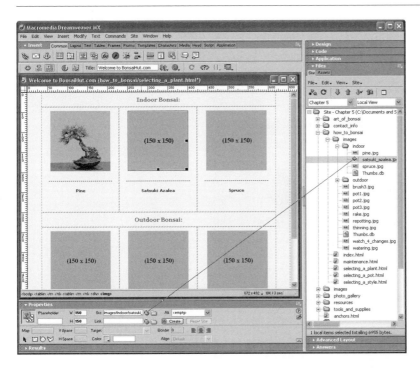

6. In the **Property Inspector**, click the **Point to File** icon next to the **Src** option and drag it over the **satsuki_azalea.jpg** and release the mouse button. This will select that image to replace the placeholder currently on your page.

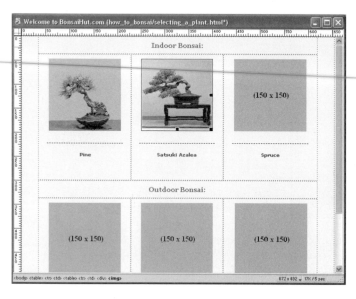

Notice that the second placeholder has now been replaced with the satsuki_azalea.jpg image.

7. Replace the other four images on this page, using the **Point to File** feature (using the preceding image as a guideline). When you are finished, your page should look like the one in Step 8. **Note:** The images for the outdoor plants are located inside the **outdoor** folder.

8. Save your work. You can close this file, because you won't need it for any other exercises in this book.

3. ————————**Browse for File and the Link History**

The **Link History** is one of those features that you probably are not aware of, but it can save you time and ensure that links are entered properly throughout your site. It will not remember links that you attach to images using the Point to File feature. If you want to enjoy the convenience of the Link History for both image and text links, you should create your links using the Browse for File feature.

This exercise shows you how to use the Link History to reproduce links throughout many pages in your site.

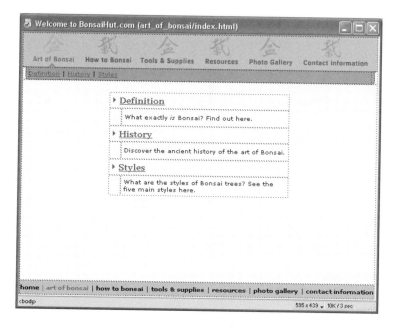

1. Make sure you have **chap_05/art_of_bonsai/index.html** file open..

2. Highlight the word **home** at the bottom of the page. Notice that art of bonsai is a different color than the other text, that's because you are already in the art of bonsai page, so you don't need to create a link to that page. This isn't a requirement, but is a common technique when setting up links on a Web page.

3. In the **Property Inspector**, click **Browse for File**.

4. Browse to **chap_05/index.html** and click **OK** (Windows) or **Choose** (Mac). This will create a link to that HTML file. Note: Make sure the Relative To: option is set to Document.

5. Highlight the words **how to bonsai** at the bottom of the page.

6. Click **Browse for File** again.

7. Browse to **chap_05/how_to_bonsai/index.html** and click **OK** (Windows) or **Choose** (Mac). This will create a link to that HTML file..

8. Using the **Browse for File** method, create a link for the rest of the text navigation:

- Link tools and supplies to **chap_05/tools_and_supplies/index.html**.

- Link resources to **chap_05/resources/index.html**.

- Link photo gallery to **chap_05/photo_gallery/index.html**.

- Link contact information to **chap_05/contact_info/index.html**.

Now that you have created the links for your site, you are ready to begin using the Link History.

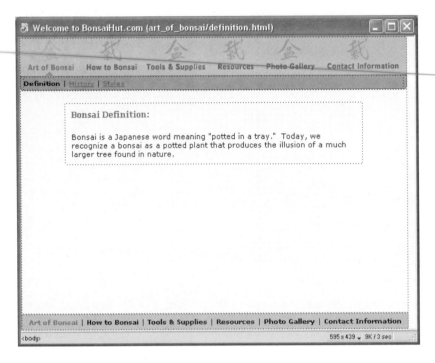

9. Open **art_of_bonsai/definition.html**. The text at the bottom of the page needs to be converted to links. In the following steps, you will use the Link History to do this very quickly.

10. Highlight the words **how to bonsai** at the bottom of the page.

You have already created a link to this file, so it is recorded in the Link History.

11. In the **Property Inspector**, click the **Link History** pop-up menu and choose **../how_to_bonsai/index.html**. This will create a link to that HTML file. Notice that each link you created using the Browse for File method is listed in the Link History.

12. Highlight the words **tools & supplies**.

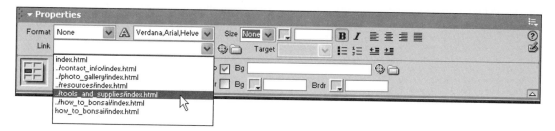

13. Click the **Link History** pop-up menu and choose **../tools_and_supplies/index.html**. This creates a link to that HTML file.

14. Highlight the word **resources**.

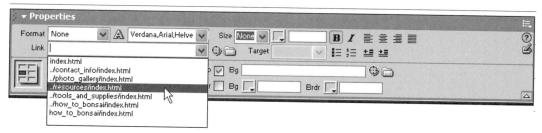

15. Click the **Link History** pop-up menu and choose **../resources/index.html**. This will create a link to that HTML file.

16. Highlight the words **photo gallery**.

17. Click the **Link History** pop-up menu and choose **../photo_gallery/index.html**. This will create a link to that HTML file.

*By now, you should be able to see how much time you can save by using the Link History. If you want more practice using the Link History, open the **index.html** page inside each folder and create links for the text at the bottom of each these pages.*

18. Press **F12** to preview your page in a browser. Make sure you check the links you created at the bottom of each page.

19. Return to Dreamweaver and **save** and **close** the file.

You did all that work in just a few minutes and no typing, browsing, or pointing was needed. Sweet!

4. —————————Creating Email Links

An **email** link will launch your end user's email application and insert the recipient's address into the **To:** field. This is convenient and doesn't require the end user to remember complex and lengthy email addresses. This exercise shows you how to create an email link.

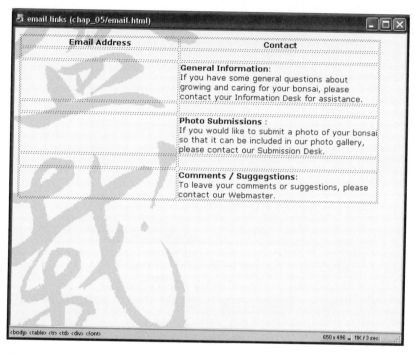

1. Open **email.html**. This file contains a table with some text and spaces for some email links. You will create those links in this exercise.

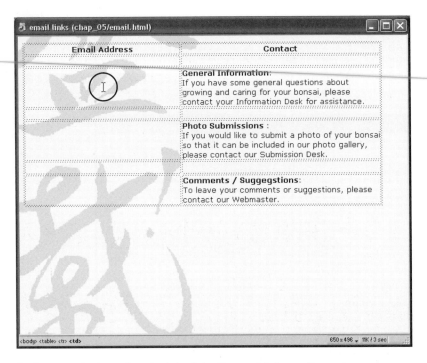

2. Click inside the cell to the left of the **General Information** column.

3. Click **Email Link** in the **Insert** panel. This will open the **Email Link** dialog box.

4. Enter Text: **General Information** and press **Tab**. Enter E-Mail: **information@bonsaihut.com**. Click **OK**.

5. Click anywhere on the email link you just inserted on the page. In the **Property Inspector**, notice that the **Link** field reads **mailto:information@bonsaihut.com**. This is the correct format for creating email links.

NOTE | Text versus Email

The Text field determines what text will be displayed on the page, whereas the E-Mail field sets the actual email address for the recipient. Sometimes, you might want to put the email address in both fields, to allow someone to copy and paste the actual email link into another document or email application.

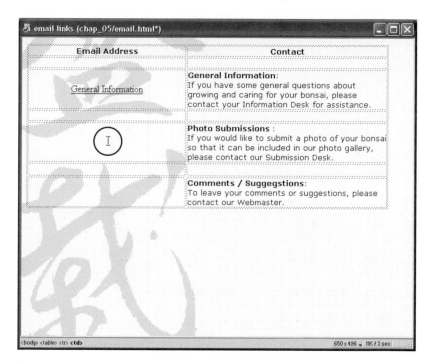

6. Click inside the cell to the left of the **Photo Submissions** cell.

7. Click **Email Link** in the **Insert** bar.

8. Enter Text: **photos@bonsaihut.com** and press **Tab**. Enter E-Mail: **photos@bonsaihut.com**. Because Dreamweaver will automatically insert any email address that you used previously, **information@bonsaihut.com** will appear in the **E-Mail:** field in the Property Inspector. Click **OK**. This will insert an email link into the empty cell.

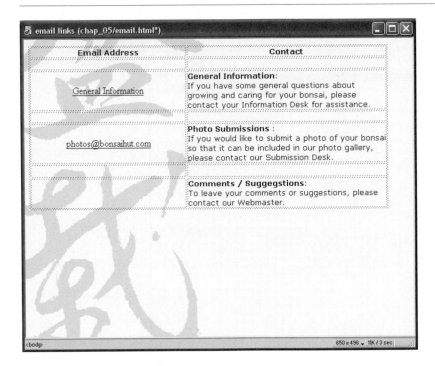

You have just created an email link that displays the email address on the page.

9. An alternate way to create an email link is to avoid the **Email Link** object and do it manually. To do this, first click inside the cell to the left of the **Comments/Suggestions** cell.

10. Type **comments@bonsaihut.com** inside the empty cell.

11. Click and drag over **comments@bonsaihut.com** to highlight the text.

12. In the **Property Inspector**, type **mailto:comments@bonsaihut.com** in the **Link** field and press **Return/Enter**. This will create an email link from the selected text.

You see, once again there are two ways to do the same operation. You learned how to create the email link using the Email Link *object and how to manually insert an email link. As your skills build in Dreamweaver MX, you will develop your own personal preferences for creating email links, just as you will develop your own preferences for assigning links.*

13. Press **F12** to preview this page in your default browser. You can click each of the email links to make sure they work.

14. When you are finished, return to Dreamweaver MX so you can **save** and **close** this file.

WARNING | Browser Email Settings

Not all site visitors use a browser for their email; they sometimes use other programs, such as Eudora, Entourage, etc. If visitors to your site click an email link and do not have their email preferences set in their browsers, they will get an error message asking them to do so. This is true for both Internet Explorer and Netscape Navigator. There's not a lot you can do about this, and it's a good reason to include email addresses in your email links, as was shown in Step 8 of the preceding exercise.

5. _____Named Anchors

Named anchors are a type of link. They are used infrequently, but when they're appropriate there's no other link quite like them. The time to use them is when you want to link to sections within a long page of content. Named anchors have two components—the **anchor** and the **link**. Working together, they make it easy to jump to specific areas of your page. This exercise shows you how to set up anchors on your page.

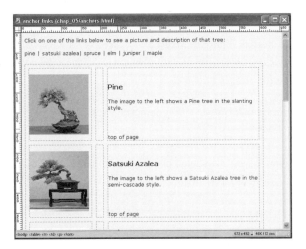

1. Open **anchors.html**. This file has a table with some images that extend down the page.

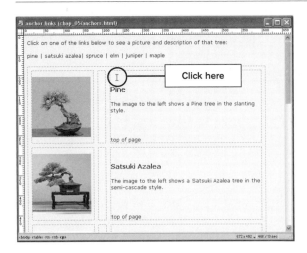

2. Click above the word **Pine**. You will learn next how to insert a named anchor here, so users can easily jump to the photo and description of this tree.

3. Click the **Named Anchor** icon in the **Insert** panel. This will open the **Named Anchor** dialog box.

4. Type **pine** and then click **OK**.

Notice the small yellow anchor marker that appears on your page where you inserted the named anchor tag? If you ever want to change the name you've set for your named anchor, click this anchor marker to access its name in the Property Inspector in order to modify it. No one but you will ever see this yellow icon; it's there for your benefit as you're creating these types of links. When you preview the page in the browser, this icon will not be visible.

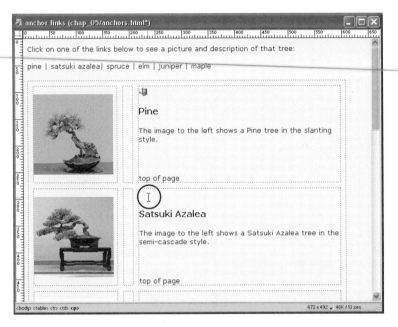

5. Click above the words **Satsuki Azalea**. You will insert another named anchor here, so users can easily jump to the photo and description of this room.

6. Choose **Insert > Named Anchor**. This will open the **Named Anchor** dialog box. Type **satsuki** and then click **OK**. If you prefer, you can use the **Named Anchor** button in the Insert panel instead of using the Insert menu.

7. Click above the word **Spruce** and choose **Insert > Named Anchor**. This will open the **Named Anchor** dialog box. Type **spruce** and then click **OK**.

8. Click above the word **Elm** and choose **Insert > Named Anchor**. This will open the **Named Anchor** dialog box. Type **elm** and then click **OK**.

9. Click above the word **Juniper** and choose **Insert > Named Anchor**. This will open the **Named Anchor** dialog box. Type **juniper** and then click **OK**.

10. Click above the word **Maple** and choose **Insert > Named Anchor**. This will open the **Named Anchor** dialog box. Type **maple** and then click **OK**.

Because you are going to be inserting several named anchors, we thought you would like to know that the keyboard shortcut for inserting named anchors is Opt+Cmd+A (Mac) or Ctrl+Alt+A (Windows). ;-)

11. Click and drag to highlight the word **pine** in the nav bar at the top of the page. Now that you have set up all of your named anchors, you need to create links to each of them.

 MOVIE | anchor.mov

To learn more about using named anchors, check out **anchor.mov** located in the **movies** folder on the Dreamweaver MX **H•O•T CD-ROM**.

12. In the **Property Inspector**, using the **Point to File** option, click and drag to the anchor marker above the text **Pine**. Release the mouse button to create the link. **Note:** Links to anchor points always begin with a pound sign (#).

13. Click and drag to highlight the words **satsuki azalea** at the top of the page.

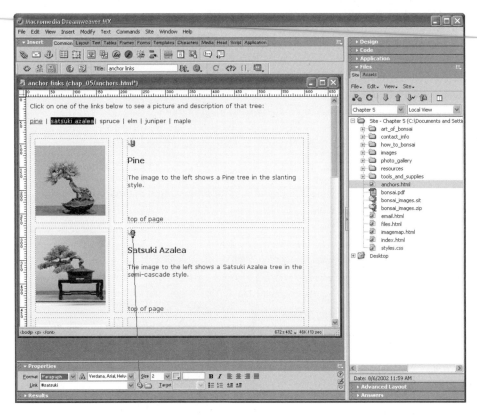

14. In the **Property Inspector**, using the **Point to File** option, click and drag to the anchor marker above the text **Satsuki Azalea**. Release the mouse button to create the link.

15. Click and drag to highlight the word **spruce** at the top of the page.

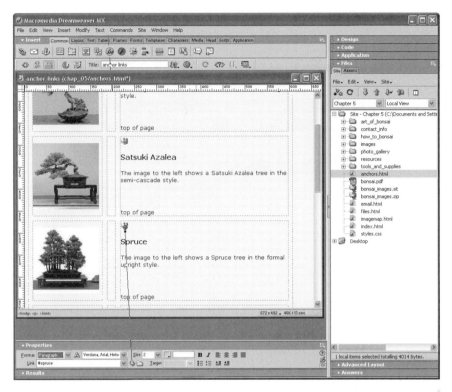

16. In the **Property Inspector**, using the **Point to File** option, click and drag to the anchor marker above the text **Spruce**. Release the mouse button to create the link.

17. Using this same process, go ahead and finish the other links at the top of the page.

18. Press **F12** to preview your page in a browser. Click each of the links at the top to see how the named anchors work.

As you can see, this is a nice way to jump to different sections within a single page. Once you are at the bottom of the page, wouldn't it be nice if you had a link to a named anchor that would take you back to the top of the page? You will learn to create that feature in the next few steps.

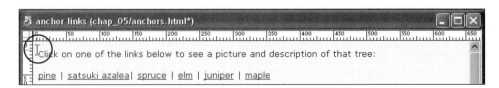

19. Return to Dreamweaver MX and click just to the left of the word **Click** at the top of the page.

20. Choose **Insert > Named Anchor**. This will open the **Named Anchor** dialog box. Type **top** for the name and click **OK**. This will insert an anchor marker at the top of your page.

21. Highlight the words **top of page** under the description of the **Pine**.

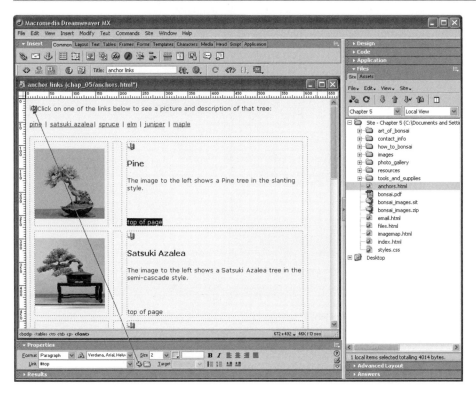

22. In the **Property Inspector**, using the **Point to File** option, click and drag to the anchor marker next to the word **Click** at the top of the page. Release the mouse button. This will create a link to the top anchor marker.

23. Repeat this process for each block of text that reads **top of page**. This will create a link to the top anchor marker, so users have a quick and easy way to get back to the top of your page. **Note:** If you find it difficult to use the Point to File method, you can simply type **#top** in the **Link** field of the Property Inspector. There is no right or wrong way to do this; it's a matter of personal preference.

24. Press **F12** to preview your page in a browser. Click the **Maple** link. This will take you to the bottom of the page. Next, click the **top of page** link. This will take you back up to the top. *Pretty slick!*

25. Return to Dreamweaver. **Save** and **close** all the work you've done in this file.

6. ——————————Image Maps

An image map contains invisible coordinates that allow you to assign multiple links to a single image. With image maps, you can specify multiple regions of a single image and have each of those areas link to a different URL. This exercise shows you how to create an image map.

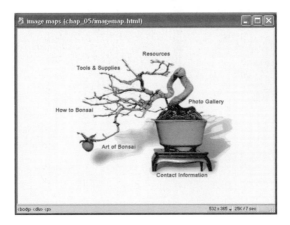

1. Open **imagemap.html**. This file contains a single image that will serve as a navigation bar for the site. In the following steps, you will create an image map so that this single image can link to multiple pages.

2. Click the image so that it is selected.

With an image selected, the Property Inspector changes to reflect options for images, which include the image map settings.

3. In the **Map** field, type **navbar**. By doing this, you are assigning a name to the image map, which is required and becomes even more important if you have multiple image maps on a single page.

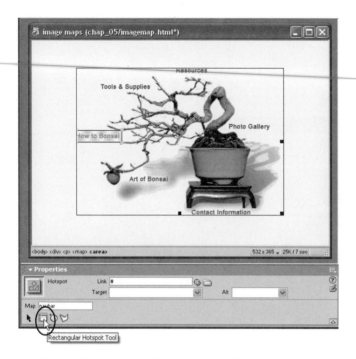

4. Click the **Rectangular Hotspot Tool**. Click and drag a rectangle around the words **How to Bonsai**. By doing this, you are defining what area of the image you want to serve as a link. When you release the mouse button, you will notice a light blue box around the image, and the options in your Property Inspector will have changed.

Note: The # mark in the Link field is used as a temporary link for the real link. If you don't remove this or add your own link, the users will still see the link icon—the little hand—when they move their cursor over the image map. It won't link to anything, though! It's just a stand-in for the real thing.

5. With the light blue rectangle selected, use the **Point to File** option to choose the **how_to_bonsai/ index.html**. This will create a link for this specific area of the image map.

6. With that image map still selected, type **how to bonsai** in the **Alt** field in the **Property Inspector** and press **Enter/Return**. In some browsers, this will display a small help tag when the user hovers over the hot area of the image map. You don't have to put anything here if you don't want to.

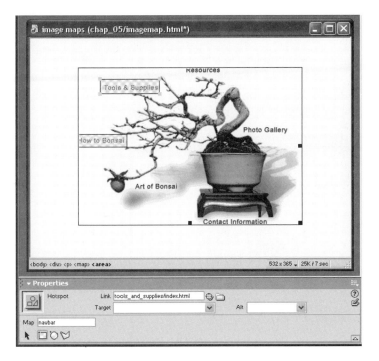

7. Click the **Rectangular Hotspot Tool** again. Click and drag a rectangle around the words **Tools & Supplies**.

8. With the light blue rectangle selected, use the **Point to File** option to choose the **tools_and_supplies/index.html**. This will create a link for this specific area of the image map.

9. Press **F12** to preview the links in a browser. Like other links, they cannot be previewed from within Dreamweaver; they must be viewed through a browser.

10. When you are finished, return to Dreamweaver. **Save** and **close** this file.

TIP | Help Tags

Have you ever held your mouse over an image map only to discover that a little tag pops up with some text inside it? This type of effect can be easily created by using the **ALT** attribute of the **HREF** tag being displayed. If you want to add an **ALT** tag to your image map, simply give each link a message inside the **ALT** field of the Property Inspector, as shown in Step 6. However, help tags do not work in all browsers. :-(

Linking to Files

In addition to creating links to HTML pages, there might come a time when you want or need to link to a file. For example, maybe you have a PDF brochure for users to download, or you want to let them download an entire folder of stuffed or zipped images. The possibilities are endless. The good news is that linking to files is just as easy as linking to other HTML pages. This exercise shows you how.

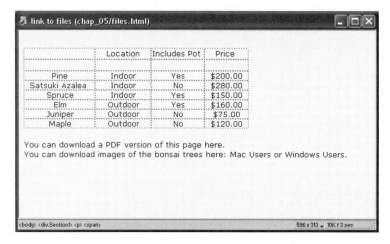

1. Open the **files.html** file from the **chap_05** folder. This page contains a table with information about some trees for sale at bonsaihut.com. You are going to create a link that will let the end user view this same content in PDF (**P**ortable **D**ocument **F**ormat), which is great for printing.

You can download a PDF version of this page here.
You can download images of the bonsai trees here: Mac Users or Windows Users.

2. At the bottom of the page, click and drag to select the words **PDF version**. Like with other text links, you need to select your text before creating the link.

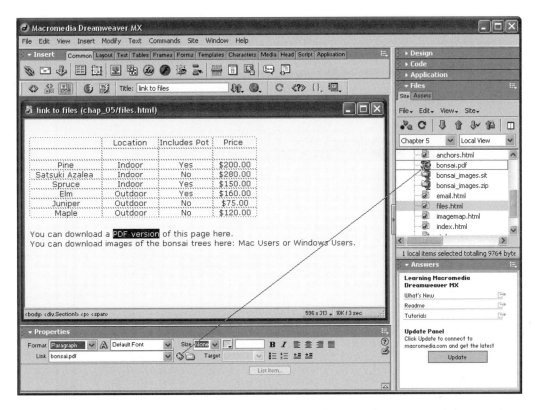

3. With the text selected, click the **Point to File** icon in the **Property Inspector** and drag to select **bonsai.pdf** inside the **Site** panel. If you are working on a Mac, the Site panel will need to be partially visible in the background to use this method of linking. Honestly, any linking method will work; it's simply a matter of which one you prefer.

4. Press **F12** to preview this page in a browser. Click the link you created at the bottom. Because the file you linked to is a PDF file, the browser will automatically launch the Adobe Acrobat Reader plug-in for your browser.

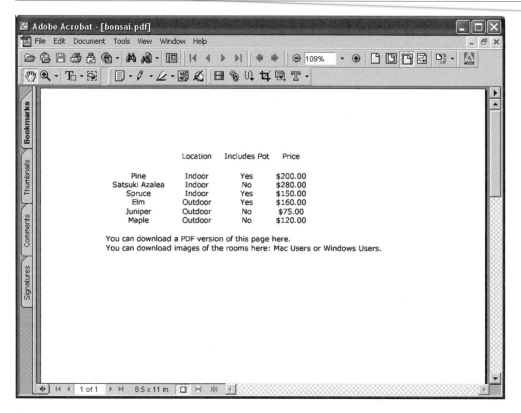

Clicking on a link that points to a PDF file will automatically launch the Adobe Acrobat Reader plug-in if it's installed in your browser. If it's not installed and you get an error when you click on the link, you'll need to go to the Adobe site to download it. The Adobe Acrobat Reader plug-in is a free download and is available at http://www.adobe.com/products/acrobat/readermain.html. You should also consider adding a link to the Adobe PDF download area to your page so users can download the plug-in if they don't already have it installed.

TIP | How Do You Create PDF Files?

In this exercise, you learned how to create a link to a PDF file and then view that link in a browser, but you did not learn how to create the PDF file we supplied for you. Creating PDF files is now a pretty easy process; you just need the right software. If you think you'll create PDF files often, you might want to purchase the full version of Adobe Acrobat. This is a PDF authoring tool sold by Adobe; it gives you the ability to create PDF files from almost any application. Alternately, you can now create PDF files online for free at Adobe's Web site at **http://createpdf.adobe.com**. Pretty neat. You might also be interested to know that we have another Hands-On Training book on Acrobat 5. Check it out at **http://www.lynda.com/books/ae5hot**.

In the following steps, you will learn how to create a link to a file of compressed images. Using a compressed file format lets you transfer large amounts of data, such as images, with a smaller file size. We have created two files—one for Mac users and one for PC users. Why? Because each operating system uses different file formats to compress files. The most common format on the Mac is the SIT (StuffIt) format; the most common format on Windows is the ZIP format.

You can download a PDF version of this page here.
You can download images of the bonsai trees here: Mac Users or Windows Users.

---

5. At the bottom of the page, click and drag to select the words **Mac Users**.

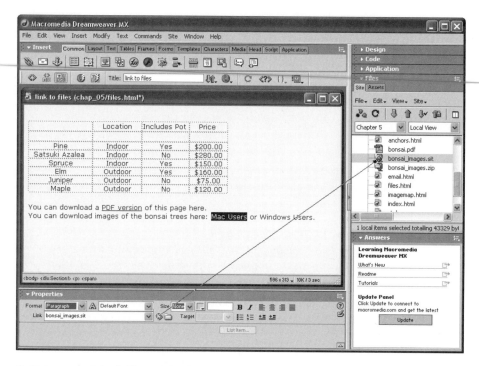

6. Using one of the linking methods you learned earlier, create a link to the **bonsai_images.sit** file located inside the **chap_05** folder. This file was compressed in the SIT format specifically for Mac users.

7. At the bottom of the page, click and drag to select the words **Windows Users**.

8. Again, using one of the linking methods you learned earlier, create a link to the **bonsai_images.zip** file located inside the **chap_05** folder. This file was compressed in the ZIP format specifically for PC users.

TIP | How Do You Create SIT and ZIP Files?

When you have a large file or a collection of files that you want to let people download, it's a good idea to compress those files so the download goes as quickly as possible. There are different file formats on the Mac and PC for compressing files: SIT and ZIP. The SIT (StuffIt) format is the most common on the Mac; the ZIP format is the most common on the PC. Several programs let you create these formats. For example, on the Mac you can use StuffIt (**http://www.aladdinsys.com**) to create SIT files, or MacZip (**http://www.sitec.net/maczip/**) to create ZIP files. On the PC, you can use WinZip (**http://www.winzip.com**) to create ZIP files.

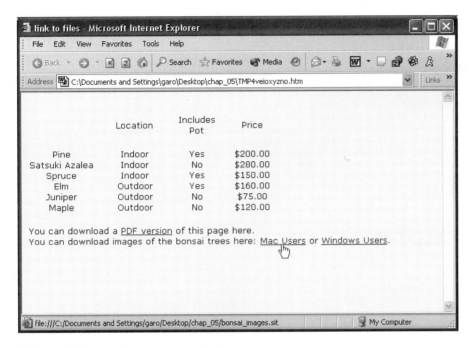

9. Press **F12** to preview your page in a browser:

- *Mac Users:* Click on the **Mac Users** link; your browser will automatically download and save the file to your desktop. In order to open this file, you will need a program capable of opening SIT files, such as StuffIt Expander.

- *Windows Users:* Click on the **Windows Users** link; you will be prompted to save this file someplace on your hard drive. Save the file on your desktop. In order to open this file, you will need a program capable of opening ZIP files, such as WinZip.

10. Save and **close** the **files.html** file; you won't be working with it any longer.

Phew, another chapter under your belt. Congratulations! When you are ready, you can move on to the next chapter. ;-)

6.

Typography

| Adding and Formatting HTML Text |
| Font Lists | Aligning Text |
| Ordered, Unordered, and Definition Lists |
| Color Schemes | Formatting Table Text |
| Applying HTML Styles | Flash Text |

chap_06

Dreamweaver MX
H•O•T CD-ROM

Most professional typographers cringe when they look at Web pages because Web browsers default to Times Roman, and most sites use the default font. Adding to the frustration is the fact that type appears differently on Mac, Windows, and UNIX platforms.

Dreamweaver MX gives you many hooks and handles for making the best of this situation. This chapter covers how to set font styles (such as **bold**, *italics*, and <u>underlined</u>), font sizes, font colors, and font faces (such as Times Roman, Helvetica, Arial, etc.). It also covers making bulleted lists, definition lists, and unordered lists. If you haven't heard those terms before, they will also be explained here. There is a great feature in Dreamweaver MX: the ability to add Flash text. This feature allows you to use any font or style you want without worrying about how it will appear on other platforms.

CSS versus FONT Element

The first part of this chapter describes how to use font formatting in Dreamweaver MX that utilizes (behind the scenes) HTML called the **FONT** element. The Web Standards Organization (**http://www.w3.org**) has eliminated the FONT element from the formal HTML specification, but it is still used on many new and old Web sites. We advocate that you use CSS (**C**ascading **S**tyle **S**heets), which you will learn about in Chapter 11, "*Cascading Style Sheets*," instead of the FONT element as you begin to code your real site. This chapter is an intermediate step toward building better type skills. It teaches you how to use Font styles, and some of the information you learn here will be very similar to what you will learn in the CSS chapter. We could have eliminated this chapter altogether, but chose not to so you could see both ways of formatting text. Because the FONT element is no longer part of HTML, there is a strong chance that future browsers will not support it. Today, browsers do support this tag, but there is wide speculation that some day they will not.

A Word About FONT FACE

The **FONT FACE** element in HTML allows you to specify a typeface other than the end user's default font. You can apply the attribute in Dreamweaver MX by creating **font lists**, which are described in the following exercise. Font lists are also used in CSS, so this knowledge will apply to future chapters as well. The caveat is that the typeface must be installed on your end user's system, or the browser will not be able to display it. It might come as a surprise that HTML text uses different sizing conventions from traditional print type sizes. Actually, all HTML text has a default size of 3, with a total range from 1 to 7.

HTML Default Text Size

FONT SIZE None

FONT SIZE 1

FONT SIZE 2

FONT SIZE 3

FONT SIZE 4

FONT SIZE 5

FONT SIZE 6

FONT SIZE 7

FONT SIZE +1

FONT SIZE +2

FONT SIZE +3

FONT SIZE +4

FONT SIZE +5

FONT SIZE +6

FONT SIZE +7

FONT SIZE -1

FONT SIZE -2

FONT SIZE -3

FONT SIZE -4

FONT SIZE -5

FONT SIZE -6

FONT SIZE -7

To change HTML text to a size other than the default of 3, you can either specify a number from 1 through 7, or + or −1 through + or −7 relative to the **BASEFONT** size (which is 3). For example, if you want your HTML text to be size 6, specify the font size to be 6 or +3. Either setting produces an HTML type of size 6. Some browsers let you set the **BASEFONT** for a page by using **<BASEFONT size = "4">**. You can specify any size you want, using one of the above-mentioned methods.

The illustration above shows an example of the **FONT SIZE** settings in Dreamweaver MX. The top example, None, is the equivalent of **FONT SIZE** 3. Notice how the type does not look different in **FONT SIZE +4** through +7, or **FONT SIZE −2** through −7? There is no difference between these settings.

I. _____**Adding and Formatting HTML Text**

In this exercise, you will learn how to add HTML text to a Web page. You will also learn how to format this text by modifying the typeface, size, style, and other attributes. As you will see, creating and formatting HTML text with Dreamweaver MX is just as easy as working with any word processing application.

1. Copy **chap_06** from the **H•O•T CD-ROM** to your hard drive. Define your site for Chapter 6 using the **chap_06** folder as the local root folder. If you need a refresher on this process, visit Chapter 3, "*Site Control.*"

2. Open the **index.html** file. This is the home page of bonsaihut.com, but it doesn't have text navigation. You are going to add this next.

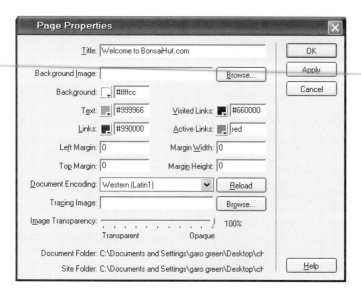

3. Open the **Page Properties** by choosing **Modify > Page Properties**. Notice that we have already set the text color properties for this page. This is an important issue to point out because as you add text and create links on this page, they will take on the color settings specified in this dialog box.

4. Click to the right of the **Contact Information** image and press **Return/Enter**. This will insert a paragraph break tag and create an extra line of space between the text and the image above.

5. Type **home | art of bonsai | how to bonsai | tools & supplies | resources | photo gallery | contact information** and press **Shift+Return/Enter**. Remember, you create the | character by pressing Shift+backslash.

6. Type **visit treebay.com to learn more about bonsai.**

7. Select the words **art of bonsai.**

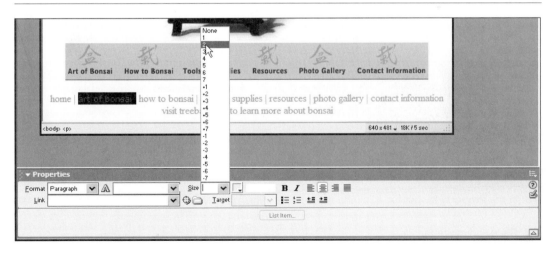

8. In the **Property Inspector**, choose the **Font List** pop-up menu and select the **Verdana, Arial, Helvetica, sans-serif** option. This will change your text to Verdana if you have that font installed; if you do not, Dreamweaver MX will display the next font in the list.

9. With **art of bonsai** still selected, in the **Property Inspector**, choose the **Size** pop-up menu and select **2.** This will change the size of your type.

10. Go to the **Size** pop-up menu again and select **−1**. Notice how the type size stays at 2. That's because all HTML text has a basefont size of 3, from which you add or subtract to make your type larger or smaller.

11. Select the words **how to bonsai**.

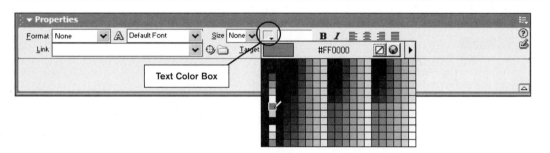

12. From the **Property Inspector**, choose the **Text Color Box**. Select a bright red color. Your text color is now red. This setting will override any text color that you might have specified under **Modify > Page Properties**.

13. Select the words **tools and supplies**.

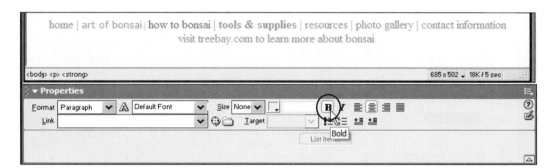

14. In the **Property Inspector**, click the **Bold** button. This will make the selected text bold.

15. In the **Property Inspector**, click the **Italic** button. This will make the selected text italic.

16. Save and **close** the file.

What Are Headings?

HTML text can also be formatted using **Heading** tags. The tags look like this: **<H1>**. They range from **1** to **6** and change the size of the HTML text. Here's a tricky thing that you might want to remember: The smaller the number next to the **H**, the bigger the text will be. For example, **<H1>** will produce the largest text, whereas **<H6>** will produce the smallest text. Generally, the **<H1>** through **<H6>** tags insert a line break before and after the text without requiring additional code. **Heading** tags can be useful for formatting large text.

Why might you use a **Heading** tag instead of a **FONT SIZE** element? Accessibility! If sight-impaired users access your Web page, they might not "see" your Web page, but will instead have a read-ing device "read" it aloud. **Heading** tags can be "read" by HTML readers as headlines, whereas large type, formatted with the size attribute, is given the same emphasis as body copy. You might not imagine that your site has much of a sight-impaired audience, and perhaps do not think this information applies to your site design strategy. In many cases, however, making your site acces-sible is not an option, but a requirement. Our advice is to use **Heading** tags instead of large font sizes for headlines. In addition, **Heading** elements can be used in CSS, so this information applies to future chapters as well.

*This image shows the range of how **Heading** tags display in a browser.*

2. _____Font Lists

In this exercise, you will learn how to add and modify the **font lists** that come with Dreamweaver MX. By specifying multiple fonts using a font list, the likelihood of visitors seeing the page in one of the typefaces you specified is higher, because you're offering more than one choice. You will learn how to modify what typefaces are in the existing font lists and how to create your own custom font list. Learning and using this technique will allow you to break out of the Times Roman mold a little bit, which is a welcome enhancement to the bland Web type landscape we all see every day. Font lists are also used in CSS.

1. Open **text2.html**.

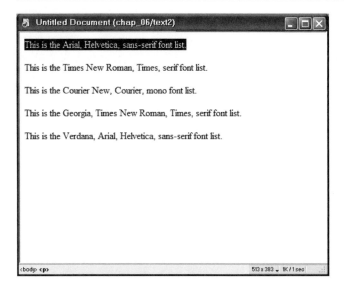

2. Select the words **This is the Arial, Helvetica, sans-serif font list**.

3. From the **Font List** pop-up menu in the **Property Inspector**, choose **Arial, Helvetica, sans-serif**. This will change your text to Arial if you have that font installed; if you do not, it will go to the next font in the list.

> **NOTE | How Font Lists Work**
>
> Font lists are a very useful way of ensuring that the HTML text on your Web page is viewed the way you intended. A Web browser will search for each font in the list until it finds one that is installed on the end user's system. Once it finds a font in the list, it will use that font to display the HTML text on your Web page. For example, if your font list were "Arial, Helvetica, sans-serif," the browser would try to use Arial first to display text. If the end user did not have Arial installed, the browser would then try to display Helvetica. If it could not find Helvetica, it would then display the first sans-serif font it found. The goal of font lists is to create sets of fonts that have similar structure and characteristics, so that there is minimal change from viewer to viewer.

4. Select the words **This is the Times New Roman, Times, serif font list**.

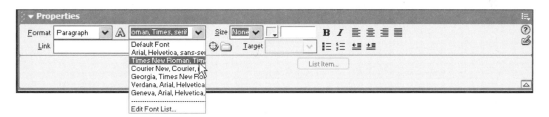

5. From the **Font List** pop-up menu, choose **Times New Roman, Times, serif**. This will change your text to Times New Roman if you have that font installed; if you do not, it will go to the next font in the list.

6. Select the words **This is the Courier New, Courier, mono font list**. From the **Font List** pop-up menu, choose **Courier New, Courier, mono**. This will change your text to Courier New if you have that font installed; if you do not, it will go to the next font.

Are you getting the idea about how this works yet? ;-)

7. Select the words **This is the Georgia, Times New Roman, Times, serif font list**. From the **Font List** pop-up menu, choose **Georgia, Times New Roman, Times, serif**.

8. Select the words **This is the Verdana, Arial, Helvetica, sans-serif font list**. From the **Font List** pop-up menu, choose **Verdana, Arial, Helvetica, sans-serif**.

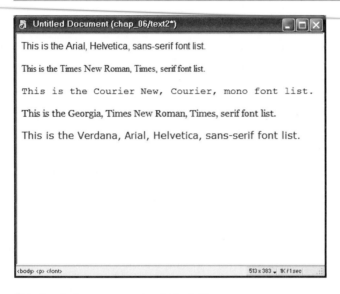

This is what your page should look like now.

9. Click off the text to deselect it, and press **Return/Enter**. Below the last sentence on the page, type **This is my very own font list**.

10. From the **Font List** pop-up menu, choose **Edit Font List**.

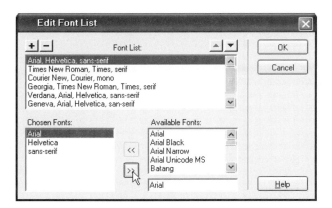

11. In the **Edit Font List** dialog box that appears, select **Arial, Helvetica, sans-serif** from the **Font List** option. Select **Arial** under **Chosen Fonts**, then click the **>>** button to remove Arial from this font list.

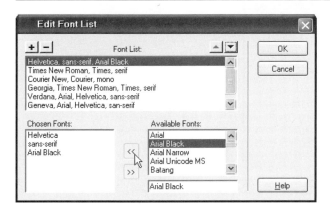

12. Select **Arial Black** under the **Available Fonts** option. Click the **<<** button to add this to the selected font list. You have just modified the fonts that will be used for this font list.

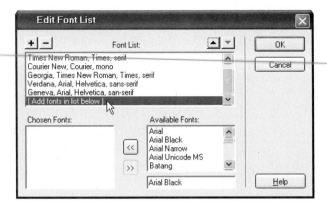

13. Select **(Add fonts in list below)** from the bottom of the **Font List** field.

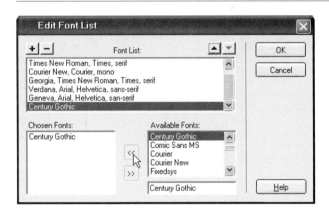

14. Select **Century Gothic** under **Available Fonts** and press the << button to add this to your list.

15. Select **Verdana** under **Available Fonts** and press the << button to add this to your list.

16. Click **OK** to add your new list to the font list.

17. In the **text2.html** file, select the words **This is my very own font list**.

18. From the **Font List** pop-up menu, choose **Century Gothic, Verdana**. This will change your text to Century Gothic if you have that font installed; if you do not, it will go to Verdana.

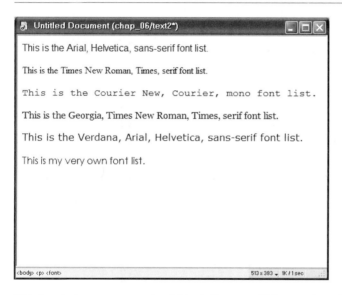

This is what your screen should look like now. This exercise gives you an example of how these font lists will display on your computer system. What you see might appear differently on other people's browsers, because they might have different fonts installed on their systems than you do.

19. Save and **close** the file.

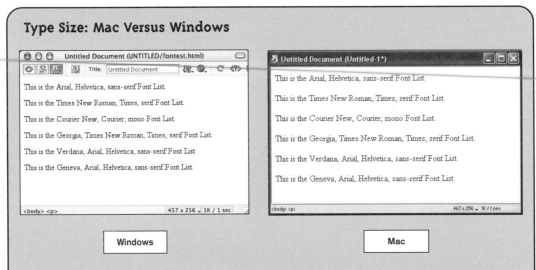

Type Size: Mac Versus Windows

Windows

Mac

Unfortunately for all of us well-intentioned Web publishers, HTML type appears much larger on Windows than it does on the Mac. Although they both display images at 72 dpi (dots per inch), Windows displays type at 96 dpi, whereas the Mac displays it at 72 dpi. This deceptively small technical difference results in much larger type on Windows.

The images above illustrate the difference in size between the two platforms. Pretty scary, huh? There is no solution to this, except to turn to **Style Sheets** (see Chapter 11, "*Cascading Style Sheets*") to size your text by using pixels, but that works only on 4.0 version and later browsers.

To compensate, we often make type smaller at −1 or −2 when we are developing pages, but doing so only results in a more appealing Windows version, and a less appealing Mac version. Ugh! The theory is that there are more Windows users than Mac users, so we've taken the tack to make the type on our pages look acceptable on Windows, and slightly small on Macs.

One other solution to the size difference issue is to use images of text instead of HTML text. Because images display at 72 dpi on either Mac or Windows, the type will look identical on either platform. Later in this chapter, you'll learn to make Flash Text, which generates an image using the SWF file format. The downside is that images are larger in file size than corresponding HTML text, and are not searchable by search engines. It's always one gotcha or another, right?

3.——————Aligning Text

In this exercise, you will learn how to align text on the page. Unfortunately, HTML does not give you much control over aligning text. You have three basic options: **Left Align**, **Center Align**, and **Right Align**. You do have some extra options when you align text next to images, which you will also explore in this exercise. If the limitations of HTML alignment features frustrate you, that's understandable. You'll learn about more exact layout techniques in later chapters.

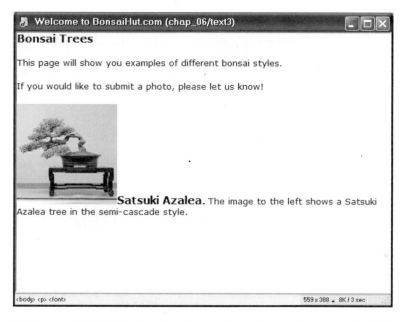

1. Open **text3.html**. Notice that the two lines of text at the top are left aligned. This is the default alignment setting for text.

2. Click anywhere within the sentence that reads, **This page will show you examples of different bonsai styles**.

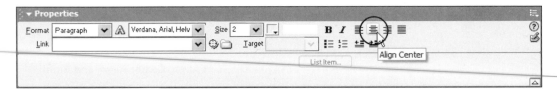

3. In the **Property Inspector**, click the **Align Center** button. This will center your text on the page. **Note:** The centering of the text is relative to the width of the browser window.

4. Click anywhere within the sentence **If you would like to submit a photo, please let us know!**

5. In the **Property Inspector**, click the **Align Right** button. This will place your text on the right edge of the page.

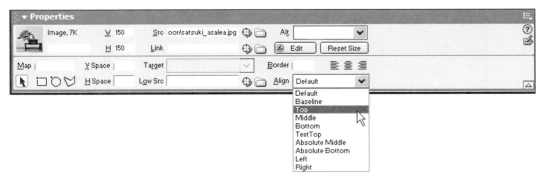

6. Click the **satsuki_azalea.jpg** image. Notice when you select an image to align with type, you have different alignment options available in the **Property Inspector**. The alignment options in this menu are strictly used when aligning text next to an image.

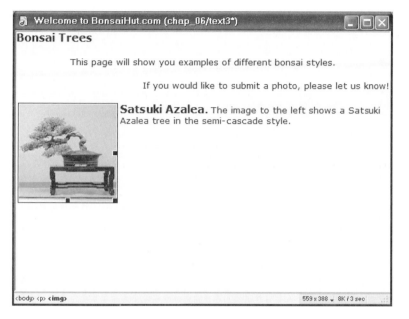

7. In the **Property Inspector**, choose the **Align** pop-up menu and select the **Left** option.

Notice that the text moves to the top-right of the image. Go ahead and play with the other align options to see how they affect the alignment of the text next to the image. Hey, if you don't want to do that, just read the upcoming chart below to learn more. ;-)

8. Save and **close** the file.

Aligning Text and Images

Dreamweaver MX offers many alignment options for text and images. The following chart defines all the alignment terms, so now you will know what you are requesting when you select one:

HTML Text and Image Alignment Options	
Alignment	**Description**
Browser Default	Varies between browsers, but usually uses the Bottom option (see below)
Baseline	Aligns the baseline of the text to the bottom of the image
Bottom	Aligns the baseline of the text to the bottom of the image (same as Baseline)
Absolute Bottom	Aligns text, including descenders (e.g., g and j), to the bottom of the image
Top	Aligns the image to the tallest part of the object (image or text)
TextTop	Aligns the image with the tallest character in the line of text
Middle	Aligns the baseline of the text to the middle of the image
Absolute Middle	Aligns the middle of the text to the middle of the image
Left	Left-aligns the image and wraps text to the right
Right	Right-aligns the image and wraps text to the left

4.—————————Ordered, Unordered, and Definition Lists

In this exercise, you will learn how to create a variety of lists—an **ordered list**, an **unordered list**, and a **definition list**. These are HTML terms that refer to whether the list is formatted with a bullet, an indent, or Roman numerals. These lists can be generated from existing text or from scratch. Ordered, unordered, and definition lists remain part of the HTML 4.01/XHTML WC3 formal recommendations and will continue to be supported by Web browsers.

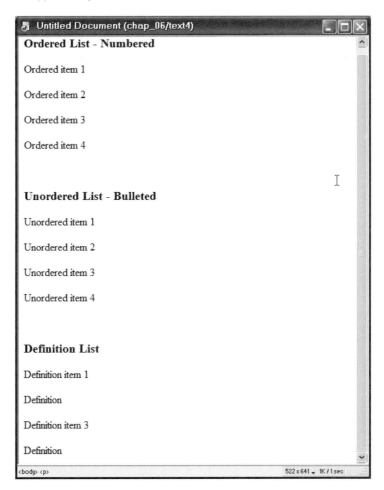

1. Open **text4.html**.

2. Select the four lines of text under the section called **Ordered List - Numbered**, which includes **Ordered item 1**, **Ordered item 2**, **Ordered item 3**, **Ordered item 4**.

3. Choose **Text** > **List** > **Ordered List**.

Ordered List - Numbered

1. Ordered item 1
2. Ordered item 2
3. Ordered item 3
4. Ordered item 4

This is what an ordered list looks like.

---

4. Select the four lines of text under the **Unordered List - Bulleted** section (**Unordered item 1**, **Unordered item 2**, **Unordered item 3**, **Unordered item 4**).

---

5. Choose **Text** > **List** > **Unordered List**.

Unordered List - Bulleted

• Unordered item 1
• Unordered item 2
• Unordered item 3
• Unordered item 4

This is what an unordered list looks like.

---

6. Select the four lines of text under the **Definition List** section (**Definition item 1**, **Definition**, **Definition item 3**, **Definition**).

---

7. Choose **Text** > **List** > **Definition List**.

Definition List

Definition item 1
Definition
Definition item 3
Definition

This is what a definition list looks like.

---

8. Save the file and **close** it. You'll find that knowing how to set up these different types of lists will come in very handy as you create your own Web pages and sites.

---

5. ——————**Color Schemes**

Color schemes are preset groups of colors that Dreamweaver MX provides for your background, text, links, active links, and visited links colors. You can apply a color scheme to a page at any time. They are useful when you are not sure which colors to use. Why is this exercise in the "*Typography*" chapter? Because color schemes affect the color of type and links on your page, that's why! You will learn how to control your own custom color schemes in Chapter 17, "*Templates and Library Items.*"

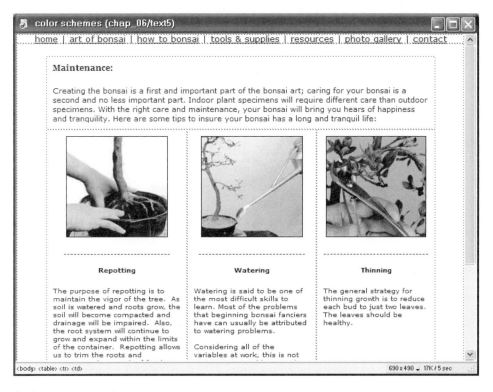

1. Open **text5.html**.

2. Choose **Commands > Set Color Scheme**.

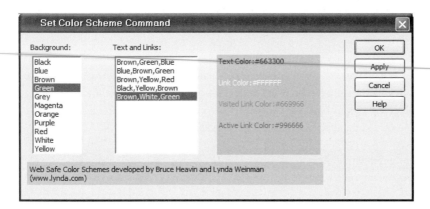

3. In the **Set Color Scheme Command** dialog box, select **Green** under the Background option. Select **Brown, White, Green** under the Text and Links option. Click **OK**.

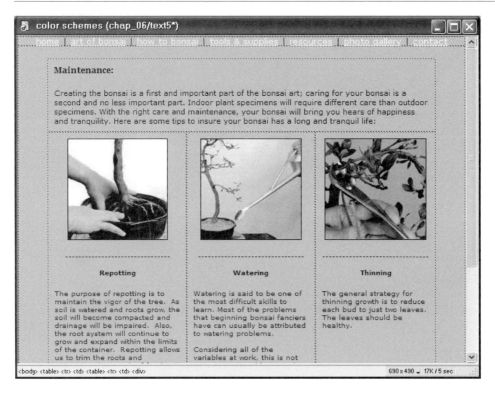

This is what the page looks like with the color scheme applied. If you do not like it, go ahead and choose another!

4. Choose **Commands > Set Color Scheme** again. Pick a different combination of colors and click **Apply**. Knock yourself out! (In other words, enjoy yourself.)

5. When you're done having fun with colors, click **OK** and **save** and **close** the file.

NOTE | Can I Create My Own Color Schemes?

One question our students always ask is, "Can I create my own color schemes?" Well, the answer is yes and no. You can't do it through the Set Color Scheme Command dialog box. However, you can do it by using templates, and we show you how in Chapter 17, "*Templates and Library Items.*"

6. ———————Formatting Text in Tables

In this exercise, you will learn to change a **table's** type, style, color, alignment, and more. In the old days, which weren't so long ago, you would have had to edit each individual cell, one at a time, and it could have taken hours to edit a large table. Not anymore! With Dreamweaver MX, you can do it with a few deft clicks and drags.

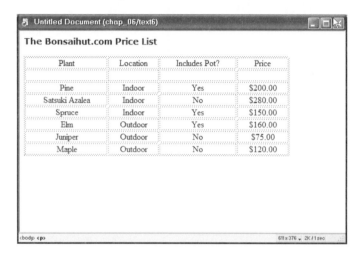

1. Open **text6.html**.

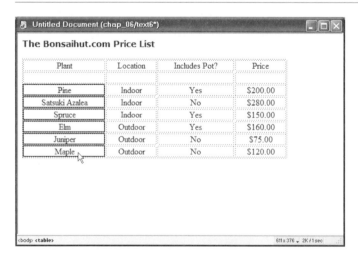

2. Click in cell 1 in row 2 (**Pine**) and drag down to the last cell in the column (**Maple**).
Note: You must be in **Standard view** to select a range of table cells.

3. In the **Property Inspector**, choose the **Font List** pop-up menu and select the **Verdana, Arial, Helvetica, sans-serif** font list. All the text in the selected column will update before your eyes. If you've ever hand-coded this sort of thing, you will be gasping in delight right now.

4. Highlight cell 1 in row 1 (**Plant**) and drag across to cell 4 (**Price**).

5. Using the **Property Inspector**, change the text style to **bold**.

6. Press **F10** to see the HTML. Look at all those **FONT** tags! Aren't you glad you didn't have to insert each one by hand? Press F10 again to close the HTML panel.

7. Save and **close** this file.

7. ——————**Applying HTML Styles**

HTML styles are a great way to quickly format text in a document. You can save specific text formatting attributes and then apply them to any text on a page or within an entire site. Unlike Cascading Style Sheets, which require a 4.0+ browser, HTML styles will work in earlier browsers, which makes them an attractive option. In this exercise, you will format some text and create an HTML style based on that formatting. Then you will apply that formatting to other blocks of text on the same page. You will quickly begin to see how HTML styles can help automate simple text formatting.

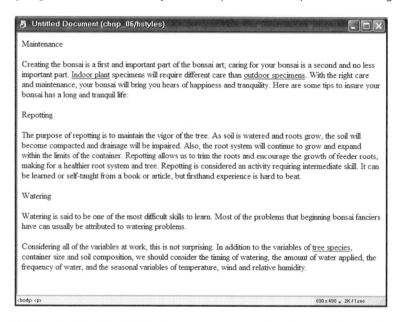

1. Open **hstyles.html**. This document contains a lot of text, and it provides a good example of when you might want to use HTML styles to apply formatting across large amounts of text.

NOTE | The Library Folder and HTML Styles

As you begin working with HTML styles, you might notice a small addition to your local root folder. When you create your first HTML style, Dreamweaver MX automatically adds to your local root folder a Library folder, inside which you will see a **styles.xml** file. All of your HTML styles will be saved in that file. The file is important to the Dreamweaver MX internal workings, but it is not necessary to upload it when you publish your site to the Web. The folder does not hurt anything by residing in your Site window. In fact, it is a needed element to ensure that HTML styles will work properly.

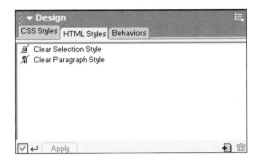

2. Make sure your **HTML Styles** panel is open. If not, choose **Window > HTML Styles**. The shortcut keys are **Ctrl+F11** (Windows) or **Cmd+F11** (Mac).

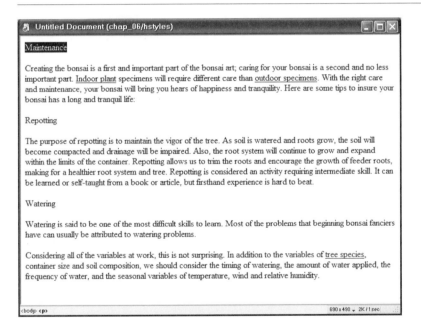

3. Click and drag to select the word **maintenance**.

4. Using the **Property Inspector**, change the font to **Verdana, Arial, Helvetica, sans-serif**, the **Size** to **4**, **Bold**, and the **color** to **blue** (any color of blue is fine).

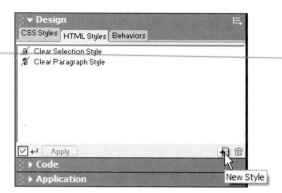

5. With your text still selected, click the **New Style** icon at the bottom of the **HTML Styles** panel. This will open the **Define HTML Style** dialog box, which allows you to define a style based on the selected text.

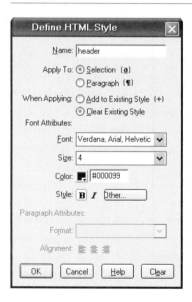

6. For **Name**, enter **header**. You can use any name you want here. Just use something that you will remember.

Tip: *We recommend that you name your HTML styles relative to something that describes how they look. Because this text is formatted as a header, we named it* header.

7. You can leave the rest of the options at their default values. Click **OK**. For an explanation of the options in the **Define HTML Style** dialog box, refer to the handy chart at the end of this section.

8. You should see your new style, **header**, listed in the **HTML Styles** panel.

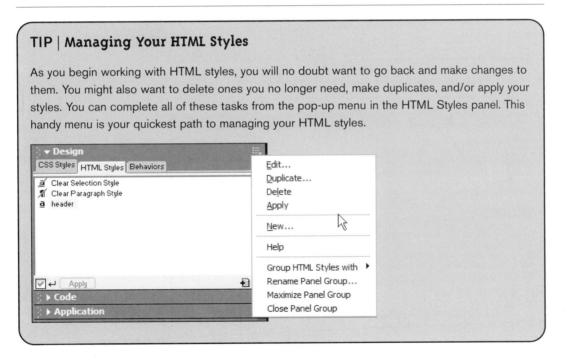

TIP | Managing Your HTML Styles

As you begin working with HTML styles, you will no doubt want to go back and make changes to them. You might also want to delete ones you no longer need, make duplicates, and/or apply your styles. You can complete all of these tasks from the pop-up menu in the HTML Styles panel. This handy menu is your quickest path to managing your HTML styles.

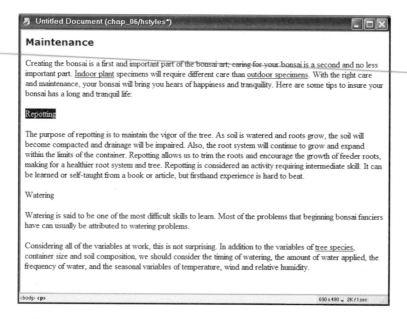

9. Select the word **Repotting** by clicking and dragging.

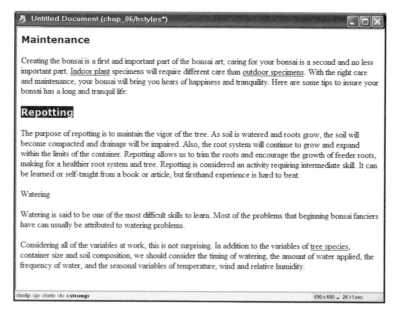

10. In the **HTML Styles** panel, click the style named **header**. This will format the selected text using the style you previously defined. Now, that is what we call quick formatting ;-).

Maintenance

Creating the bonsai is a first and important part of the bonsai art; caring for your bonsai is a second and no less important part. <u>Indoor plant</u> specimens will require different care than <u>outdoor specimens</u>. With the right care and maintenance, your bonsai will bring you hears of happiness and tranquility. Here are some tips to insure your bonsai has a long and tranquil life:

Repotting

The purpose of repotting is to maintain the vigor of the tree. As soil is watered and roots grow, the soil will become compacted and drainage will be impaired. Also, the root system will continue to grow and expand within the limits of the container. Repotting allows us to trim the roots and encourage the growth of feeder roots, making for a healthier root system and tree. Repotting is considered an activity requiring intermediate skill. It can be learned or self-taught from a book or article, but firsthand experience is hard to beat.

Watering

Watering is said to be one of the most difficult skills to learn. Most of the problems that beginning bonsai fanciers have can usually be attributed to watering problems.

Considering all of the variables at work, this is not surprising. In addition to the variables of <u>tree species</u>, container size and soil composition, we should consider the timing of watering, the amount of water applied, the frequency of water, and the seasonal variables of temperature, wind and relative humidity.

`<body> <p> <font> <b> <strong>`   690 x 490 ▾ 3K / 1 sec

11. Go ahead and repeat this process for **Watering**. When you are finished, your page should look like the one above.

---

12. Now the only real way you are going to learn this is by doing it on your own. So, see if you can make another HTML style and then apply that to the other paragraphs. Don't worry; if you get stuck, just refer to the beginning of this exercise.

---

13. When you are finished exploring this feature, **save** and **close** the file. You won't need it for future exercises.

HTML Style Options

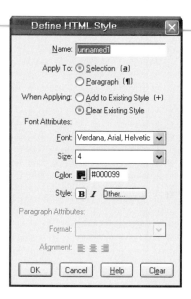

Here is a quick definition for each of the options in the Define HTML Style dialog box:

HTML Styles	
Option	**Description**
Name	This is the name of your style that appears in the **HTML Styles** panel.
Apply To: Selection	With this option selected, the formatting will be applied only to the text you have selected.
Apply To: Paragraph	With this option selected, the formatting will be applied to everything within the paragraph (**<p>**) tag.
When Applying: Add to Existing Style	With this option selected, the formatting will be added to any formatting that has already been applied to the selected text.
When Applying: Clear Existing Style	With this option selected, the formatting will replace any formatting that has already been applied to the selected text.
	continues on next page

HTML Styles *continued*	
Option	**Description**
Font Attributes: Font:	This allows you to specify what font is used with the style.
Font Attributes: Size:	This allows you to specify what font size is used with the style.
Font Attributes: Color:	This allows you to specify what font color is used with the style. You can choose from the swatch or enter in a hexadecimal value.
Font Attributes: Style:	This allows you to specify which font styles (bold, italic, etc.) are used with the style. The **Other** pop-up menu displays less frequently used options.
Paragraph Attributes: Format	Available only if Apply To: Paragraph is selected, this lets you choose formatting options such as Heading 1, Paragraph, etc.
Paragraph Attributes: Alignment	Available only if Apply To: Paragraph is selected, this lets you specify the alignment settings for the style.

What Is Flash Text?

It's pretty hard to be involved in Web design today and not hear the word "Flash." It has become widely adopted in the Web design industry as an alternative and/or adjunct to HTML formatting. Macromedia Flash MX is a vector-based drawing, animation, and interactivity program. It can be used to create something as simple as a button for a Web page or as complex as an entire video game that can be played on the Web. Macromedia Flash MX uses a proprietary file format called SWF (pronounced "swiff"). Macromedia Flash MX content that gets uploaded to the Web always ends in the .swf suffix.

In order to view Macromedia Flash MX content on the Web, you must have the Flash MX plug-in installed in your browser. If you don't have this plug-in, you can download it for free at **http://www.macromedia.com/software/flashplayer**.

The **Flash Text** feature in Dreamweaver MX lets you create text and text rollovers for your Web pages, using any font on your system, in the SWF file format. Flash Text is a good feature for creating text rollovers and small lines of text, such as headlines for your body text. It is not searchable by search engines and should not be used for large bodies of text. Before you move on to the exercise and learn the nuances of Flash Text, here's a handy list that outlines some of the pros and one very big con of this feature.

Using Flash Text	
Pros	**Explanation**
Font integrity	With Flash Text, you can use any font installed on your system, and the visitors to your page don't need to have that font installed, as they do with regular HTML text. This gives you much more flexibility when you are designing your pages.
Text rollovers	Creating text rollovers usually requires that you use a separate image editing program to create the necessary images. With Flash Text, you can create text rollovers without ever leaving Dreamweaver MX.
Con	**Explanation**
Plug-in required	All Macromedia Flash MX content on the Web requires a plug-in to be viewed properly. Flash Text is no different and requires that the Flash plug-in be installed in the browser.

8. _____Creating Flash Text

In this exercise, you'll get to use Flash Text. Flash Text lets you use any font you want without worrying whether the visitors to your site will have it installed on their systems. It also lets you easily create rollovers without using any JavaScript. It's really easy to learn and use—read on and try it out to see what we mean!

1. Open **flashtext.html**. This page contains a simple layout that was created using tables to control the position of the images on this page. You will learn more about tables in the next chapter, we promise!

2. Click inside the **first cell** at the top. This will place a blinking I-beam cursor in that cell and lets Dreamweaver MX know that this is where you want to place your object, which is Flash Text in this case.

3. From the **Media** tab in the **Insert** panel, click the **Flash Text** icon. This will open the Insert Flash Text dialog box.

4. Select a font for your text from the **Font** drop-down menu. We are using a font called SimSun. You can use whatever font you want. The point is to use a font that isn't common to that many people.

Make sure you choose a font that you don't think end users will have on their computers. One of the advantages of using Flash Text is that the font is embedded in the SWF file and does not have to be installed on the end user's computer. So, now you can feel free to use just about any font you have on your computer!

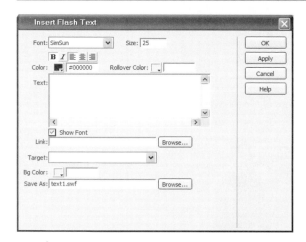

5. Set the **Size** option to **25**. This option sets the size of your text in points. Click the **Bold** button to make the text bold.

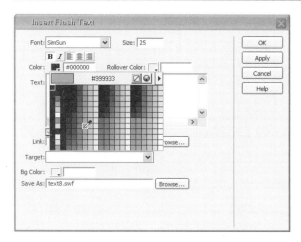

6. Click the **Color** option and select an olive color. We used **#999933**, but you are welcome to use any color you like.

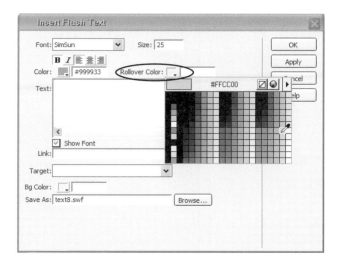

7. Click the **Rollover Color** box and select a bright orange color. Setting this color will automatically create a rollover effect for your Flash text. Pretty simple, huh? ;-)

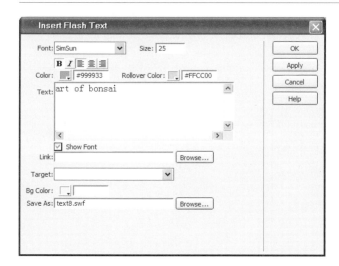

8. In the **Text** field type **art of bonsai**. By default, the **Show Font** checkbox is checked; this will give you a preview of the text in the font you selected. If the font you selected is not being displayed, make sure the **Show Font** checkbox is checked.

Warning: This dialog box will not give you a preview of the size you specified; you can only see the actual size in the document itself. We think that it would be nice if the next version let you preview the size of your text in this dialog box.

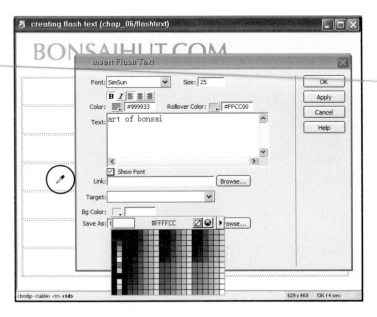

9. Click the **Bg Color** color box and move the eyedropper over the background of the document window and click. This will let you sample and select the background color of your page so that it matches the background color of your Flash Text.

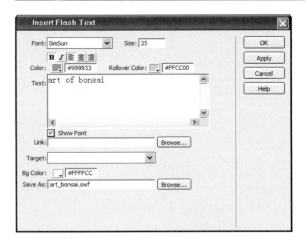

10. In the **Save As** field, type **art_bonsai.swf**. Good file management principles dictate that you give your files names that reflect their content. **Note:** If you are using a Mac with OS X, you should click Browse before entering the name for the SWF file.

Notice that you can easily add a link to the Flash Text using the Link field option.

11. Repeat Steps 2 though 10 to create Flash Text for **how to bonsai**, **tools and supplies**, **resources**, **photo gallery**, and **contact info**. When you're finished, your page should look similar to the one shown below.

This is what your page should look like when you are done. Remember, we used the SimSun font, so yours will display whatever font you selected.

12. Press **F12** to preview your page in a browser. Return to Dreamweaver MX and **save** the changes to this file. You can **close** this file; you won't be working with it any longer.

Woo-hoo! You are done with another chapter; you can take a nap or keep on moving to the next chapter! I don't know about you, but we sure could use a little nap after all that talk about text. ;-)

7.

Tables

| Creating, Sorting, and Modifying a Table |
| Using Tables to Align Images and Text |
| Assembling Seamless Images | Combining Pixels and Percentages |
| Inserting Tabular Data | Nested Tables and Borders |
| Rounded-Corner Tables |

chap_07

Dreamweaver MX
H·O·T CD-ROM

We were very excited when HTML tables were introduced back in Netscape 1.2. Tables are a way to display and organize charts and data. They were most commonly used in financial or database spreadsheets because they provided defined columns and rows. The HTML engineers who created tables for the Web did not predict that developers would use tables to align images, not just to display text and numbers. Tables have, however, become the standard method used by designers to position and anchor content to Web pages. You'll learn about both uses for tables: a formatting device for data, and a layout device for custom positioning of images.

This chapter shows you how to create custom tables, insert rows and columns, come up with color schemes, and handle formatting and sorting tasks. You will also learn how to use tables to align and position images. Tables are a critical item in your Web design toolbox, and Dreamweaver MX gives you great control and techniques for mastering them. Towards the end of this chapter, we show you two table tricks: one for creating custom table borders, and another for making rounded table corners. Don't worry, the fun doesn't stop there; you will get to work with tables some more in Chapter 8, "*Layout*."

What Is a Table?

A table is a highly versatile feature in HTML. It can be useful for organizing data or positioning images. What does a table look like under the hood of Dreamweaver MX? It is comprised of a combination of HTML tags.

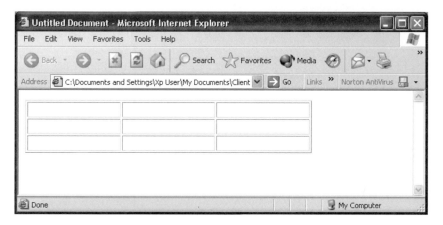

A table in the browser.

```
<table width="75%" border="1">
  <tr>
    <td> </td>
    <td> </td>
    <td> </td>
  </tr>
  <tr>
    <td> </td>
    <td> </td>
    <td> </td>
  </tr>
  <tr>
    <td> </td>
    <td> </td>
    <td> </td>
  </tr>
</table>
```

Here's the HTML for the table above. Tables always begin with a **<table>** *tag. The width and border elements are attributes of the* **<table>** *tag.* **<tr>** *stands for* **t**able **r**ow, *and* **<td>** *stands for* **t**able **d**ata.

Anatomy of a Table			
	Column		
Row			
			Cell

A table contains rows, columns, and cells. If these terms are unfamiliar to you, this diagram should help.

I. ——————————Changing the Border of a Table

This first exercise helps you build your table formatting skills on a premade table. It also alerts you to a common HTML problem relating to empty table cells. You see, even if a table cell is empty, you have to put something in it to preserve the table formatting. That "something" can be a single-pixel transparent GIF, which is a small image file that has been set to be fully transparent, or invisible. It serves as a placeholder to keep the table formatting from collapsing with empty cells. You'll learn how to add a transparent GIF in a few moments, once you get going with this exercise.

1. Copy **chap_07** from the **H•O•T CD-ROM** to your hard drive. Define your site for Chapter 7 using the **chap_07** folder as the local root folder. If you need a refresher on this process, visit Exercise 1 in Chapter 3, "*Site Control.*"

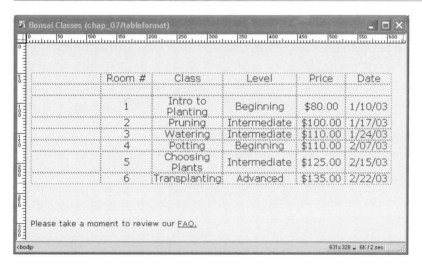

2. Open **tableformat.html**. The dotted lines that you see around each cell are just table border guides, and will not show up inside the browser.

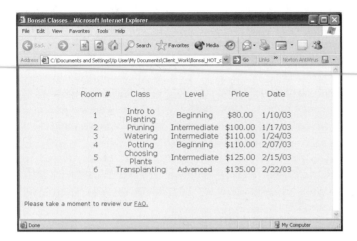

3. Press **F12** to preview this file in your Web browser. Notice how the dotted lines don't appear in the browser? In this file, the **border** setting was changed to **0** in order to make the formatting guides disappear, because Dreamweaver MX uses a default setting of **1** for table borders. The results of this change are visible only in the browser, not in the authoring environment of Dreamweaver MX. Next you'll learn how to control the weight of the lines with the **border** property.

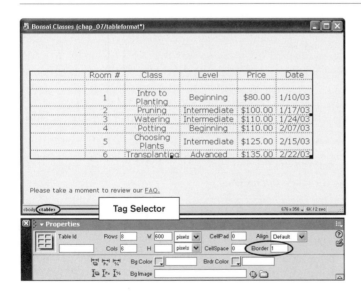

4. Return to Dreamweaver MX and select the entire table. You can do this by using the **Tag Selector** at the bottom left of the document window. Click anywhere inside the table. You should see the word **<table>** appear as a Tag Selector. Click the **<table>** element in the Tag Selector, and the entire table should become selected. With the table selected, in the **Property Inspector**, enter **Border: 1** and then press **Return/Enter**.

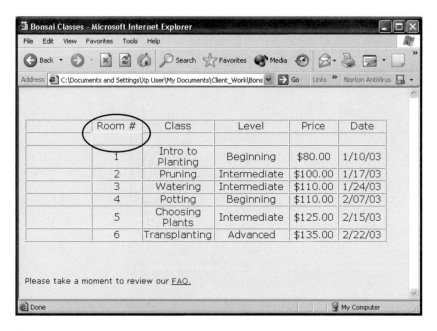

5. Press **F12** to preview the results. See how the border value affected the appearance? This is one of the many controls that you have over the appearance of tables.

Note: Some browsers display the cell underneath Room # *in a different way from the other table cells. In every other row there is content, but the cell without content looks different, or "bloated" because it is empty. The following steps will show you how to correct this problem.*

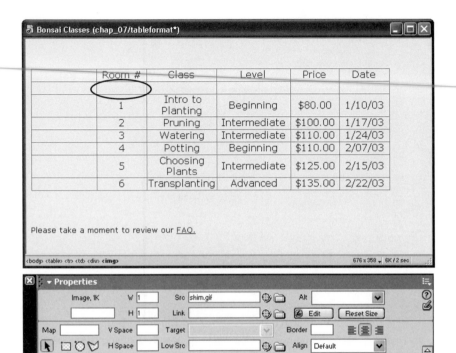

6. In Dreamweaver MX, click inside the cell below the **Room #** cell (column 2, row 2). Choose **Insert > Image**, browse to **shim.gif** located inside the **chap_07** folder, and click **Open**. Be careful to deselect the image after you insert it. If you press **Return** or **Enter** with it selected, it will disappear!

The file that you just inserted (shim.gif), contains a single-pixel transparent GIF, which is invisible to your end user. By placing it inside the empty table cell, you fool the browser into thinking there is content, even though your audience will never see that content. The sole purpose of inserting the graphic is to fix the appearance of the empty table cell.

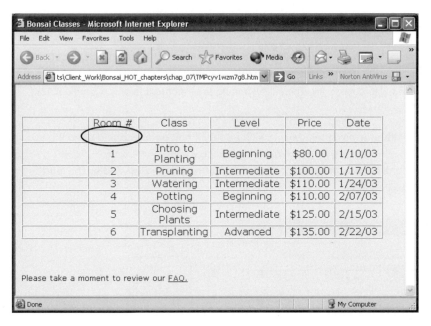

7. Save the changes to the border. Press **F12** to preview the results. See, no more funky pixels, Mom! The empty cell looks like every other cell, which is just the way it should look! Return to Dreamweaver MX and leave this document open for Exercise 2.

NOTE | What Is a Transparent GIF?

The GIF file format supports a feature called transparency, which is a term for a mask. Transparency makes it possible to specify areas in a GIF graphic to disappear in a Web browser. A single-pixel transparent GIF is a graphic that contains only a single pixel that has been instructed to disappear. You can create transparent GIF files in Fireworks, Photoshop, ImageReady, or a host of other graphics applications. Methods for making them vary in each program, so consult the user manual of whichever graphics application you own. If you like, you can store the file **shim.gif** for Web projects other than this book, and that way you will always have a single-pixel transparent GIF on hand.

Note: "Shim" is a term used in carpentry to hold things in place. You may name your single-pixel transparent GIF anything you like. "Shim" was just a name we chose.

2. ——————Sorting the Table

In version 2.0, Macromedia introduced the capability to sort the content of tables both alphabetically and numerically in Dreamweaver. Before this feature existed, if you wanted to sort a table, you had to copy and paste each row or column manually. Thankfully, sorting table content is only a simple dialog box away.

1. The document **tableformat.html** should still be open. If not, go ahead and open it again.

2. Make sure that the table is selected and choose **Commands > Sort Table**. The **Sort Table** dialog box will open.

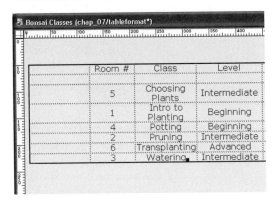

3. Change the settings to **Sort By: Column 3, Order: Alphabetically Ascending**. Click **OK**.

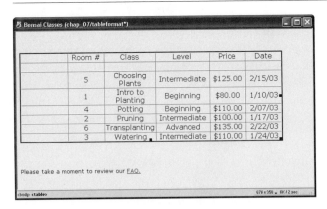

Notice that the file has been sorted differently from when you first opened it? The third column is now in alphabetical order. You can arrange table contents through this kind of command. Try doing this manually, and you'll really appreciate this feature!

4. Save the file and keep it open for the next exercise.

The Sort Table Dialog Box

The **Sort Table** dialog box has a variety of options to help you modify the appearance of tables. See the chart below for an explanation of all its features:

Sorting Features	
Feature	**Definition**
Sort By	Use this option to select which column you would like to use to sort the table.
Order	Use these two pull-down menus to choose Alphabetically or Numerically and Ascending or Descending.
Then By	Use this option to sort multiple columns in your table.
Options: Sort Includes First Row	If this box is checked, the first row in your table will be sorted. This option is off by default because most often the first row is used as a header for the table.
Sort THEAD Rows (If Any):	If this box is checked, all the rows in the table's **<thead>** section (if any) will be sorted using the same criteria as the body rows.
Sort TFOOT Rows (If Any):	If this box is checked, all the rows in the table's **<tfoot>** section (if any) will be sorted using the same criteria as the body rows.
Options: Keep TR Attributes With Sorted Row	If this box is checked, and a row is moved around due to sorting, all the attributes for that row will also move (e.g., color, font, etc.). **<tr>** stands for **t**able **r**ow in HTML.

3. —————————Changing the Color Scheme

Next on the list of table building skills is learning how to apply color formatting. This exercise shows off Dreamweaver MX's color-picking features for tables. Dreamweaver MX offers a variety of ways to get the job done. When it comes to coloring your tables, you may use Dreamweaver MX's automatic color features or set whatever custom colors you desire.

In this exercise, you will learn how to manually apply color to the background of tables, columns, rows, and cells by using the Property Inspector.

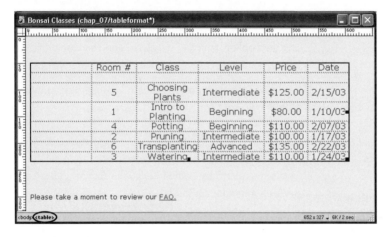

1. With **tableformat.html** still open from the previous exercise, select the **<table>** tag in the **Tag Selector**.

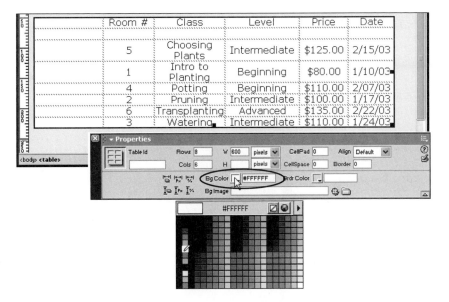

2. In the **Property Inspector**, click on the **Bg Color** box for the table and select white **#FFFFFF** from the **color cube**. The background color of the table changes.

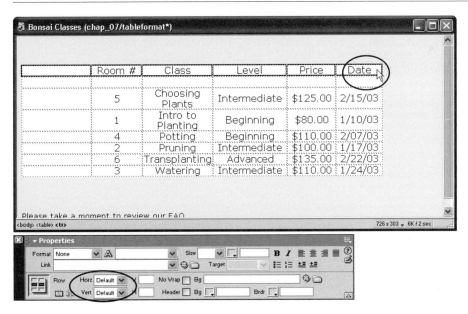

3. Starting at the upper-left corner of the table, click and drag across the top row to select that entire row. Notice that the lower-left portion of the **Property Inspector** displays properties for the selected row.

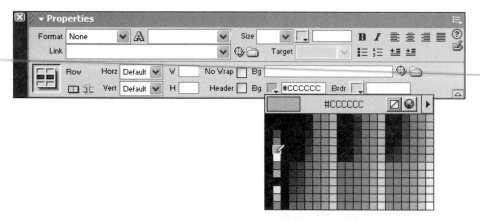

4. In the **Property Inspector**, click the **Bg** color box and choose gray **#CCCCCC** from the color cube.

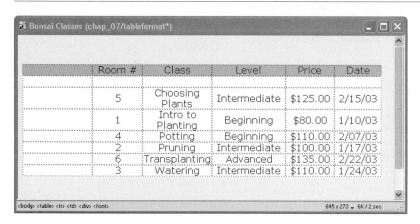

Here's what your table looks like now. You can color table columns and individual cells in much the same way.

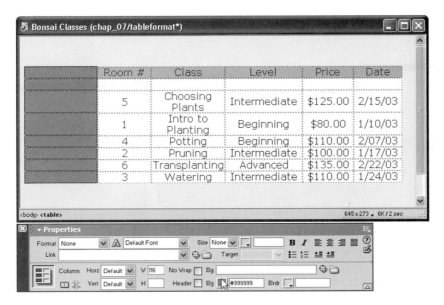

5. Click inside the **first cell** in **row 1** and drag down to select the **first column**. In the **Property Inspector**, click on the **Bg** color cube for the column and pick gray **#999999** from the color cube.

6. Save and **close** this file, you won't need it any longer.

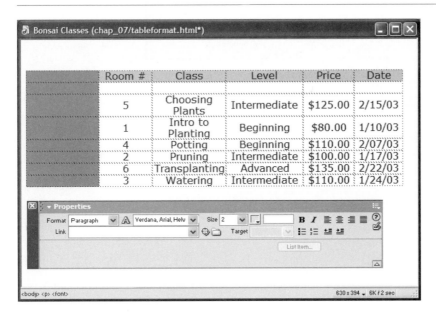

The table should now look like this.

The Format Table Command

But wait there's more! Dreamweaver MX provides yet another way to customize your table's color settings. The Format Table command is quick and easy to use; plus, it is great if you have trouble with or plain don't like choosing colors. By choosing **Commands > Format Table**, you can open the **Format Table** dialog box.

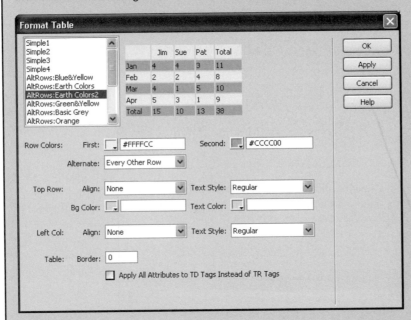

The Format Table dialog box gives you access to a bunch of preset color themes that can be applied to your tables. As you click through the various themes, notice how the table preview in the middle changes so you can preview that theme. These color combinations are part of Dreamweaver MX and can be applied to any table. Additionally, if you want, you can customize the color theme by clicking on a **Row Colors** box and selecting a color from the picker.

4. _____Creating and Modifying a Table

This exercise shows you how to create your own table from scratch and how to modify it. You will learn to work with a combination of the **Insert Table** object, the **Modify > Table** menu, and the Property Inspector. You won't be building a finished page yet. Instead, you'll have a chance to explore many of the different table options first.

1. Create a new document and save it as **firsttable.html**.

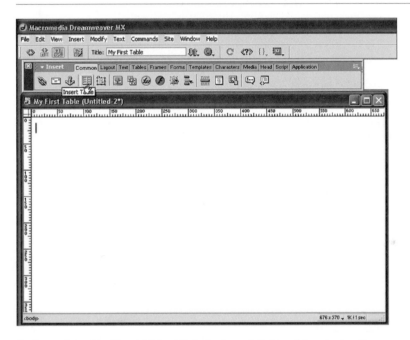

2. Enter **Title: My First Table**. Click the **Insert Table** object in the **Common** tab in the **Insert** panel or choose **Insert > Table**. The **Insert Table** dialog box will appear.

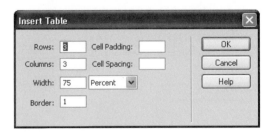

3. Make sure your settings match the settings above, then click **OK**.

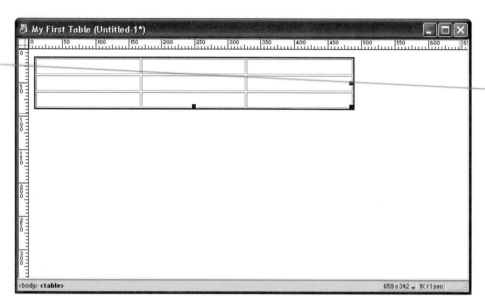

The Insert Table dialog box's default settings result in a table that is three rows high and three columns wide.

4. Select the left column by clicking inside the top-left cell and dragging down to the bottom row with your mouse button still depressed. Don't worry, it's not sad. ;-)

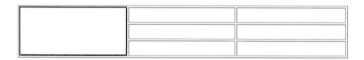

5. Choose **Modify > Table > Merge Cells**. This will result in a table with three columns, with the left column made of only one cell and the other two columns containing three rows of cells.

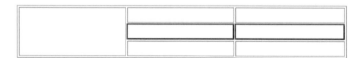

6. Select the middle row by clicking inside the left-middle cell and dragging over to the right-middle cell while leaving your mouse button depressed.

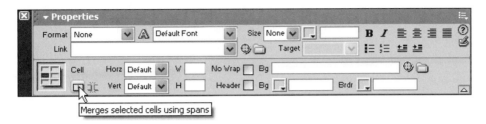

Merges selected cells using spans

7. In the **Property Inspector**, click the **Merge Cells** button. This achieves the same effect as the **Modify** menu did in Step 5. As with many things in Dreamweaver MX, there are multiple ways to accomplish the same task. We prefer to use the **Property Inspector** to merge cells, though you may prefer to use the **Modify** menu method.

Just as you can merge cells in rows and columns, you can also add and delete entire rows and columns. However, selecting rows and columns can be tricky at times. For example, to select the column on the far left, you will find that you can no longer click and drag inside it because now it is only a single cell.

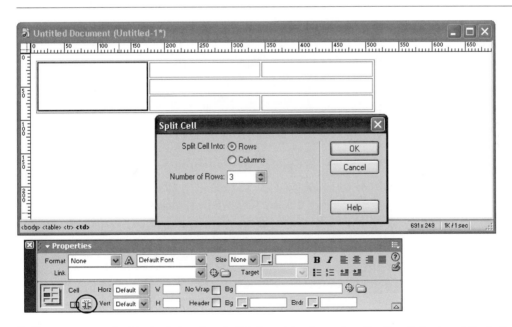

8. Put your cursor inside the left cell and click the **<td>** element on the **Tag Selector** at the bottom of the document (remember, **<td>** stands for table data). In the **Property Inspector**, click the **Split Cell** button. This brings up the **Split Cell** dialog box. Enter **3**, if it's not already entered, and make sure the **Rows** radio button is selected, then click **OK**.

You just added back to this table the three cells that you merged in Step 5. See how flexible this table editor is?

9. To delete the left column completely, select it again and choose **Edit > Cut**. The shortcut keys for this are **Ctrl+X** (Windows) and **Cmd+X** (Mac). You can delete rows or columns by selecting them and cutting them out at any time.

Insert Rows or Columns

Insert: ⦿ Rows
⚬ Columns
Number of Rows: 1
Where: ⚬ Above the Selection
⦿ Below the Selection

OK
Cancel
Help

10. Add a new row by clicking inside the upper-right cell and choosing **Modify > Table > Insert Rows or Columns**. Select **Insert: Rows, Number of Rows: 1**, and **Where: Below the Selection**. Click **OK**.

11. Here are the results of that action. You can also select other options, of course. Dreamweaver MX offers a lot of flexibility when it comes to formatting tables, which you'll likely find useful for the variety of table-related tasks that will arise over the course of your future Web-design projects. **Save** and **close** the file.

NOTE | Contextual Table Menus

Time and again, Dreamweaver MX lets you accomplish the same task in many different ways. For example, Exercise 4 showed you how to merge and split cells by using the **Modify > Table** menu or the **Property Inspector**. Alternately, you could select the column and **Ctrl+click** (Mac) or **right-click** (Windows) to access the **contextual** menu. There you will find a handy list of everything you'd ever want to do to a table.

You can use any of three ways to access this same information (Property Inspector, Modify menu, or contextual menu), depending on your preference.

5. ——————— Aligning Images and Text with Tables

Many people use tables to align images and text because they offer the ability to position artwork freely on a page. This next exercise shows you how to work with a page layout and modify the alignment through adjusting the height and width of table rows and columns.

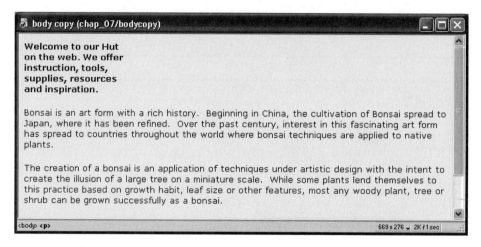

1. Open **bodycopy.html**. Press **F12**. This is a text file that has no table formatting. Resize the browser window and watch how the width of the text within the document extends to the width of the browser. This is default alignment behavior, and the problem with it is that it can create very wide layouts on large monitors.

Most design experts agree that column widths should be limited in order to make reading text easier. You don't see books that are 21 inches across with text stretching side-to-side. That's because it's hard for people to read lines of text that extend more than 3–4 inches across the screen. In order to create a narrower column, you will need to learn how to create a table with fixed-pixel widths.

2. Return to Dreamweaver MX. Create a new document and save this file in the **chap_07** folder as **align.html**.

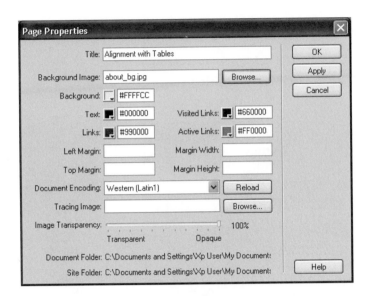

3. Choose **Modify > Page Properties** and enter **Title: Alignment with Tables**. Set the **Background** color to **#FFFFCC**, the **Text** color to **#000000**, the **Links** color to **#990000**, the **Visited Links** color to **#660000**, and the **Active Links** color to **#FF0000**. Click **Browse** to the right of the **Background Image** field and browse to **about_bg.jpg**. Click **Open**. You will be returned to the Page Properties dialog box. Click **OK**.

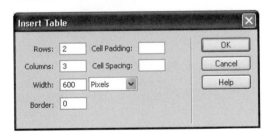

4. Choose **Insert > Table** and change the settings to **Rows: 2, Columns: 3, Width: 600 Pixels** (make sure you change this to Pixels, not Percent), and **Border: 0**. Click **OK**.

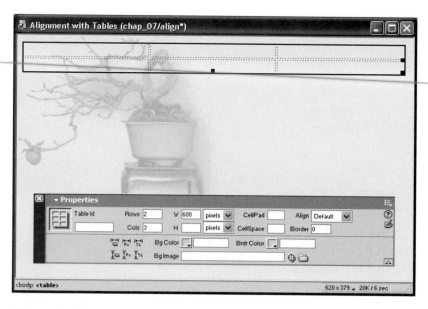

The result of these settings should look like this. You are laying down the framework for a fixed-pixel table that is suitable for aligning objects.

5. Choose **Window > bodycopy.html** (located at the bottom of the **Window** menu, which lists all the open documents). If for some reason **bodycopy.html** is not open, go ahead and open it from the **Site** window (F8).

6. Select and **copy** just the text that contains the Welcome statement. The image above shows you the text that should be selected.

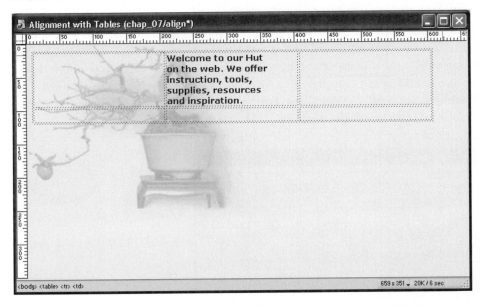

7. Choose **Window > align.html** to bring forth the **align.html** document. Click inside **column 2, row 1** and paste the text into that cell.

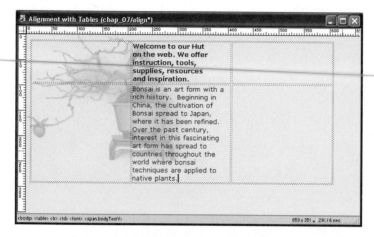

8. Switch back to the **bodycopy.html** document by choosing **Window > bodycopy.html**. *Note:* If you are using Windows and have your document window maximized, you could go back and forth between these two documents by clicking on the small tabs in the lower-left corner of each document window. Select and copy the first paragraph. Switch back to the document with the table in it by choosing **Window > align.html**. Click inside **column 2, row 2** and paste the text into that cell. The image above shows what your page should look like at this point.

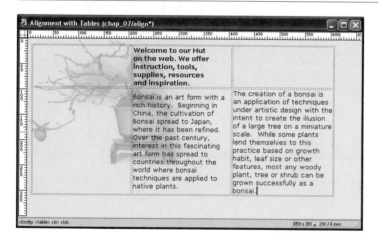

9. Switch between the two documents, using the **Window** menu, to copy and paste the second paragraph into column 3, row 2 of the table, as shown above. Close **bodycopy.html**. You're finished with copying and pasting.

Notice that the top of column 2, row 2 does not align with the top of column 3, row 2? This is an example of default table formatting, which vertically centers the text in a table cell unless otherwise instructed. In order to fix this, you'll need to adjust the table-alignment settings. The next step shows you how.

Collapsed cell

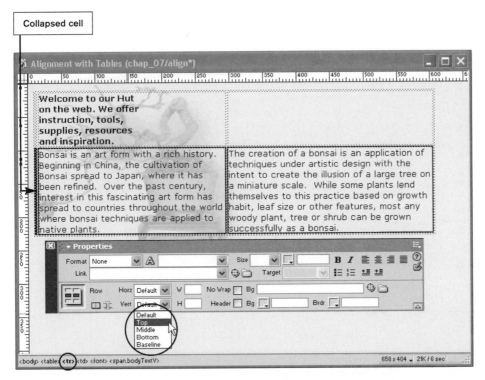

10. Click anywhere in the second row of the table. Click the **<tr>** tag in the **Tag Selector** to select the entire second row. Change the **Property Inspector's Vert** setting to **Top**. As you can see, this corrects the irregular alignment, but it also collapses the empty cell on the far left.

As you now know, empty cells in Dreamweaver MX and in browsers are certainly problematic, aren't they? The only solution is to insert a transparent GIF again, which you'll do in the following step.

11. If your rulers aren't visible, choose **View > Rulers > Show**. The rulers help you see the page's pixel dimensions.

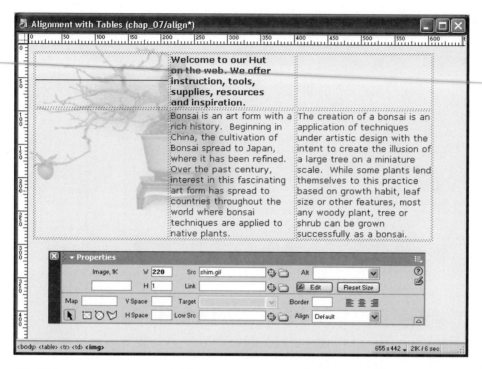

12. Click inside the cell with the Welcome statement and press **Shift+Tab**. This will move your cursor into the collapsed cell. Choose **Insert > Image**, and browse to **shim.gif**, then click **Open**. The **shim.gif** will be selected, and you should see its settings inside the Property Inspector. **Hint**: If the **shim.gif** accidentally gets deselected, click inside its table cell and select the **<img>** element in the **Tag Selector** to reselect it. In the **Property Inspector**, enter **W: 220**. This should stretch the single-pixel GIF to hold the left-hand cell's dimension open.

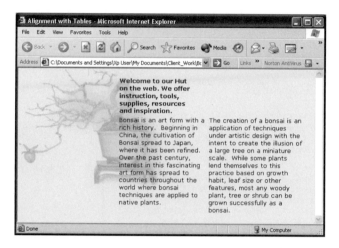

13. Press **F12** to preview the results. This layout is starting to look good, but the space between the table cells feels a little cramped, doesn't it?

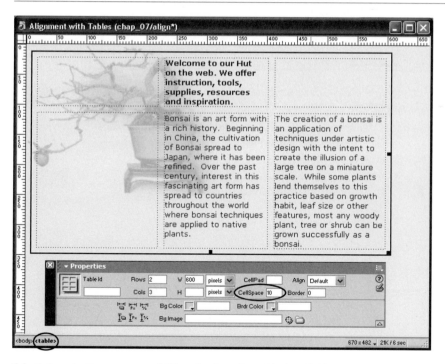

14. Return to Dreamweaver MX and select the table by clicking anywhere inside it and choosing the **<table>** element inside the **Tag Selector**. In the **Property Inspector**, enter **CellSpace: 10**. As you will see, **CellSpace** controls the amount of space between cells. Press **F12** to preview the results.

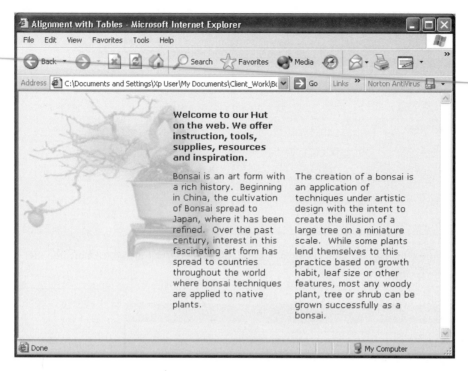

Here are the results of changing the CellSpace attribute. The change is subtle, but it is different. If you want to experiment further with this file, try changing the dimensions of the shim.gif or the CellSpace or CellPad settings. You are in total control over the alignment of this page. By leaving the rulers turned on, you can get a better idea of what values to enter into the settings.

15. Save and **close** all the open documents before you begin the next exercise.

NOTE | Using Rulers

Rulers in Dreamweaver MX are helpful for getting a sense of scale. You can access rulers by choosing **View > Rulers > Show**.

NOTE | Fixed Pixels Versus Percentages in Tables

You can size your tables in two ways: by percentages or by pixels. A percentage-based table will stretch with the width of the browser, meaning that its size will vary depending on the size of the browser window. If you specify that a table uses a width of 75%, for example, it will stretch to fill three-fourths of the horizontal space regardless of the browser window size. This can be a great thing in some cases, but not in others. When you want to restrict the size of a table, regardless of the browser window size, pixel-based tables are the way to go. When you want the table to stretch to the size of the browser window, percentage-based tables are best. To complicate matters, it's possible to nest a pixel-based table inside a percentage-based table or vice versa. By the time you've finished the exercises in this chapter, you will have some concrete examples as to why and when to choose which type of table, and how to combine the two for more complex formatting.

NOTE | CellPad Versus CellSpace

Using CellPad and CellSpace settings alters the amount of space between table cells. CellPad adds room inside the cell, whereas CellSpace adds to the space between cells. When used with table borders set to **0**, CellSpace and/or CellPad achieve the identical result, by interjecting more space between the data and the edge of each cell.

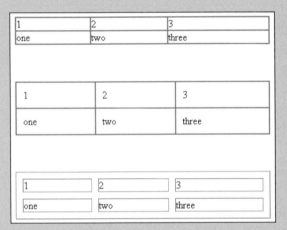

The top table uses neither CellPad nor CellSpace, the middle table uses a CellPad setting of 10, and the bottom table uses a CellSpace setting of 10.

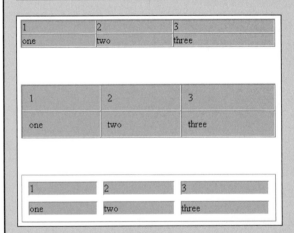

With colored table cells, the differences between CellPad (middle) and CellSpace (bottom) are more noticeable.

6. _____Percentage-Based Table Alignment

In the last exercise, you worked with a table that was fixed at 600 pixels. When you want to control your alignment precisely, fixed pixels are the way to go. There's another way to achieve alignment with tables that is based on percentages. This next exercise uses percentage-based tables to ensure that the page elements will be centered on any size browser window.

1. Create a new document and save it into the **chap_07** folder and name it **center.html**.

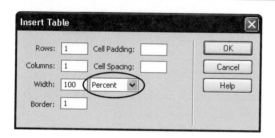

2. Choose **Insert > Table** and change the settings to **Rows: 1**, **Columns: 1**, **Width: 100 Percent**, and **Border: 1**. For this exercise to work, it's imperative that the width be set to Percent and not Pixels. Click **OK**.

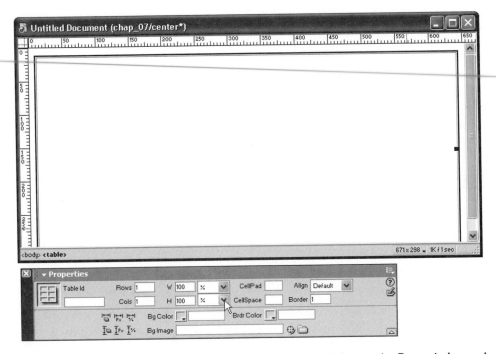

3. Select the **<table>** tag at the bottom of the document and change the **Property Inspector's** height setting (**H**) to **100%**. The Property Inspector's width setting (**W**) should already be set to **100%**. Press **F12** to preview this page in a browser.

Note: When you press F12 to preview this page right now, you can move the browser window size around, and you'll see the table stretch. What's happening? You specified that the width and height of this table would fill 100% of the browser's shape, regardless of its size. This is critical to the success of this exercise, because you are now going to align an image to this table, and the image will be aligned in relationship to the size of the browser, regardless of its shape.

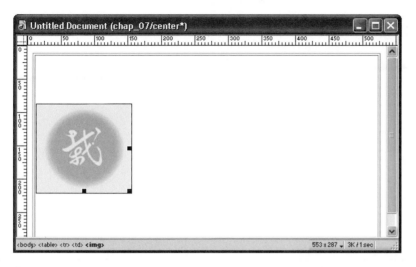

4. Return to Dreamweaver MX. Click inside the giant table cell. Choose **Insert > Image**, browse to **bonsai_symbol.jpg**, and click **Open**.

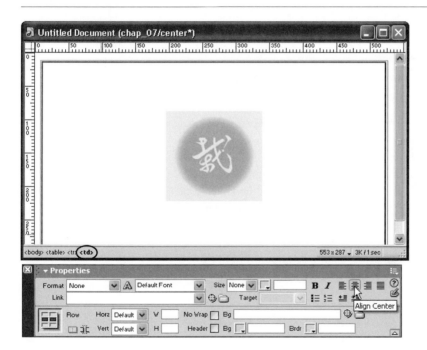

5. In the **Tag Selector**, click on the **<td>** tag to select the table cell, and then in the **Property Inspector**, click the **Align Center** button. The image will pop into the center of the large table.

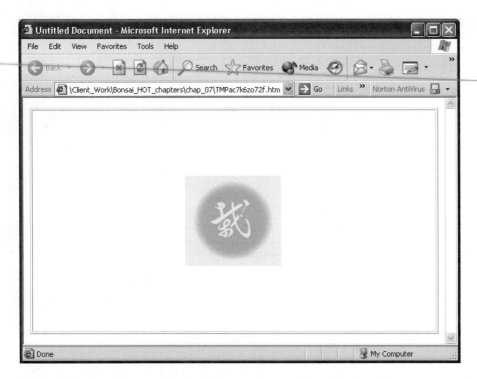

6. Press **F12** to preview and try stretching the browser to different positions. No matter how you set the browser window, this image will always be perfectly centered!

This is just one example of percentage-based table alignment. You could center an image to a pixel-based table, but because the table wouldn't stretch to the size of the browser window, the image would center to the table's shape, not the browser's shape.

7. To finish the effect, return to Dreamweaver MX. Select the table by clicking inside it and highlighting the **<table> Tag Selector**. Change the **Property Inspector Border** setting to **0**. This will turn off the border.

8. Choose **Modify > Page Properties**, enter **Background: #FFFFCC**, and click **OK**.

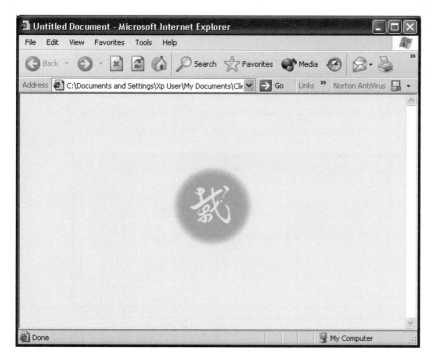

9. Press **F12** to see the results. People who view this page will never know you used a table, yet the image will always be centered.

What's so great about hiding the table from viewers? Because you've just created a layout that is centered regardless of the size or shape of the browser window, and people who view this page won't be distracted by a table border at the edge of the browser screen.

10. Return to Dreamweaver MX. **Save** and **close** this file.

7. ————————Seamless Image Assembly

If you've looked around the Web much, you've probably noticed that tables are sometimes used to assemble multiple images so that they look like a single image. Why would anyone want to do this? Tables can ensure that artwork stays aligned and grouped, whereas HTML without tables can be subject to movement depending on the size of the browser window. This exercise shows you how to reassemble multiple images into a pixel-based table so that they won't be misaligned.

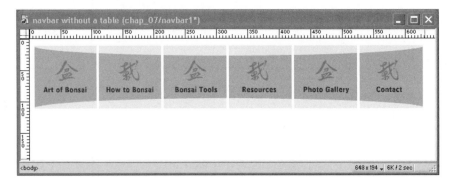

1. Open **navbar1.html**. Notice the gaps between each of the images? This can be the result of putting images next to each other without a table.

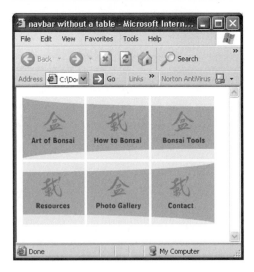

2. Press **F12** to preview this document, then make your browser window smaller. Notice how the row of images gets disrupted? By placing them inside a table, they will become grouped, and won't be able to move around like this.

3. Return to Dreamweaver MX. Click each image once (don't double-click!), and you'll see its dimensions inside the **Property Inspector**. You have six images, which are each 100 pixels wide. Multiplying 6 by 100 gives you 600, so you'll need to create a 600-pixel-wide table in order to assemble these as one seamless-looking image.

4. Position your cursor after the last image and press **Return** or **Enter**, so your insertion cursor appears below the images on the screen and on the left.

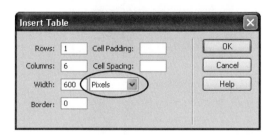

5. Choose **Insert > Table** and change the settings to **Rows: 1**, **Columns: 6**, **Width: 600 Pixels** (not Percent!), and **Border: 0**. Click **OK**.

6. Click inside the far-left bottom cell, and choose **Insert > Image**. Browse to **navbar1.gif** inside the **chap_07** folder and click **Open**. The table formatting between cells has shifted, but the image is now inside the appropriate cell.

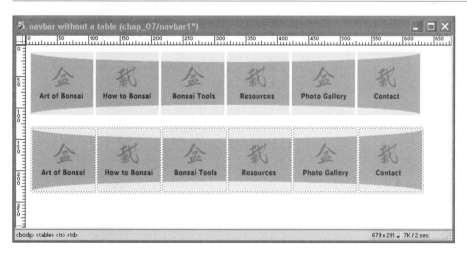

7. Once you insert all the other images into the appropriate cells, the table should appear like this. The names of the files, from left to right, are **navbar1.gif**, **navbar2.gif**, **navbar3.gif**, **navbar4.gif**, **navbar5.gif**, and **navbar6.gif**.

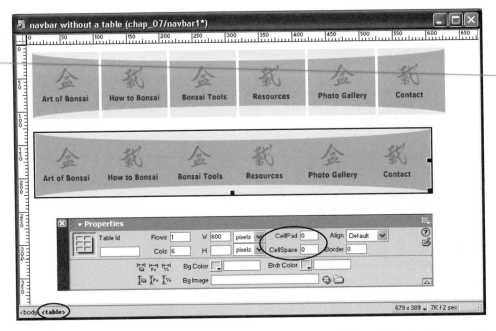

8. To get rid of the gaps between the cells, select the entire table by clicking inside any cell and selecting the **<table>** **Tag Selector**. Once you've selected it, change the **Property Inspector** setting to read **CellPad: 0** and **CellSpace: 0**. The table will come together seamlessly.

9. Press **F12** to preview your seamless table. Now that is what a navigation bar ought to look like!

10. Save this file and leave it open for the next exercise.

8. ————————Combining Pixels and Percentages

This next exercise demonstrates how to combine a pixel-accurate table, like the one you just created in Exercise 7, with a percentage-based table like you created in Exercise 6. Why would this be important? Let's say that you had a navigation bar, like the one you just built, that you wanted to be center aligned regardless of whether it was seen on a small or large monitor. Combining the last two techniques lets you do just that.

1. Create a new document and save it into the **chap_07 folder** and name it **navbar2.html**.

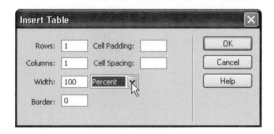

2. Choose **Insert > Table** and change the settings to **Rows: 1, Columns: 1, Width: 100 Percent** (not Pixels!), and **Border: 0**. Click **OK**. By using **Percent** for width, the table will always be horizontally centered on the page.

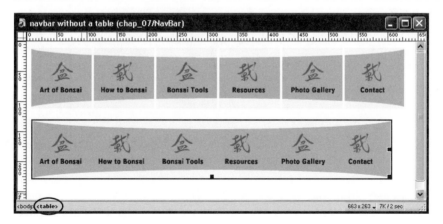

3. Return to **navbar1.html** (use the Window menu and look at the bottom to locate it) and select the bottom table. Remember that you can click anywhere in the table to access the Tag Selector in order to select it. With the table selected, choose **Edit > Copy**.

4. Now switch over to **navbar2.html** and click inside the centered table. Choose **Edit > Paste**.

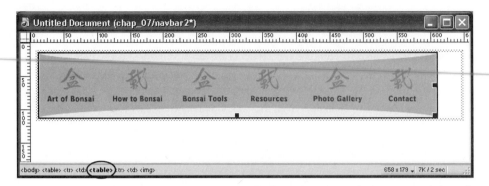

5. Select the table that you just pasted. Again, if you click inside it you can use the **<table> Tag Selector** to select it. Notice there are two **<table>** tags in the **Tag Selector** now. This happens because you have one table nested inside another.

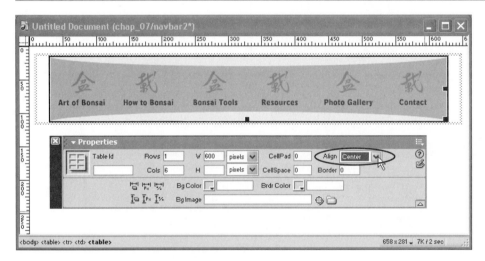

6. With the nested (navigation bar) table selected, change the **Property Inspector Align** setting to **Center**.

7. Preview in the browser (**F12**), and you should see that the navigation bar remains centered regardless of how wide you drag your browser window out. Congratulations again, you've just made a nested table using a combination of pixels and percentages. Sounds impressive, but even better than that— it's useful!

8. Return to Dreamweaver MX. **Save** and **close** the **navbar1.html** and **navbar2.html** files.

9. ————————Inserting Tab-Delimited Data

As you just learned, creating tables from scratch can be quite a chore. So anything that helps stream-line the process is a dream. Dreamweaver MX gives you the ability to easily insert delimited text files. This is great for people who use Excel and other office applications, because now it's simple to get that data into Dreamweaver MX. This exercise shows you how to import a delimited text file into a table.

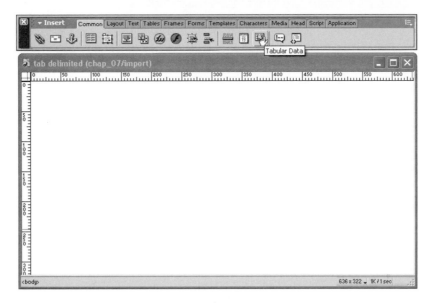

1. Open **import.html**. This is just a blank file that we created for you. Click the **Tabular Data** object in the **Insert** panel to open the **Import Tabular Data** dialog box.

2. Click **Browse** and navigate to **tabdelimited.txt** from the **chap_07** folder. Click **OK** to select that file.

Import Tabular Data Settings

You won't be changing most of the default settings in this exercise, but you should know what those options mean. Here's a handy chart that explains what you can do in the **Import Tabular Data** dialog box.

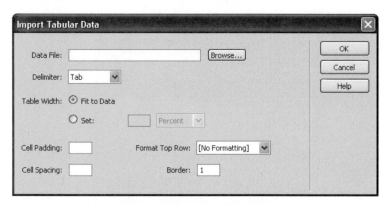

Import Tabular Data Settings	
Setting	**Function**
Data File	Use this option to browse to the delimited file on your hard drive.
Delimiter	This option specifies the type of delimiter used in the imported file, such as tabs or commas.
Table Width: Fit to Data	This option will create a table large enough to fit the data in the imported file.
Table Width: Set	This option lets you specify how wide to make the table that holds the imported data. You can choose either percent or pixel widths.
Cell Padding	Controls the CellPad value for the table that holds the imported data.
Cell Spacing	Controls the CellSpace value for the table that holds the imported data.
Format Top Row	You can apply a number of different formatting options to the first row of data in your table.
Border	Controls the table's border width.

3. Leave the rest of the settings at their default settings. Click **OK**. This will import the data into Dreamweaver MX inside a custom table.

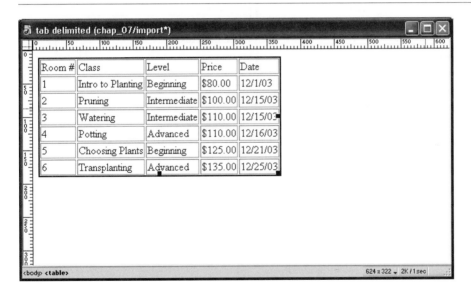

This is what your page should look like at this point.

4. Save and leave this file open for the next exercise.

10. _____Nested Tables and Borders

As you learned earlier, it is possible to modify the size and appearance of table borders through changing the width and border in the Property Inspector. In this exercise, we show you how to produce an outline appearance around the border of the table. This technique isn't accomplished through the Property Inspector; it's created instead through nesting tables. If you like this technique, don't forget to share this trick with someone you know. ;-)

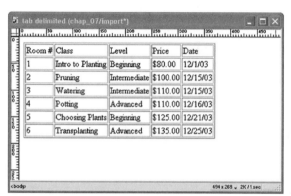

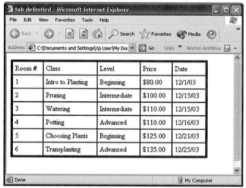

The table on the left uses standard table properties to create its appearance. The table on the right uses nested tables to create the appearance of a stroked outline around the border of the cells and outer table. This technique offers an attractive alternative to the boring old tables we see everywhere.

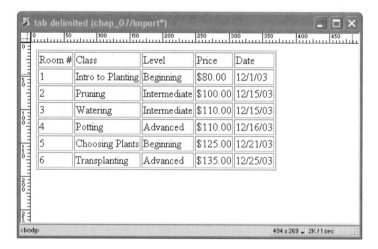

1. The file from the previous exercise should be open; if it's not, go ahead and open the **import.html** file located inside the **chap_07** folder.

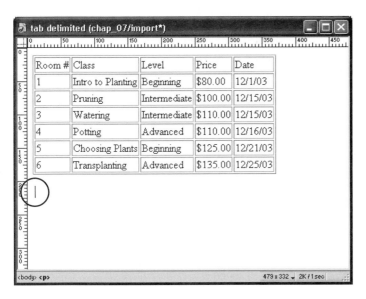

2. Click to the right of the table to place your blinking cursor outside the table. Press **Return/Enter** to move your cursor down.

3. Click the **Insert Table** object in the **Common** tab in the **Insert** panel. This will open the **Insert Table** dialog box.

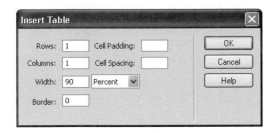

4. Create a table with **1 Row, 1 Column, 90% Width**, and **0 Border**. Your dialog box should look just like the one shown above. Click **OK**.

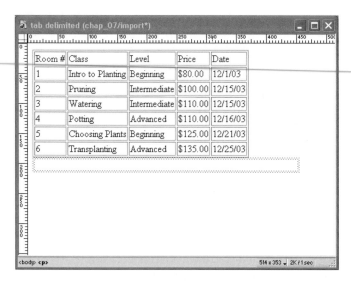

This is what your page should look like after the new table has been added. Don't worry, you are going to make it look much better than this!

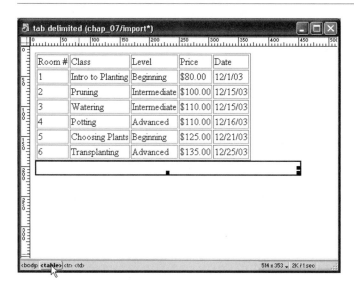

5. Click inside the new table you just created. In the **Tag Selector**, click on **<table>** to quickly select the entire table.

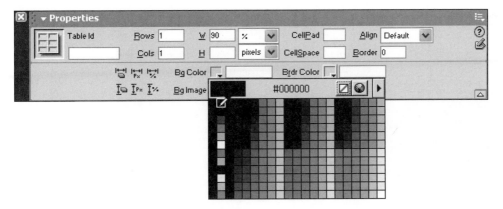

6. In the **Property Inspector**, click the **Bg Color** option and select **black**. The color you select for the background will also be the color of your table borders.

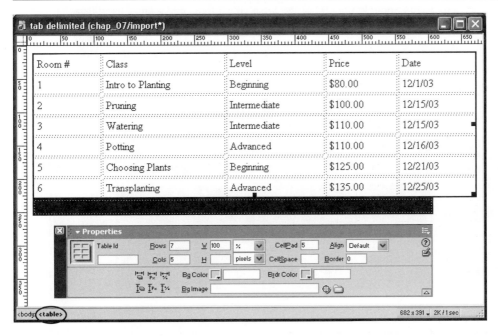

7. Select the top table using the **Tag Selector**, just like you did in Step 5. In the **Property Inspector**, change the **Width** to **100%, CellPad** to **5**, and the **Border** option to **0**.

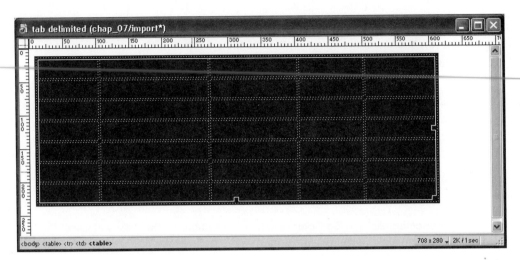

8. Move your cursor to the upper-left corner of the table until it turns into a small hand (Mac) or a four-headed arrow (Windows). Then, click and drag the upper table into the lower table.

Your nested tables should look like the one shown above. Everything will turn black! Don't worry, you'll fix this soon.

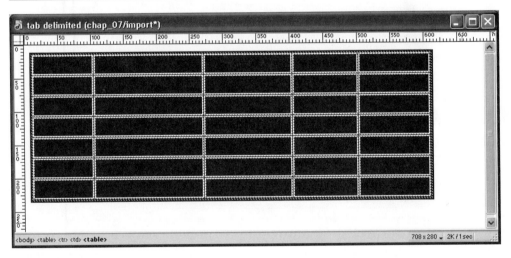

9. Click inside the upper-left cell and drag to select all of the cells in the table.

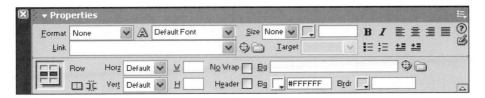

10. In the **Property Inspector**, set the **Bg Color** option to **White**. This will change the background of each individual cell to white so you can see your text and the black table borders.

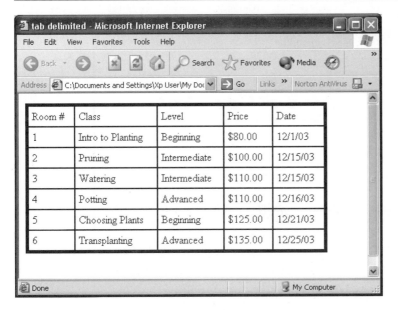

Room #	Class	Level	Price	Date
1	Intro to Planting	Beginning	$80.00	12/1/03
2	Pruning	Intermediate	$100.00	12/15/03
3	Watering	Intermediate	$110.00	12/15/03
4	Potting	Advanced	$110.00	12/16/03
5	Choosing Plants	Beginning	$125.00	12/21/03
6	Transplanting	Advanced	$135.00	12/25/03

11. Press **F12** to preview this page in your default browser. Here, you can clearly see how the inner table is used to color the border of the outer table. Pretty neat, huh?

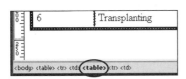

12. Click anywhere inside the table so the **Tag Selector** looks like what you see here. In the **Tag Selector**, click the second instance of the **<table>** tag to select the inner table.

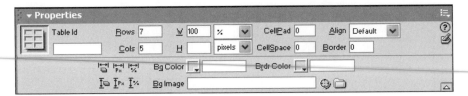

13. Try setting the **Cell Padding** and **Cell Spacing** of the inner table to **0**. Then preview the page again in a browser. Another cool effect. Go ahead and experiment with other settings. You can't break anything, so just have some fun.

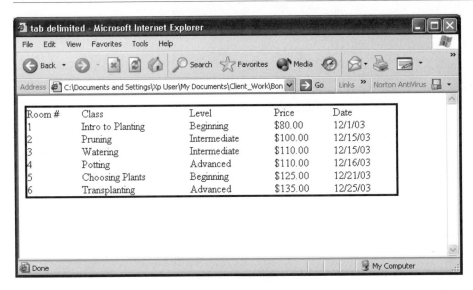

This is what the page looks like with the Cell Padding and Cell Spacing set to 0. As you can see, by adjusting these two options, you can dramatically change the appearance of the table border.

14. Return to Dreamweaver MX. **Save** and **close** this file.

II. —————————**Rounded-Corner Tables**

Tables, like most things on the Web are square. Images are square, frames are square, the browser window is square; it seems like almost everything on the Web is square. It's no wonder Web designers are always looking for ways to make things look less square. This handy little trick is one way to make your tables look less boxy. This is another one of those custom tricks you might want to share with your friends, or perhaps not share with your competitors!

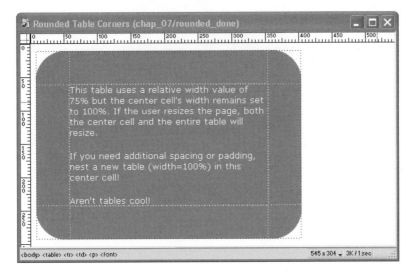

1. Open the **rounded_done.html** file located inside the **chap_07** folder. This is the completed file for this exercise, so you can see the effect you're aiming for in this exercise.

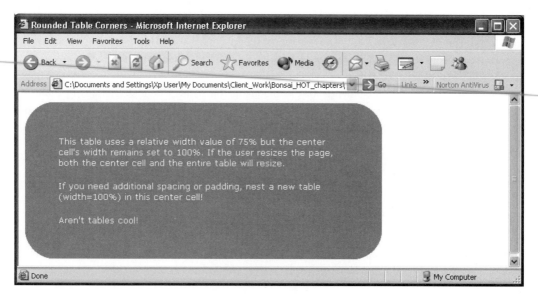

This is what the finished table looks like in the browser. Notice that as the browser window changes size, so does the table.

2. Press **F12** to preview this page in a browser. Go ahead and resize the window of your browser; notice how the table size adjusts with the size of the window. This occurs because the table is set to a percentage width, in this case 75%.

3. Return to Dreamweaver MX.

Now you know where this exercise is going, it's time to get started. The following steps walk you through the whole process of creating this same table.

4. Create a new document and save it inside the **chap_07** folder as **round.html**.

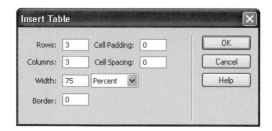

5. Create a new table that has **3 Rows**, **3 Columns**, **Width 75 Percent**, **Borders 0**, and **Cell Padding** and **Cell Spacing** of **0**. Your dialog box should look just like the one shown above.

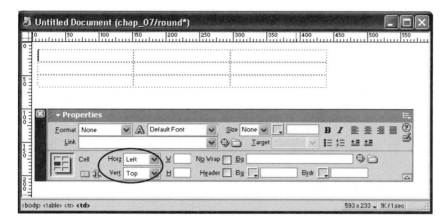

6. Click inside the upper-left cell. In the **Property Inspector**, set the **Horz** option to **Left** and the **Vert** option to **Top**. This will ensure that the images you insert into this cell are aligned in the upper-left corner of the cell.

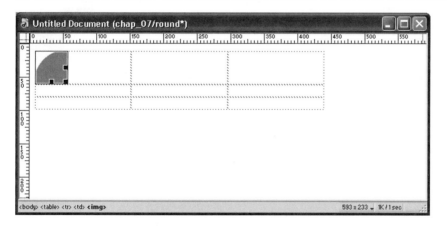

7. Click the **Insert Image** object on the **Common** tab in the **Insert** panel and browse to the **chap_07/images** folder. Click to select the **topleft.gif** file and click **Open**. This will insert that image into the table cell.

8. Click inside the upper-right cell. In the **Property Inspector**, set the **Horz** option to **Right** and the **Vert** option to **Top**. This will ensure that the images you insert into this cell are aligned in the upper-right corner of the cell.

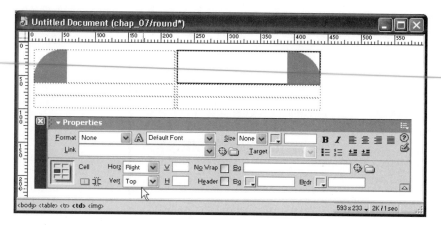

9. Click the **Insert Image** object and browse to the **chap_07/images** folder. Click to select the **topright.gif** file and click **Open**. This will insert that image into the table cell.

10. Click inside the lower-left cell. In the **Property Inspector**, set the **Horz** option to **Left** and the **Vert** option to **Bottom**. This will ensure that the images you insert into this cell are aligned in the lower-left corner of the cell.

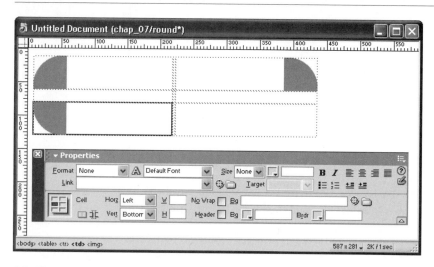

11. Click the **Insert Image** object and browse to the **chap_07** folder. Click to select the **bottomleft.gif** file and click **Open**. This will insert that image into the table cell.

12. Click inside the lower-right cell. In the **Property Inspector**, set the **Horz** option to **Right** and the **Vert** option to **Bottom**. This will ensure that the images you insert into this cell are aligned in the lower-right corner of the cell.

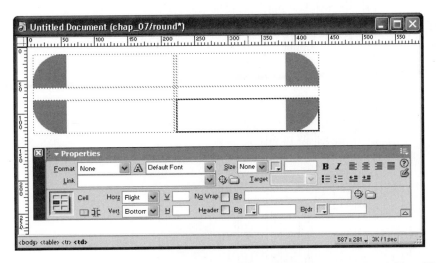

13. Click the **Insert Image** object and browse to the **chap_07/images** folder. Click to select the **bottomright.gif** file and click **Open**. This will insert that image into the table cell.

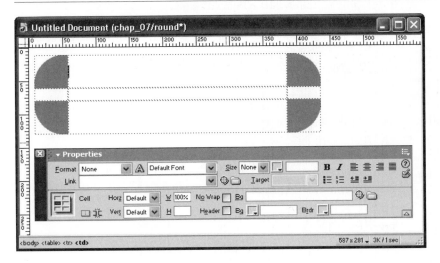

14. Click in the upper-middle cell. In the **Property Inspector**, type **100%** for the **Width** option. This will cause the center cell to expand with the width of the table.

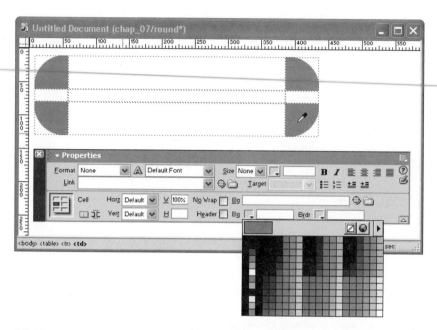

15. Use the **Bg** color option to sample the color of one of the green images. This will change the background color of that cell so that it matches the corner images.

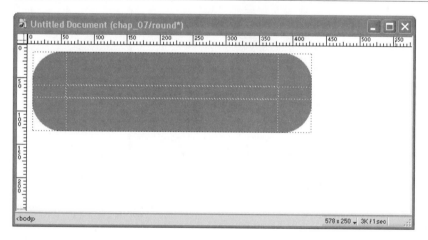

16. Use this same process to color the other cells. When you are finished, your table should look like this.

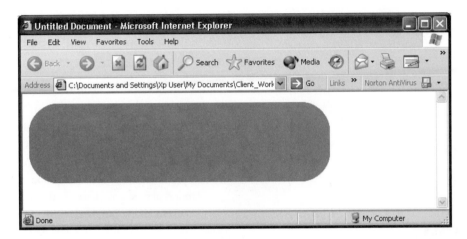

17. Press **F12** to preview this page in a browser. Resize the browser window. Notice how the table changes size and the corners all stay in their correct positions.

18. Return to Dreamweaver MX. If you want to experiment, try adding some text to the middle cell. There are lots of variations on this technique. **Save** and **close** this file.

Phew, you made it again, another chapter under your belt! You deserve a break; this was a long chapter!

8.

Layout

Tracing Images	Using Layers
Converting Layers to Tables	Converting Tables to Layers
Creating Layout Tables	Creating Layout Cells
Modifying Layout Cells	Creating Autostretch Cells

chap_08

Dreamweaver MX
H•O•T CD-ROM

In traditional layout programs, such as Adobe PageMaker, inDesign, and QuarkXPress, most people take it for granted that they can move blocks of text and images around almost anywhere on the screen. Unfortunately, standard HTML doesn't contain any tags that allow you to easily position elements. You've learned how you can use tables to position your elements both horizontally and vertically on your Web pages, but creating a basic table still doesn't give you the precision that you get in traditional print layout programs. This has caused considerable frustration among Web page designers.

Fortunately, Dreamweaver MX has built-in functions that help you work in a visual mode to create precise alignment for your text and images. You'll learn how to align your images using tracing images and layers, which you can then convert into tables that can be viewed on nearly any browser. Dreamweaver MX has an alternative layout feature called **layout cells**— which gives you the freedom of absolute positioning while still conforming to strict HTML table guidelines!

In this chapter, you'll learn several techniques that allow you to position elements anywhere on your Web page, such as tracing images and layers, converting layers to tables, and working with layout tables and layout cells. After completing these exercises, you can decide for yourself which method you prefer when building your own pages.

What Are Tracing Images, Layers, and Tables?

The following chart outlines the concepts behind tracing images, layers, and tables, which you will learn about in the following exercises:

Tracing Images, Layers, and Tables Defined	
Item	**Definition**
Tracing image	An image (GIF, JPEG, or PNG) that can be loaded into the background of your Web page to serve as a reference for layout. Consider this the blueprint you follow to build your pages.
Layer	This is where you put your text and images so you can move them around freely. The downside to using layers is that they work only on 4.0 browsers and above.
Table	Tables can hold images and text in place, but they are not intuitive or flexible when it comes to positioning them on the screen. However, Dreamweaver MX offers some helpful features that give you more flexibility, including the ability to convert layers to tables, and innovative table drawing tools.

I. _____Applying a Tracing Image

Imagine that you have mocked up a wonderful layout for a Web page in Photoshop, Fireworks, Illustrator, or any drawing or painting program of your choice. Wouldn't it be great if you could take that mockup and put it up on the Web? If you save your mockup as a GIF, JPEG, or PNG, you can work with it easily as a tracing image. Dreamweaver MX's **tracing image** feature allows you to place any GIF, JPEG, or PNG into a tracing layer on your page, which can then be used as a reference for you to use to align your HTML elements to match up to it perfectly.

In this exercise, you will learn how to apply a tracing image to your Web page, as well as how to change its transparency and position on the page. You'll work with a tracing image that is supplied from the **H•O•T CD-ROM**. If you were to create your own tracing image, you would create a composite of your Web page in a graphics application of your choice, such as Photoshop, Fireworks, Illustrator, or whatever, and save it as a GIF, JPEG, or PNG. You would then specify your design as a tracing image in Dreamweaver MX, so that you could use it as your guide to re-create your page design.

A tracing image is visible only in Dreamweaver MX. Visitors to your site cannot see it. Keep in mind that when you are viewing the tracing image in Dreamweaver MX while building your page, you cannot see the background image or background color that you are setting, unless you decrease the tracing image's transparency setting. You'll learn to do this in the following exercise.

> **1.** Copy **chap_08** from the **H•O•T CD-ROM** to your hard drive. Define the site for Chapter 8 using the **chap_08** folder as the local root folder. If you need a refresher on this process, visit Exercise 1 in Chapter 3, "*Site Control.*"

> **2.** Open **index.html**. This page is empty except that it already contains the Title "Chapter 8" and the colors for Text, Links, Visited Links, and Active Links have been preset for you. **Choose Modify > Page Properties** to see these settings. The shortcut keys for this are **Cmd+J** (Mac) and **Ctrl+J** (Windows).

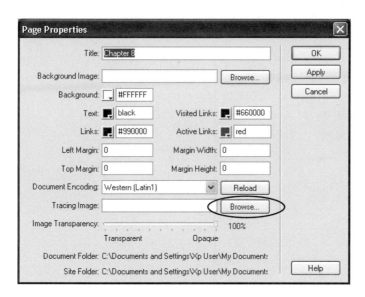

3. Click **Browse** next to the **Tracing Image** field.

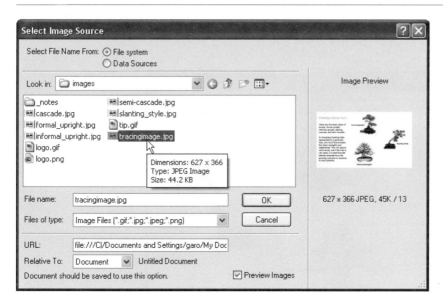

4. Browse to **tracingimage.jpg** inside the **images** folder and click **OK**.

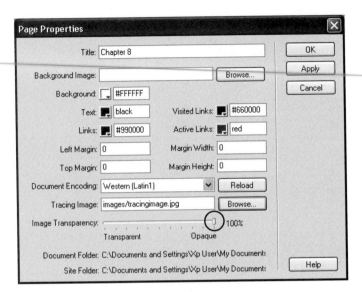

5. For this exercise, make sure the **Image Transparency** slider is at **100%**. This will enable your tracing image to be visible in the document window of Dreamweaver MX.

6. Click **OK** to close the **Page Properties** dialog box.

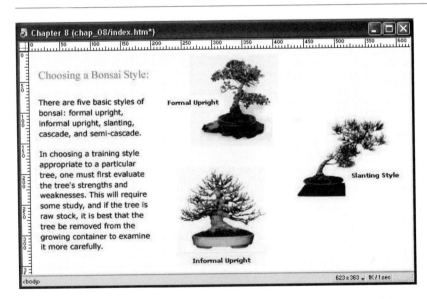

This is what your page should look like with the tracing image applied. It was inserted at 100% opacity in the Page Properties dialog box, which makes it opaque.

NOTE | Browser Offset

The white space you see above and to the left of the tracing image is the result of an offset that Dreamweaver MX created. By default this offset is X:8 Y:11. This means that the image is offset 8 pixels from the top and 11 pixels from the left of the document. You can modify this offset by choosing **View > Tracing Image > Adjust Position**.

Why does Dreamweaver MX introduce such an offset? The program is emulating what would happen in a Web browser. For some kooky reason, browsers do not display foreground images flush top and left, but that's exactly how they display background images—flush top and left. This means that any image in the foreground (meaning it is not a background image) will always be displayed in the browser with this offset. Dreamweaver MX allows you to get rid of the offset; however, the offset is intentionally there to show you how the foreground artwork will align in a Web browser.

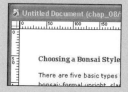

Dreamweaver MX offsets tracing images from the top-left corner to emulate an offset that exists in 3.0 or older Web browsers. You can get rid of this offset if you like. We usually leave the offset alone, because it represents what will happen in a browser, anyway. If you have not accounted for this offset in the design of your tracing image, we suggest you don't change this setting.

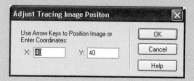

You can use the **Adjust Tracing Image Position** dialog box to set the offset anywhere you want. In some cases, you may want to set the image to **X:0** and **Y:0**. For this example, bring up this dialog box, choose **View > Tracing Image > Adjust Position** and enter **X:40** and **Y:40**. This will move the tracing image towards the center of the document.

7. Press **F12** to preview this page in a Web browser (if you have not defined a browser yet, this is explained in Chapter 2, "*Interface*"). When you do this, notice that the page appears as a blank screen. This is supposed to happen! The tracing image appears only in Dreamweaver MX, and it won't be visible to your end user.

8. Return to Dreamweaver MX and choose **Modify > Page Properties** to access the tracing image settings again.

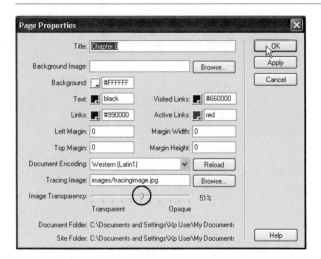

9. Drag the **Image Transparency** slider down to **50%** and click **OK**.

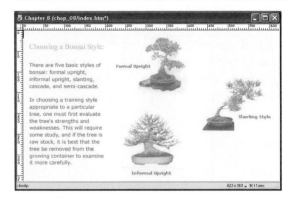

With the opacity reduced, it's much easier to use the tracing image as a guide because it doesn't compete with foreground images and text that are by default set to full opacity.

10. Choose **File > Save** and leave this file open for the next exercise, in which you'll add images to match this layout.

Tracing Images, Background Colors, and Images

Once you apply a tracing image to your page, it will hide the background color and background images while you are editing the document inside Dreamweaver MX. However, if you view the page that contains the tracing image from a browser, the background color and/or background image will be visible, and the tracing image will not. In other words, tracing images are only visible to you while you're working in Dreamweaver MX. This is a good thing, because you don't want people seeing your blueprint—you want them to see the final results.

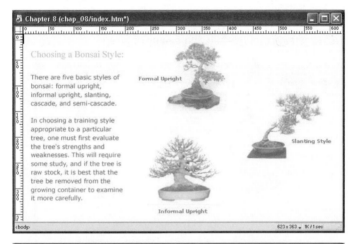

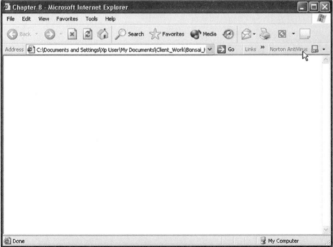

Remember, the tracing image is an internal function of Dreamweaver MX to help you follow a preconceived layout. When you preview the Dreamweaver MX file above in a browser, it appears empty because there is no placed artwork yet.

2. _____Adding Layers

In previous chapters, you have been putting artwork and text directly on your page or inside tables. With that method, you can right-, left-, or center-align elements, and that's the end of the story. This frustrates most people because it would be much easier if you could stick that artwork or text anywhere you wanted on the page and have it stay there. Layers are your friends, because they can be positioned anywhere without restriction. Rather than simply placing artwork and text on a page, as you have been doing so far, you can put your content into layers and move it anywhere you want.

In this exercise, you will learn how to create layers on your page and insert images and text inside them. Then—presto, you'll be able to move everything around. Ahh, the beauty of layers!

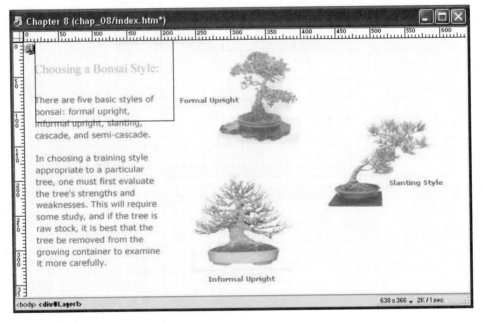

1. With **index.html** still open from the last exercise, choose **Insert > Layer**. If you prefer, you can select the **Layer** object from the **Insert** panel and hand draw your layer by clicking and dragging a box onto the document window.

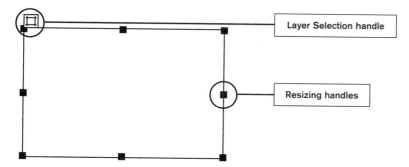

When a layer is selected, the layer handle and eight resizing handles will appear around the border of the layer.

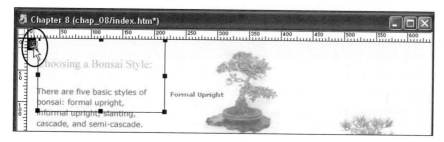

Notice the yellow thingie in the upper-left corner? It's called an invisible element in Dreamweaver MX. If you deselect the layer by clicking outside its boundaries, you'll see that the invisible element is deselected as well. For more on invisible elements, see the "Invisible Element Markers" sidebar later in this chapter.

2. Next, you will move the layer to a new position on the page. Because the layer handle is hiding at the top of the document, you need to select the layer using the invisible element marker. Make sure that visual aids are enabled so that you can see them. If necessary, select **View > Visual Aids > Invisible Elements**.

Click on the **small yellow icon** that appears at the top of your page. This will cause eight resizing handles to appear around the layer.

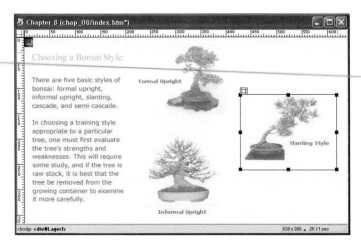

3. Move your cursor over the edge of the layer and click and drag to move the layer so that its upper-left corner aligns with the photo of the slanting style bonsai that is visible in the tracing image. Using the bottom-right resizing handle, resize the layer so that it fits around the edge of that tree's image.

4. Click inside the layer. You should see a blinking I-beam cursor inside the layer.

5. Open the **Assets** panel if it is not already open. Click the **Images** radio button to select **Image Assets**. Select the **slanting_style.jpg** and drag it into the selected layer.

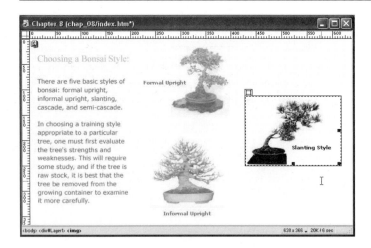

An image is now inside the layer. Notice how this image is darker, whereas the tracing image is screened back? That's because you set the tracing image's opacity to 50% in the last exercise. This makes it easy to distinguish between the layout and the final artwork, doesn't it?

WARNING | Invisible Element Markers

As mentioned earlier, when you create a layer in Dreamweaver MX, a small yellow icon appears at the top of your page. This is referred to as an invisible element marker. Each time you create a layer, a yellow marker will be inserted. By selecting these markers, you can easily select the associated layers. When the yellow icon is selected, it becomes a blue icon, by the way!

You will see these markers in the **index.html** document after you have completed Exercise 2. If you find that these markers get in your way, choose **View > Visual Aids > Invisible Elements** to hide/show them all. You can turn off invisible elements permanently if you want, by choosing **Edit > Preferences > Invisible Elements**.

This is what an invisible element marker looks like in Dreamweaver MX.

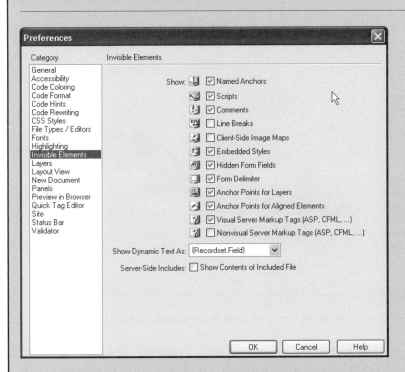

You can turn invisible elements on or off permanently in Dreamweaver MX's Preferences, available under the Edit menu. You can also choose View > Visual Aids > Invisible Elements to turn the Invisible Elements view on and off as you need to.

Draw Layer

6. In the **Insert** panel, click the **Draw Layer** object. If you have a different Insert panel visible, click on the small tab at the top of the panel and select **Common** to switch back to it.

---

7. With the **Draw Layer** tool selected, draw a layer around the image of the **Informal Upright bonsai**.

You've just inserted a layer by using the Insert panel instead of the Insert menu. Either way works fine, and you have now been exposed to both.

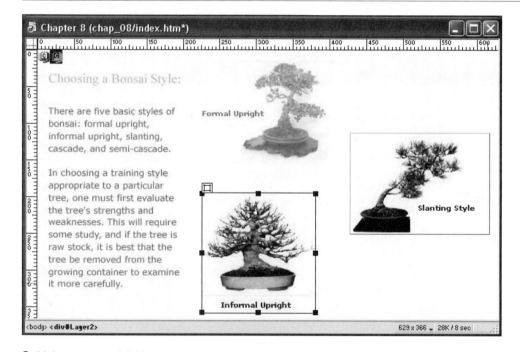

8. Make sure your blinking cursor is inside the layer and drag the **informal_upright.jpg** into this layer.

---

9. Add another layer around the remaining tree. You can use either the **Insert** panel or the **Insert** menu to accomplish this.

---

10. Drag the **formal_upright.jpg** image from the **Assets** panel into this layer.

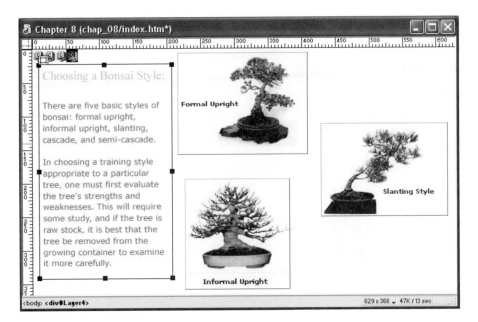

11. So far you have inserted images into layers. Inserting text is just as simple. Add another layer around the **Choosing a Bonsai Style** text panel at the left side of the page.

---

12. Click inside the layer and type the text as you read it on the screen, or you can open the **style.txt** file with a text editor, select all the text, copy it, and paste it into the layer.

Normally you would now format this text. However, for the purpose of this exercise, don't worry too much about matching the type of the original layout. If you need a refresher on type, revisit Chapter 6, "Typography."

---

13. At this point, you will probably want to adjust the position of the layers to more closely match the tracing image. To do this, click on the layer's selection handle to select the whole layer and its content. Then you can either drag the layer to a new position, or you can use the arrow keys on your keyboard to nudge the layer around the document one pixel at a time. **Tip:** Holding the Shift key while pressing the arrow keys will move the selection in 10-pixel increments.

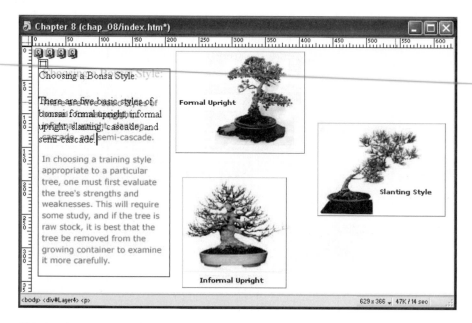

This is what your page looks like now. Most likely, your text won't perfectly match the tracing image. That's all right—the tracing image is there only as a guide.

14. Press **F12** to preview this page in a browser. Notice once again that the tracing image disappears. Only this time, you've re-created the layout using layers. When you are finished marveling at this accomplishment, return to Dreamweaver MX and save the file. Leave this document open for the next exercise.

MOVIE | layers.mov

To learn more about using layers, check out **layers.mov** located in the movies folder on the Dreamweaver MX **H•O•T CD-ROM**.

3. Converting Layers to Tables

You've just positioned artwork precisely to match a specific layout. As you may recall from the introduction to this section, layers display only on version 4.0+ browsers. People using earlier browsers will see the content of the layers all jumbled up along the left side of your page, which, of course, is not cool at all! We're guessing that you want the luxury of freely positioning artwork with layers, but still want people with older browsers to view your site. This exercise will show you how to convert layers to standard HTML tables, so anybody can see your perfect layout, no matter what browser they're using.

1. With **index.html** still open from the last exercise, choose **Modify > Convert > Layers to Table**. The **Convert Layers to Table** dialog box will open.

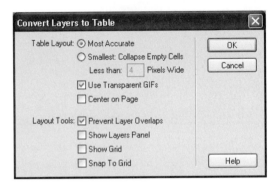

2. Click **Table Layout: Most Accurate**. Check the **Prevent Layer Overlaps** checkbox. This setting is required because layers can overlap, but tables cannot. Leave the **Use Transparent GIFs** option selected. This will insert a transparent GIF into your layout as needed to ensure that your table doesn't collapse in some browsers. Click **OK**.

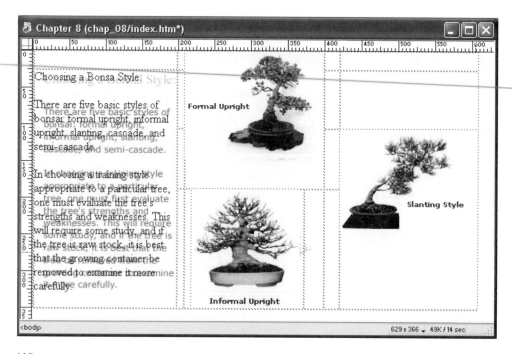

When you convert your layers to tables, by default Dreamweaver MX will set the table borders to 0, as shown above in the Property Inspector. Why? You do not want to advertise that you are using tables. The 0 gives you an invisible border, creating the illusion of floating background images and text on your Web page.

You can access the table properties by clicking anywhere in the table, and then selecting the **<table>** tag at the bottom of the document. The Property Inspector will reveal the different table settings.

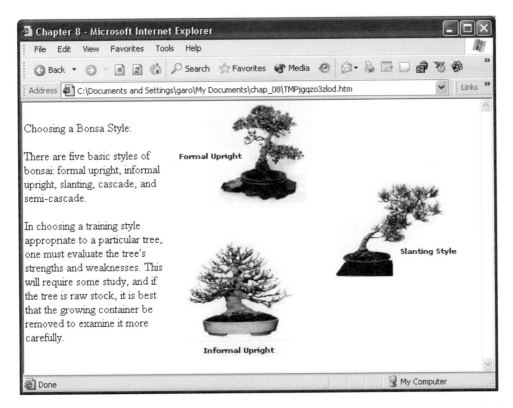

3. Preview the results in a browser by clicking **F12**. Notice that in the browser you can't tell whether layers or tables were used. Converting layers to tables affects the compatibility of the HTML document, not the appearance. Return to Dreamweaver MX.

4. For a final touch, choose **Modify > Page Properties** and change the background color to **#FFFFCC** (or you can sample the yellow color that surrounds the tree images).

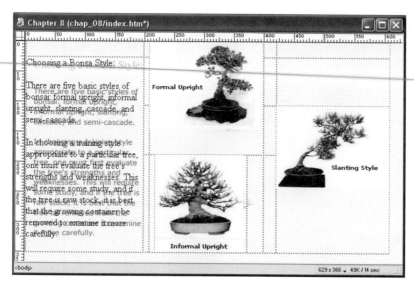

This is more or less what your page looks like now. The outcome of the new table will vary depending on how the edges of the layer boxes are aligned.

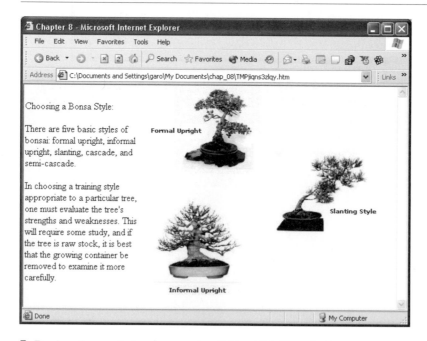

5. Preview the results in a browser by clicking **F12**. Now the images appear seamless against the background of the page. Return to **Dreamweaver MX**. **Save** the file and leave it open for the next exercise.

Convert Layers to Table Options

The **Convert Layers to Table** dialog box has several options to help you control how your layers are converted. The following chart explains how these features work:

Convert Layers to Table Options	
Option	**Description**
Most Accurate	This default option creates a table cell for each layer and all the cells necessary to maintain the layer structure. More information about tables and cells can be found in Chapter 7, "*Tables*."
Smallest: Collapse Empty Cells	This option sets the edges of the layers to align if they are within a certain pixel range of each other. This typically results in fewer columns and rows. This can be a good thing, because fewer columns and rows equate to faster downloading; or it can be bad thing, because it can potentially disrupt your layout's appearance. We recommend experimenting to see which suits your needs best.
Use Transparent GIFS	This option inserts transparent GIFs in each of the empty cells. This helps maintain the table structure across browsers. Tables can collapse in some browsers if they don't contain content, and transparent GIFs can fill in as content, though they are invisible.
Center on Page	This option centers the table on the page.
Prevent Layer Overlaps	Table cells cannot overlap. This option prevents you from overlapping your layers by warning you about which layers, if any, overlap.
Show Layers Panel	This opens the Layer panel, which allows you to rename or reorder your layers.
Show Grid	If it's not already visible, this will turn on the grid for the page.
Snap To Grid	This snaps the layer to the nearest snapping point on the grid. This can be useful for aligning objects.

Converting Tables to Layers

In this exercise, you will convert the table version of your page back to layers, modify the layout, and then convert it back to tables for browser compatibility. You will turn the tracing image off and be encouraged to modify the page's layout however you want. When you are finished, you should definitely appreciate how powerful these features are in helping you create and modify the layout of your pages.

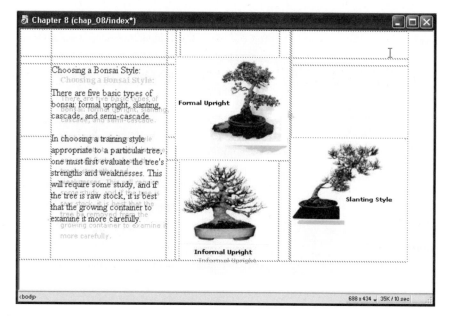

1. With **index.html** still open from the last exercise, choose **Modify > Convert > Tables to Layers**. The **Convert Tables to Layers** dialog box will open.

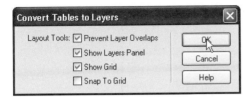

2. Remove the checkmark in the **Snap To Grid** checkbox. If checked, this option will force your layers to snap to a grid, sometimes causing unwanted shifting of page elements. For this reason, we prefer to not use this option. Make sure that your settings are like those shown above and click **OK**.

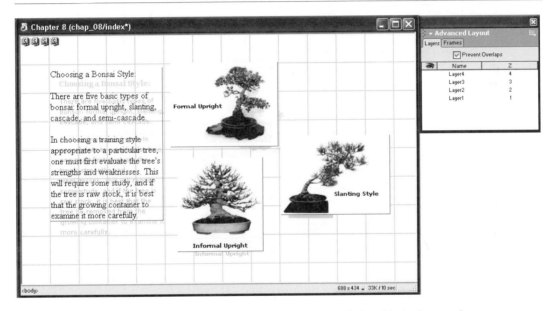

Your table is converted into layers, and the grid is turned on to help with the layout of your page. If you want to change the layout, you'll find that it's much easier to do so with layers than with tables! If the grid bothers you, turn it off by choosing View > Grid > Show Grid. We find it helpful, so we leave it on.

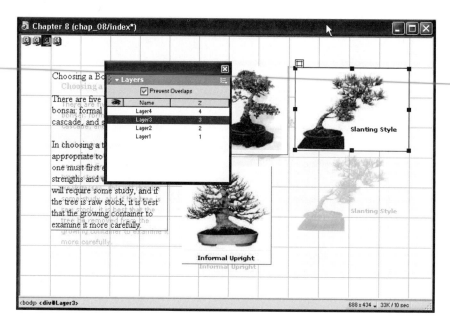

3. Click the layer that contains the **Slanting Style** image. Use the **Layer Selection Handle** to drag this layer up so that the top of it aligns with the top of the **Formal Upright** image.

Note: When you click and drag on a layer, it becomes highlighted in the Layers panel.

4. Select the layer containing the **Informal Upright** image. Use the layer selection handle to drag this layer to the right so that it is centered below the other two images.

5. Select the layer with the text in it. Align it with the top of the tree in the **Formal Upright** image. We decided it was time to format the text, so for the headline **Choosing a Bonsai Style**, we used **Georgia**, **Bold**, size **2**. For the rest of the copy, we used **Verdana**, size **2**.

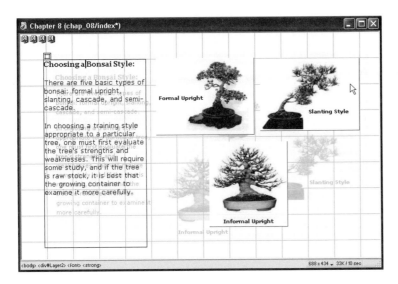

Here is the new layout in Dreamweaver.

6. Choose **Modify > Convert > Layers to Table**. Click **OK**.

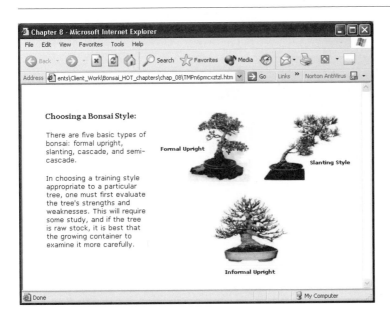

7. Press **F12** to preview the file in a browser.

8. Save and **close** the file.

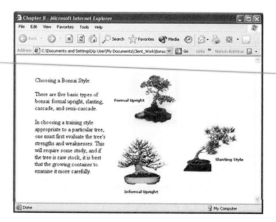
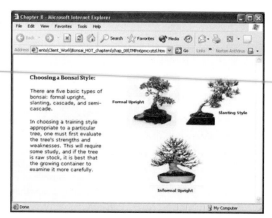

You can start to see how easy it is to change the layout of your pages by converting back and forth between layers and tables. On the left is the original page and on the right is the new page, with the artwork rearranged.

What is the Layout View?

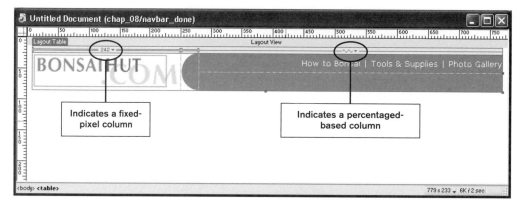

Dreamweaver MX contains a great way to create the layout for your Web pages. The **Layout** view feature allows you to create layout cells and tables by drawing them exactly where you need them, at exactly the size that you want. This technique was introduced in Dreamweaver 4 as a more visual way to design your layouts while creating clean and optimized table code behind the scenes. Although converting from layers to tables is convenient and easy, it does not write nested tables (tables that are within other tables). Instead, it must produce table code that is not as "clean" or as optimized as possible. Layout cells and tables, on the other hand, are written in a very clean manner and can include nested tables.

Layout tables and cells are indicated by different symbols to describe what kind of table cell (fixed-pixel or percentage-based) is being used.

Layers to Tables versus Layout View

During the course of this chapter, you were shown how to create Web-page layouts using two different methods; first, with layers and then converting layers to tables. Next, you'll learn how to create layouts with the Layout view using layout cells and layout tables. At this point, you might be scratching your head and wondering which one you should be using for your page layouts. Although there are some pros and cons to both, much of it boils down to a matter of preference. We always suggest that you find a workflow that makes you comfortable and stick with it. Just because there are many ways to accomplish the same thing doesn't mean you have to use them all. The following table outlines some of the pros and cons of each workflow:

Layers to Tables versus Layout View		
Item	**Pros**	**Cons**
Layers to Tables	Easy to use and do not require knowledge of table behaviors and restrictions.	The table code generated in this process is often overly complex.
	Easy to save a layer-based and table-based version of your page.	More difficult to create layouts with percentage based-designs.
Layout view	Easy to create layouts with percentage-based designs.	Requires knowledge of table behavior and restrictions.
	Table code is optimized and very clean.	
	Will automatically create and insert **spacer.gif** into your layout.	

Layout Tables and Layout Cells

This exercise shows you how to use layout cells and layout tables to create a navigation bar that stretches with the width of the browser window. It combines the use of fixed table cells and percentage-based table cells using the **Layout Cell** editor.

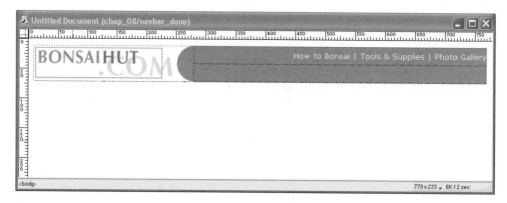

1. Open the **navbar_done.html** file located inside the **chap_08 folder**. This is the finished version of the file you will create in this exercise.

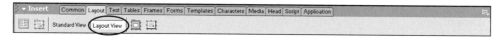

2. Click the **Layout** tab on the **Insert** panel and then click the **Layout View** button. This will switch the view of your document to the Layout view.

Layout View vs. Standard View

| A page as it appears in Standard view | A page as it appears in Layout view |

You learned earlier that Dreamweaver MX has three different views for your document window: the Design view (default), Design and Code view, and Code view. In addition to this, there are two ways to view the Design view: the Standard view (default) and the Layout view. The Standard view is where you will do most of your work, such as inserting objects, text, and links. The Layout view is an alternative, flexible mode for constructing the layout of your page. However, while in the Layout view, you cannot use the Insert Table object or create layers. Despite these few limitations, the Layout view lets you design your pages in a visual manner while creating clean and optimized table code behind the scenes.

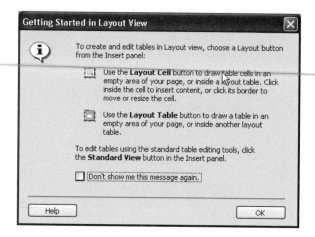

3. The **Getting Started in Layout View** dialog box will appear. This is just a simple introduction and explanation of the Layout view, layout tables, and layout cells. Once you've read this, you probably won't want to read it again, so we suggest you select the **Don't show me this message again** checkbox.

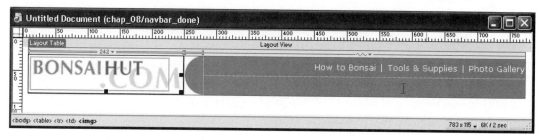

This is what the page looks like in Layout view. Notice that the appearance of the table has changed quite a bit. By the end of this exercise, you will know what this change in appearance means and how to work in this mode.

4. Press **F12** to preview this page in a browser. Resize your browser window. Notice that the text content stretches with the size of the browser window. This design is effective because it can accommodate almost any resolution. Woo-hoo!

5. Return to Dreamweaver MX. Close **navbar_done.html**.

The following steps will walk you through the process of creating this page using layout tables and cells in the Layout view.

6. Create a new document and save it inside the **chap_08** folder as **navbar.html**.

7. At the bottom of the **Insert** panel, click the **Layout View** button.

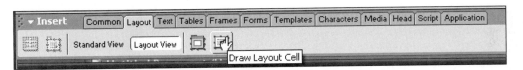

8. Click the **Draw Layout Cell** icon on the **Insert** panel. This will let you draw a table cell in your document window.

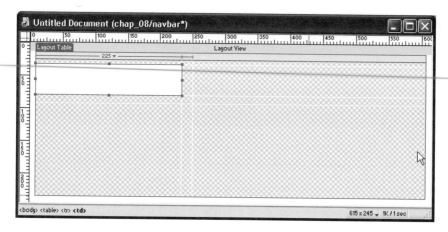

9. Starting from the upper-left corner of your document, click and drag to create a cell that is approximately 242 x 60 pixels. Don't stress yourself out trying to get it exact. You will learn how to adjust the size in a few steps—just get as close as you can.

Table cells cannot exist without a table—that's a fact of Web design. So, when you create a table cell, Dreamweaver MX will automatically create a table to hold the cell, as dictated by HTML guidelines. That's exactly what happened here and that's what you see on your screen. A green Layout Table tab will appear in the upper-left corner, indicating that a table has been created. The table cell will appear with a light blue border around it.

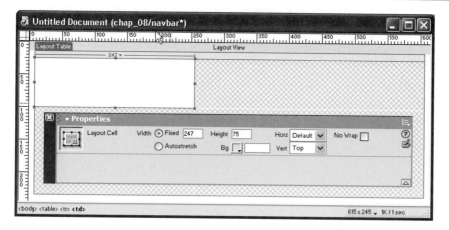

10. Move your cursor over the edge of the layout cell. The border of the layout cell will turn red indicating that you will select that cell if you click. Well, guess what? Click to select that layout cell. ;-)

The Property Inspector will change to display the editable options for the layout cell. Notice that you can numerically adjust the width and height of the cell here.

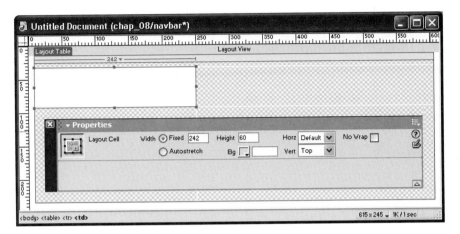

11. In the **Property Inspector**, change the **Width** to **242** and press **Return/Enter**. Then change the **Height** to **60** and press **Return/Enter**.

12. Click the **Draw Layout Cell** icon in the **Insert** panel again.

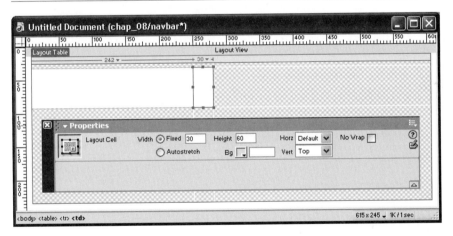

13. Click and drag another layout cell to the right of the first cell. This cell should be **30 x 60** pixels. If you don't get it exactly right, use the **Property Inspector** to adjust the **Width** and **Height**.

Notice how the cell snaps to the guidelines? This will help ensure that your tables aren't overly complex.

TIP | Drawing Multiple Layout Cells

As you work with the layout cells feature, you will find yourself creating several cells at once. However, each time you draw a cell, you need to reselect the Draw Layout Cell object before you can create another one. This can get annoying and slow down your workflow quite a bit. Don't worry, there is a solution! If you hold down the **Cmd** (Mac) or **Ctrl** (Windows) key while you draw a layout cell, you can draw as many cells as you want without having to reselect the object each time. Nice.

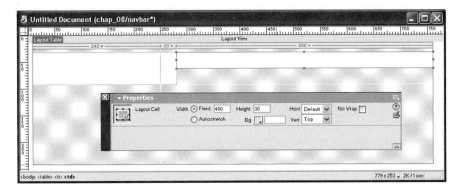

14. Click the **Draw Layout Cell** icon in the **Insert** panel again and draw a cell to the right that extends to the end of the table. It should have a height of **30** pixels.

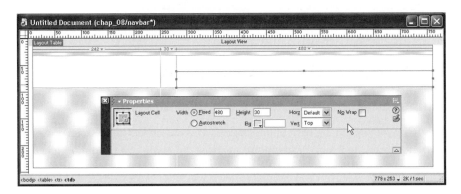

15. Click the **Draw Layout Cell** icon in the **Insert** panel and draw another cell right below that is the same size.

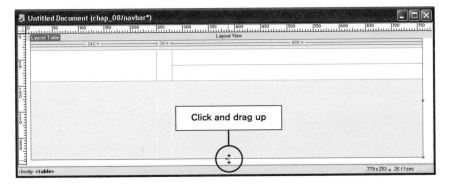

16. Click the green **Layout Table** tab in the upper-left corner to select the **Layout Table**. Click and drag the middle resize handle at the bottom of the table to bring it up to the bottom of the cells. You don't want the table to be any bigger than necessary.

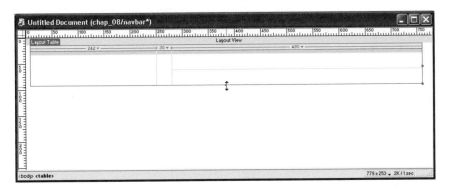

This is what your layout should look like at this point.

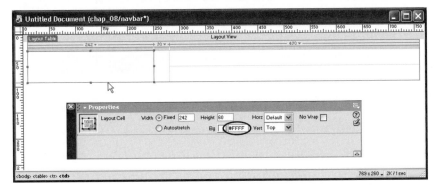

17. Click the border of the large cell on the left to select it. In the **Property Inspector**, change the background color of this cell to **#FFFFCC**, which is a nice shade of yellow.

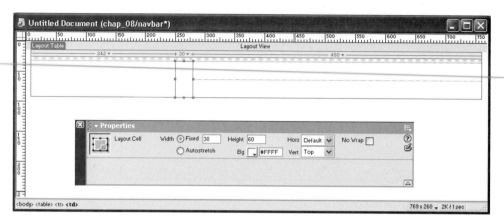

18. Click the border of the middle cell to select it. In the **Property Inspector**, change the background color of this cell to **#FFFFCC**.

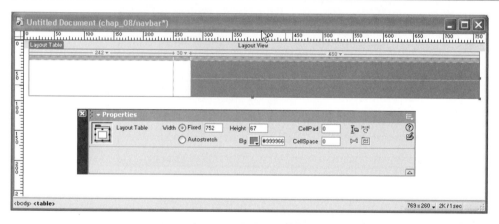

19. Using this same process, change the background of the two long horizontal cells to **#999966**.

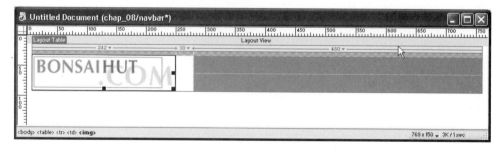

20. Click inside the large cell on the left and insert the **logo.gif** image into that cell.

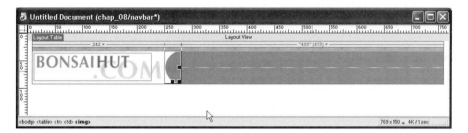

21. Click inside the middle cell and insert the **tip.gif** image into that cell.

22. Click to select the border of the upper-right horizontal cell. You are going to insert some text into this cell, so you will first modify its alignment properties.

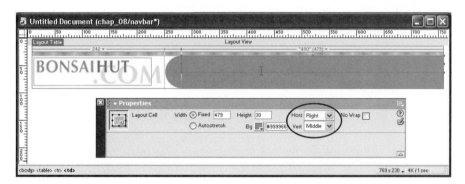

23. In the **Property Inspector**, change the **Horz** alignment to **Right** and the **Vert** alignment to **Middle**. This will place any text in this cell in the middle and align it to the right side of the cell.

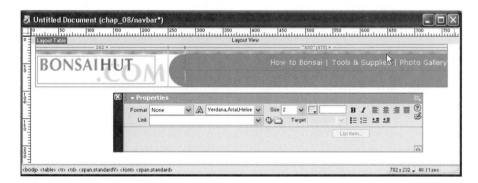

24. Click inside the upper-right cell and create a text navigation like the one shown above. Make sure you change the text color to white or some other light color. We changed the font to **Verdana** at a size of **2**. If you are using a Mac, you may want to use size **1** for the text.

25. Press **F12** to preview your page in a browser. Things look good, but the table doesn't stretch with the browser window. The following steps will show you how to make the table stretch with the browser window.

26. Return to Dreamweaver MX.

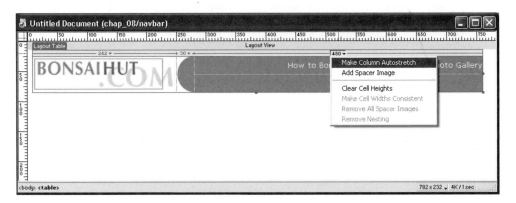

27. Click the green arrow above the middle of the upper-right cell. Select **Make Column Autostretch**. This option will set the right column to 100% so that it stretches with the browser window. Simple huh?

In order to prevent the table from collapsing in some browsers, Dreamweaver MX needs to insert an invisible GIF inside the cells with no content. Don't worry if you don't have an invisible GIF file, Dreamweaver MX will even create one for you. The following dialog box displays the different options available to you.

28. Make sure the **Create a spacer image file** radio button is selected and click **OK**. This will cause Dreamweaver MX to create a **spacer.gif** file—a transparent GIF image—and insert it into the cells with no content.

29. Browse to the **images** folder inside the **chap_08** folder and save the **spacer.gif** file there.

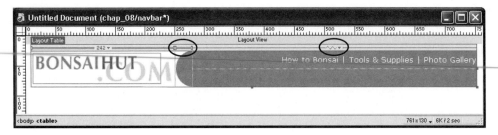

Notice that the tops of all the cells have changed. The following chart explains what each of these different visual cues mean.

Anatomy of Layout Cells	
Item	**Description**
	A layout cell with a numeric value displayed at the top means that the cell has a specific width value set in pixels. This value can be changed with the resize handles or in the Property Inspector.
	A layout cell with a numeric value and a thick double line is an indication that the cell is set to a specific pixel value, and it also contains a **spacer.gif**. This occurs when another column has been set to Autostretch.
	A layout cell with a little squiggle at the top is an indication that this column has been set to Autostretch, which means that it will stretch to fill the remaining horizontal space in the browser window. This setting can be changed to a fixed-pixel value in the Property Inspector.

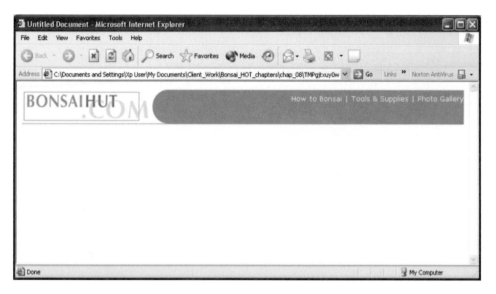

30. Press **F12** again to preview this page in a browser. Voila, your table will now stretch to the width of the browser window.

31. Return to Dreamweaver MX and **save** and **close** this file.

MOVIE | layoutview.mov

To see this exercise in action, check out **layoutview.mov** located in the movies folder on the Dreamweaver MX **H•O•T CD-ROM**.

You finished yet another chapter… congratulations, you might want to take a short break before moving onto Chapter 9, "Frames."

9.

Frames

| What Are Frames? | The Pros and Cons of Frames |
| Saving Frames | Coloring Frames | Links and Targets |
| Adding a Background Image |
| Background Images in Frames | Frame Objects |

chap_09

Dreamweaver MX
H•O•T CD-ROM

So far in this book, you've learned to insert text, tables, and images into individual HTML pages. The concept of **frames** is a little more challenging because, in effect, a frame is an HTML page inside another HTML page. Why would anyone want to put an HTML page inside another HTML page? So that one part of a page can update independently from another.

Let's say that you've created an image that belonged at the bottom of an HTML page. If your site contained 100 pages, and you wanted to put that same image at the bottom of all of them, you would need to insert that image 100 times into each of those 100 individual pages.

Frames allow you to reuse a single HTML page by nesting it inside another HTML document (otherwise known as a **frameset**). This would make it possible to create that image at the bottom of an HTML page only once, but allow 100 other pages to load up above it. If it sounds complex, it is. Frames have a high learning curve, but fortunately this chapter is here to walk you through every step of the way.

What Are Frames?

Lynda's husband Bruce came up with this wonderful metaphor for teaching frames. Imagine a TV dinner. You've got your peas and carrots, an entrée and, if you are really lucky, a dessert. Don't forget, though, about the tray that holds all these food items together! A frameset, if you will, is the TV dinner tray that holds together multiple HTML documents.

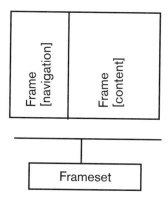

If you were to build a frameset that contained two frames, a left frame for your Web navigation element and a right frame for your content, visitors to your site would see only two frames. What's hidden is that your visitor would actually be working with three documents: a frameset (think TV dinner tray) and two frames (the content HTML page and the navigation HTML page). Every time you come to a page that contains frames, it always includes a frameset that holds the frames in place. If this sounds confusing at all, welcome to frames! Conceptually, they can be a bit of a brain twister.

We promise that the exercises in this chapter will help you unravel these concepts. You'll learn that frames are controversial creatures, and that they are either loved or hated by most people. We do our best to fill you in on the pros and cons of using frames, as well as a variety of techniques for using them effectively and creatively. In the end, you will have the honor of deciding if they are right or wrong for your site. Hey, we just teach this stuff!

Frames: A Love-or-Hate Proposition

First, a word from our sponsors (the venerable authors of this book). Frames are controversial—most people either love or hate them. You may want to consider the pros and cons before you use them in your site. Here are two charts to help you if you're weighing the decision to use or not use frames:

Love Frames	
Pro	**Explanation**
Good workflow	It's easier to update a single page than hundreds, right? If you put a navigation element (all your links) into a single frame of a frameset, and then your site's navigation changes, you have to update only that one page.
Fixed navigation	The entire page doesn't have to reload each time a link is clicked, only sections of the page. This means that you can anchor a navigation page so it doesn't have to be reloaded with each new page click and always stays consistent throughout your site.
Special effects	Frames let you do cool special effects, such as putting a single background into multiple frames for aesthetic purposes. You'll learn this technique in this very chapter!

Hate Frames	
Con	**Explanation**
Confusing	If not well implemented, frames can create confusing navigation for your audience. However, this chapter teaches you how to implement frames well, of course!
Printing hassles	It is not possible to print an entire frameset. That would be like printing three or more HTML pages at once. Your end user can print an individual frame, but frames are often transparent to the end user so this can prove challenging. Our suggestion? If you think people are going to print a page from your site, don't put it in a frameset.
Bookmark hassles	The only part of a framed page that can be bookmarked easily is the frameset. Let's say you have 20 pages that load into a single frameset. If one of your end users wanted to bookmark page 11, he/she would not be able to do so, because only the first page that loads into the frameset could be bookmarked. We have no remedy for this problem, except to say that you should make it very clear how to get to the other 19 pages within that frameset, by adding a simple navigation path, a horizontal listing of links of all previously visited pages, on the first page.
Hidden security issues	At the **lynda.com** Web site, we once made the mistake of placing a secure order form into an insecure frameset. Some of our customers complained because they couldn't see the lock symbol at the bottom left of their browsers that ensures a page is secure. Although the order form page was in fact secure, we eventually took it out of the frameset so our customers would see the lock symbol and feel more confident buying from us.
Too boxy	Frames divide an already small amount of screen real estate into smaller regions, which causes a boxy effect. You'll learn how to make framesets without unsightly scrollbars and borders. That will help eliminate the ugly boxy effect.
Accessibility	Frames can be very problematic from an accessibility perspective. They can be difficult, if not impossible, to view on some devices, such as screen readers. Navigating from frame to frame can be difficult for some devices as well.

I. —————————Saving Your First Frameset

This chapter is going to build your frame-making skills gradually. This first exercise shows you how to save a set of frames properly. Sound simple? Unfortunately, saving frames is one of the more difficult aspects of learning how to build framesets. By taking you slowly through the process, our hope is that you'll get through these hurdles without a problem.

1. Copy **chap_09** from the **H•O•T CD-ROM** to your hard drive. Define your site for Chapter 9 using the **chap_09** folder as the local root folder. If you need a refresher on this process, visit Exercise 1 in Chapter 3, "*Site Control.*"

2. Start this exercise with a blank untitled document. Don't save this page just yet. You may be surprised by this advice, given our past warnings, but saving now will cause Dreamweaver MX to believe that this is a single HTML page (which it is not!). You are going to divide this into a frameset and frames before you save.

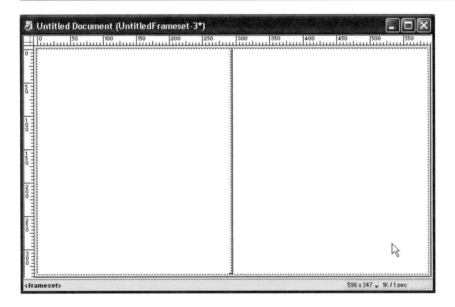

3. Choose **Modify > Frameset > Split Frame Left**. This puts a vertical frame divider through your page. What's more, it switches you from looking at one page to looking at three: the **frameset**, the **left frame**, and the **right frame**.

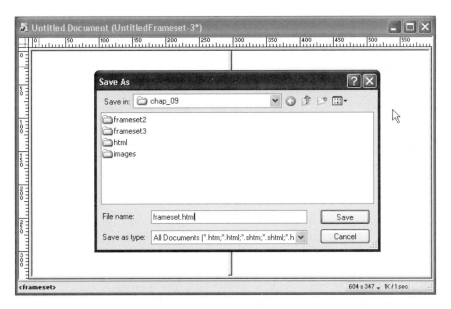

4. Choose **File > Save Frameset As** and save the file as **frameset.html** inside the **chap_09** folder. The frameset document will be the container for the other HTML files.

Note: *If you wanted this frameset to be the first page in your site (often referred to as the home page), you would save the frameset as* index.html.

 MOVIE | saving_frames.mov

To learn more about saving frames, check out **saving_frames.mov** located in the **movies** folder on the Dreamweaver MX **H•O•T CD-ROM**.

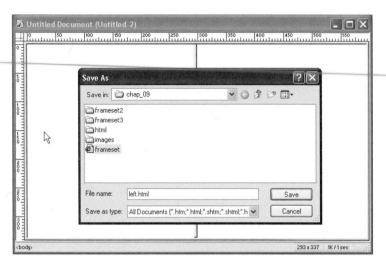

5. Click inside the **left frame** and select **File > Save Frame As** and save the file as **left.html**. Make sure you are saving this file in the same location as the **frameset.html** file.

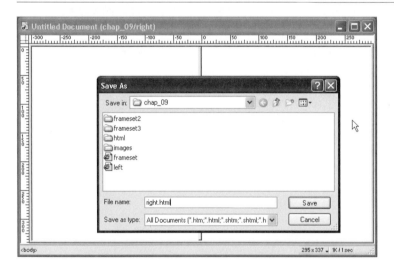

6. Click inside the **right frame** and select **File > Save Frame As** and save the file as **right.html**. Make sure you are saving this file in the same location as the **frameset.html** file.

Even though you just saved these files, notice that it says Untitled Document at the top of each document window. What's up with that? As you learned in Chapter 4, "Basics," you've saved and named the HTML document, but have not assigned the title yet. To set the title, be sure to follow the exact directions in the following steps, because you are juggling three HTML documents and you want to put the title in the outermost page (frameset.html).

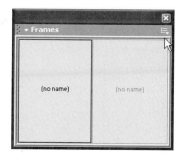

7. Select **Window > Others > Frames** to open the **Frames** panel. This panel will give you a preview of your frameset structure and can be helpful for selecting different portions of your frameset.

8. Click on the outermost border around the edge of the **Frames** panel. It has a thick black edge when it is selected. This is a quick way to select the frameset. In the toolbar at the top of the document, enter in the **Title** field: **My First Frameset**, and press **Enter**. The default untitled document title should be instantly replaced by your new title. **Note:** Press **Enter** only after you deselect your new title; otherwise, it will be deleted!

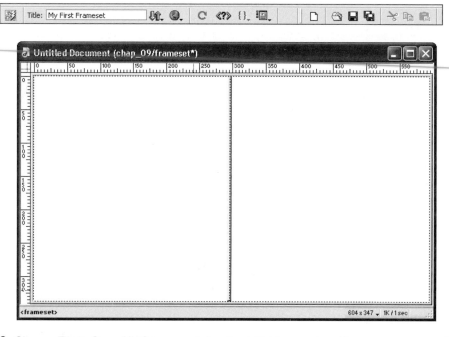

9. Choose **File > Save All**. Once you define the initial frameset and frames, you can perform one simple **Save All Frames** operation to save the changes to all the files and be done. Leave this file open for Exercise 2.

Different Ways to Save Frames

This exercise taught you to save frames by choosing **File > Save Frame As**. There are a few different ways to save them besides this, but the way we already showed you is the best because you always know what file you are saving. All three ways are listed in the handy chart below.

Ways to Save Frames	
Option	**Explanation**
File > Save Frame **File > Save Frame As**	To save a document inside a frameset, click the cursor in the frame and use this method.
File > Save Frameset **File > Save Frameset As**	To save a frameset file only, you may choose to use either of these methods.
File > Save All Frames	To save all open files at once, use this method. However, we don't recommend this method. There's a known bug on the Mac that doesn't give you a good visual cue about which file is being saved using this method. Using the **File > Save All Frames** method *after* you've saved the first time using the other listed methods is fine. Just don't start the process with a **File > Save All Frames**, or you'll potentially get confused by the process.

2. ——————————Coloring Frames

Coloring frames is challenging because you're manipulating multiple HTML documents in one Dreamweaver MX window. This exercise teaches you how to color two frames independently. You'll also learn how to turn off the borders between them, which can help eliminate that boxy appearance that many people don't like about frames.

1. You should still have **frameset.html** open from the last exercise. In the document window, click on the **left frame** and make sure you see the text-insertion cursor blinking.

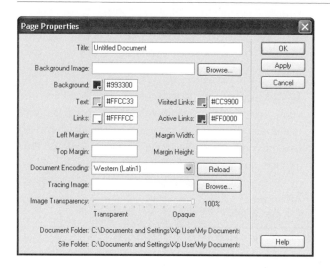

2. Choose **Modify > Page Properties** (Ctrl+J [Windows] or Cmd+J [Mac]). Make the **Background** a dark brown, the **Text** yellow-orange, the **Links** pale yellow, the **Visited Links** light brown, and the **Active Links** red. You can use the colors shown above or pick your own colors. Click **OK**.

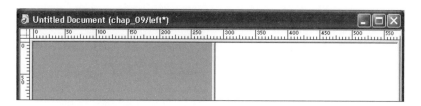

The left frame should be brown at this point.

3. In order to change the color for the right side, click in the **right frame** and make sure you see the text-insertion cursor blinking. **Choose Modify > Page Properties** yet again.

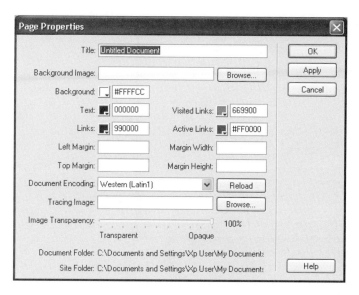

4. Make the **Background** pale yellow, the **Text** black, the **Links** dark red, the **Visited Links** medium green, and the **Active Links** red. You can use the colors shown above or if you are feeling wild, go ahead and pick your own colors. ;-) Click **OK**. The right frame should turn pale yellow.

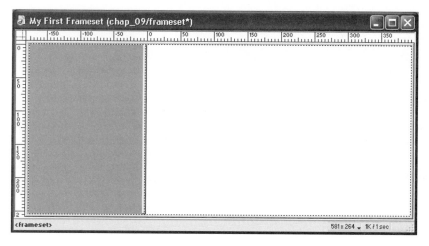

The left side of the document should be brown, and the right side yellow

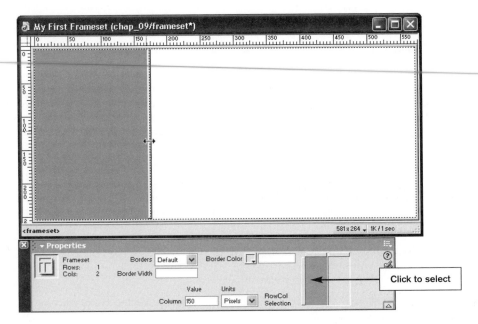

5. Click on the middle dividing frame border. Make sure the left frame in the **Property Inspector** is selected and enter the value **150** into the **Column** setting in the **Property Inspector**. Then press **Enter**.

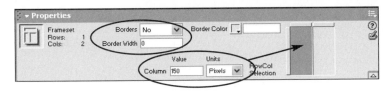

6. We don't know if you agree with us, but part of what we do not like about frames is their boxy appearance. To turn off the border on the frame divider, select **Borders: No**, and **Border Width: 0** in the **Property Inspector**. Now the dividing border should be gone. Choose **File > Save All** and leave this document open for the next exercise.

3.————————**Links and Targets**

You've gotten through the hardest part of making a frameset, but there's still more distance to go to the finish. This exercise shows you how to insert a link into the left side page of the frameset. You've learned about making links, so much of this should be familiar. This exercise introduces a new concept, however—using a "target"—which allows you to specify which frame the link will trigger in your frameset.

1. Click inside the left frame and make sure you see the blinking text-insertion cursor. Type the words **Bonsai Tools**.

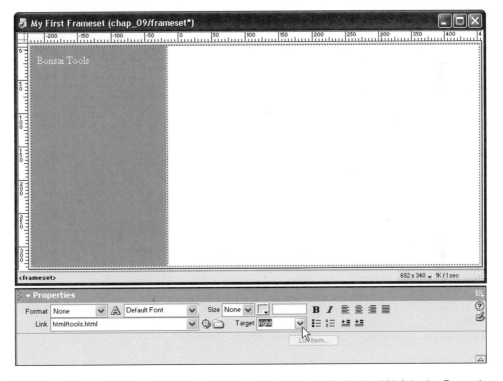

2. Select the words **Bonsai Tools** and click on the folder to the right of **Link** in the **Property Inspector**. Browse to the **html** folder inside the **chap_09** folder and select **tools.html**. Click **Open**. **Bonsai Tools** should now appear as an underlined link.

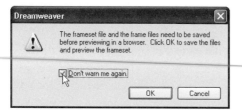

3. You can't preview links in Dreamweaver MX, so press **F12** to preview in your browser. You'll be prompted to save your files before you preview them in a browser, so click **Save**. **Note:** We suggest that you click the **Don't warn me again** checkbox so you don't see this message every time you test your frameset in a browser.

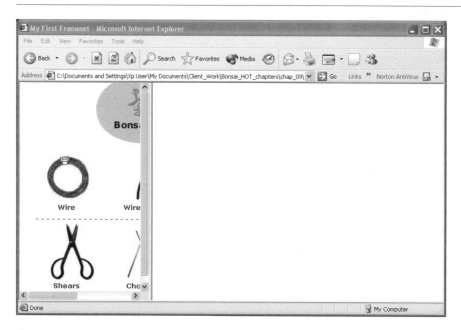

4. Once in the browser, go ahead and click the link **Bonsai Tools**. You might be surprised that the **tools** page appears in the left frame, the exact frame where the link was in your file! Just like in any other Web page, once you click on a link, it's replaced with whatever content to which it was linked. However, in this situation, the narrow left frame isn't where you want that linked page to appear. The left frame should remain stationary, and the linked pages should open on the right. The way to make this happen is by setting up a target for the link.

If you'd prefer (as we do) that the link load in the larger right side of the frameset, you must first name the two frames. Giving a name to an element in HTML is something you haven't done yet, but you'll see that it is necessary in certain instances throughout the exercises in this book. In this situation, you can't target the right frame to receive the results of the link without first giving it a name.

Note: *The directive to give the frame a name, because you've already saved all the documents with file names,* frameset.html, left.html, *and* right.html, *might confuse you. You also gave a title,* My First Frameset, *to the* frameset.html *document. Giving a "name" to an element in HTML, in order to set custom targets in links, is something totally different, however.*

5. Return to Dreamweaver MX to fix the target problem. Make sure the **Frames** panel is open. If it's not, choose **Window > Frames** to bring it up. Notice that it reads **(no name)** on both the right and left sides? Click on the **left side** and it will become outlined with a dark line, as shown above.

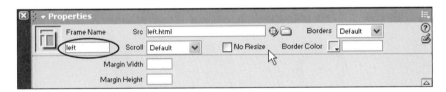

6. The **Property Inspector** should now display the setting for the **Frame Name** field. Enter **left**. You could name it anything you want. However, you should name it something meaningful because this name will appear in a menu later on, and you'll want to easily remember what it meant.

7. Click on the **right side** of the **Frames** panel and look at the **Property Inspector** again. This time there is no frame name because you haven't given the right side of the frameset a name yet. Enter **right** into the **Frame Name** field. The Frames panel should now read **left** and **right** in faint letters. Leave the Frames panel open—you'll need it shortly.

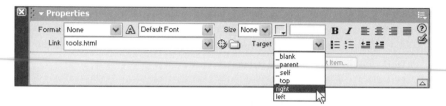

8. Select the words **Bonsai Tools** in the left frame. Click on the arrow next to the **Target** field to access the pop-up menu. Select **right** from the menu. The word **right** should pop into the **Target** field.

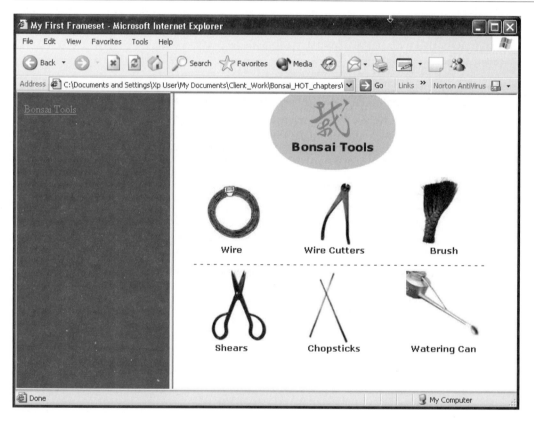

9. Press **F12** to preview the page again. Click on the link. If you're prompted again to save your files, click **Save**. This time the results should appear on the right side. You've just set up your first target in your first frameset. And you're on your way to mastering frames, which is no small accomplishment!

10. Return to Dreamweaver MX and keep the files open for the next exercise.

Target Names

A further explanation of target names is in order, because in the last exercise you used only the **Custom Target** feature.

When you access the pop-up menu for **Target**, you may wonder what the terms **_blank**, **_parent**, **_self**, and **_top** mean. You created the targets **right** and **left**, and those names are in the menu because you added them. The other names, however, are part of the HTML specifications. Below you will find a chart that explains their meanings.

HTML Specifications for Target Names	
Target Name	**Significance**
_blank	Loads the link into a new browser window. This is the target to use if you want to keep someone inside your site, and show them another site at the same time. It opens a new browser window, so that two windows are on the screen at the same time—one containing your site, and the other containing the URL of the site you linked to.
_parent	Used when framesets are nested, to send your end user to the parent of the nested framesets. It's possible to put a frameset inside another frameset, but that's more advanced frameset building than this book covers. Frankly, we rarely use this target, because we rarely work with nested framesets.
_self	Used when you want the results of the link to load in the same page that the link was in. That's the default behavior of HTML anyway, so we never use this.
_top	Transports the end user from a frameset to a single HTML page. This breaks the frames and loads all of the results into a single page, in the same window. Use this target when you want to exit a frameset.

NOTE | To Scroll or Not to Scroll?

We keep harping on the fact that frames can look boxy, and you've already learned how to remedy this by turning off the border on the frameset. What about scrollbars, which can also make a frameset look boxed in? Scrollbars are necessary if your content is larger than the size of the frame. You can turn scrollbars off completely or allow them to appear automatically, which is the Dreamweaver MX default. We suggest you leave the program at its defaults. If the content is big enough to warrant scrollbars, they'll appear.

Scrollbars are set in the Property Inspector.

To access the Property Inspector's Frame Scroll *options, click on the right or left region of the Frames panel. Scrollbars are set independently for each frame. It is not necessary to do this at all unless you want to force scrollbars on or off via the* Scroll *option.*

4. —————————Adding a Background Image

You've learned how to color the background of each frame, but what about adding a **background image**? This is similar to coloring the background of each frame, which you already did in Exercise 2. There can be unexpected alignment problems with this process, however, if the frameset clips the background image on one of the frames. In this exercise, you will learn how to set the left frame to a specific size so that it doesn't cut off the background image unexpectedly.

1. Click inside the **left frame** and make sure you see the text-insertion cursor blinking to the right of the linked words **Bonsai Tools**. Choose **Modify > Page Properties**.

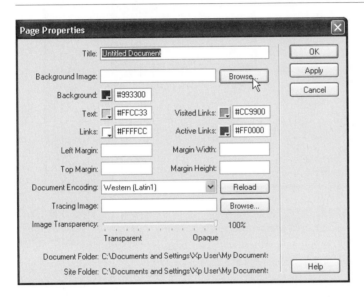

2. Click the **Browse** button to the right of the **Background Image** field to browse to the **images** folder, and select **bg_symbol.jpg**. Click **Open**, and then **OK** in the **Page Properties** dialog box. The background image should appear in the left side of the frameset.

3. Click inside the frame named **right.html** and make sure you see the text-insertion cursor blinking, then choose **Modify > Page Properties**.

4. Click the **Browse** button to the right of the **Background Image** field to locate once again **bg_symbol.jpg** in the **images** folder where you just were. Click **Open**, and then **OK**. The background image should appear in the right side of the frameset.

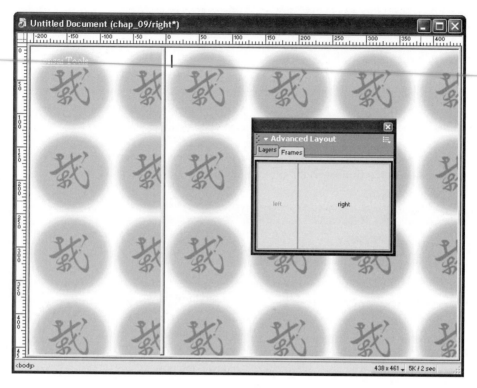

There's just one problem. It doesn't look that great, does it? The background image has been clipped by the size of the two frames. To correct the problem, it's essential to know the dimensions of both the graphic and the frameset. The following steps walk you through this process.

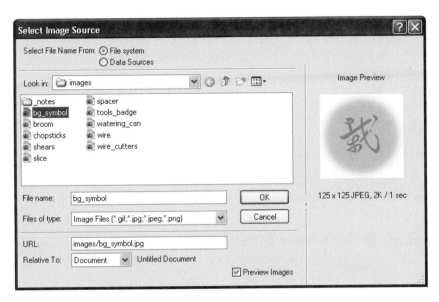

5. To establish the size of the background image, click on the **left.html** frame again and make sure you see the blinking text-insertion cursor. Choose **Modify > Page Properties** again. Click on the **Browse** button to the right of the **Background Image** field to locate **bg_symbol.jpg**. Make sure that you check the **Preview Images** checkbox in the **Select Image Source** dialog box. Notice that the dimensions **125 x 125** appear in the **Select Image Source** preview window? You now know that the width of the image is 125 pixels. Click **Cancel** twice to return to the document window.

Why cancel? The sole purpose for doing this step was to read the dimensions of the graphic, not to actually reinsert the background image! Often, we will insert an image just to learn more about its size or downloading speed, and then cancel out of the process once the information is gathered.

Next, you'll want to make the left column of the frameset match the size of that background image. Because the background image is 125 pixels wide, you could make the left.html column 250 pixels wide, and it would tile twice perfectly. Question is, how do you get to the information that shows the left column's size? Frankly, it's a bit tricky and takes some clicking around.

6. In the **Frames** panel (if it's not visible, go to **Window > Frames**), click on the outer border of the panel. Your Frames panel might already look like this before you read this step. If so, click on the left side, and then click on the outer border again.

Sometimes you have to toggle the outer border of the Frames panel on and off to get it to show the correct information settings in the Property Inspector. What's the goal of doing this? Changing your Property Inspector to show you the frameset's column size.

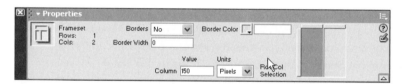

The goal of clicking on the outer border of the Frames panel is to change your Property Inspector so that it looks like this, which gives you access to the column value. *With the left column selected in the Property Inspector, you can see that the* Column *setting is 150 pixels, which is the setting that you created way back in Exercise 2. You'll want to change this to accommodate the size of the background image in this exercise. The next steps walk you through this process.*

MOVIE | frames_settings.mov

To learn more about frames, check out **frames_settings.mov** located in the **movies** folder on the Dreamweaver MX **H·O·T** CD-ROM.

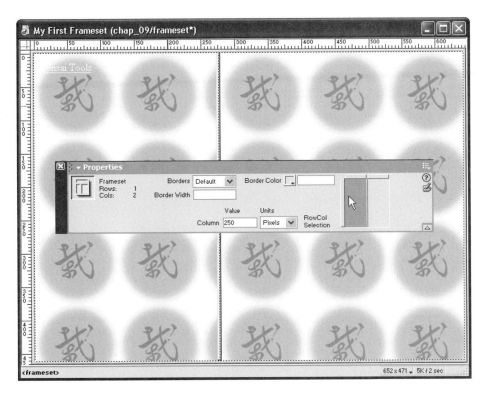

7. Enter the value **Column: 250** into the **Property Inspector** and press **Enter**. The left column should have just shifted a bit to the right. Things still don't fit properly because there are more steps to follow.

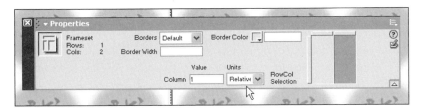

8. In the **Property Inspector**, click on the right **Column** icon, at the right of the panel. Select **Units: Relative**. Now to remove the border between the two frames. Make sure the frameset borders are selected using the **Frames** panel. From the **Borders** pop-up menu, select **No**. Type **0** for the **Border Width**.

Bingo! The background image now tiles perfectly!

9. Select **File > Save All** and press **F12** to preview in your browser.

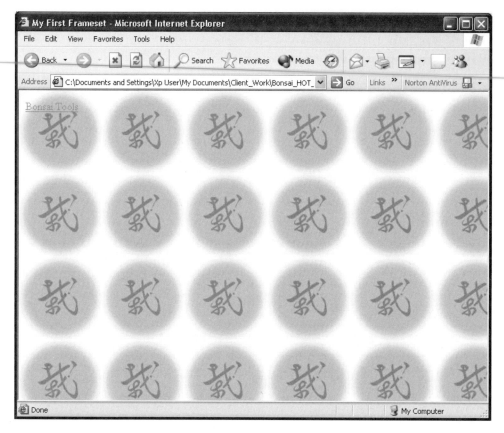

10. Close the file.

If the directions in Exercise 4 seemed odd and/or mysterious to you, it's because they are a little odd and mysterious! Perhaps this review will help: Clicking on the right side of the Property Inspector's Column icon allowed you to change the settings for the right column. Choosing Relative Units makes HTML allocate to the right column whatever space is left over from the fixed-pixel left column. In Exercise 4, you wanted the left side to be fixed, but the right side to scale proportionately depending on the size of the end user's monitor.

TIP | Specifying a Frame Size

The last exercise showed how to specify the left frame to be 250 pixels wide. Here are step-by-step directions to access the frame size settings.

1. Make sure the **Frames** panel is open (**Window > Frames**).

2. Click on the outer region of the **Frames** panel. **Tip:** You might have to click on an inner region and then an outer region to jog the Property Inspector to show the correct setting.

3. Click on the icon to the far right of the **Property Inspector** to select the appropriate frame. In this instance, it's the **right** one.

4. Enter the **Column Value** of your choice. You can select units in either **Pixels**, **Percent**, or **Relative**. See the chart on the next page for a description of each.

Units

Below is a chart that defines the choices you have when specifying a frame size in the Property Inspector:

Frame Size Settings	
Units	**Function**
Pixels	Sets the size of the selected column or row at an absolute value. This option is the best choice for a frame that should always be the same size, such as a navigation bar. If you set one of your frame regions to **Pixels**, all the other frames will have to yield to that size. In other words, **Pixels** takes priority over all other settings.
Percent	Specifies that the current frame take up a specified percentage of the frameset. This causes frames to dynamically resize according to the width or height the end user's browser was opened to. If you mix **Pixels** and **Percent**, **Pixels** will be honored first.
Relative	Allocates space after frames with **Units** set to **Pixels** and **Percent** are satisfied. These frames are designed to take up all the remaining space in the browser window.

NOTE | Frame Properties

What do the frame settings mean in the Property Inspector? On the following page you will find a chart to help you understand them.

Frame Properties In Dreamweaver MX

Setting	Description
Frame Name	Sets the name of the current frame so you can use targets (remember _blank, _parent, _self, and _top?) when setting up links. This name must be a single word or use underscores (my_name) or hyphens (my-name). Spaces are not allowed.
Src	Sets the source document for each frame. Enter a file name or click the folder icon to browse to and select the file. You can also open a file in a frame by clicking the cursor in the frame inside the document window and choosing **File > Open in Frame**.
Scroll	Determines whether scrollbars appear when there is not enough room to display the content of the current frame. Most browsers default to **Auto**. This is a good thing, because you only want scrollbars if they are necessary. Scrollbars aren't pretty, but they are necessary when there's more content than the frameset column size can display.
No Resize	Prevents a frame from being resizable in browsers. **Tip:** If you turn the borders off in your frameset, end users won't be able to resize them even if the **No Resize** option is left off.
Borders	Controls the border of the current frame. The options are **Yes**, **No**, and **Default**. This choice overrides border settings defined for the frameset. It's important to set the borders to **No** even if you've set them to **0**, because of differences between Netscape and Explorer. Netscape honors **0**; Explorer honors **No**.
Border Color	Sets a border color for all borders adjacent to the current frame. This setting overrides the border color of the framesets. It's supported only on 4.0+ browsers, so if you choose to use it at all, we don't recommend that you make it an integral part of your design.
Margin Width	Sets in pixels the width of the left and right margins (the space between the frame border and the content). The default is that the frame border and content are aligned, so unless you want an offset, you don't need to adjust this setting.
Margin Height	Sets in pixels the height of the top and bottom margins (the space between the frame border and the content). The default is that the frame border and content are lined up, so unless you want an offset, you don't need to adjust this setting.

5. ——————Seamless Background Across Two Frames

In the previous exercise, you learned to put the identical background image into two frames and how to set a frameset's column width. Next, you'll produce a similar exercise that uses different artwork to further alter the appearance of the frameset. In this example, the background image art was created at a size large enough to fill the entire screen (800 x 600 pixels), then sliced into two pieces, and then reassembled inside the frameset to appear as a seamless image. This technique successfully hides the unwanted boxy appearance that results so often when creating frames.

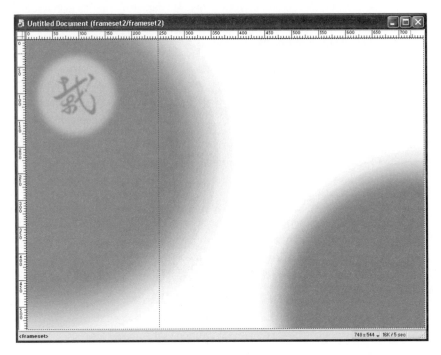

You may not realize that this page is composed of frames. That's because this frameset uses two different background images that have been cut up to appear as a single background image. You'll learn how to accomplish this technique by following the steps in this exercise.

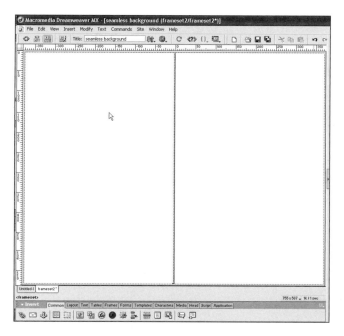

1. Open **frameset2.html** from the **frameset2** folder. This is similar to the document you made before, but a lot of the early steps are already completed. Click on the **left frame** in the document window. Next, choose **Modify > Page Properties**.

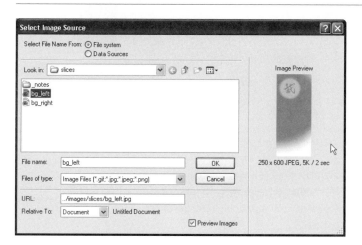

2. Click on the **Browse** button to the right of the **Background Image** field and browse to the **images** folder and then the **slices** folder. Select **bg_left.jpg**. Notice that the dimensions appear in the **Image Preview** of the **Select Image Source** window and that the width of this image is **250** pixels. Click **Open**, then **OK**.

3. Click on the **right frame** of the frameset and choose **Modify > Page Properties**. Select **bg_right.jpg** (from the **slices** folder you'll find inside the **images** folder) as your background image. Notice that the dimensions appear in the **Image Preview** of the **Select Image Source** window and that this image is 850 pixels wide. Click **Open**, then **OK**.

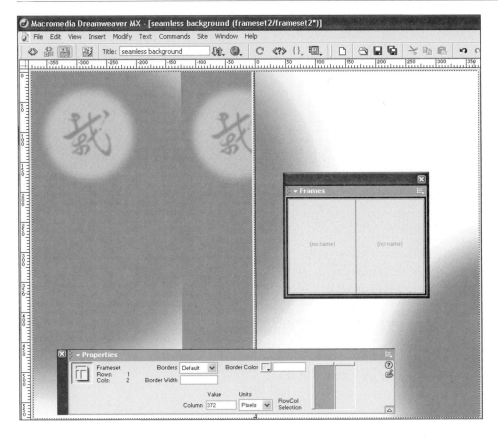

Your screen should look funky because you haven't set the frameset's dimensions yet.

4. Make sure the **Frames** panel is open (**Window > Frames**), and click on the outer region (if you've forgotten how, check Exercise 4, Step 6) to make your **Property Inspector** display the frameset's dimensions. Click on the left side of the **Column** icon and select **Borders: No**. Then enter **Border Width: 0**, **Column Value: 250**, and **Units: Pixels**.

5. Click on the right side of the **Column** icon, and enter **Units: Relative**.

6. Remove the frame border the same way that you did in the previous exercise.

7. Press **F12** to preview in your browser. When you are satisfied, **save** and **close** the file.

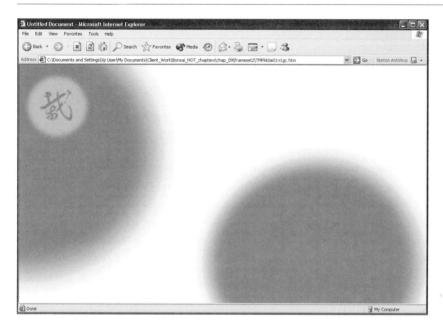

If your screen looks like this, you did everything right! If it doesn't, go back and reread all the steps (especially the part about setting the right side to Relative!) It looks like a single page with a single background, does it not? If your audience hates the way frames look, they should have no complaints with this little sleight of hand.

6. ——————Frames Objects

The previous examples taught you a lot about the basics of frames. Now that you have that knowledge under your belt and understand the concepts behind frames, you will be able to fully understand the power of the **Frames** panel. This exercise shows you how to use it.

1. Open a new blank document.

2. Make sure the **Insert** panel is showing, if it is not, go to **Window > Insert**. Click on the **Frames** tab to display the frame icons on the **Insert** panel.

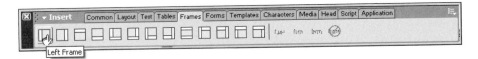

3. Click on the first icon on the left column side of the panel. This will make Dreamweaver MX create a frameset similar to the icon.

Note: This step is an alternate method to Step 3 in Exercise 1. You don't have to choose Modify > Frameset Split Frame anymore if you use these handy objects on the Insert panel.

TIP | What Does the Blue and White Mean?

You might have noticed that the icons in the Frames Insert panel are colored in blue and white. This has significant meaning: It tells you how the different areas have been specified with regard to size. The blue areas are set to a relative size, and the white areas have been set to an exact pixel size.

What you spent several steps establishing in Exercise 4 by setting the frames to be either relative or pixel-based is accomplished automatically by using one of these frames objects from the Insert panel. This is a huge improvement in Dreamweaver MX. Don't hate us for making you go through all those steps in Exercise 4, though. As teachers, we decided it was good for your education to appreciate the frames features in Dreamweaver MX by learning how to do it manually and painfully first. Sorry 'bout 'dat, but not really. Just think, "no pain, no gain." ;-)

This is what your page should look like at this point.

4. With the **frameset** still selected, choose **File > Save Frameset As**. This works just like the procedure you learned in Exercise 1.

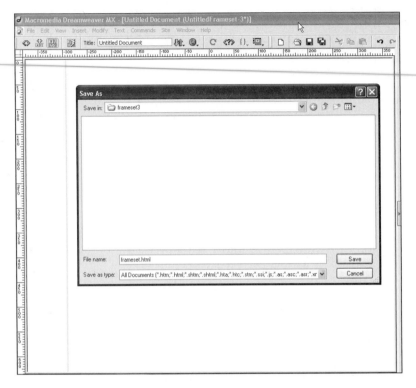

5. The first file you are going to save is the frameset file. It contains all of the information on how the entire structure of the page is set up. Save this file as **frameset.html** inside the **frameset3** folder.

6. The next file you are going to save is the **left frame** of your frameset. Click inside the left frame of the document window and choose **File > Save Frame As**. Save this file as **left.html** inside the **frameset3** folder.

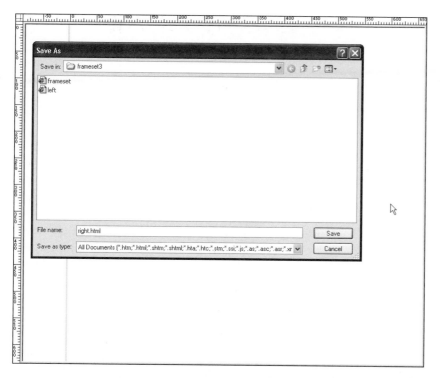

7. The next file you are going to save is the **right frame** of your frameset. Click in the right frame of the document window and choose **File > Save Frame As**. Save this file as **right.html** inside the **frameset3** folder.

As you can see, using a frames object from the Insert panel is a pretty simple way to create a frameset. But you still need a working knowledge of framesets, so that's why we chose to wait until the end of this chapter to show you this option. Now that you know it's here, use it!

8. Close this file. You are done working with it.

Phew, this was a long chapter. Take a quick break, and then it's time to move on to the next chapter.

IO.

Rollovers

Creating a Simple Rollover	Animated Rollovers!
Creating Pointer Rollovers	Creating Multiple-Event Rollovers
Creating Flash Buttons	Inserting a Navigation Bar Rollover
Inserting Fireworks HTML

chap_10

Dreamweaver MX
H•O•T CD-ROM

One of the key challenges in Web development is to invent artwork that clearly communicates how to navigate through your site. **Rollover** graphics, which change when the end user's mouse goes over them, are great for adding visual cues that ensure your audience knows an image has special meaning or that it is a link. Rollovers are also great if you have limited space, because you can put extra information within the changing graphic. For example, you could make a button that says "Services," and when visitors place their mouse over the word, it could change to list the services you offer.

What you might not realize is that rollovers are not written in standard HTML. Instead, rollovers are written in a widely used scripting language invented by Netscape, called JavaScript.

Dreamweaver MX automatically writes beautiful JavaScript rollovers for you without you ever having to write the scripts or even understand how they are constructed. This is great news, because a lot of people, ourselves included, don't know how to write JavaScript from scratch. Alternately, we have trained many programmers who do know how to write JavaScript by hand, but enjoy Dreamweaver MX for its rollover capabilities because it can literally save days of programming work. For this reason, the Dreamweaver MX rollover feature is helpful to both the designer and the programmer.

Rollover Rules

Although this book provides many exercises that teach you how to implement rollovers, it is our hope that you'll move beyond the exercises to create your own custom rollover graphics once you get the hang of this feature. If you plan to make your own rollovers from scratch, you should be aware of a few important concepts.

Rollovers require a minimum of two graphics—an "off" state and an "on" state. Because this is a book on Dreamweaver MX, it doesn't cover how to make the graphic component of rollovers. You would need an imaging program, such as Fireworks or Photoshop, to make the images.

If you are going to make your own rollover graphics in an image editor, one important rule to understand is that the graphics for the "off" state and "on" state for each of your rollover images must be the same size in dimensions, or you risk that they will look distorted. JavaScript requires **WIDTH** and **HEIGHT** information, which Dreamweaver MX will add for you automatically. If you have two different-sized pieces of artwork, the JavaScript will scale both to the same width and height, causing distortion. For this reason, all the images that are provided in this chapter's exercises share the same dimensions, as they should. ;-)

I. ——————Creating a Simple Rollover

This first exercise shows you how to create a simple rollover. These types of rollovers involve two pieces of artwork. The first graphic appears on the screen initially, and the second appears when the mouse "rolls over" it. In JavaScript terminology, this is called a swap image. But you will not be writing any JavaScript from scratch, because Dreamweaver MX makes creating a simple rollover easier than many other operations you've already learned.

1. Define your site for **Chapter 10**. If you need a refresher on this process, revisit Exercise 1 in Chapter 3, "*Site Control*."

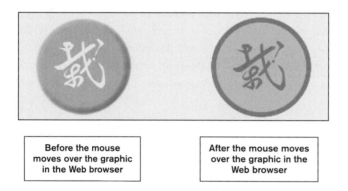

| Before the mouse moves over the graphic in the Web browser | After the mouse moves over the graphic in the Web browser |

2. Open **basicroll_final.html** in the **html** folder. Move your mouse over the symbol. Nothing happens, right? Press **F12** to preview the page. When you move your mouse over it in your Web browser, it changes to an alternate version of the symbol. You can only view a rollover inside a browser because Dreamweaver MX cannot preview rollovers within its authoring environment. Return to Dreamweaver MX and close the file. You'll get to build this same file from scratch in the following steps.

3. Create a new blank HTML page and then save it as **simple_roll.html**. Saving a file before you begin working with it is always a good practice. If you don't save it, Dreamweaver MX will bug you with annoying error messages.

4. Display the **Insert** panel by choosing **Window > Insert** if it is not already showing. Click the **Rollover Image** object on the **Common** panel.

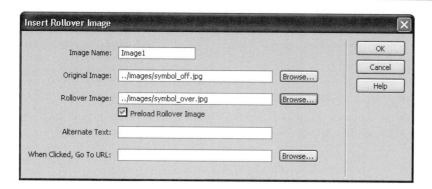

5. The **Insert Rollover Image** dialog box will appear. For the **Original Image**, click **Browse** to select **symbol_off.jpg** located inside the **images** folder. For the **Rollover Image**, click **Browse** to select **symbol_over.jpg** located inside the same folder. Make sure your dialog box looks just like the one above and click **OK**.

MOVIE | rollover_list.mov

To see this exercise in action, check out **rollover_list.mov** located in the movies folder on the Dreamweaver MX **H•O•T CD-ROM**.

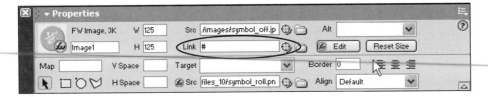

With the image still selected, notice the hash mark (#) inside the Link area of the Property Inspector? Dreamweaver MX inserted this symbol in order to create a link even though you didn't specify one. Why? Because a link is necessary for the JavaScript rollover to work. Putting a hash mark in the Link area inserts a stand-in link that doesn't link to anything. It simply acts as a placeholder so that you can still click it and see the rollover.

6. In the **Property Inspector**, click the **Browse for File** (small folder) icon to the right of the **Link** field, and browse to select **brush.html** located in the **chap_10** folder. Press **F12** to preview the rollover. Click the symbol and voilà, **brush.html** will appear!

7. Return to Dreamweaver MX and **save** and **close** the document.

NOTE | JavaScript and Java: Separated at Birth?

You might wonder if JavaScript bears any relation to the popular programming language Java, developed by Sun Microsystems. Only in name. Netscape licensed the name from Sun in hopes that the Web community would embrace its scripting language more quickly if it had a recognizable name. Ironically, since then, JavaScript has become more widely embraced than Java, and has taken on a life and following all of its own.

One important distinction between JavaScript and Java is that the code for JavaScript is placed inside your HTML pages, whereas Java is compiled as a separate program, meaning that you can't see the code for it inside an HTML page. This means that you can see JavaScript code inside HTML documents if you view the source code, whereas the code within a Java applet is hidden. This has made JavaScript immensely popular among Web authors, because many people were able to teach themselves the language by looking at other people's Web-page source and by copying, pasting, and experimenting.

2. ——————Animated Rollovers!

This next exercise uses the same technique as Exercise 1, only instead of two static images, the rollover image is an animated GIF. You'll be putting the rollover graphics inside a table to ensure that they don't move around once they're in place. Working with animated rollovers may look complicated, but it's just as easy as the last exercise you completed.

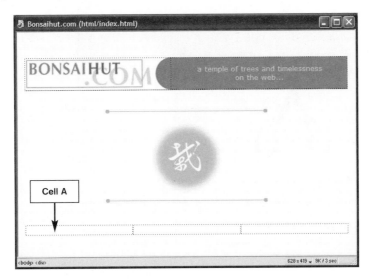

1. Open **index.html** located in the **html** folder. Notice the empty table where the navigation elements belong? This is where you're going to insert rollovers for each button. Click inside **Cell A** and click the **Insert Rollover Image** object in the **Common** panel.

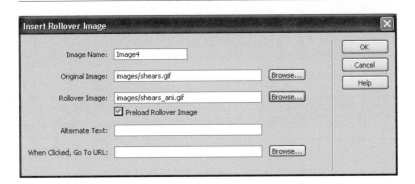

2. The **Insert Rollover Image** dialog box will appear. For the **Original Image**, click **Browse** to select **shears.gif** located in the **images** folder. For the **Rollover Image**, click **Browse** to select **shears_ani.gif** located in the same folder. Click **OK**.

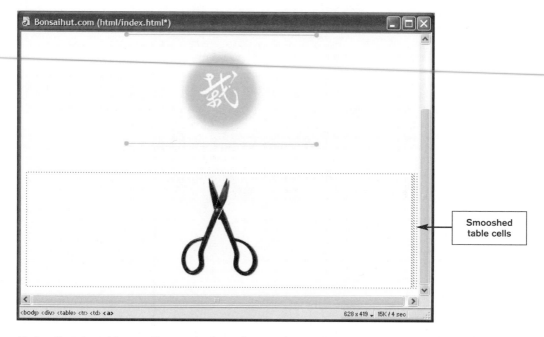

Notice that the table got all smooshed up after you inserted the image? You'll fix that shortly, so don't worry about it just yet.

3. Unfortunately, you can't preview the results of what you just did in Dreamweaver MX, so press **F12** to view it in a browser. Move your mouse over the **shears** image. Notice that the rollover state is an animated GIF? Dreamweaver MX treats the animated GIF as it would any other GIF, yet the result when previewed in a browser is different from that of a rollover created from two static GIFs. This technique produces a simple, novel effect.

4. Return to Dreamweaver MX and click to the right of the **shears** (shears.gif) graphic to make sure it is deselected. Press **Tab** to insert your cursor in the next cell, which is now scrunched up with the other cells on the right-hand side of the table.

5. Once your cursor is in **Cell B**, click the **Insert Rollover Image** object on the **Common** panel. For the **Original Image**, click **Browse** to select **pot.gif** located in the **images** folder. For the **Rollover Image**, click **Browse** to select **pot_ani.gif** located in the same folder. Click **OK**.

6. Click to the right of the **pot** (pot.gif) image to deselect it. Press **Tab** to insert your cursor in **Cell C** (row 1, column 3), then click the **Insert Rollover Image** object on the **Common** panel. For the **Original Image**, click **Browse** to select **care.gif** located in the **images** folder. For the **Rollover Image**, click **Browse** to select **care_ani.gif** located in the same folder. Click **OK**.

7. Press **F12** to preview the results. We hope you agree that this was simple to execute and impressive upon completion. Return to Dreamweaver MX, then **save** and **close** your document. Fun isn't it!

 MOVIE | **smooshed_table.mov**

To see a movie of how to insert these rollovers into the table, check out **smooshed_table.mov** located in the **movies** folder on the Dreamweaver MX **H•O•T CD-ROM**.

WARNING | **Animated GIF Rollovers and Preload**

The previous exercise used animated GIF files for one of the rollover states. Dreamweaver MX regards these files no differently from static GIFs. If you make your own animated GIF files in an image editor and use them in Dreamweaver MX as rollover states, there's a problem that we would like to warn you about.

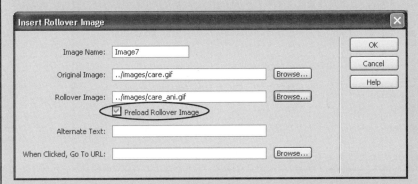

Notice that Dreamweaver MX automatically checks the **Preload Rollover Image** checkbox in the **Insert Rollover Image** dialog box? What does that mean, exactly? The browser is being instructed to wait until all the graphics for the rollover have been downloaded before the rollover functions.

Animated GIFs can be set to play once, any number of times (2x, 3x, etc.), or loop indefinitely. If when you create your animated GIF files you set them to loop indefinitely, then leaving the Preload Rollover Image box checked will work just fine, as it did here. However, if you have your animated GIF play only one time, it will play when it's preloaded and by the time your end user looks at your rollover it will no longer animate! The rule of thumb is this: leave **Preload Rollover Image** on for looping GIFs, and uncheck **Preload Rollover Image** if your GIF is set to play only one time.

3.———————Creating Pointer Rollovers

This next exercise shows you how to create pointer rollovers. Pointer rollovers reuse one piece of artwork (in this example, the symbol that follows the mouse as you move over each word. This type of rollover involves making a table to hold all the artwork in place. You'll also get to use the **Behaviors** feature, instead of the Insert Rollover Image object from the Insert panel. Are you feeling macho, or what?

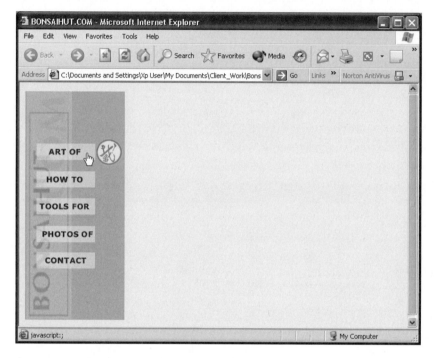

1. View the finished file first. Open **pointer_final.html** located in the **html** folder and press **F12** to preview it inside a browser. When you're finished, return to Dreamweaver MX and close the file. You're going to re-create it from scratch.

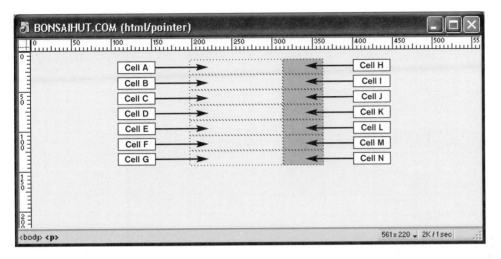

2. Open **pointer.html** from the **html** folder, which already contains an empty table with seven rows and two columns. When you are finished, you will have created a navigation bar that uses pointer rollovers as a visual navigation aid. Notice that the right column of the table has a green background color applied to it. These colored cells match the background of the graphics you will be inserting here. We could have had you create this table from scratch, but we wanted to help you get to learning about programming the rollovers faster.

3. Click inside **Cell I** and choose **Insert > Image**. Select **blank_p.gif** from the **images** folder, then click **Open**. The goal of the first part of this exercise is to insert the same **blank_p.gif** image in every location that the pointer will appear. Why? Because rollovers require two images: the original state and the rollover state. In this instance, the original state looks like nothing, because it is a transparent GIF, which lets the background color show through.

4. Repeat this process four more times, inserting the same **blank_p.gif** file inside **Cells J**, **K**, **L**, and **M**.

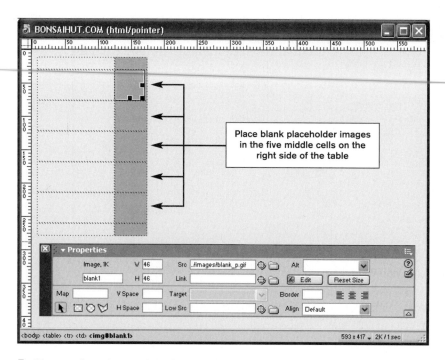

Place blank placeholder images in the five middle cells on the right side of the table

5. After you have inserted the **blank_p.gif** image into the middle five cells on the right column of the table, click inside **Cell I**, as shown above. In the **Property Inspector**, give it the name **blank1**. It is essential that you assign a unique name to each image by selecting each instance of **blank_p.gif** and naming it respectively **blank2**, **blank3**, **blank4**, and **blank5**. Make sure to highlight the appropriate **blank_p.gif** image when naming each graphic.

Note: In Exercise 1, Dreamweaver MX gave the rollovers names automatically. When you use the Swap Image behavior, you have to manually give each image a unique name, or the behavior will not work. Be aware that names in Dreamweaver MX (or HTML) cannot contain any spaces.

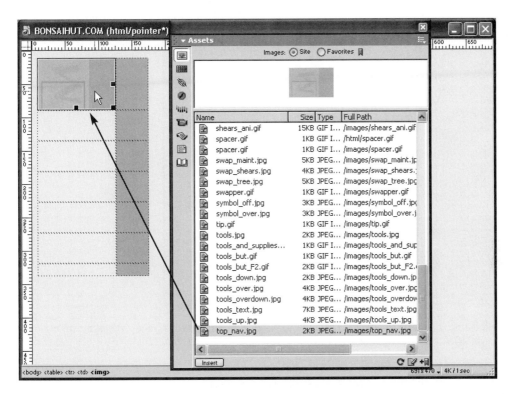

6. From the **Assets** panel, click the **Images** button if it is not already showing the image files. Click inside **Cell A** and then drag the **top_nav.jpg** from the **Assets** panel into this cell.

7. With **top_nav.jpg** selected, enter the name **top** inside the **Property Inspector**.

Note: Naming each image is essential to working with rollovers in Dreamweaver MX. This is because JavaScript requires a unique name for each source graphic in order to perform rollover functions. For this reason, you will need to add a unique name for every image that you insert into this table.

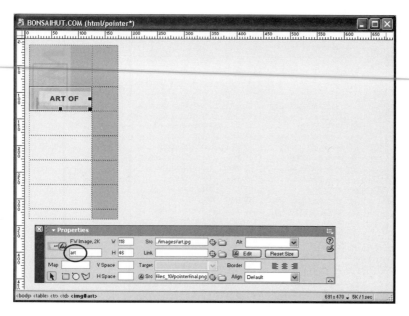

8. Click **Cell B** and insert the image **art.jpg** by dragging it from the **Assets** panel. While **art.gif** is selected, enter the name **art** inside the **Property Inspector**.

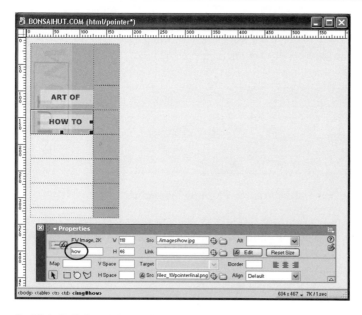

9. Click **Cell C** and insert the image **how.jpg** by dragging it into the cell from the **Assets** panel. While **how.jpg** is selected, enter the name **how** inside the **Property Inspector**.

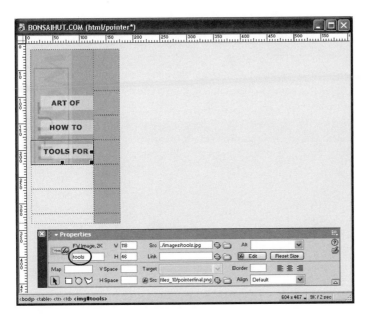

10. Click **Cell D** and insert the image **tools.jpg** by dragging it into the cell from the **Assets** panel. While **tools.jpg** is selected, enter the name **tools** inside the **Property Inspector**.

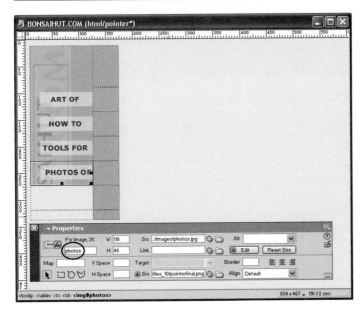

11. Click **Cell E** and insert the image **photos.jpg** by dragging it into the cell from the **Assets** panel. While **photos.jpg** is selected, enter the name **photos** inside the **Property Inspector**.

12. Click **Cell F** and insert the image **contact.jpg** by dragging it into the cell from the **Assets** panel. While **contact.jpg** is selected, enter the name **contact** inside the **Property Inspector**.

13. Click **Cell G** and insert the image **bottom_nav.jpg** by dragging it into the cell from the **Assets** panel. While **bottom_nav** is selected, enter the name **bottom** inside the **Property Inspector**.

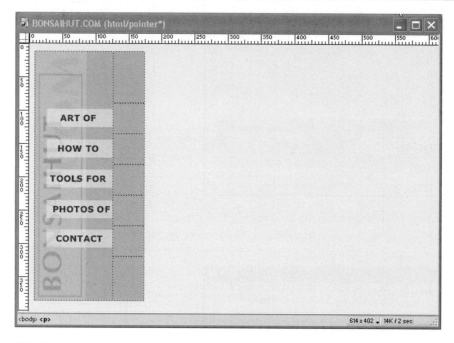

This is what the pointer.html looks like now.

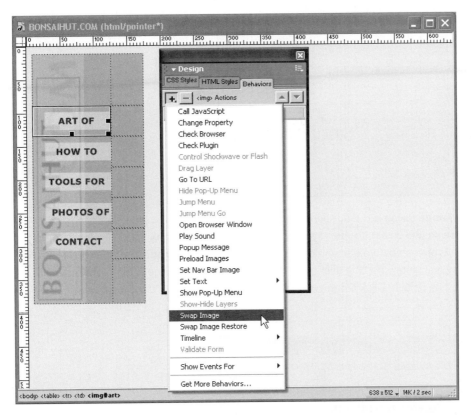

14. Next, you will set the rollovers. Click **art.jpg** (Art of) to select it. Open the **Behaviors** panel (if it isn't already open) by selecting **Window > Behaviors** or using the shortcut key (**Shift+F3**).

15. With **art.jpg** (Art of) still selected, click the **plus** sign above the **Events** column and select **Swap Image** from the pop-up menu.

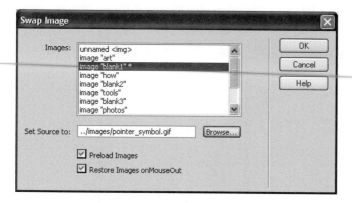

16. In the **Swap Image** dialog box that opens, make sure the **blank1** image name is highlighted at the top. Click **Browse** and select **pointer_symbol.gif** located in the **images** folder. **Preload Images** allows all images to preload before a user mouses over them. **Restore Images onMouseOut** returns images to their original state when the user takes the mouse off of the image. Both of these checkboxes are checked by default. Click **Open** (Windows) or **Choose** (Mac). In the **Swap Image** dialog box, click **OK**.

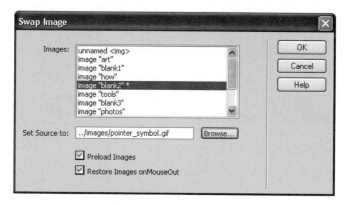

17. Next, select **how.jpg** (How to) and click the **plus** sign in the **Behaviors** panel to select **Swap Image**. Select image **blank2** from the **Images** list and click **Browse** to locate **pointer_symbol.gif**. Click **Open**. Back in the **Swap Image** dialog box, click **OK**.

18. Repeat this process three more times as follows:

For **tools.jpg** (Tools for), selecting **image "blank3"**.

For **photos.jpg** (Photos of), selecting **image "blank4"**.

For **contact.jpg** (Contact), selecting **image "blank5"**.

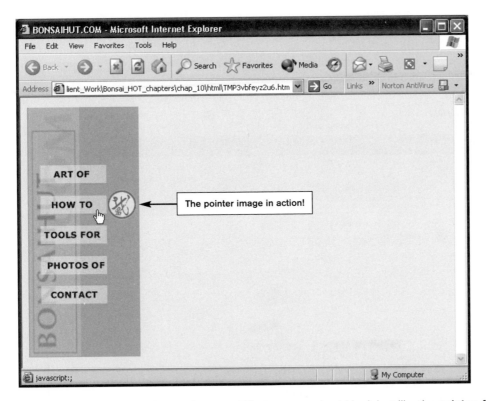

The pointer image in action!

19. Press **F12** to preview in your browser. What you see should look just like the **pointer_final.html** document you opened and previewed at the beginning of this exercise. To make yourself feel really good, return to Dreamweaver MX and press the **Code View** button to view the code. Hey, you didn't have to write any of that! Press the **Design View** button to return to the Design view. **Save** and **close** the file to move on to the next exercise.

In this exercise, you learned the benefit of using a table to hold together multiple graphics. It also reinforced that you need two images for a rollover—the original state and the rollover state. In this instance, the original was a blank image. When you program rollovers from the Behaviors panel, you also must give them a name, which you did several times in this exercise!

Creating Multiple-Event Rollovers

A multiple-event rollover uses more than two pieces of artwork in the Swap Image behavior. In this example, three different pieces of artwork change for every rollover. If that sounds complicated, it is! Assembling this type of rollover can be tedious, but not nearly as tedious as writing all the HTML and JavaScript from scratch.

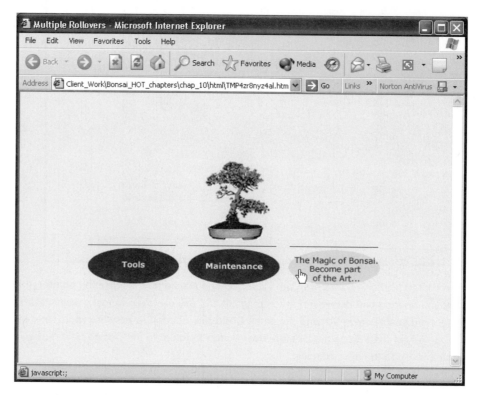

1. Open **multiple_final.html** located in the **html** folder, and preview this finished exercise in your browser. Roll your mouse over each item in the list and watch the oval button change and an image appear at the top center of the navigation bar. This is a very impressive type of rollover, and you (yes you!) are going to know how to do it as soon as you follow along. Close this file.

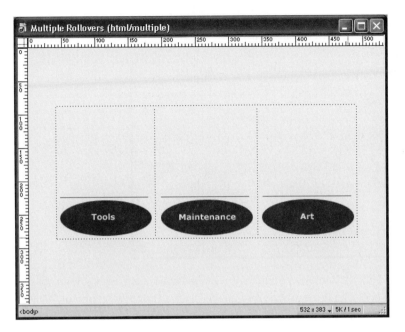

This image shows what the page looks like in Dreamweaver MX.

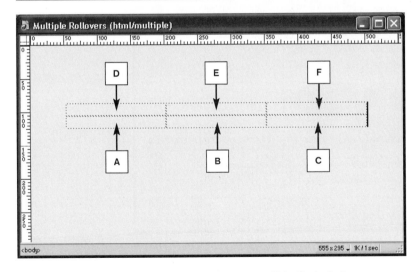

2. Open **multiple.html** located in the **html** folder. This file includes an empty, prebuilt table. You learned to make a tables similar to this in Chapter 7, "*Tables*."

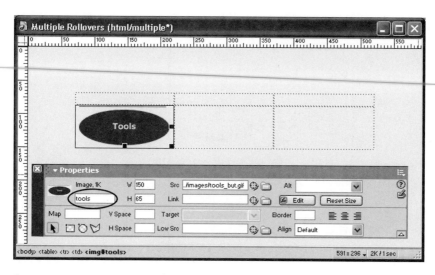

3. Display the **Assets** panel and click the **Images** button if the images are not already showing. Click inside **Cell A** (row 2, column 1) and drag **tools_but.gif** into the cell. In the **Property Inspector**, name the image **tools**.

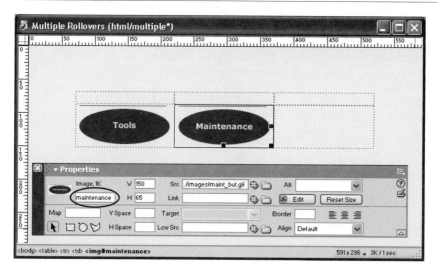

4. Click inside **Cell B** (row 2, column 2) and drag the image **maint_but.gif** from the **Assets** panel into the cell. In the **Property Inspector**, name the image **maintenance**.

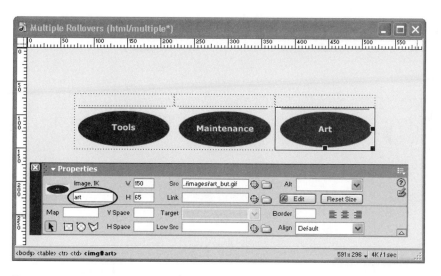

5. Click inside **Cell C** (row 2, column 3) and drag the image **art_but.gif** from the **Assets** panel into the cell. In the **Property Inspector**, name the image **art**.

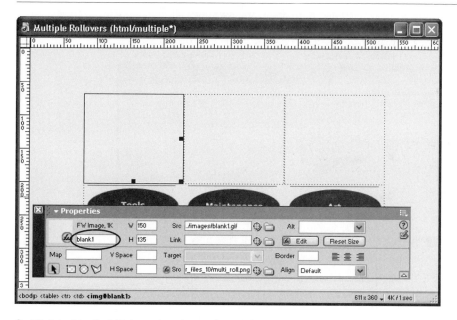

6. Click inside **Cell D** (row 1, column 1) and drag the image **blank1.gif** from the **Assets** panel into the cell. In the **Property Inspector**, name the image **blank1**.

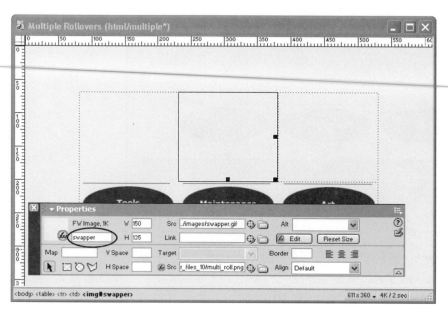

7. Click inside **Cell E** (row 1, column 2) and drag the image **swapper.gif** from the **Assets** panel into the cell. In the **Property Inspector**, name the image **swapper**.

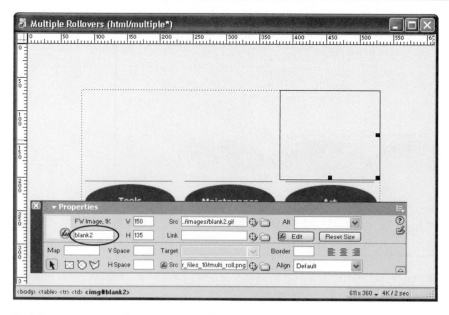

8. Click inside **Cell F** (row 1, column 3) and drag the image **blank2.gif** from the **Assets** panel into the cell. In the **Property Inspector**, name the image **blank2**.

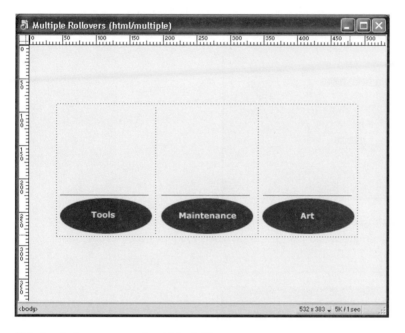

This is what your page should look like now.

9. If the **Behaviors** panel is not open, press **Shift+F3** to open it. Select the image in **Cell A** (row 2, column 1). With the image selected, click the **plus** sign in the **Behaviors** panel to select **Swap Image**. In the **Swap Image** dialog box that opens, notice that **tools** is selected in the **Images** list.

Be sure not to click OK until we say so.

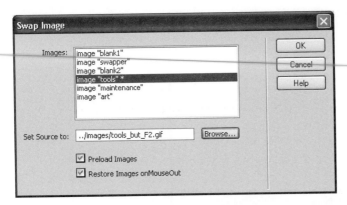

10. Click **Browse** to **Set Source** to **tools_but_F2.gif**. This sets the rollover for the graphic **tools** (tools_but.gif) to change to an alternate version of the button when you move your mouse over it. Don't click **OK** yet!

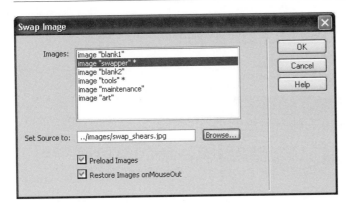

11. Select **swapper** from the same **Images** list. Click **Browse** again to **Set Source** to **swap_shears.jpg**, then click **Open**. You just instructed the behavior to swap the **swapper** (swapper.gif) artwork with the picture of the **pruning shears** (swap_shears.jpg). Click **OK**!

The rollover now triggers two behaviors: the Tools button has been instructed to switch, and an image of the pruning shears will appear when the mouse moves over the original Tools button image.

12. Press **F12** and test your first rollover! Move your mouse over the **Tools** button. The button now contains a brief description, the text will turn red, and the ellipse shape becomes a pale green color. You've just set the rollover for the **Tools** button.

There are only two more items on the list to go.

13. Return to Dreamweaver MX and repeat this process for the next image. Select the **Maintenance** image in **Cell B**. With the image selected, click the **plus** sign in the **Behaviors** panel and select **Swap Image**. In the **Swap Image** dialog box that opens, notice that **maintenance** is selected in the **Images** list.

14. Click **Browse** to **Set Source** to **maint_but_F2.gif**. Don't click **OK** yet.

15. Select **swapper** from the **Images** list. Click **Browse** to **Set Source** to **swap_maint.jpg**. Click **OK**!

One more item to go!

16. Select the Art graphic. With the image selected, click the **plus** sign in the **Behaviors** panel to select **Swap Image**. In the **Swap Image** dialog box that opens, notice that **art** is selected in the **Images** list.

17. Click **Browse** to **Set Source** to: **art_but_F2.gif**. Don't click **OK** yet.

18. Select **swapper** from the **Images** list. Click **Browse** to **Set Source** to **swap_tree.jpg**. Click **OK**.

19. You're done. Press **F12** to preview your work in a browser, then **close** the file and move on to the next exercise.

 MOVIE | **swap_image.mov**

This isn't the most intuitive operation in the universe, so don't kick yourself if you don't get it right the first time. If it didn't work, please view the movie **swap_image.mov**, located in the movies folder on the Dreamweaver MX **H•O•T CD-ROM**.

What Are Flash Buttons?

Dreamweaver MX lets you create something called **Flash Buttons**. These buttons have very similar characteristics to other rollovers you have worked with in this chapter. For example, like other rollovers, Flash Buttons have an Up state and Over state. They can be set up to link to other pages, both internal and external. However, unlike other buttons, they are created from within Dreamweaver MX. This means that they can be quickly changed with just a few clicks, which can save you time. You don't need to use an image editor like Fireworks or ImageReady to work with Flash Buttons.

Creating Flash Buttons is fairly simple, as you will see by following the next exercise. What is different is that Dreamweaver MX creates the rollover images in the SWF file format, instead of GIF or JPG, once you click **OK** in the easy-to-use Flash Button interface. In other exercises, you have simply worked with existing images and set the behavior to write the necessary JavaScript to enact a rollover. With Flash Buttons, you are creating actual image files from Dreamweaver MX. This can be wonderfully convenient!

In order to view Flash content on the Web, you must have the Flash plug-in installed in your browser. If you don't have this plug-in, you can download it for free at **http://www.macromedia.com/software/ flashplayer/**.

Creating Flash Buttons	
Pros	**Explanation**
Font integrity	With Flash Buttons, you can use any font installed in your system, and the visitors to your page don't need to have that font installed. This gives you much more flexibility when you are designing your pages.
Easily updated	With just a few clicks, you can change the text and entire look of your Flash Buttons. This can save you a lot of time when you need to make changes to your site.
Complex animations	Some of the Flash Buttons available to you in Dreamweaver MX have more complex animation than you could easily achieve with animated GIF files.
Design consistency	Because a navigation system that uses Flash Buttons can be set up in minutes, it's easy to get a consistent look and feel to your site without a spending a lot of time designing your own rollover art. This helps to bring consistency to the overall design of your site.

Using Flash Text	
Cons	**Explanation**
Plug-in required	All Flash content on the Web requires a plug-in in order to be viewed properly. Flash Buttons are no different, and require that the Flash plug-in be installed in the browser.

5. —————————Creating Flash Buttons

Dreamweaver MX enables you to create Flash rollover buttons from a predefined set of styles, without ever leaving Dreamweaver MX. This exercise shows you how to work with this cool feature.

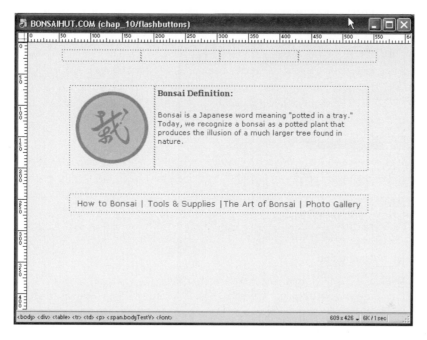

1. Open the **flashbuttons.html** file located inside the **chap_10** folder. This page contains a table at the top that is set up to hold the Flash Buttons you will create this exercise.

2. Click inside the first cell of the table. You should see a blinking cursor inside the cell. This indicates that your content will be inserted in this cell.

WARNING | Flash Plug-In Required

One advantage of Flash Buttons is that you can use any font you want and end users do not have to have that font on their computers. All Flash content on the Web requires that end users have the Flash plug-in installed in their browsers. According to Macromedia, about 436 million people have a version of the plug-in installed. That's a lot of people. We talk about ways to detect whether users have this plug-in installed in Chapter 14, "*Behaviors*."

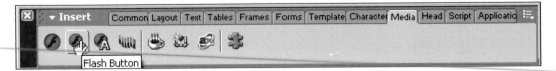

3. In the **Media** panel, click the **Flash Button** object. This will open the **Insert Flash Button** dialog box.

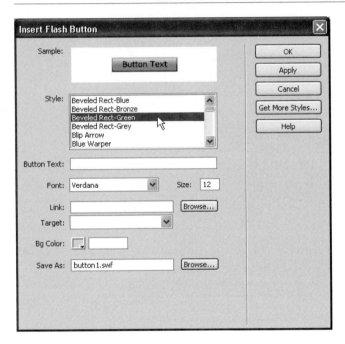

The Insert Flash Button dialog box will display a preview of the button settings at the top of this dialog box. As you select different styles, the Sample area will change. Moving your cursor over the Sample area will display a preview of the rollover effect.

4. Under the **Style** option, select **Beveled Rect-Green**. This will change the Sample area at the top. Move your mouse over the **Sample** area to preview the rollover effect for this style. For the **Button Text** option, type **How to Bonsai**. This option defines the text you want to appear on the button. If you leave this option blank, no text will appear on the button. Make sure the **Font** option is set to **Verdana** and the **Size** option is set to **12**.

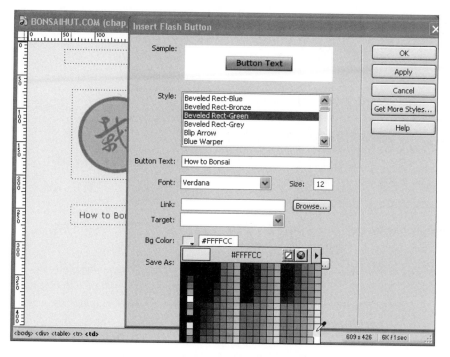

By default, the Flash Buttons will have a white background. You can use the eyedropper to match the background of the buttons with other colors in your site, such as the background color.

5. Click the **Bg Color** box and move your mouse over the background of your document. This will let you sample the yellow color so that both backgrounds match.

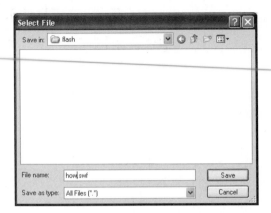

6. Click the **Browse** button to the right of the **Save As** option. Browse to the **flash** folder located inside the **chap_10** folder. Name the file **how.swf** and click **Save**.

Note: If it seems odd to save this file, let us take a moment to explain what is happening. Not only are you creating settings for the Flash text, but you're actually creating and saving the Flash file from directly within Dreamweaver MX. The Flash file format is SWF. If you choose not to manually set where to save the SWF file, it will be saved in the same location as the HTML document. This is OK, because the Flash Button file will work either way; however, we created a flash folder to hold the SWF files for this exercise because it is a good work habit to keep the files organized. Although it's not necessary, many developers like to create separate folders for images and content (such as Flash).

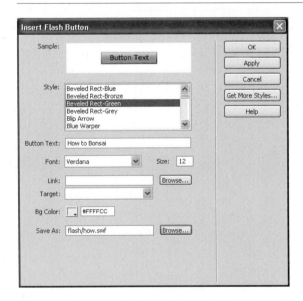

This is what the dialog box should look like at this point in the exercise.

7. Click **OK** to complete this process and create the Flash Button.

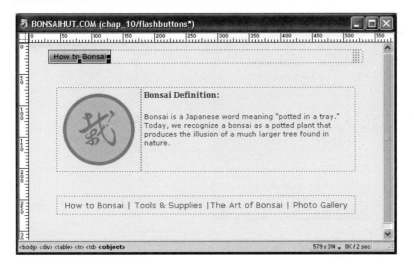

This is what your page should look like when the first button is inserted.

8. Press **Tab** to move your cursor to the next table cell.

9. Using the same steps, create a Flash Button for the following options: **Tools & Supplies**, **The Art of Bonsai**, and **Photo Gallery**. Don't forget to save each file, with a unique name, inside the **flash** folder.

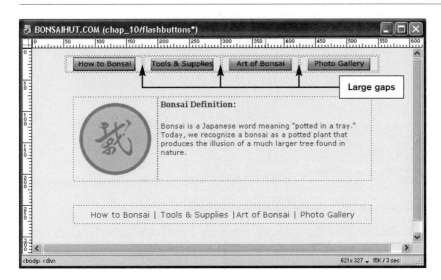

This is what your page should look like after you have added the other Flash Buttons.

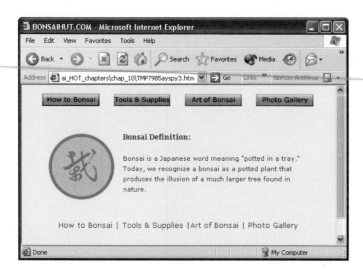

10. Press **F12** to preview this page in a browser. Notice the rather large spaces between the buttons? You will learn how to get rid of those next.

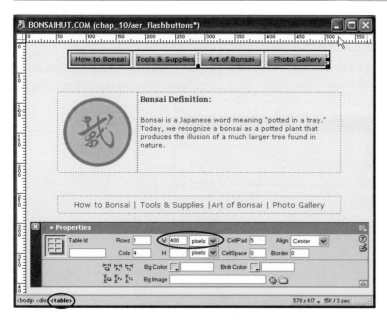

11. Return to Dreamweaver MX. Using the **Tag Selector**, select the entire table. In the **Property Inspector**, set the table width (**W**) to **400**. This will set the table and graphics to fit exactly inside of the table. Try experimenting with the **CellSpace** and **CellPad** options to adjust the spacing between the buttons how you like them. We think a CellPad of 5 looks right.

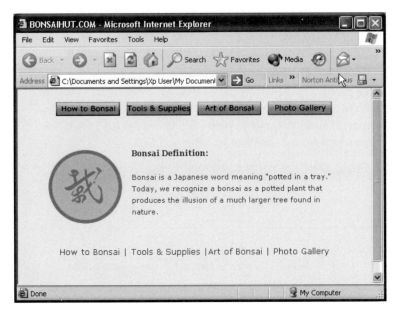

12. Press **F12** to preview the page again in a browser. Looking good!

13. Return to Dreamweaver MX. **Save** and **close** this file.

6. ————Inserting a Navigation Bar Rollover

So far, you have created simple rollovers, animated rollovers, and multiple-event rollovers. You have one more type of rollover to learn to create before you finish this chapter—the **navigation bar** rollover. A navigation bar-style rollover allows each button to display four **states**: **up**, **over**, **down**, and **over while down**. Instead of working with two images for each rollover, this type of rollover requires that you work with four, one for each separate state. This might sound intimidating, but the Dreamweaver MX **Insert Navigation Bar** feature makes it much easier than you might imagine.

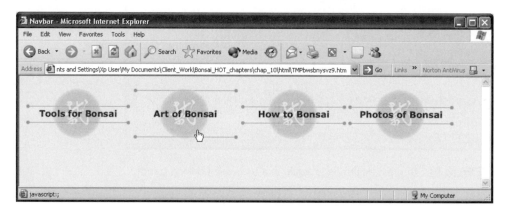

1. To view a sample of what you are about to create, open **navbar_final.html** located in the **html** folder. Press **F12** to preview this page in a browser. Move your mouse over the images and click a few as well. Notice there are more than two rollover states? This is what you'll learn to build in this exercise. Pretty neat-o!

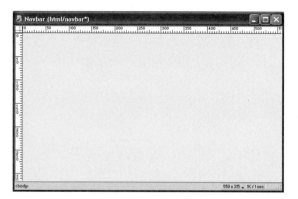

2. Return to Dreamweaver MX. Close **navbar_final.html** and open **navbar.html** located in the **html** folder. This is simply a blank file that has been saved for you already. You are going to use it as a starting point to create your own navigation bar.

3. Click the **Navigation Bar** object in the **Common** panel. As an alternative, you could select **Insert > Interactive Images > Navigation Bar**. Either way is fine and will open the **Insert Navigation Bar** dialog box (and a big dialog box it is at that!).

Different Rollover States

Keeping track of the different types of rollover states can be a little tricky. Heck, we have a hard enough time keeping track of our car keys, not to mention our rollover states. So, we have included the following chart to help you with this task:

Rollover States	
State	**What It Does**
Up	The graphic that appears on the Web page when it is loaded. This is also referred to as the "static" or "off" state.
Over	The graphic that appears when the end-user's mouse moves over the image. Most often, this image will revert back to the Up state when the mouse is moved off of the image. This is sometimes referred to as the "on" state.
Down	The graphic that will appear after the end user has clicked on the Over state. This state will not change again until the end-user's mouse moves over this image or clicks on another image.
Over While Down	This appears when the end-user's mouse moves over the Down state. It works just like the Over state, except that it works on the Down state only. Because the user's mouse is only depressed on a button for a short time, this state is not used very often.

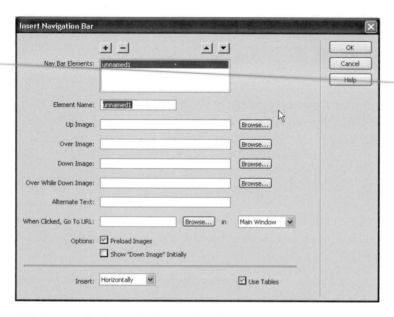

This is what the Insert Navigation Bar dialog box looks like by default.

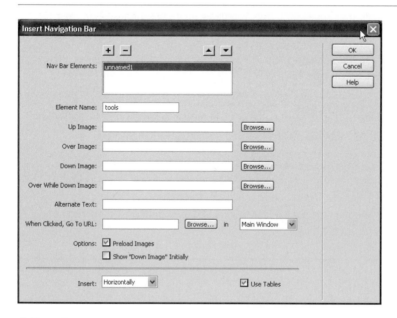

4. Enter **Element Name: tools**. This assigns a name to the first rollover image in this navigation bar. Each element (rollover) must have a unique name. We suggest you name them in relationship to their function on the page. The first button will access the **Tools for Bonsai** page, so you will name this first element **tools**.

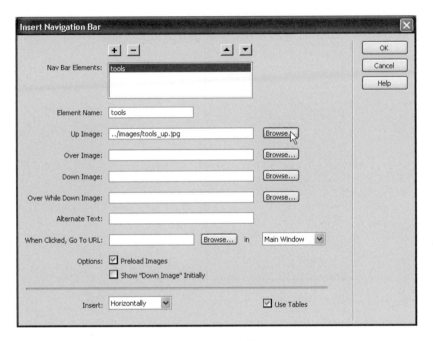

5. Click **Browse** next to the **Up Image** field. Browse to the **images** folder and select **tools_up.jpg**. Click **Open** to select this image. You've just specified the image for the Up state of the rollover.

---

6. Click **Browse** next to **Over Image**. Browse to the **images** folder and select **tools_over.jpg**. Click **Open** to select this image. You've just specified the image for the Over state of the rollover.

---

7. Click **Browse** next to **Down Image**. Browse to the **images** folder and select **tools_down.jpg**. Click **Open** to select this image. You've just specified the image for the Down state of the rollover.

---

8. Click **Browse** next to **Over While Down Image**. Browse to the **images** folder and select **tools_overdown.jpg**. Click **Open** to select this image. You've just specified the image for the Over While Down state of the rollover.

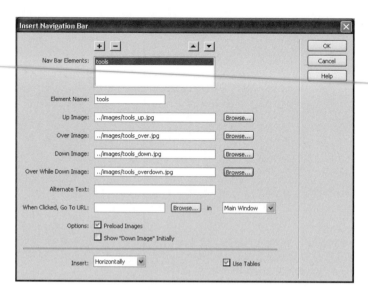

This is what your screen should look like at this point in the exercise.

Now that you have added the first rollover button in your navigation, it's time to add the next one. By the end of this exercise, this will all be second nature to you!

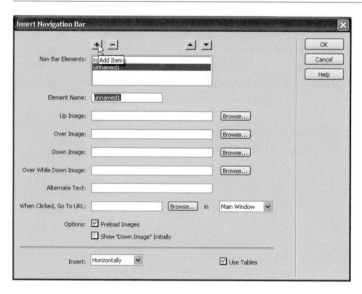

9. Click the **plus** sign at the top of the dialog box. You will see that a new unnamed element is added. This will let you add the second rollover image to the navigation bar.

10. Enter **Element Name: art**. This will assign a name to the second rollover image in this navigation bar. Remember, each element must have a unique name.

11. Click **Browse** next to **Up Image**. Browse to the **images** folder and **select art_up.jpg**. Click **Open** to select this image. This option lets you specify the image for the Up state of the rollover for the second element in the navigation bar.

12. Click **Browse** next to **Over Image**. Browse to the **images** folder and select **art_over.jpg**. Click **Open** to select this image. This option lets you specify the Over state of the second rollover.

13. Click **Browse** next to **Down Image**. Browse to the **images** folder and select **art_down.jpg**. Click **Open** to select this image. This option lets you specify the Down state of the second rollover.

14. Click **Browse** next to **Over While Down Image**. Browse to the **images** folder and select **art_overdown.jpg**. Click **Open** to select this image. This option lets you specify the Over While Down state of the second rollover.

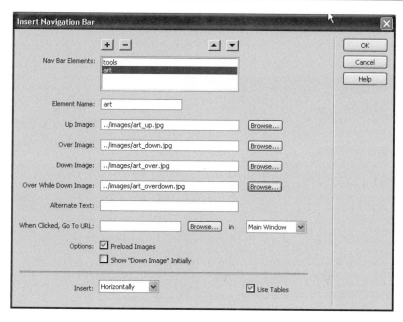

This is what your dialog box should look like with the second rollover settings.

Adding Elements to the Navigation Bar		
Element	**State**	**File**
how	Up	how_up.jpg
	Over	how_over.jpg
	Down	how_down.jpg
	Over While Down	how_overdown.jpg
photos	Up	photos_up.jpg
	Over	photos_over.jpg
	Down	photos_down.jpg
	Over While Down	photos_overdown.jpg

15. Now that you know how to add new elements to the navigation bar, go ahead and add two more four-state buttons, using the chart above.

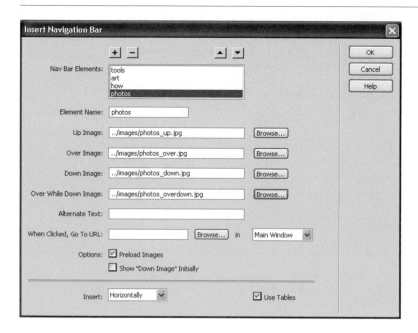

This is what the dialog box should look like when you are finished.

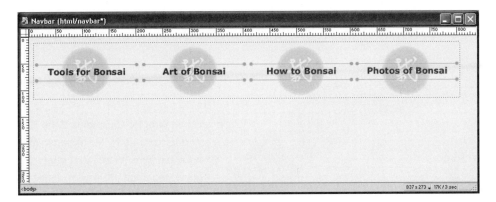

16. After you have added the fourth element, click **OK**. Dreamweaver MX will automatically create a table, insert the images you specified, and create all of the complex JavaScript necessary for the rollovers to function. It does all of this in about two seconds. We dare any JavaScript programmer to compete with this time!

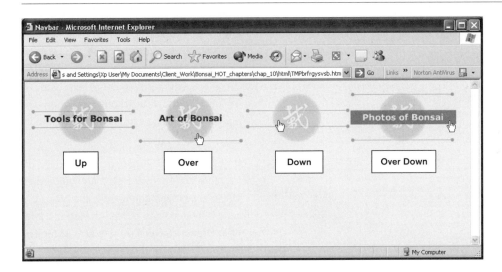

Here you can see the four possible states in the navigation bar.

17. Go ahead and press **F12** to preview your navigation bar in a browser. Make sure you roll over each of the images, click them, and then roll over them again to see the four different states of each.

18. Return to Dreamweaver MX. **Save** and **close** the file.

Wow, another chapter under your belt, congratulations. We know it was a lot of hard work, but you are well on your way to becoming a Dreamweaver MX expert.

II.

Cascading Style Sheets

| Redefining HTML with Style Sheets |
| Making Classes | Using Selectors |
| Affecting Links with Selectors |
| Linking to a Style Sheet |

chap_II

Dreamweaver MX
H•O•T CD-ROM

CSS, which stands for **C**ascading **S**tyle **S**heets, is a standard defined by the World Wide Web Consortium (W3C) that offers a more flexible and accurate way to define the appearance of your text and formatting than standard HTML. If, for example, you wanted all the text in your document to be blue and all the headlines to be green, with standard HTML you would have to go through the elements on the page one by one and assign those colors to the text. Using **style sheets**, you can redefine all the body elements in the entire document to turn blue with just one instruction and then perform the same single step for the headlines to turn green.

The style sheets specification also offers more control over type than standard HTML. With styles, you can specify the amount of space between lines of type (called the **line height** in Dreamweaver MX), the size of the type in pixels instead of points, and specific fonts for specific page elements. Anyone yearning for more control over typography is going to be drawn to using styles as opposed to the type attributes discussed in Chapter 6, "*Typography*."

Support for CSS

There is a slight disadvantage to CSS because they are supported only by 4.0 or later browsers. And to complicate matters, these browsers don't offer full support for the entire CSS1 or CSS2 specifications. At the time we were writing this book, Netscape 7.0 was in beta, so the likelihood of someone viewing your page with a non-4.0 browser is becoming less of an issue as the next generation of browsers are released. So, as you can probably guess, we are strong advocates of using CSS on your pages. But, if someone looks at your styles-based page with an older browser, they will not see any formatting whatsoever beyond the normal HTML formatting. Of course, Dreamweaver MX has a great solution to this. It's the only program we know of that can convert styles to HTML tags automatically. Dreamweaver MX offers the best of both worlds—it allows you to design with styles and convert to backward-compatible HTML. CSS also plays an important role in developing accessible Web pages. We discuss this side of CSS in Chapter 18, "*Accessibility*." As you will see, CSS is an important part of the Web design process.

Levels of CSS

You should know that the W3C has released two recommendations for Cascading Style Sheets, CSS1 and CSS2. The CSS1 recommendation was formalized on December 17, 1996 and revised on January 11, 1999. It contains about 50 properties. The CSS2 recommendation was formalized on May 12, 1998. It contains about 120 properties, including those of the CSS1 recommendation. We suggest that you take the time to read these recommendations to learn what's possible with CSS, see CSS code examples, and learn about compatibility issues. However, we should warn you that these documents are really technical and might be hard for you to digest. If you can't make any sense from them, you should invest in a good CSS book. We really like *Cascading Style Sheets–Designing for the Web (Second Edition)* written by Hakon Wium Lie and Bert Bos.

You can find the recommendations online at:
http://www.w3.org/TR/REC-CSS1
http://www.w3.org/TR/REC-CSS2

The Cascading Part of Style Sheets

The term "cascading" in style sheets has to do with how browsers interpret the style sheet code. Sometimes, when multiple style sheets are used (such as inline and external, which you'll learn about very soon in this very chapter!), the browser might not know which style sheet to honor. The "cascading" part of CSS has to do with what rules the browser should follow when it encounters conflicting CSS information. The rules are complex, and describing them would require more space than we have room for in this book. Furthermore, not all browsers support the cascading aspect of CSS. If you are interested in learning more about the rules for the "cascading" structure, visit **http://www.htmlhelp.com/reference/css/structure.html**.

Types of Style Sheets

Before you jump right into the exercises in this chapter, you should have some background information about the different type of styles and when you would use each. Knowing the difference between them is important so you can decide which one is best for your Web projects. The table below outlines the different types of style sheets:

Types of Style Sheets	
Style Sheet Type	**Description**

Embedded	This type of style sheet is an internal part of the HTML document. All of the code is written inside the **<head>** tag of the document and affects only this one page. Some sample embedded CSS code looks like this:
	
	`<STYLE TYPE="text/css">`
	`<!–`
	`H1 {color:blue; font-family: verdana}`
	`–>`
	`</STYLE>`
	
	This type of style sheet is useful if you want to apply this style to a single page only.

External	External style sheets are the most powerful type of style sheet. One single file can be used to format hundreds, thousands, and even millions of pages. Then, with one change, all of those pages can instantly be changed to have a new style. The contents of an external CSS file look just like the embedded code, except that they are not part of the HTML page. Instead, they are stored in a separate file with a .css extension instead of an .html extension. This file simply contains a list of styles, with no other HTML code. Instead of embedding the code in the HTML document, you make a link to the external CSS file. Here's an example: `<LINK REL=stylesheet HREF="mystyles.css" TYPE="text/css">`

continues on next page

Types of Style Sheets *continued*	
Style Sheet Type	**Description**
Inline	This type of style sheet is useful when you have multiple pages that share the same style(s). Inline styles are similar to embedded styles, in that they are part of the HTML document. However, they are written directly in the **<body>** of the page, not the **<head>** section. This is what some sample code would look like:

```
<BODY>
<H1 STYLE="color: orange; font-family: verdana">This is some
sample text.</H1>
</BODY>
</HTML>
```

Inline styles are much less powerful than embedded and external style sheets. Why? Because if you ever want to change the style, you would have to do it every place the inline style appeared in your document.

Inline styles do have a purpose, however. For example, they can be used to override styles from an external style sheet.

Note: Dreamweaver MX does not have any way of creating inline styles. You will have to know the correct syntax and enter the code manually.

Anatomy of a Style Sheet

Now, it's time for CSS Anatomy 101. The anatomy of a style sheet includes some terminology that is likely new to you, such as **declarations** and **selectors**. Here are some examples of how these terms relate to style sheet programming.

At the very core of CSS are rules. Here is an example of a simple CSS rule:

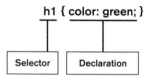

Rules consist of two parts, the selector and the declaration. In this example, the **<h1>** tag is the selector— the HTML object being modified; the color is the declaration—how the selector is being changed.

This is an example of a CSS declaration:

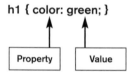

The declaration has two parts: the **property** and the **value**. In this example, property is the color of the **<h1>** tag that is being modified. The value is set to green, which specifies how the property is being modified.

I. ──────────Redefining HTML with Style Sheets

As we pointed out, there are multiple ways to implement styles in Dreamweaver MX. In this exercise, you'll learn how to assign font attributes—such as color and size—by redefining HTML tags. You will also learn how to create an embedded style sheet, where the CSS code is written inside the **<head>** tag of the document.

1. Copy the **chap_11** folder from the **H•O•T CD-ROM** to your hard drive. Define your site for Chapter 11, using the **chap_11** folder as the local root folder. If you need a refresher on this process, visit Exercise 1 in Chapter 3, "*Site Control.*"

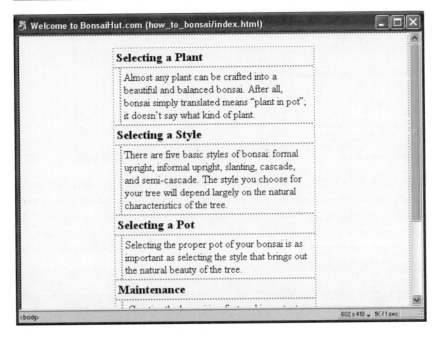

2. Open **chap11/how_to_bonsai/index.html**.

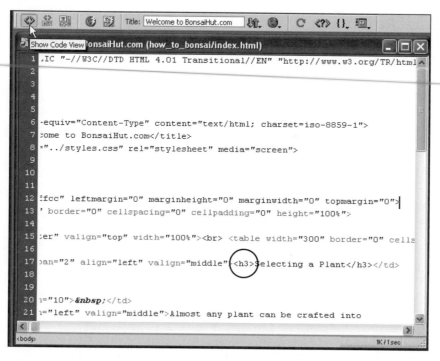

3. Click the **Show Code View** button to look at the HTML code for this document. Notice that it uses **<h3>** as the headers for the title of each section. Also, notice that no **<font>** tags have been used to format the text on the page. Click the **Show Design View** button to return to the design view.

TIP | HTML and CSS Together

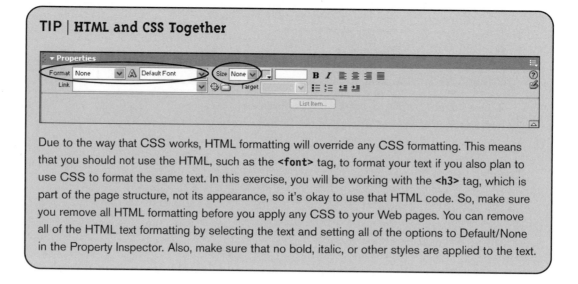

Due to the way that CSS works, HTML formatting will override any CSS formatting. This means that you should not use the HTML, such as the **<font>** tag, to format your text if you also plan to use CSS to format the same text. In this exercise, you will be working with the **<h3>** tag, which is part of the page structure, not its appearance, so it's okay to use that HTML code. So, make sure you remove all HTML formatting before you apply any CSS to your Web pages. You can remove all of the HTML text formatting by selecting the text and setting all of the options to Default/None in the Property Inspector. Also, make sure that no bold, italic, or other styles are applied to the text.

4. Make sure your **CSS Styles** panel is open. If it is not, choose **Window > CSS Styles** (**Shift+F11**). Click the **New CSS Style** button at the bottom of the panel. The **New CSS Style** dialog box opens.

5. Choose **Redefine HTML Tag**. Click the arrow next to the **Tag** option and select **h3**, if it's not already selected. Make sure **This Document Only** is selected for the **Define In** option. This option tells Dreamweaver MX to create an embedded style sheet. Click **OK**.

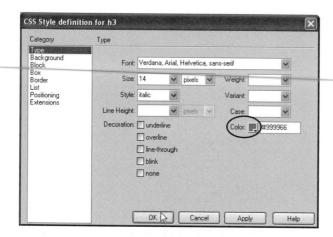

6. Select **Font: Verdana, Arial, Helvetica, sans-serif** and **Size: 14 pixels**. Choose **Style: italic**. Change **Color** to olive by clicking on the **Color Well** (shown above) and selecting your own color or by typing in the value **#999966**. Click **OK**.

Note: For the Font setting, Dreamweaver MX defaults to pixels rather than points, because this results in better consistency between the Mac and Windows platforms. Unfortunately, as we discussed in Chapter 6, "Typography," Windows renders type at 96 dpi, whereas Macs render it at 72 dpi. By default, Internet Explorer 5, on the Mac, will display HTML text at 96 dpi, too, which causes the fonts on Explorer to be larger than in Netscape. Egads—it's an awful frustration for those of us who want consistent type between browsers and platforms! Setting the type to pixels eliminates this problem, but only for 4.0+ browsers.

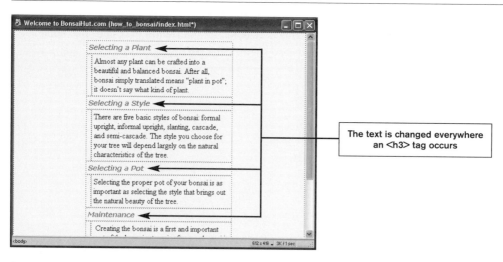

This is what the results of your labor should look like so far.

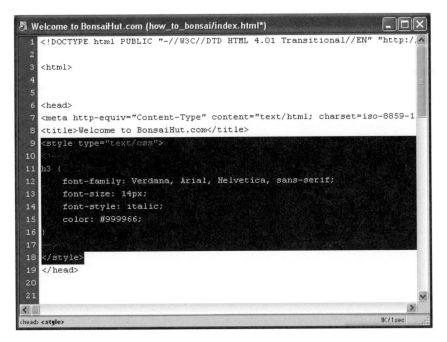

```
 1  <!DOCTYPE html PUBLIC "-//W3C//DTD HTML 4.01 Transitional//EN" "http://
 2
 3  <html>
 4
 5
 6  <head>
 7  <meta http-equiv="Content-Type" content="text/html; charset=iso-8859-1
 8  <title>Welcome to BonsaiHut.com</title>
 9  <style type="text/css">
10  <!--
11  h3 {
12      font-family: Verdana, Arial, Helvetica, sans-serif;
13      font-size: 14px;
14      font-style: italic;
15      color: #999966;
16  }
17  -->
18  </style>
19  </head>
20
21
```

7. Click the **Show Code View** button to check out the code. Notice all the style sheet information that was added to the **<head>** of the document? Pretty darn cool of Dreamweaver MX to write all of that for you, wasn't it? This is what the code of an embedded style sheet looks like.

8. Save and **close** this document.

What was the point of all this, you might ask? Styles offer a different method for formatting your documents. They ensure consistency and can save a lot of time by formatting global changes. As you will soon see, redefining HTML is just one way to apply styles. The next exercises show you how to make changes that are local (that apply to individual text characters or words instead of entire tags).

TIP | Instant CSS Reference

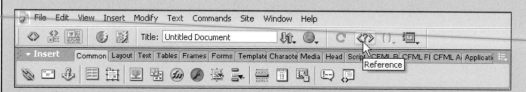

If you are new to CSS or just need a quick reference, you might be happy to know that Dreamweaver MX includes a copy of the O'Reilly CSS reference guide (and a bunch of other O'Reilly guides!). How convenient is that? No more lugging around fat books. It is really simple to access, too. In the toolbar, click the Reference button, which will open the Reference panel— go figure.

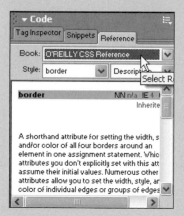

The Reference panel gives you really quick access to the O'Reilly CSS reference guide and a bunch of other ones, too.

2. _____Defining a Custom Class

You just learned to redefine the default formatting of an HTML tag with style sheets. Now it's time to move on to learn to make a custom style sheet class. A style sheet class is a set of specifications that can be applied to any tag on the page. Why would you use a class instead of redefining the formatting of an HTML tag, as you did in the last exercise? Perhaps you would like to randomly apply a set of styles, such as a particular color and text size, without having them automatically applied to every instance of a particular HTML tag. For example, maybe you don't want all the **<h3>** tags to automatically be green, and perhaps you want some **<h4>** tags to be green, as well. Rather than redefining an existing HTML tag, you can use a class to apply the same style to different tags on your page. In other words, a class can be applied to any tag at any time, rather than the global application of redefining a tag. If this sounds confusing, try the exercise and it will likely make more sense. This exercise also shows you how to create an external style sheet, which is how style sheets are used most often. You will learn more about the power of external style sheets in Exercise 5.

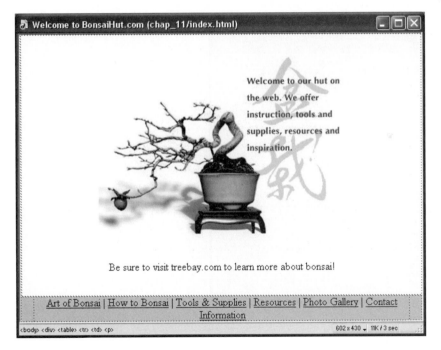

1. Open **chap_11/index.html**. This is a simplified version of the bonsaihut.com home page with no CSS applied.

---

2. Make sure your **CSS Styles** panel is open. If it is not, choose **Window > CSS Styles** (**Shift+F11**). Click the **New CSS Style** icon to open the **New CSS Style** dialog box.

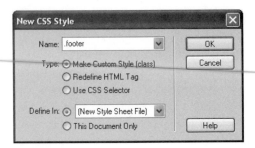

3. You should have **Make Custom Style (class)** selected. Enter **Name: .footer**. Make sure you put a period before the word **footer**. All class names must start with a period. Make sure that the **Define In** option is set to **(New Style Sheet File)**. Click **OK**.

This option creates an external style sheet file, which is where style sheets become really powerful. Why? Because multiple files can be linked to one external style sheet, so when the style sheet is modified, that change is applied to every sheet that links to it.

4. Browse to the **chap_11** folder and save this file as **customclass.css**. This creates an external style file that any page within your site can link to.

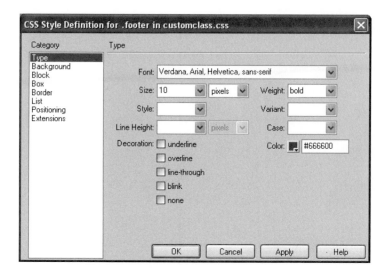

5. Fill out the **Style Definition for .footer** dialog box, using the image above as a reference for the settings to use. **Note:** Clicking **Apply** will have no effect in this instance, because you aren't redefining an existing tag. Therefore, click **OK** when you're finished.

Your CSS Styles panel should now contain the word "footer" in it. **Note:** *The proper syntax for a style sheet class is to contain a period in front of the class name, such as .footer. Even though the period is necessary, it doesn't show up in this panel. Dreamweaver MX is well aware of this, and the needed period will still appear in the code.*

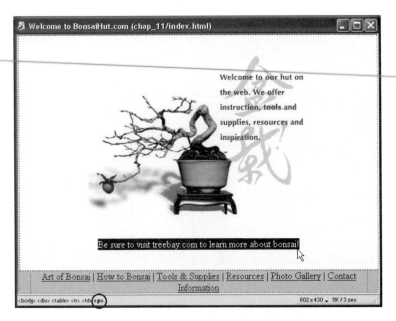

6. Click and drag to select the text: **Be sure to visit treebay.com to learn more about bonsai**. Before you apply a custom class, you must first select the object(s) you want to format.

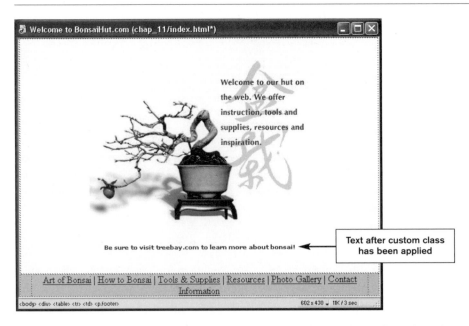

Text after custom class has been applied

7. In the **CSS Styles** panel, click the **.footer** class. This will apply that style to the selected block of text.

8. If you click the **Show Code View** button, as shown above, you can see the style code that Dreamweaver MX inserted. Classes can be applied to lines of text or even to individual words or characters. Go ahead and click on different bits of type on your page and click the **.footer** class to see what happens.

Congrats! You've just created classes and applied them to a document.

---

9. Save and **close** the document.

 MOVIE | customclass.mov

To learn more about custom classes and external CSS, check out **customclass.mov** located in the **movies** folder on the Dreamweaver MX **H•O•T CD-ROM**.

3. _____Using Selectors to Group Tags

In the last two exercises, you learned how to apply styles to redefine an HTML tag as well as how to create custom classes and apply them to selected text. What if you want to apply a single style to multiple HTML tags? Let's say you wanted to reformat both the **<h3>** and **<h4>** tags at the same time. **CSS selectors** are the answer, because they allow you to apply styles to multiple HTML tags at once.

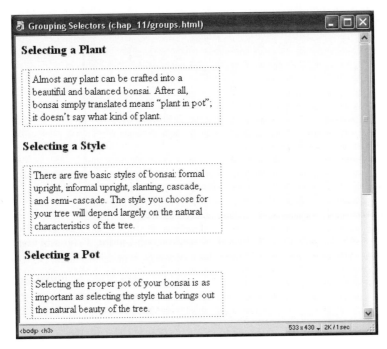

1. Open **chap_11/groups.html**. This file is similar to the one you worked with in Exercise 1.

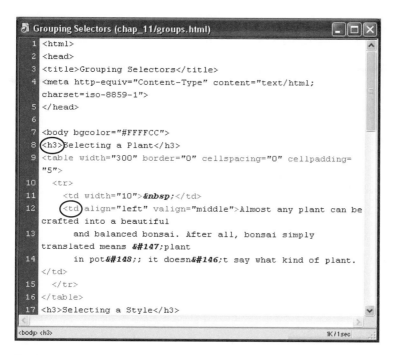

2. Click the **Show Code View** button in the **Document toolbar** to view the code for this page. Notice that this page consists of text that has been formatted with **<h3>** tags and text is inside the **<td>** tag because it is inside table cells.

3. Make sure your **CSS Styles** panel is open. If it is not, **choose Window > CSS Styles (Shift+F11)**. Click the **New CCS Style** icon at the bottom of the **CSS Styles** panel.

4. Click **Use CSS Selector**. Enter **h3, td** in the **Selector** field to select tags **<h3>** and **<td>**. Note that there is a comma and a space between the two tags. Click **OK**.

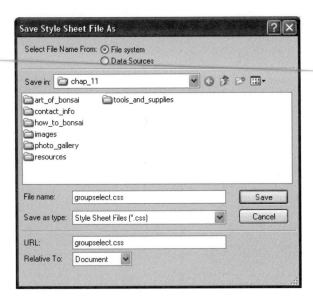

5. Save the file as **groupselect.css** inside the **chap_11** folder. Again, this will save an external style sheet file that other HTML pages could eventually link to.

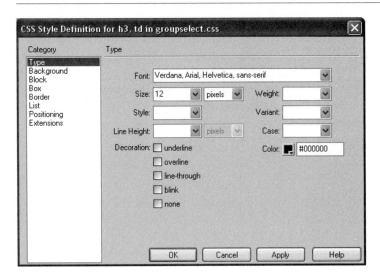

6. Set the formatting options as shown above. If you are feeling crazy and wild, go ahead and use any formatting options you want. ;-) Click **OK**.

All of the text inside the **<h3>** *and* **<td>** *tags has been formatted using the CSS properties specified above. As you can see, grouping selectors can be a quick way to format a lot of text at once. Also, it lets you retain certain structure properties, such as the* **<h3>** *tag, which can play a role in accessibility. You will learn more about that issue in Chapter 18, "Accessibility."*

7. Click the **Show Code View** button to see the CSS code that Dreamweaver MX created. Click the **Show Design View** button to return to the visual view. **Close** and **save** this file.

4. Affecting Links with Selectors

The default appearance of a link in standard HTML is that it is formatted with an underline. Some reasons people use style sheets is to turn off the underlining and/or create rollover effects. We're not sure we think removing the underline is a good idea, because many people rely on the visual cue of underlined text to know that it is truly a link. Regardless, some of you may want to remove it anyway, so this exercise shows you how. Not only that, you'll get to use the CSS selector feature again! Will the fun ever stop? ;-)

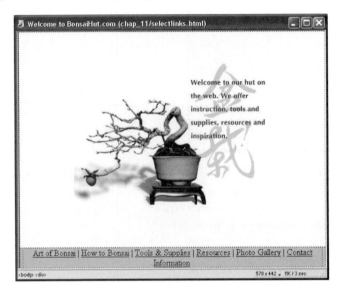

1. Open **chap_11/selectlinks.html**. As you can see, this is another version of the home page, and by the underlined text, this document contains some links.

2. Make sure your **CSS Styles** panel is open. If it is not, choose **Window > CSS Styles** (**Shift-F11**). Click the **New CSS Style** button at the bottom of the CSS Styles panel. The **New CSS Style** dialog box opens. Click **Use CSS Selector** and select **a:link**. This allows you to define the **<a>** (anchor) tag's link properties. Make sure **(New Style Sheet File)** is selected, and click **OK**.

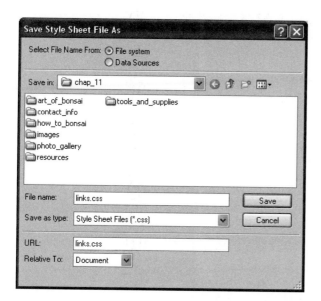

3. Save the file as **links.css** inside the **chap_11** folder.

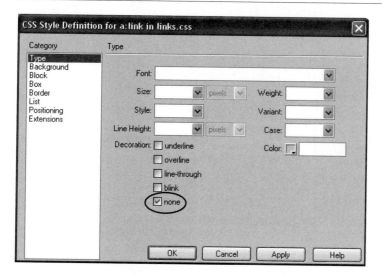

4. Check **Decoration: none** and click **OK**. You are returned to the document window. The term "Decoration" refers to how the link is displayed. In this case, because an underline is not wanted, this option is set to **none**. Dreamweaver MX gives you a preview of what the effect will look like in a browser. Sweet.

Note: This change can be seen only from a 4.0+ browser. If you have an earlier browser, you will not be able to see it even though you made it. Such is life in the not-so-fair world of never-ending browser incompatibility.

5. Click the **New CSS Style** button at the bottom of the **CSS Styles** panel. The **New CSS Style** dialog box opens. Click **Use CSS Selector** and select **a:hover**. This allows you to define the **<a>** (anchor) tag's link properties when the mouse moves over the link. Many people use this feature to create a link that changes appearance when the mouse moves over it, sort of like a rollover but made entirely from text. You'll be doing this soon! Make sure **links.css** is selected, and click **OK**.

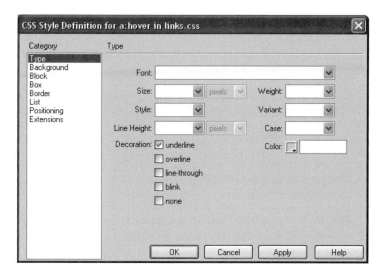

6. Check **Decoration: underline**. This will make an underline appear under each link when the mouse is moved over the link.

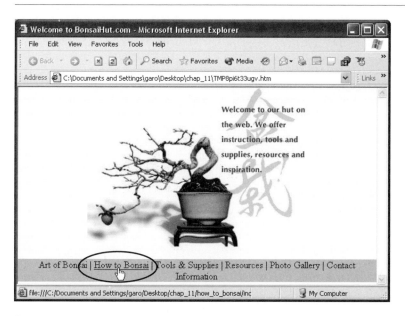

7. Press **F12** to preview this page in a browser. Notice how the underline appears when the mouse is over (hovers over) the link. **Close** the browser and return to Dreamweaver MX. **Close** and **save** this file.

Redefine HTML, Custom Class, or Selector?

Now that you've learned to create styles based on redefining HTML, a custom class, and a CSS selector, here is a handy chart that helps to explain when to use which type of style.

Creating Styles in Dreamweaver MX	
When to Use?	**For What Purpose?**
Redefine HTML tag	Use when you want to change the appearance of content based on a certain tag. For example, everything with an **<h1>** tag could be made to look consistent.
Create a custom class	Use when you want to change the appearance of your document, but not have it dependent on a tag. Use also when you want to make certain words a particular color—regardless of whether they are in the headline or the body copy.
Selector	A selector can change the appearance of multiple HTML tags all at once. Use this feature when you want to make appearance changes based on tags, but on more than one tag at a time. Dreamweaver MX also includes the **a:Selectors** as a way to change the appearance of linked text (turning off the underline, for example).

5. ————————Linking to a Style Sheet

Most of the exercises in this chapter have had you create external style sheets, so at some point different pages in your Web site could share the same style information. We had you do this because external style sheets are very powerful, because you can base all the style information in one document. If you make a change, you just have to change it there, instead of in each individual document that references it. This exercise shows you how to create another external style sheet and then how to link several pages to it once it's created.

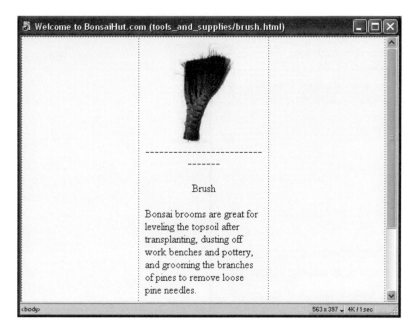

1. Open the **tools_and_supplies/brush.html** file. This page contains a simple layout with some HTML text. You are going to format the text using an external style sheet. Three other pages share the same layout and color scheme in this folder, chopsticks.html, pliers.html, and saws.html. You can look at these files to see that we're telling the truth about sharing the same color scheme. If you open any other files, make sure you close them and leave only the **brush.html** file open before you continue.

2. At the bottom of your **CSS Styles** panel, click the **New CSS Style** icon. The **New CSS Style** dialog box opens.

3. Click **Make Custom Style (class)** and enter **Name: .header**. Make sure that the **Define In** option is set to **(New Style Sheet File)**. Click **OK**. A **Save Style Sheet File As** dialog box opens. This style will be used to format the name of each tool.

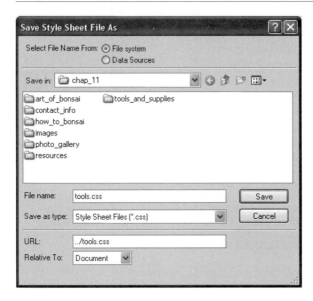

4. Save this file as **tools.css** inside the **chap_11** folder. This will be the external style sheet file to which you will link the other pages later in this exercise.

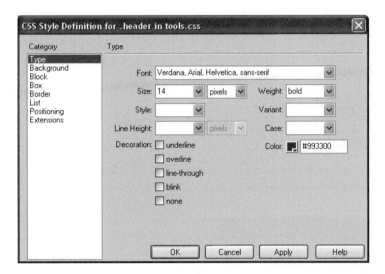

5. Set the formatting options as shown above. This style will be used to define the tool name. Click **OK**.

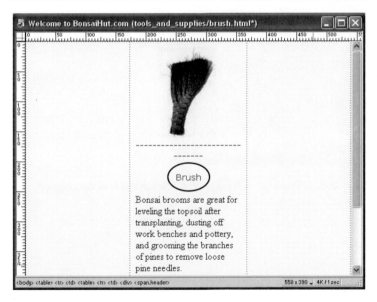

6. Click and drag to highlight the word **Brush**, and click the **.header** style in the **CSS Styles** panel. This formats that word with the **.header** style.

7. At the bottom of your **CSS Styles** panel, click the **New CSS Style** icon. The **New CSS Style** dialog box opens.

8. Click **Make Custom Style (class)** and enter **Name: .body**. Make sure that the **Define In** option is set to **tools.css**. Click **OK**. This style will be used to format the description of each tool.

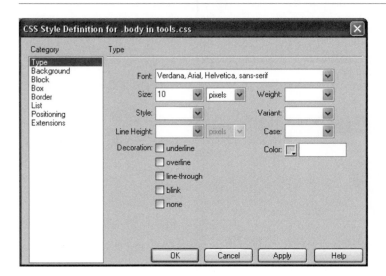

9. Set the formatting options as shown above. This style will be used to define the tool description. Click **OK**.

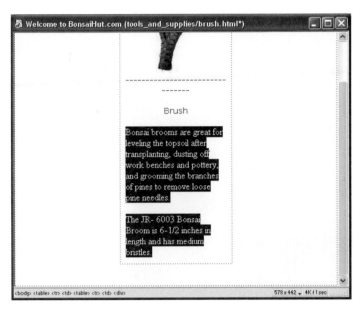

10. Click inside the table cell and then click and drag to select the entire description of the brush. Click the **.body** style in the **CSS Styles** panel. This formats all the text in that paragraph. Nice and easy.

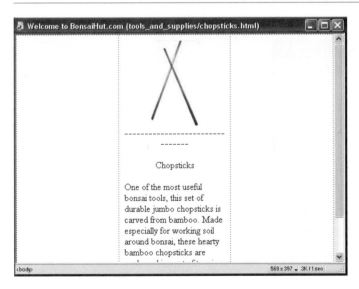

11. Open the **tools_and_supplies/chopsticks.html** file. This page is just like the **brush.html** file. It is formatted exactly as **brush.html** was before you changed it. That's fine for now, because next you'll learn how to attach it to the external CSS document you made in the last few steps. This will cause both **brush.html** and **chopsticks.html** to share the same style sheet information.

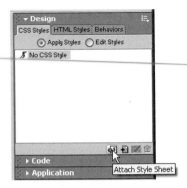

12. In the **CSS Styles** panel, click the **Attach Style Sheet** button.

13. This will open the **Link External Style Sheet** dialog box, which lets you attach an external style sheet to the HTML file. Click **Browse**.

14. Browse to the **chap_11** folder and select the **tools.css** file. Click **OK**. This attaches the **tools.css** file to the **chopsticks.html** file. This page does not look like the brush page. Hmmmm.

15. Click **OK** in the **Link External Style Sheet** dialog box.

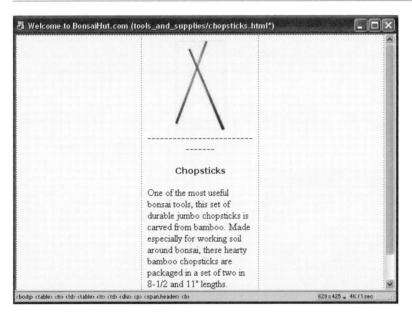

16. Click and drag to select the tool name line, and click the **.header** style in the **CSS Styles** panel. This formats that word with the .header style. Click and drag to select the description of the tool. Then, click the **.body** class in the **CSS Styles** panel.

So far, you have two HTML files linked to the external style sheet: brush.html and chopsticks.html. You could easily continue this process and link pliers.html and saw.html to the same style sheet file. In fact, that's what the next step is going to have you do.

17. Using these same steps, go ahead and link the **tools.css** file to **pliers.html** and **saws.html**. Make sure you format the tool name with the **.header** class and the tool description with the **.body** class, just as you did in **brush.html** and **chopsticks.html**.

When you are done, brush.html, chopsticks.html, pliers.html, and saw.html should be linked to the tools.css file, and the tool name should be styled using the .header class and the tool description should be styled using the .body class. To fully illustrate the power of external style sheets, the following steps will show you how to change the external CSS file and how those edits will propagate throughout all four HTML files.

18. From the **CSS Styles** panel, choose the **Edit Styles** radio button. This will display the linked style sheet information and the styles within that style sheet. In the image above, you can see the two styles you created earlier in this exercise.

19. Double-click on the **.body** style. This opens the **CSS Style Definition** dialog box so you can make changes to the style.

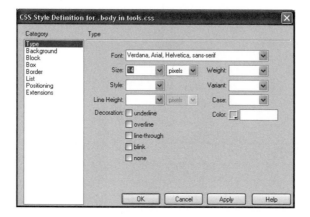

20. You can make any change you want in this dialog box. To make the change really obvious, increase the size of the **.body** class to **14 pixels**.

21. Click **OK** to save the changes you just made to this class.

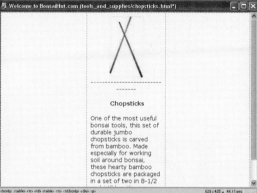

With a single click, all of the pages that linked to the tools.css external style sheet were updated. Cool, huh? This is the true power of external style sheets!

21. When you are done, **save** and **close** all of the open files.

 MOVIE | linkedcss.mov

To learn more about external CSS, check out **linkedcss.mov** located in the **movies** folder on the Dreamweaver MX **H•O•T CD-ROM**.

Converting from CSS to HTML

Now that you've successfully created internal and external style sheets, you ought to be feeling pretty proud. You may be feeling so good, in fact, that you have forgotten that some people are still using browsers that don't support style sheets—who would do such a thing? ;-) What's a conscientious Web designer to do? Dreamweaver MX has a great solution—you can convert the CSS to HTML! The only caveat is that HTML doesn't support certain things, such as links with no underlines or font sizes in pixels

Choose **File > Convert > 3.0 Browser Compatible**. After the **Convert to 3.0 Browser Compatible** dialog box opens, choose **CSS Styles to HTML Markup** and click **OK**. This creates a new document window with only HTML code and no CSS. How much easier can it get?

This chapter should help you better understand CSS and how easy it is to implement in Dreamweaver MX. You deserve a little break. But, hey, don't let us stop you if you want to move on to the next chapter!

12.

HTML

| Viewing HTML Code | Editing in Code View |
| Using the Quick Tag Editor |
| Cleaning Up HTML | Cleaning Up Word HTML |

chap_12

Dreamweaver MX
H•O•T CD-ROM

We are frequently asked whether it's necessary to know HTML to be a successful Web designer. Several years ago, the answer was a resounding yes, because there were no alternatives to writing HTML code to create Web pages. However, since the introduction of WYSIWYG HTML editors such as Dreamweaver MX, Web developers are shielded from writing the HTML code and can create Web pages in a completely visual environment. The invention of the WYSIWYG editor brought Web page publishing within the reach of almost anyone. However, it's still our belief that a basic understanding of HTML is beneficial to anyone planning to work in this field professionally. This book doesn't teach HTML, but you can teach it to yourself by looking at the code while building pages visually within Dreamweaver MX. This chapter shows you how to do this, of course!

Dreamweaver MX gives you three ways to view the document window, combining the best of both the visual and the code environment. The **Design** view is the visual WYSIWYG editing environment where you will do most of your work. The **Code** view lets you use Dreamweaver MX like other full-featured text editors that specialize in HTML, such as BBEdit or HomeSite. The **Code and Design** view lets you work with both the code and the visual elements of your page within the same document window.

A lot of what is covered in this chapter will appeal to people who already know how to hand-code their pages, but don't be afraid to read on and dig into the exercises in this chapter, even if you are not familiar with HTML.

I. ———————Viewing HTML Code

The Dreamweaver MX interface has three extremely useful buttons: the **Show Design View** button, the **Show Code View** button, and the **Show Code and Design Views** button. The ability to toggle quickly between editing your code and working in the visual editing environment makes working with the HTML code intuitive for anyone. For those of you who are familiar with HTML code, you won't feel so far from home when using Dreamweaver MX. Those of you who are less familiar with HTML will find that you can watch Dreamweaver MX create the HTML code as you use the visual editing environment. Observing this process is actually a great way to teach yourself HTML.

This first exercise exposes you to the Design view, the Code view, and the Code and Design view to show you how to edit your HTML code. Even if you don't know a whole lot about HTML, you should still work through this exercise. It's not that hard, and it will show you that learning HTML is truly within your reach.

1. Copy **chap_12** from the **H•O•T CD-ROM** to your hard drive. Define your site for Chapter 12, using the **chap_12** folder as the local root folder. If you need a refresher on this process, visit Chapter 3, "*Site Control.*"

2. Open the **inspector.html** file from the **chap_12** folder. This is just a blank file that has been saved for you. By default, your page will open in what's known as the Design view.

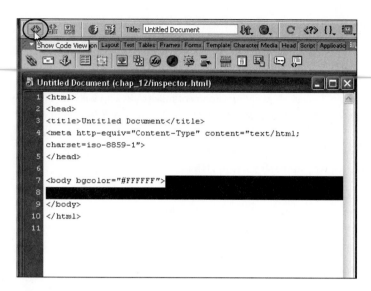

3. Click the **Show Code View** button to view the HTML of your document window. Even though the page looks empty in the Design view, there is some base HTML that already exists in the Code view. This window doesn't have much in it, but neither does your page yet!

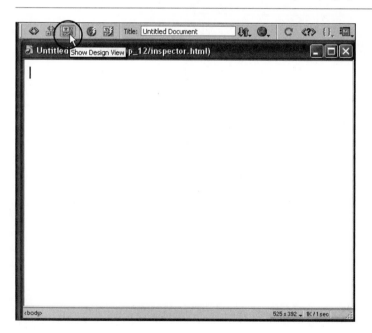

4. To return to the Design view, click the **Show Design View** button. As you can see, switching between the different views is really easy.

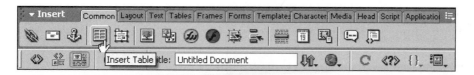

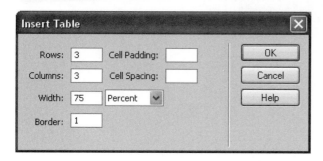

5. Click on the **Insert Table** object in the **Insert** panel. When the **Insert Table** dialog box appears, make sure the settings match the dialog box above, and then click **OK**.

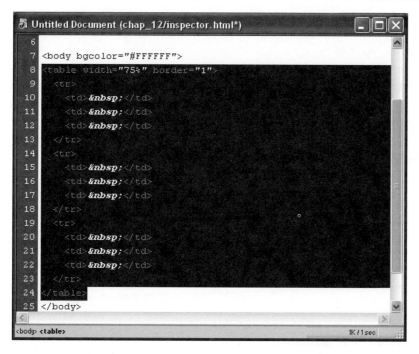

6. Click the **Show Code View** button. Check out all the code that was generated to create the table. Would you like to have typed all this? Your answer most likely is heck, no!

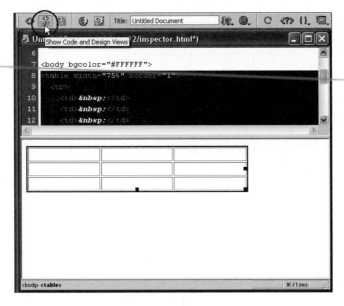

7. Click the **Show Code and Design Views** button so that you can see the code and the table on your page at the same time. This splits your document window so you can see both the code and the visual elements. Pretty neat, huh?

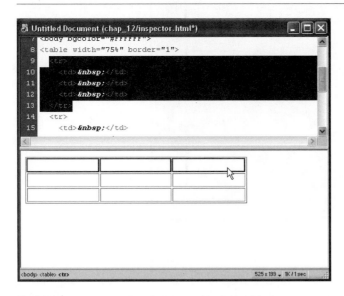

8. Click in the first cell and drag to the right. This lets you select the entire first row. Notice that the associated HTML code is also selected. This level of visual feedback is really great for identifying how the code and the visual results are joined at the hip. Nice!

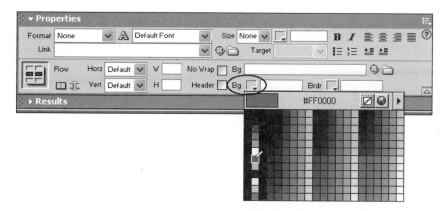

9. In the **Property Inspector**, click the **Bg** color swatch and choose any color of red. This changes the background of the selected row.

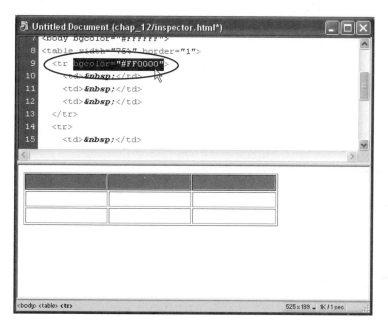

Look at the Code window. See how the HTML code is updated to reflect the changes you just made? This is a great way to learn HTML. You can literally watch the code being generated as you add, modify, and remove content from your page. Go ahead and make some more changes to your page, but leave the Code window open so you can watch all the HTML being created. To think that people used to type all of this by hand! We are sure glad we don't have to do that anymore.

10. When you are finished, **save** your changes and leave the file open for the next exercise.

Options in the Code View

Several options are available in the Code view. The following table outlines each of these options.

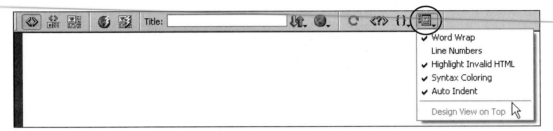

Code View Options	
Option	**Description**
Word Wrap	Wraps code within the window so you don't have to scroll to the left and right, making large amounts of code easier to see.
Line Numbers	Adds line numbers along the left side of the window. This is especially helpful when you need to identify a specific line of code, such as when troubleshooting an HTML error. The numbers won't appear in the final HTML output; they're just there for your own reference.
Highlight Invalid HTML	Invalid HTML code will be highlighted in yellow. This is really helpful when you are looking for errors in your code. When bad code is selected, look in the Property Inspector for ways to correct the problem.
Syntax Coloring	Color-codes parts of your HTML based on your Code Color preferences. This helps you quickly spot the different elements of code.
Auto Indent	Automatically indents code, which helps with readability.
Design View on Top	Available only in Code and Design view, this option inverts the positioning in the document window.

The Code Inspector

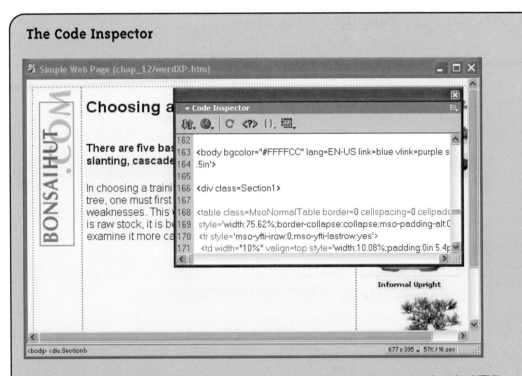

Although the three document views are really useful, there is one more way to view the HTML code of your pages. The **Code Inspector** is identical to the Code view, with the exception that the Code Inspector is a floating window above the document window. You can access the **Code Inspector** by choosing **Window > Others > Code Inspector** or by pressing **F10**. This floating window can be resized and moved around the screen without affecting the main document window. This can be nice if you have a large monitor and want to see the code next to the visual editing environment.

2. _____Editing in Code View

Now that you have an idea of how the Code window works, you will learn how to use it to modify your page. In fact, if you wanted to hand-code a page, you could create your entire page right within the HTML Code window.

In this exercise, you will use the Code window to add content to your page and then make modifications to it. The purpose of this exercise is to make you more comfortable with the Code window.

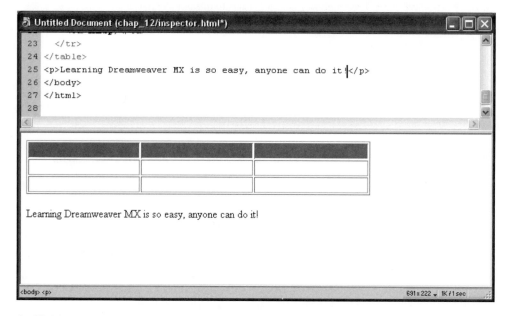

1. Click anywhere below the table and type **Learning Dreamweaver MX is so easy, anyone can do it!** Look inside the **Code** window and watch as your text is created.

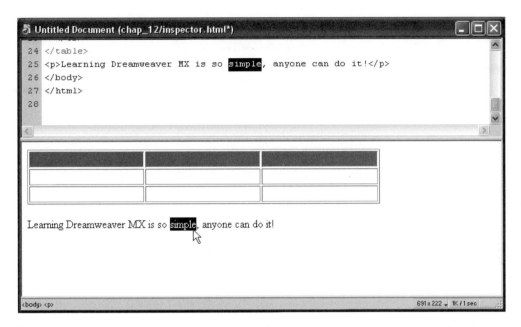

2. Inside the **Code** window, click and drag to select the word **easy**. Once you have it selected, type **simple**. When you are done typing, click anywhere in the **Design** view portion of the document window to see the changes updated.

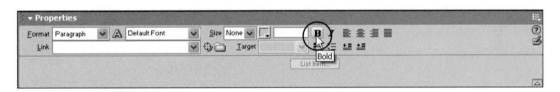

3. In the document window, click and drag to highlight the word **simple**. With the word highlighted, click the **B** button in the **Property Inspector** to make the word bold. Notice that the **<strong>** tags were added around the word in the **Code** window, which shows you the tag required to achieve bolding of text.

```
24  </table>
25  <p>Learning Dreamweaver MX is so <strong>simple</strong>, anyone can do it!</p>
26  </body>
27  </html>
28
```

```
24  </table>
25  <p>Learning Dreamweaver MX is so <i>simple</i>, anyone can do it!</p>
26  </body>
27  </html>
28
```

4. In the **Code** window, change the **<strong>** tags to **<i>** tags. The **<i>** tag will format the text so it's in italics instead of bold, whereas the **<strong>** tag was used to bold the text.

You don't have to know HTML tags, such as **<strong>** *and* **<i>**, *but if you do know them you can type them right into the code. We think it's easier to use the Property Inspector for this type of formatting. This exercise is here simply to show you that you can edit the code directly if you want to, and it achieves the same result as if you had used the Property Inspector.*

TIP | Code Preferences

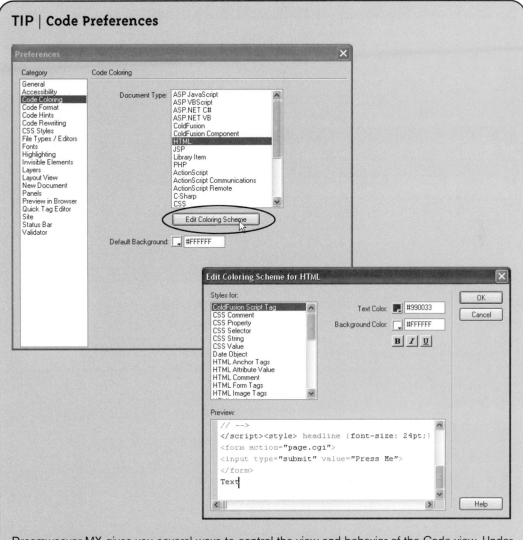

Dreamweaver MX gives you several ways to control the view and behavior of the Code view. Under Edit > Preferences, you can use the **Code Coloring**, **Code Format**, **Code Hints**, and **Code Rewriting** options to set everything from how the HTML code appears to how it is formatted. So if you find yourself working in the Code view a lot, be sure to look over these different options.

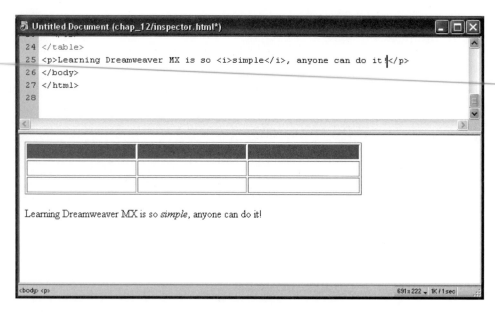

You can begin to see how you can use the Design window and the Code window in tandem to create and modify your documents.

5. When you are finished, **save** your changes and **close** this file.

Working with XHTML

Earlier we discussed the fact that HTML is being replaced by XHTML, which is basically HTML that follows XML syntax rules. Whether you want to create new XHTML documents or convert existing HTML documents into XHTML, Dreamweaver MX has multiple ways for you to make your Web pages XHTML compliant.

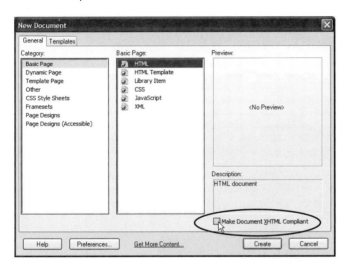

When creating new documents, you can make them XHTML-compliant by simply checking the **Make Document XHTML Compliant** checkbox. It's that simple!

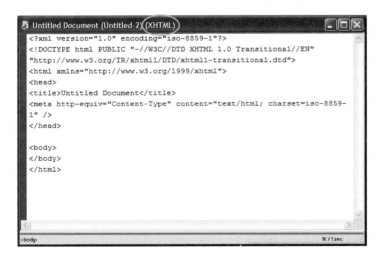

You can convert existing HTML pages into XHTML compliant pages by choosing **File > Convert > XHTML**. When you do this, **(XHTML)** will appear at the top of the document window.

3. ────────Using the Quick Tag Editor

The **Quick Tag Editor** gives you instant access to the HTML code on your page without forcing you to access the Code window or an external HTML editor. This is great if you want to make a quick change to a tag or attribute. This exercise will show you how to use the Quick Tag Editor to make changes to a file.

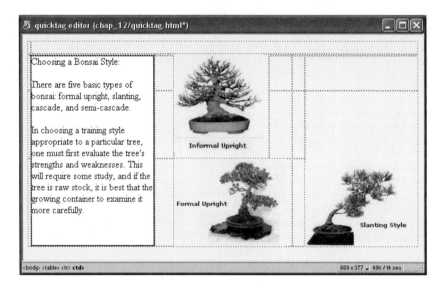

1. Open the **quicktag.html** file from the **chap_12** folder.

This file needs a few changes. First, the large cell on the left has a white background and is not allowing the yellow background to show through. Second, the image of the slanting style tree is aligned with the bottom of the table cell and should be aligned with the top of the table cell. These problems can be easily fixed with the Quick Tag Editor.

First click here

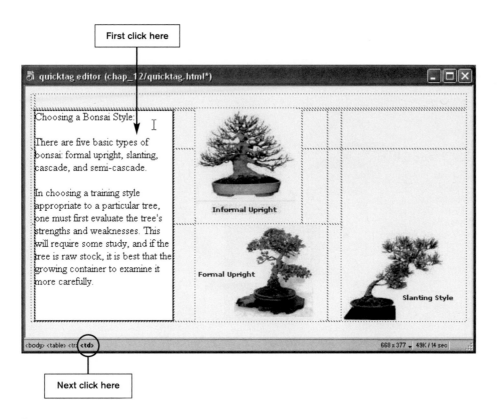

Next click here

2. Click inside the large white cell on the left side of the table, so that your cursor is blinking inside the cell. Next, click on the **<td>** (**t**able **d**ata) tag in the **Tag selector** at the bottom of the document window. This selects the entire large white cell.

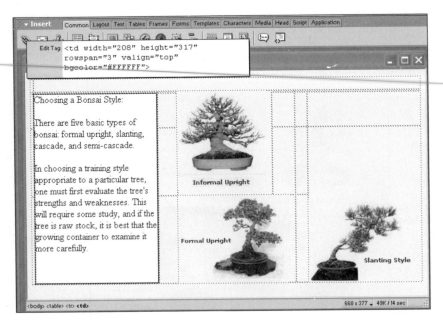

3. Press **Ctrl+T** (Windows) or **Cmd+T** (Mac) to access the **Quick Tag Editor**. (You could also choose **Modify > Quick Tag Editor**.) The Quick Tag Editor appears at the top of the document window. It currently displays the active attribute settings for the selected **<td>** tag. Notice that the **bgcolor** attribute is set to **#FFFFFF**, which is the hexadecimal value for white.

NOTE | What Are HTML Attributes?

HTML consists of a series of HTML tags. These tags define how your page is formatted in a browser. Attributes attach to these HTML tags to further define the appearance of your page. For example, **<table>** is a standard HTML tag. The **<table>** tag has several different attributes that can be used to further define its appearance, such as **width**, **height**, **bgcolor**, and so on.

Dreamweaver MX comes with the complete O'Reilly HTML Reference Guide. This guide can help you learn more about specific HTML tags. You can access this guide by choosing Window > Reference and then choosing O'Reilly HTML Reference from the Book drop-down menu. It's a great resource for learning more about HTML!

For some great references on HTML tags and their associated attributes, make sure you check out the following links:

http://www.w3.org/MarkUp/

http://www.htmlhelp.com/

Edit Tag: `<td width="208" height="317" rowspan="3" valign="top" bgcolor="#FFFFFF">`

Select the tag exactly as shown here.

---

4. Click and drag inside the **Quick Tag Editor** to select the **bgcolor** attribute. Be sure to select it exactly as you see here—don't select the last close bracket. Press the **Delete/Backspace** key to remove this attribute. Press **Return/Enter** to accept the changes you made. With the **bgcolor** attribute removed, the tan background is allowed to show through the table cell.

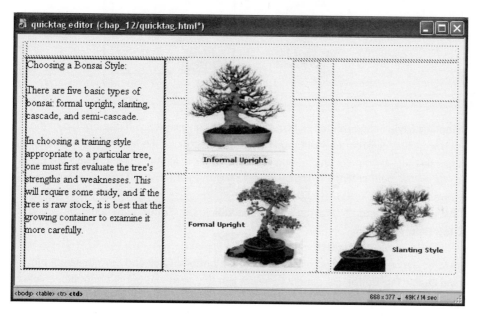

*This is what your page should look like with the **bgcolor** attribute removed.*

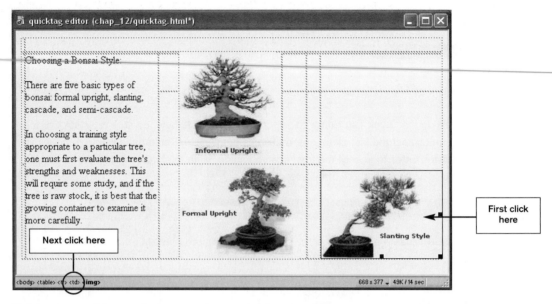

5. Click on the **Slanting Style** image (on the right), which is currently aligned with the bottom of the cell. With the image selected, click on the **<td>** tag in the **Tag selector**, at the bottom of the document window. This selects the cell so you can change the vertical alignment attribute tag by using the Quick Tag Editor.

6. Press **Ctrl+T** (Windows) or **Cmd+T** (Mac) to access the **Quick Tag Editor**. (You could also choose **Modify > Quick Tag Editor**.)

7. The image should be aligned with the top of the cell, not the bottom. Click and drag to select the word **bottom** in the **Quick Tag Editor**. Be careful to select just the word and not the quotation marks that surround it.

```
Edit Tag: <td width="188" height="259"
          rowspan="2" valign="top">
```

8. Delete the word **bottom**, then double-click on the word **top** in the small pop-up menu that appears. This changes the **VALIGN** (vertical alignment) attribute to **top** and moves the image accordingly. Press **Return/Enter** to accept your changes.

The Quick Tag Editor is a great tool if you want quick access to the HTML code. As you just saw, you can make changes to the HTML code without ever leaving the visual environment, which is very cool!

9. Save your changes and **close** this file.

The Code Validator

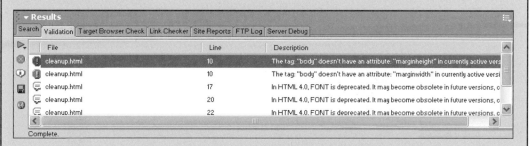

With the release of each new browser, knowing what code works in what browser can be a challenging task for even the veteran Web designer. Fortunately, there is a feature in Dreamweaver MX that will let you validate your HTML code. This lets you identify potential problems with your HTML code before you even test it in a browser. Sweet. You can access the Code Validator by choosing File > Check Page > Validate Markup. A listing of potential problems will be listed in the Results panel, which identifies the problem and the exact line of code where the error occurs.

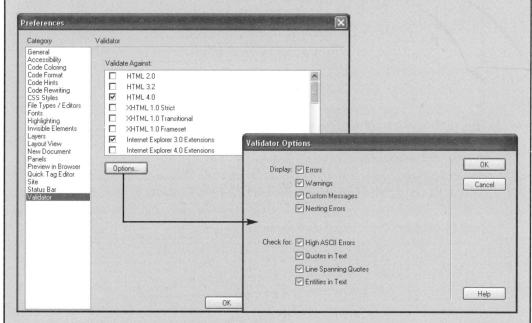

The Validator Preferences let you choose how your code is validated. For example, you might choose not to validate your code for 2.0 and 3.0 browsers because few people are using those early browsers. This flexibility makes the validation process more efficient by letting you exclude certain code environments. The Validator can even validate server-side code, such as ASP, CFM, etc.

4.——————————**Cleaning Up HTML**

There might be times when you have to work with HTML that was written by another person or in a program other than Dreamweaver MX. The HTML may not be the best code you have ever seen and might need to be cleaned up a little. Dreamweaver MX has a useful command called **Clean Up HTML** that automatically removes empty tags, redundant nested tags, non–Dreamweaver MX HTML comments, Dreamweaver MX HTML comments, nested font tags, and any tag you specify. This exercise shows you how to use the feature.

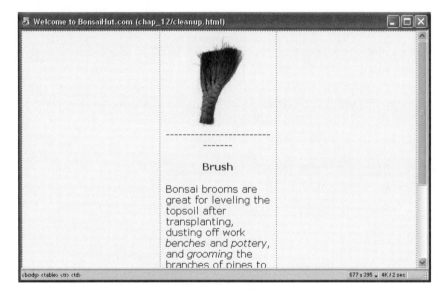

1. Open the **cleanup.html** file from the **chap_12** folder. The text on this page has been formatted extensively using the **<font>** tag. In Chapter 11, "*Cascading Style Sheets*," we told you that mixing the **<font>** tag with CSS can cause problems. So, to prepare this page for CSS, you will learn how to quickly remove the **<font>** and all HTML formatting tags from this page by using the Clean Up HTML command.

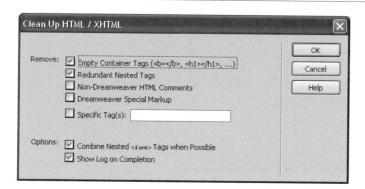

```
    Welcome to BonsaiHut.com (chap_12/cleanup.html)
15  <table width="195" border="0" cellspacing="0" cellpadding="10">
16      <tr>
17        <td valign="top"> <div align="center"> <img src="images/brush.jpg" a
18        ---------------------------<br>
19        <br>
20        </font><font color="#990000" face="Verdana, Arial, Helvetica, sans-s
21      <div align="left">
22        <p><font face="Verdana, Arial, Helvetica, sans-serif">Bonsai brooms
23          are great for leveling the topsoil after transplanting, dustin(
24          off work <em>benches</em> and <em>pottery</em>, and <em>groomi|
25          the branches of pines to remove loose pine needles.</font></p>
26        <p><font face="Verdana, Arial, Helvetica, sans-serif">The
27          <b>JR- 6003 Bonsai Broom</b> is 6-1/2 inches in length and has
28          medium bristles.</font></p>
29        </div></td>
30      </tr>
31      </table>
32      <br> </td>
33    </tr>
34  </table>
<body> <table> <tr> <td>                                          1K / 1 sec
```

2. Click the **Show Code View** button to show the Code window. Notice the **<font>** tag that has been used throughout this page. As you can imagine, it would be rather painful to remove all of those tags one at a time.

3. Click the **Show Design View** button to return to the visual editing environment.

4. Select **Commands > Clean Up HTML** to open the Clean Up HTML dialog box. This is where you can specify the parts of the HTML you want to clean up.

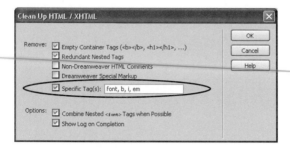

5. Click on the **Specific Tag(s)** checkbox to put a check there. In the text field, enter **font, b, i, em**. These are the HTML formatting tags that were used on this page. Click **OK**.

6. Dreamweaver MX analyzes the HTML code in your document and cleans it up based on the selections you made. It also produces a dialog box with a brief summary of the actions performed. Click **OK**.

```
Welcome to BonsaiHut.com (chap_12/cleanup.html*)
10    <body bgcolor="#ffffcc" text="black" link="#990000" vlink="#660000" alink='
11
12 <table width="100%" border="0" cellspacing="0" cellpadding="0" height="100%">
13    <tr>
14    <td align="center" valign="top" width="100%">
15 <table width="195" border="0" cellspacing="0" cellpadding="10">
16       <tr>
17          <td valign="top"> <div align="center"> <img src="images/brush.jpg" a.
18          -------------------------------<br>
19          <br>
20          <strong>Brush</strong></div>
21       <div align="left">
22          <p>Bonsai brooms are great for leveling the topsoil after transp.
23          dusting off work benches and pottery, and grooming the branche:
24          of pines to remove loose pine needles.</p>
25          <p>The JR- 6003 Bonsai Broom is 6-1/2 inches in length and has m
26          bristles.</p>
27       </div></td>
28       </tr>
29    </table>
<body> <table> <tr> <td> <table> <tr> <td> <div> <p>                     1K / 1 sec
```

7. Open the **Code** window again by clicking the **Show Code View** button. Scroll down and look for the **<font>** tag, or any of the other HTML formatting tags. Notice that they have all been removed. As you can imagine, the Clean Up HTML command can be a very useful tool, especially when you get a file that was not written properly.

8. Save and **close** this file.

Options for Cleaning Up HTML

The following chart lists the different options available in the Clean Up HTML dialog box and outlines what each does:

Options in the Clean Up HTML Dialog Box	
Option	**Purpose**
Remove: Empty Container Tags	Removes any tags that have no content between them. For example, **<i></i>** would be removed because there is nothing between the two tags.
Remove: Redundant Nested Tags	Removes tags that are redundant and not needed. For example, **<b>**This**<b>** is a **<b>**redundant**<b>** **<b>**tag**</b>**, has two redundant **<b>** tags that would be removed because they are not needed.
Remove: Non-Dreamweaver HTML Comments	Removes any comment tags that are not specific to Dreamweaver MX, but does not remove comments that are native to Dreamweaver MX. **<!--#EndEditable "image"-->**, for example, would not be removed, because it is used native to Dreamweaver MX to designate the end of an editable area of a template.
Remove: Dreamweaver Special Markup	Removes all HTML comments that are native to Dreamweaver MX. However, it does not remove standard HTML comments.
Remove: Specific Tag(s)	Removes specific tags that you specify in the text field. For example, you could remove all of the **<blink>** tags in a document, or any other tag that you specify.
Options: Combine Nested <font> Tags When Possible	Combines nested tags when they control the same block of text.
Options: Show Log on Completion	Summarizes how the HTML was modified, in a small dialog box, after the Clean Up HTML command has been applied.

5. _____Cleaning Up Word HTML

Dreamweaver MX lets you import HTML files that were saved in Microsoft Word. This is a nice feature, because more and more business professionals are using Word to author Web pages. However, Microsoft Word has a reputation for generating a lot of unnecessary HTML code. Fortunately, the **Clean Up Word HTML** command will help you remove this extra code to ensure that your pages are written in the most appropriate and concise manner. This exercise walks you through the process of using the Clean Up Word HTML command.

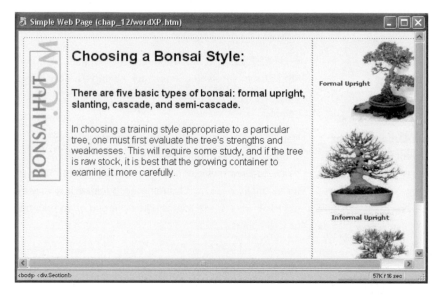

1. Open the **wordXP.htm** file from the **chap_12** folder. This file was created in Microsoft Word 2002 (XP) on a Windows machine.

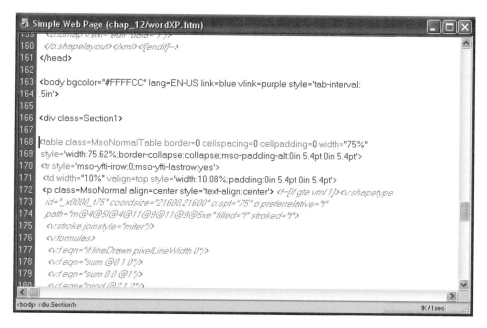

2. Click the **Show Code View** button to display the Code window. Scroll down to the bottom of the window. This page has more than 275 lines of HTML code If you are using a Mac, you might have fewer lines of code. Regardless, that's an awful lot for this very simple page.

3. Click the **Show Design View** button to return to the Design view.

WARNING | Make a Backup

Before you use the Clean Up Word HTML command, make sure you have a backup copy of the file. When you apply this command, it will make changes to the HTML that will cause it to look different if opened in Microsoft Word. You never know when you might need to refer back to the original Word file.

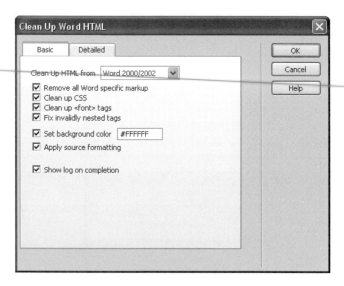

4. Select **Commands > Clean Up Word HTML**. This opens the Clean Up Word HTML dialog box, which may take a few seconds to appear while Dreamweaver MX tries to detect which version of Word the file was created in.

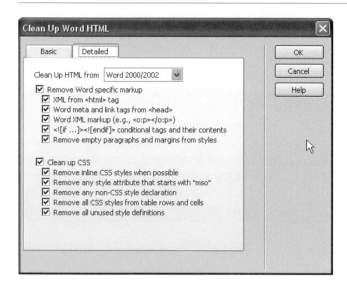

5. Click on the **Detailed** tab at the top of the dialog box. This displays the more advanced options you can control with this command. Unless you are really comfortable with XML and CSS, we suggest you leave these values at their default settings.

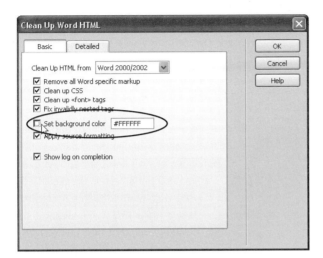

6. Click on the **Basic** tab to return to those options. Uncheck the **Set background color** checkbox. The background color for this page was set properly in Microsoft Word, so there is no need to change it here. Click **OK**.

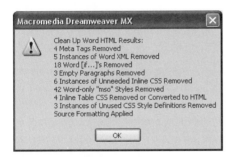

7. A dialog box appears summarizing the modifications that were made to the page. When you are finished reviewing this information, click **OK**.

8. Click the **Show Code View** button to open the Code window. You should see significantly less HTML code now. The HTML was reduced from more than 238 lines down to 36. Now, that's something you'll want to show all your friends! **Note:** If you are using the Macintosh version of Dreamweaver MX, your numbers may vary slightly.

9. Save and **Close** this file.

That's all for now. If you were intimidated by editing HTML before you read this chapter, we hope you are more at ease with it now. Move on to the next chapter if you have the stamina—there's still more to learn! Otherwise, pick this up another day.

13.

Forms

| Working with Form Objects |
| Creating a Form | Creating a Jump Menu |

chap_13

Dreamweaver MX
H•O•T CD-ROM

Forms are one of the most important elements of a Web site, because they enable you to ask questions of your end user and receive answers. Forms can be identical to those we're accustomed to in the nonvirtual world (think IRS, car insurance, or loan paperwork), but they can also be used for more exciting things, such as voting, guestbooks, interactive poetry, or e-commerce. In general, forms-based pages are much more interactive than other types of HTML pages, because they can collect and report information to you.

There are two aspects to creating forms: creating the **Form objects** (text fields, checkboxes, Submit buttons, and so on) and making the forms function properly. This chapter focuses on the creation of Form objects, not on the programming required to make forms transmit data to and from your server. Unfortunately, making the forms operational involves programming that goes beyond the scope of Dreamweaver MX and this book. At first, forms might not sound like much fun, but they are at the heart of what makes the Web different from paper and publishing mediums of the past.

The Forms Panel

The objects you use to create a form, in Dreamweaver MX, are referred to as Form objects. These include text fields, checkboxes, images, buttons, and so on. You'll find all the Form objects on the **Forms** panel. Instead of working with the Common panel, as you have in most of the other chapters so far, this chapter requires that you set your Insert panel to Forms. This will display the Form objects, as shown below.

If the Insert panel is not visible, go to **Window > Insert**. To access the Forms objects, you need to change your Insert panel from its default setting (Common) to **Forms**. You do this by clicking on the **Forms** tab at the top of the panel.

Form Objects

The following table outlines the different objects available on the Forms panel. As you become more familiar with forms, you will not need this table. Meanwhile, it should help you get a better idea of what each of the Objects does:

	Form Objects in Dreamweaver MX	
Icon	**Name**	**Function**
	Form	This is the very first step in creating a form. It inserts the <form> tag into your document. If you do not place all of your objects inside the <form> tag, your form will not work!
	Text Field	Inserts a Text Field object on your form.
	Hidden Field	Stores information that does not need to be displayed but is necessary for processing the form on the server.
	Textarea	Inserts a Multiple-line text field at the insertion point.
	Checkbox	Inserts a Checkbox object on your form. These checkboxes are used to select an option on a form.
		continues on next page

Form Objects in Dreamweaver MX *continued*

Icon	Name	Function
	Radio Button	Inserts a Radio Button object on your form. Radio buttons are used to select one item out of a list of available options.
	Radio Group	Inserts a group of Radio Button objects on your form.
	List/Menu	Inserts a List object or Menu object on your form. These two objects (list or menu) allow you to make single or multiple selections in a small area of space.
	Jump Menu	Inserts a jump menu that allows the user to select a URL from the menu and then jump to that page.
	Image Field	Inserts an image on a form, which the user can click. This can be used to make graphic-based buttons.
	File Field	Inserts a text box and button that lets the end user browse to a file on his or her hard drive, for uploading.
	Button	Inserts a Submit Button object (Dreamweaver MX default) on your form. You can also make this a Reset button, or set it to None.
	Label	Allows you to set an association of the text label for a field with the field itself.
	Fieldset	Inserts a Container tag for a logical group of form elements.

NOTE | Making Forms Function with CGI

Dreamweaver MX gives you complete control over the layout of your form and the creation of Form objects. This is great, but the truth is that there is a bit more to creating forms than just a pretty interface.

Forms are interactive elements that are driven by "scripts." This means that when the Submit or similar button is clicked, the information from the form is sent to your server or database, at which point the form is processed. This processing is more than HTML alone can handle. So, in order to process forms, you need to use some type of additional scripting beyond HTML. Although it is possible to process form data through JavaScript or even Java, most Web developers agree that the most foolproof way to program forms is through CGI, PHP, or ASP.

CGI stands for Common Gateway Interface. In essence, CGI is a protocol to send information to and from a Web server. CGI scripts can be written in a variety of programming languages, ranging from Perl to C to AppleScript. If that doesn't sound complicated enough for you, consider that different types of CGI scripts work with different Web servers, ranging from UNIX to Mac OS to Windows NT.

If you have a Web site, chances are very high that your Internet service provider or Web administrator has existing CGI scripts that you can use. Because there are so many variables to CGI, and it is outside the scope of Dreamweaver MX, it will be up to you to coordinate obtaining the scripts and implementing the processing of your forms.

Here are some online resources for CGI scripts:

FreeScripts.com
http://www.freescripts.com

The CGI Resource Index
http://www.cgi-resources.com/

Free Code
http://www.freecode.com/

—————————————**Working with Form Objects**

I.

In this exercise, you will get hands-on experience with each of the various form elements. You won't be adding any scripts because doing that would require another book, but you will get everything set up so that when you do want to add a CGI script, your pages will be ready!

1. Copy the contents of **chap_13** from the **H•O•T CD-ROM** to your hard drive, and press **F8** to define the site. If you need a refresher on this process, revisit Exercise 1 in Chapter 3, "*Site Control.*"

2. Open the **objects.html** file. It's just a blank page, but at least we put in a page title for you!

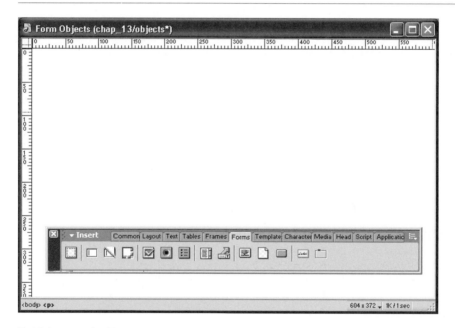

3. Make sure the **Forms** panel is visible.

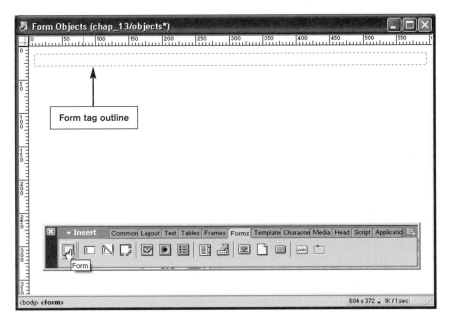

4. Click on the **Form** object in the **Forms** panel. This inserts the **<form>** tag into your document. You should see red dashed lines on your page. If you do not see them, select **View > Visual Aids > Invisible Elements**.

The visibility of the Form object doesn't matter in terms of its functionality. It's a preference of ours to turn its visibility on so we can ensure that it was added properly. You can work with it off or on; just know that it's there for the viewing if you feel more secure seeing it, as we do!

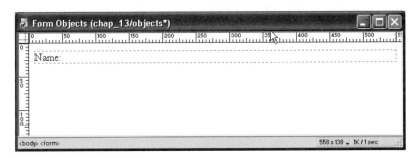

5. Position your cursor inside the red dashed lines, and type **Name:**. Press the **spacebar** once to create a single space.

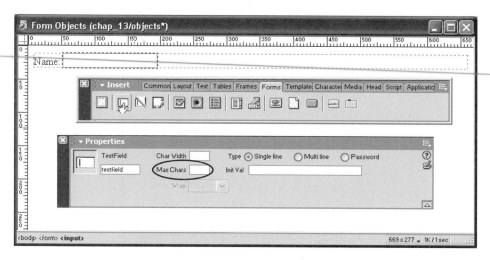

6. Click on the **Text Field** object in the **Forms** panel. This inserts a blank text field onto your page. With the text field highlighted, notice that the Property Inspector options change. Also notice that the **TextField** name is set at the default name, which is **textfield**. This needs to be changed to something that is more descriptive of the content that will be entered by the user.

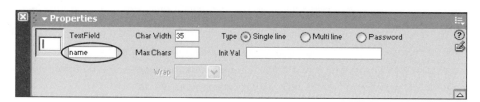

7. In the **TextField** field in the **Property Inspector**, replace the existing text with the word **name**. This gives a unique name to the text field. Enter **Char Width: 35**. This sets the length of the text field. It does not limit the amount of text that your user can enter, just how much will be visible in the browser. To limit the amount of text entered, you would enter a value for **Max Chars**. Because we don't want to limit the text, leave **Max Chars** blank.

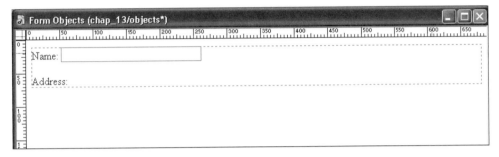

8. Click to the right of the text field in your document and press **Return/Enter**. Type **Address:** and press the **spacebar** to create one space.

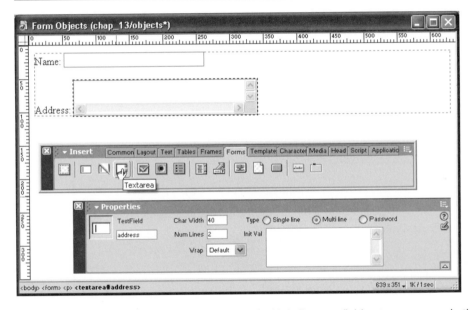

9. Click on the **Textarea** object. This inserts a multiple line text field onto your page. In the Property Inspector, enter the word **address** in the **TextField** field. Choose **Type: Multi line**, set **Num Lines: 2**, and set **Char Width: 40**. This Form object is great for larger areas of text when you don't know how much will be inserted.

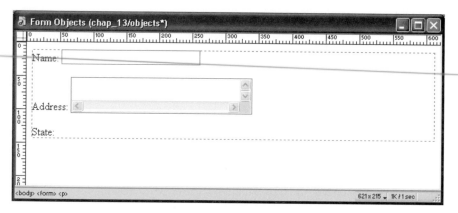

10. Click to the right of the **Multi line** text field in your document, and press **Return/Enter**. Type **State:** and insert one space by pressing the **spacebar**.

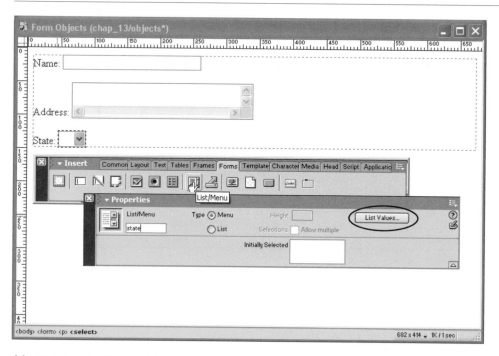

11. Click the **List/Menu** object. By default, this inserts a Menu object onto your form. In the **Property Inspector**, type **state** in the **List/Menu** field. Next, click the **List Values** button.

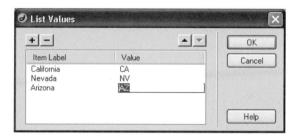

12. For the first **Item Label**, type **California**, and then press **Tab**. For the first **Value**, type **CA**, and then press **Tab**. Repeat this same process for **Nevada** and **Arizona**, using the information from the image above. This Form object will give you a pop-up menu displaying the information in the **Item Label** column. The information in the **Value** column is what a CGI or JavaScript program would process with the Form. Click **OK**.

13. In the **Property Inspector**, select **Initially Selected: California**. This determines what menu item is visible before the user clicks on the pop-up menu.

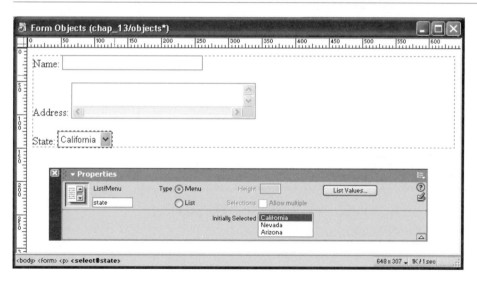

14. Click to the right of the **State** pop-up menu, and press **Return/Enter**.

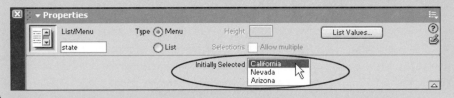

TIP | Initially Selected Values in Menus

Sometimes, when you are creating menus, you would like a default value to appear in the menu. For example, if you were building a menu with a list of all U.S. states, you might want to have California appear in the menu automatically. Selecting the value from the Initially Selected option in the Property Inspector can do this. The value you select here appears as the default value for the menu.

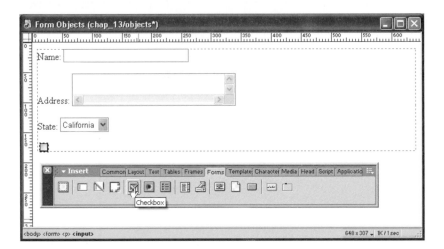

15. Click the **Checkbox** object. This inserts a checkbox onto your page.

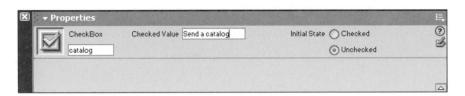

16. In the **Property Inspector**, name the checkbox **catalog**. For the **Checked Value**, type **Send a catalog**. The Checked Value information will appear next to the checkbox name when a CGI script processes the form. This information is hidden from your end user, but it is useful to a programmer who is setting up the CGI because it tells him or her what the checkbox relates to.

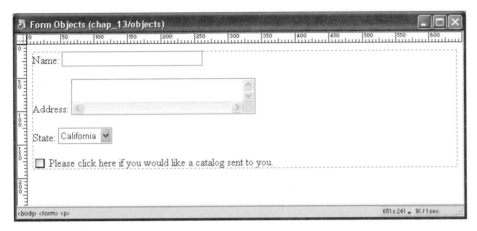

17. Click to the right of the checkbox and type **Please click here if you would like a catalog sent to you**. This will help end users understand what information they are requesting by checking this box. Press **Return/Enter**.

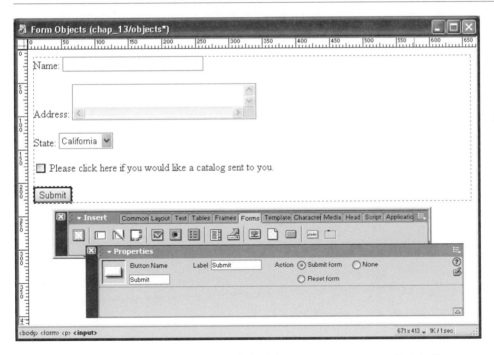

18. Click the **Button** object. This inserts a Submit button on your page, which is Dreamweaver MX's default button type. Because you need to have a button to submit the form, leave the options at their default values.

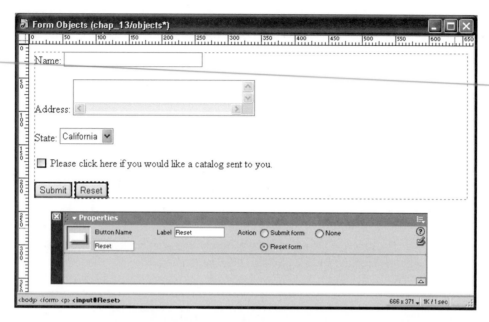

19. Click to the right of the **Submit** button. Click the **Button** object again. This inserts another Submit button on your page. In the **Property Inspector**, change the **Action** to **Reset form**. This creates a button that clears the form, just in case your end user makes a mistake and wants to start over. Change the **Button Name** to **Reset**.

20. Save your file. Press **F12** to preview your form in a browser. Remember, the **Submit** button will not work because you did not attach any CGI scripts.

21. Return to Dreamweaver MX. **Save** and **close** the document.

As you have just seen, the purpose of this exercise was to get you comfortable inserting different Form objects and modifying some of their properties. Remember, to make a form perform its functions, you would need to attach a CGI or other scripting program to it.

2. _____Creating a Form

This exercise is designed to help you become more familiar with creating a layout for your forms. Forms can combine other HTML elements such as background images and tables. By the end of this exercise, you should be comfortable combining your new form-creation skills with your existing Web-layout skills.

1. Open the **form.html** file. Notice that it already contains a background image, a graphic, and a table. Click your cursor in the bottom cell of the table.

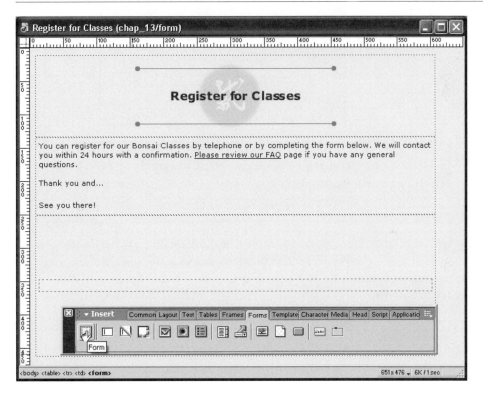

2. Click on the **Form** object in the **Forms** panel. Red dashes should appear in the table cell, indicating that you have inserted a **<form>** tag. If you don't see these red dashes, select **View > Visual Aids > Invisible Elements**.

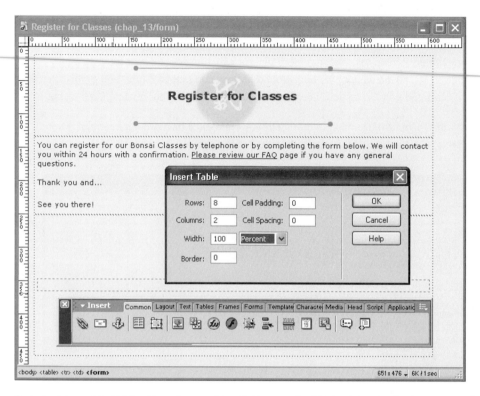

3. Select **Insert > Table**. (If you're used to clicking on the Table object in the **Insert** panel, you would need to switch it back to **Common**. For convenience's sake, just use the Insert menu right now.) Change the settings to **Rows: 8, Cell Padding: 0, Columns: 2, Cell Spacing: 0, Width: 100 Percent**, and **Border: 0**. Click **OK**.

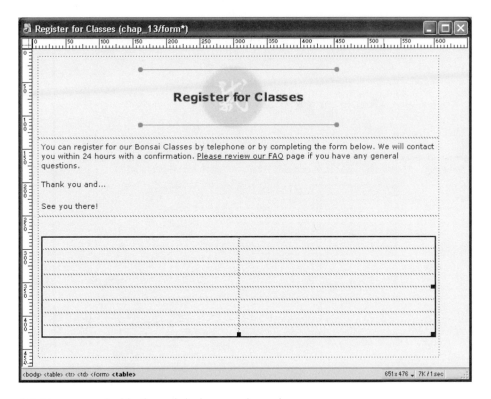

A table appears inside the red dashes, as shown here.

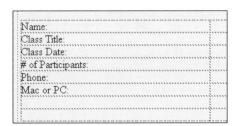

4. Click inside the first cell in column 1 and type **Name:**. Click inside the second cell in column 1 and type **Class Title:**. Click inside the third cell in column 1 and type **Class Date:**. Click inside the fourth cell in column 1 and type **# of Participants:**. Click inside the fifth cell in column 1 and type **Phone:**. Finally, click inside the sixth cell in column 1 and type **Mac or PC:**.

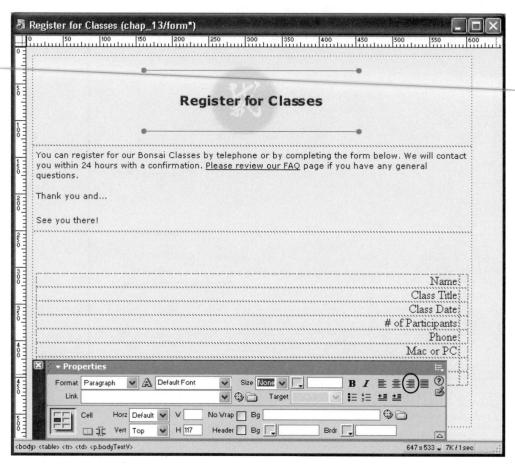

5. Click and drag to select all the cells in column 1. Then click the **Align Right** button in the **Property Inspector**.

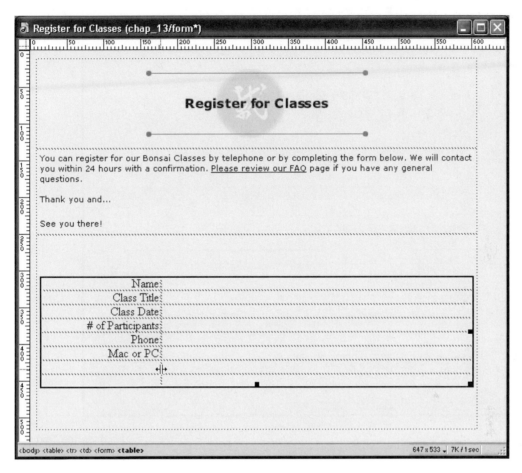

6. Click and drag the middle divider between the two columns to move it over to the left.

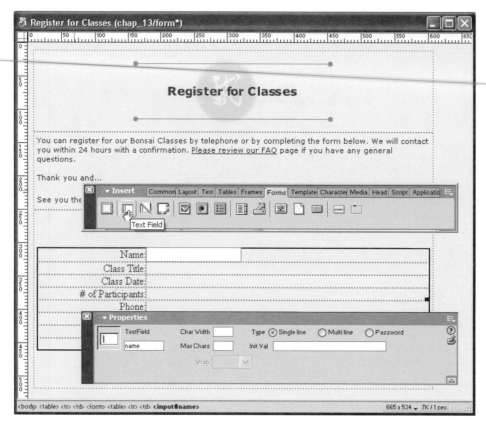

7. Next, you'll add some entry fields to the **form**. Click inside column 2, row 1, and choose the **Text Field** object in the **Insert** panel. In the **Property Inspector**, name the **TextField: name**.

8. Repeat this same process for the next five cells in column 2. Make sure you give each text field a unique name that describes the associated column.

WARNING | Strange Table Behavior

As you work with forms and tables in Dreamweaver MX, you might notice that sometimes it looks as though your Form objects are jumping out of their cells. Don't worry; they really haven't moved at all. This is just a little visual glitch in Dreamweaver MX. You can get them back to their correct places by simply clicking outside the table.

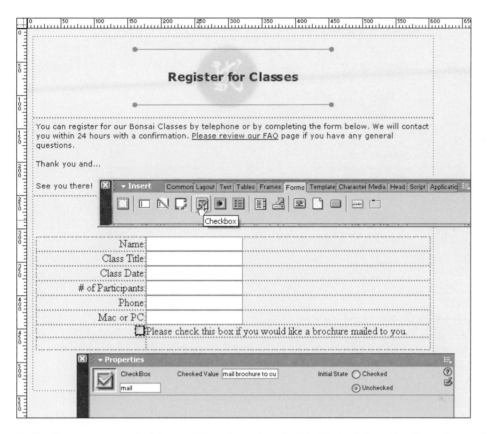

9. Position your cursor inside row 7 in column 1 and click. Next, click on the **Checkbox** object in the **Insert** panel. In the **Property Inspector**, change the **CheckBox Name** to **mail** and the **Checked Value** to **mail brochure to customer**. Then, click to the right of the checkbox, row 7 in column 2, and type **Please check this box if you would like a brochure mailed to you.**

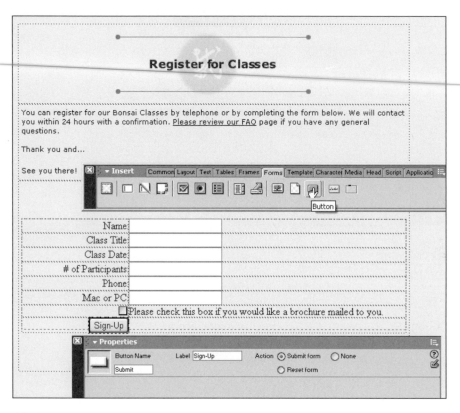

10. Click in row 8 in column 1, then click the **Button** object in the **Insert** panel. In the **Property Inspector**, change the **Label** to **Sign-Up**. The **Action** should be set to **Submit form**.

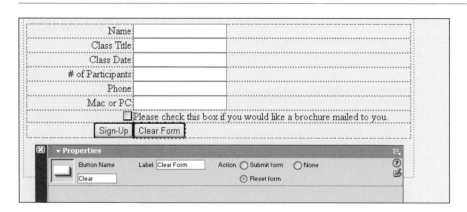

11. Click in row 8 in column 2, then click the **Button** object in the **Insert** panel again. In the **Property Inspector**, change the **Action** to **Reset form**, the **Label** to **Clear Form**, and the **Name** to **Clear**.

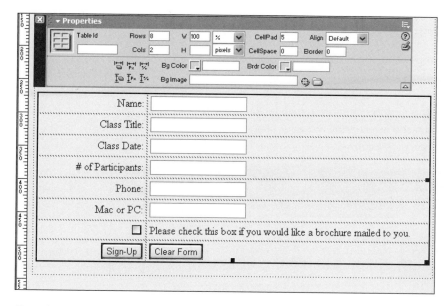

For a finishing touch, adjust the Table's padding to 5 in the Property Inspector, and voila! You have done it! You've just designed a custom-formatted form using form and table elements.

12. Save and **close** this file; you won't be needing it again.

3. —————————Creating a Jump Menu

Dreamweaver MX's **jump menu** object combines a forms element for lists and a JavaScript behavior that causes the menu to go to its target without the use of a Go button. Adding this specialized kind of form can be very useful when you have a small amount of screen real estate in which to place a lot of navigation choices. This exercise shows you how to use Dreamweaver MX to create a jump menu on your page. The jump menu works really well as a navigation tool within framesets, which is what you'll get to try in this hands-on exercise.

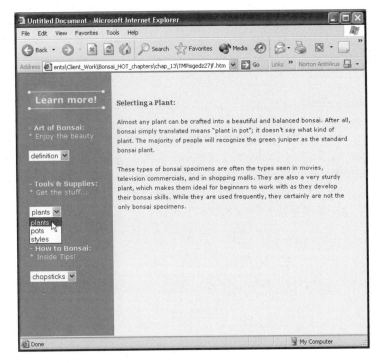

Here's a look at the jump menu you will learn to build in this exercise. The jump menu *is a special kind of Dreamweaver MX object that combines a form element with JavaScript. It allows the visitor to a page to select a choice and have that choice load without having to first click a Go button.*

1. Open the **frameset_done.html** file located inside the **chap_13** folder. Press **F12** to pre-view and play with the file in the browser. When you are finished exploring, close the file.

2. Open the **frameset.html** file located inside the **chap_13** folder. This is a frameset that we have created for you. You will add the three jump menus to this page to match the result in the opening image.

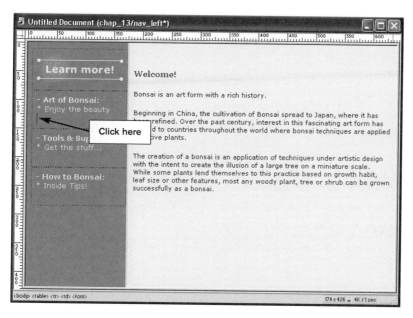

3. Click beneath **Enjoy the beauty** in the left frame. Select **Insert > Form Objects > Jump Menu**. This opens the **Insert Jump Menu** window. As an alternative, you could have clicked on the **Jump Menu** object in the **Forms** panel.

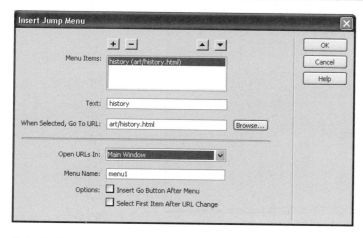

4. In the **Text** field, type **history**. This option sets the actual text that appears in the menu when the user clicks on it.

5. Click on the **Browse** button next to the **When Selected, Go To URL** field. This lets you browse to the HTML file you want to jump to when this menu item is selected.

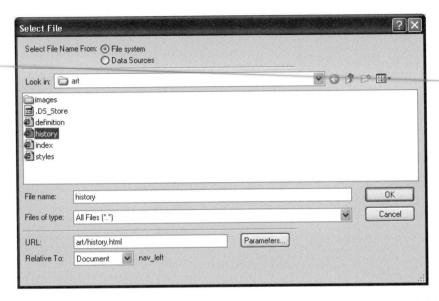

6. Navigate to **history.html** file located inside the **art** folder inside the **chap_13** folder. Select it and click **OK**.

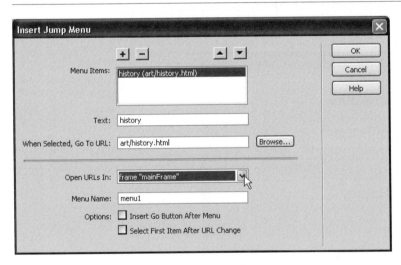

7. Click on the pop-up menu next to the **Open URLs In** option and select **frame "mainFrame"**. This option determines what frame the Web page will load into.

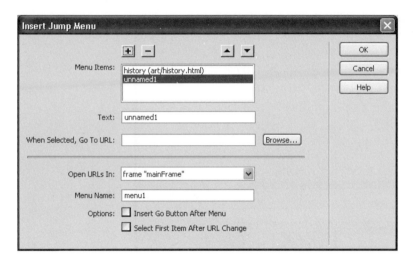

8. Click on the **plus** button at the top of the dialog box to add another item to your jump menu. This interface is very similar to the Insert Navigation Bar dialog box you learned about in Chapter 10, "*Rollovers*." It's nice to see the continuity in the interface; you gotta love it!

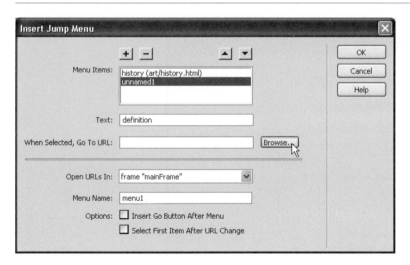

9. Enter **definition** for the **Text** field. Click on the **Browse** button next to the **When Selected, Go To URL** option.

10. Browse to the **definition.html** file located inside the **art** folder inside the **chap_13** folder. Select it and click **OK**.

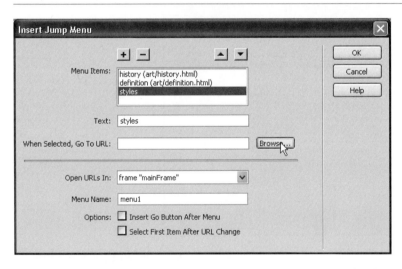

11. Click on the **plus** button at the top of the dialog box. Enter **styles** for the **Text** field. Click on the **Browse** button.

12. Browse to the **styles.html** file from the art folder inside **chap_13** folder. Select it and click **OK**.

13. You've just finished setting up your jump menu. Click **OK**. Notice how Dreamweaver MX automatically added the **<form>** tag. Nice.

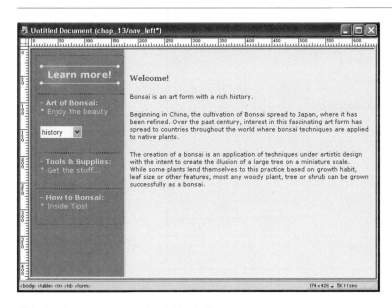

This is what your page should look like now.

14. Save your work. Press **F12** to preview your page in the browser.

15. Click on the menu and select **definition**. This will jump you to the **definition.html** page. You can click on the other options as well to test them.

16. Now, return to Dreamweaver MX and add two more jump menus.

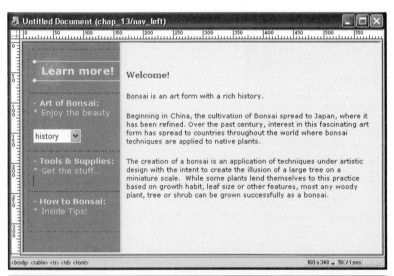

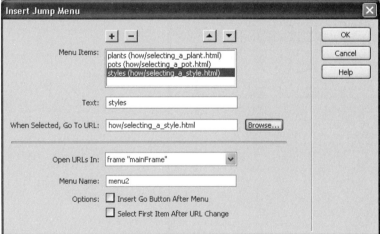

17. Click beneath **Get the stuff** and add a jump menu containing menu items for **plants**, **pots**, and **styles**. Link them to their respective pages found in the **how** folder inside the **chap_13** folder. Make sure you set **Open URLs In** to **frame "mainFrame"** for each.

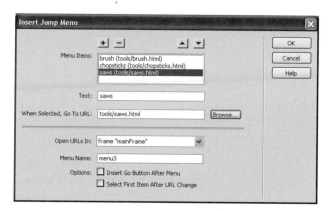

18. Click beneath **Inside Tips!** and add the last jump menu containing menu items for **brush**, **chopsticks**, and **saws**. Link them to their respective pages found in the **tools** folder inside the **chap_13** folder. Make sure you set **Open URLs In** to **frame "mainFrame"** for each.

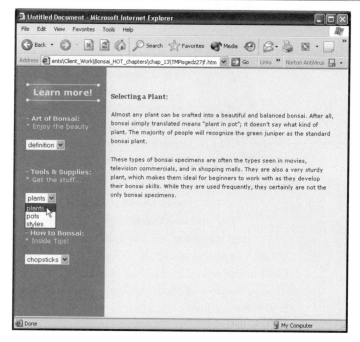

19. Save your work. Press **F12** to preview and play with your final result in the browser. Pretty cool navigation system!

20. Return to Dreamweaver MX and **close** the document.

Phew! Another chapter under your belt. Move to the next chapter if you feel ready.

14.

Behaviors

What is a Behavior | Checking for Browser |
| Setting Status Bar Text | Setting Text Field Text |
| Opening a New Browser Window | Validating Forms |
| Downloading and Installing Dreamweaver MX Extensions |

chap_14
—————————————————
Dreamweaver MX
H•O•T CD-ROM

Dreamweaver MX **behaviors** are prebuilt scripts written in JavaScript that extend HTML to do things that it can't do on its own. Dreamweaver MX ships with a variety of behaviors that allow you to do all kinds of cool things, such as open a browser in a smaller window or detect the version of your end-user's browser.

The **Macromedia Extension Manager** is a program that lets you easily install and remove extensions from Dreamweaver MX. In previous versions of Dreamweaver, you had to download and install the Extension Manager application yourself. In Dreamweaver MX, the Extension Manager is preinstalled for you and ready to be used.

This chapter shows you how to use some of the behaviors that ship with Dreamweaver MX right out of the box. You'll also learn how to download additional behaviors from Macromedia Exchange, a free online service bureau that Macromedia provides, which houses hundreds of additional Dreamweaver MX behaviors that don't ship with the program!

I. ‎‎‎‎‎‎‎‎‎‎‎‎Creating a Check Browser Behavior

As you start adding different features and technologies to your site, such as DHTML and JavaScript, you might want to make sure that the people viewing your pages are using a browser that can see these features (4.0 browsers and later). This exercise shows you how to use the **Check Browser** behavior to determine which browser and version the user has and then redirect the user to another page. This technique is very useful if you want to create different versions of your site: one that works with 4.0 or later browsers and one that works with earlier browsers. Even though fewer 3.0 browsers are in use today, knowing how to set up this behavior is still a good thing.

Note: In order to check the success of this exercise, you must have either Netscape Navigator 3.0+ and 4.0+ or Internet Explorer 3.0+ and 4.0+ installed on your computer. If you don't have both versions of one of these browsers and you wish to complete this exercise, please install both of these browser versions before continuing. We've included copies of Netscape Navigator and Internet Explorer 3.0 and 4.0 on the Dreamweaver MX **H•O•T CD-ROM** in the Software/Browsers folder. **Tip:** Windows users should install these browsers into separate directories to avoid accidentally overwriting other previously installed browsers.

1. Copy the **chap_14** folder from the **H•O•T CD-ROM** to your hard drive. Define your site for Chapter 14. If you need a refresher, visit Exercise 1 in Chapter 3, "*Site Control*." Browse to **checkbrowser.html** and open it. This file contains some text in a table.

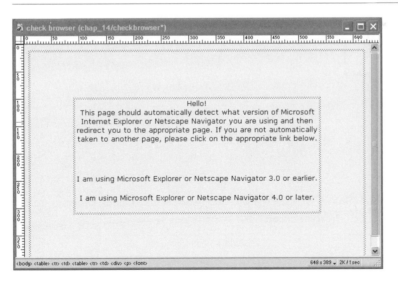

This is what checkbrowser.html *looks like at the beginning of this exercise. It's a page with a table that has text in it. You'll add the Check Browser behavior to it, which will determine the user's browser and version and then redirect the user to another page.*

2. Click on the **<body>** tag in the **Tag Selector** at the bottom of the document window. If you can't see the **<body>** tag in the Tag Selector, simply click anywhere inside the document window. You want to attach the **Check Browser** behavior to the **<body>** tag of the document so that the behavior can run when the page is first loaded.

3. In the **Behaviors** panel (**Shift+F3**), click the **plus** sign and choose **Check Browser** from the pop-up menu. This opens the Check Browser dialog box.

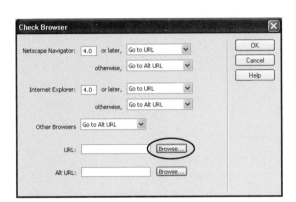

4. Click **Browse** near the bottom next to the **URL** field. Browse to **version4.html** in the **chap_14** folder and click **OK**. This will be the page your end users will see if they are using Netscape or Explorer 4.0 or later. Don't click OK just yet.

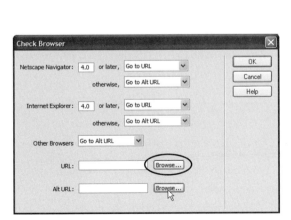

5. Click **Browse** at the bottom next to the **Alt URL** field. Browse to **version3.html** in the **chap_14** folder and click **OK**. The Alt URL is the page your end users will see if they are using something other than Netscape or Explorer 4.0 (e.g., Netscape 3.0, Explorer 2.0, etc.).

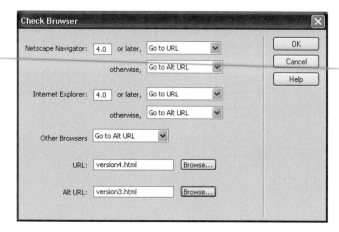

This is what your Check Browser dialog box should look like at this point.

6. Click **OK** to accept these settings. You won't detect any visual changes to your page, but a whole bunch of complex JavaScript was just added to it.

7. Notice that the **Check Browser** behavior now appears in the **Behaviors** panel. Also, notice that its event is automatically set to **onLoad**. This means that when the Web page is loaded, it will perform the Check Browser behavior. Cool!

TIP | Events and Actions

Each behavior has two components: the **event** and the **action**. Events are defined by a user's mouse state (such as onClick) or a browser's load state (such as onLoad). Actions, on the other hand, are blocks of prewritten JavaScript that are executed when the event occurs. In the context of a rollover, when the event is completed (the user's mouse moves over the graphic), the action takes place (one image is swapped with another). Although the terms "event" and "action" might sound like Greek to you right now, once you see how easy behaviors are to use, you'll find the learning curve to be remarkably low.

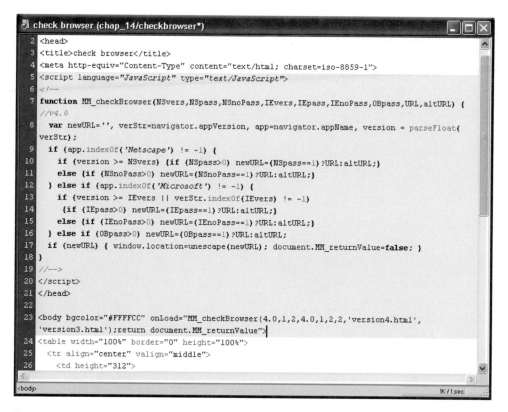

```
 2  <head>
 3  <title>check browser</title>
 4  <meta http-equiv="Content-Type" content="text/html; charset=iso-8859-1">
 5  <script language="JavaScript" type="text/JavaScript">
 6  <!--
 7  function MM_checkBrowser(NSvers,NSpass,NSnoPass,IEvers,IEpass,IEnoPass,OBpass,URL,altURL) {
    //v4.0
 8    var newURL='', verStr=navigator.appVersion, app=navigator.appName, version = parseFloat(
    verStr);
 9    if (app.indexOf('Netscape') != -1) {
10      if (version >= NSvers) {if (NSpass>0) newURL=(NSpass==1)?URL:altURL;}
11      else {if (NSnoPass>0) newURL=(NSnoPass==1)?URL:altURL;}
12    } else if (app.indexOf('Microsoft') != -1) {
13      if (version >= IEvers || verStr.indexOf(IEvers) != -1)
14        {if (IEpass>0) newURL=(IEpass==1)?URL:altURL;}
15      else {if (IEnoPass>0) newURL=(IEnoPass==1)?URL:altURL;}
16    } else if (OBpass>0) newURL=(OBpass==1)?URL:altURL;
17    if (newURL) { window.location=unescape(newURL); document.MM_returnValue=false; }
18  }
19  //-->
20  </script>
21  </head>
22
23  <body bgcolor="#FFFFCC" onLoad="MM_checkBrowser(4.0,1,2,4.0,1,2,2,'version4.html',
    'version3.html');return document.MM_returnValue">
24  <table width="100%" border="0" height="100%">
25    <tr align="center" valign="middle">
26      <td height="312">
```

8. Click the **Show Code View** button to open the Code window. Notice all the JavaScript that was added to your page. Could you imagine having to create all of that code from scratch? Part of the power of behaviors is that they shield you from such tedious tasks. Click the **Show Design View** button to return to the Design view.

9. Save the changes you made to **checkbrowser.html** and close the file.

Now that you've added the Check Browser behavior to your page, you're ready to check your work by opening this page in both the version 3 and version 4 browsers. Will the correct version load? Stay tuned.

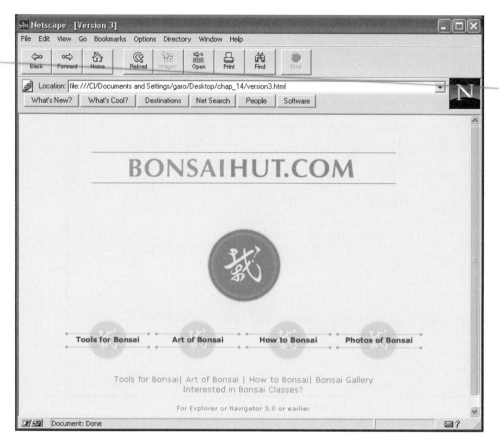

10. Launch Navigator 3.0+. Select **File > Open File**. Browse to the **chap_14** folder, select **checkbrowser.html**, and click **Open**. Notice that you are immediately taken to **version3.html**. Exit the browser.

WARNING | JavaScript Potential Problem

There's a potential problem with using this type of browser detection. Because this detection is constructed with JavaScript, and users can disable JavaScript in their browser preferences, this script may not always work properly. As a safeguard against this, you'll finish this exercise by learning how to give the user an option to load the appropriate page by clicking a link. This will prevent anyone from being locked out of your site, which is a very good thing.

11. Launch Explorer 4.0 (shown above) or Navigator 4.0+. Select **File > Open > Page in Navigator** (Mac) or **File > Open Page** (Windows). Browse to the **chap_14** folder, select **checkbrowser.html**, and click **Open**. Notice that you are immediately taken to **version4.html**. Exit the browser and return to Dreamweaver MX.

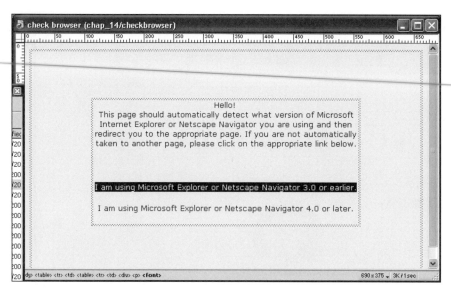

12. In the Dreamweaver MX **checkbrowser.html** document, click and drag to select the words **I am using Microsoft Explorer or Netscape Navigator 3.0 or earlier**. Now you'll use the Property Inspector to make this text into a hyperlink to **version3.html**.

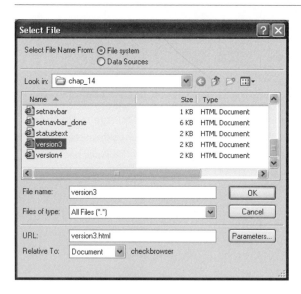

13. In the **Property Inspector**, click the **Browse for File** folder icon to the right of the **Link** field. Browse to **version3.html** and click **OK**.

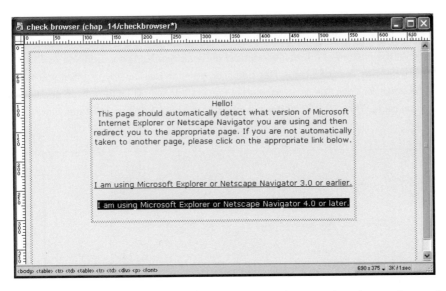

14. In the **checkbrowser.html** document, click and drag to select the text **I am using Microsoft Explorer or Netscape Navigator 4.0 or later**.

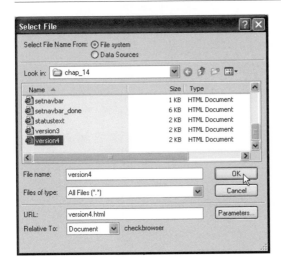

15. In the **Property Inspector**, click the **Browse for File** folder icon again. This time, browse to **version4.html**. Click **OK**.

Setting up these two links is a good idea, because if users don't have JavaScript turned on, they will still have a way to get into the site.

16. Save and **close** this file. You won't be working with it anymore.

2. ———————————Creating a Set Text of Status Bar Behavior

The **status bar** is located at the bottom of a browser window and can display text in addition to what is on the Web page. Using the **Set Text of Status Bar** behavior, you can display any text that you want in the status bar of the browser window. This is often used in conjunction with links to provide additional detail about the destination page. This exercise shows you how to add the Set Text of Status Bar behavior to a page.

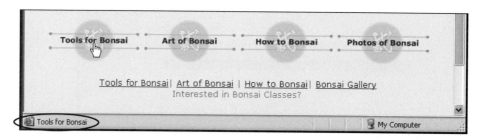

This is what the status text looks like in a browser status bar.

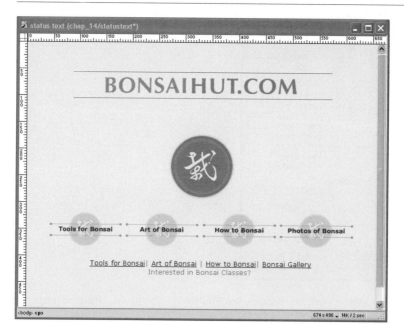

1. Open **statustext.html** from the **chap_14** folder. You are going to add the Set Text of Status Bar behavior to several of the links on this page to provide additional feedback to the user.

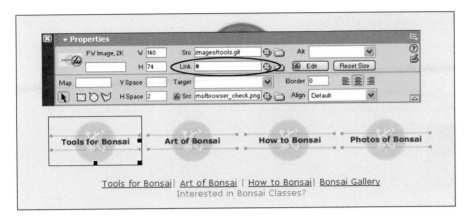

2. Click the **Tools for Bonsai** (tools.gif) image to select it. In the **Property Inspector**, notice that this image has a hash mark (**#**) in the **Link** field. This is referred to as a "nowhere" link. It's a link that goes, well, nowhere. The only reason you need it is that certain behaviors (such as the one you're about to add) must be attached to links.

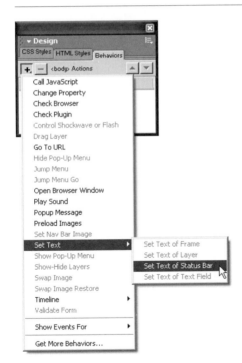

3. With the image still selected, in the **Behaviors** panel, click the **plus** sign to access the pop-up menu, and choose **Set Text > Set Text of Status Bar**. This opens the **Set Text of Status Bar** dialog box.

4. Enter **Message: Tools for Bonsai**. Click **OK**.

5. Notice that the **Set Text of Status Bar** behavior now appears in the **Behaviors** panel with the **onMouseOver** event.

6. Repeat this process for each of the other buttons, adding a short description for each one.

7. When you're finished, press **F12** to preview your page in a browser. Move your mouse over any of the four images and look at the text that is displayed in the browser window's status bar.

8. Return to Dreamweaver MX and **save** your changes and **close** this file. You won't need it any longer.

3. ────────**Creating a Set Text of Text Field Behavior**

Earlier, in Chapter 13, "*Forms*," you learned how to create forms. This exercise shows you how to create preset content that will fill specific form fields as the user interacts with your form. It uses the Set Text feature of the Text Field behavior.

1. Open **register_done.html**. This is what your file will look like when you finish this exercise. Press **F12** to preview this in a browser.

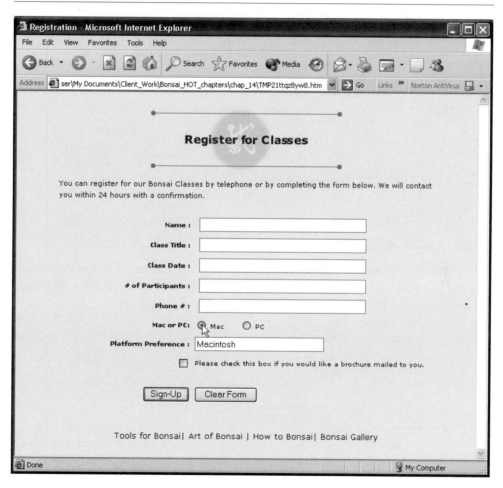

2. Click the **Mac** or **PC** radio button. Notice that text automatically appears in the **Platform Preference** text field. This effect was created using the Set Text behavior, which ships with Dreamweaver MX. Close this file for now. You will create this effect in the steps that follow.

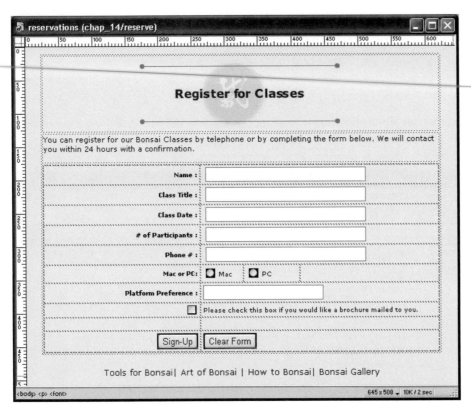

3. Return to Dreamweaver MX and open **register.html**, from the **chap_14** folder. This file consists of a form that we created for you. You will learn how to use the Set Text of Text Field behavior to dynamically update this form as the user interacts with it.

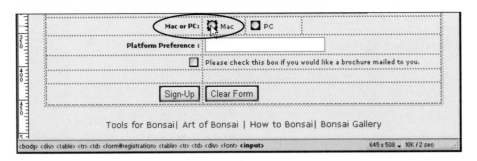

4. Click the radio button next to **Mac**. You are going to apply the Set Text of Text Field behavior to this form element so that the Platform Preference text field is automatically updated when a user selects this button in the browser.

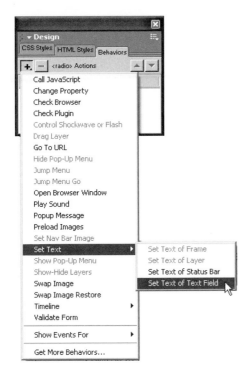

5. From the **Behaviors** panel, click the **plus** sign and choose **Set Text > Set Text of Text Field** from the pop-up menu. This opens the Set Text of Text Field dialog box.

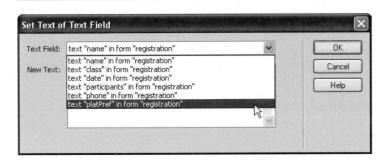

6. Click the **Text Field** pop-up menu at the top and choose **text "platPref" in form "registration"**. Don't click OK just yet.

The pop-up menu lists each of the form objects with their newly assigned names. As you can see, it's a good idea to use descriptive names that relate to the information being requested so they can easily be found and identified in this dialog box. The Text Field option determines which text field in the Registration form will automatically display the text.

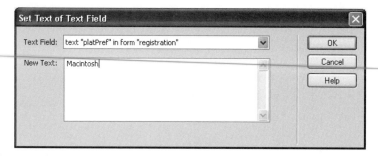

7. Enter **Macintosh** in the **New Text** field. This will replace any text that is in the Platform Preference text field when the user clicks the Mac button. Click **OK**, and you're ready to set up the next button.

8. Click the radio button next to **PC**.

9. From the **Behaviors** panel, click the **plus** sign and choose **Set Text > Set Text of Text Field** from the pop-up menu. This opens the Set Text of Text Field dialog box.

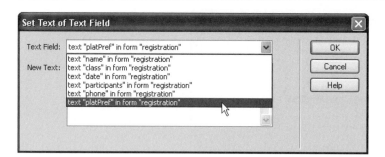

10. Click the **Text Field** pop-up menu at the top and choose **text "platPref" in form "registration"**. Don't click OK just yet.

11. Enter **Personal Computer** in the **New Text** field. This will replace any text that is in the Platform Preference text field of the form when the user clicks the PC button. Click **OK**.

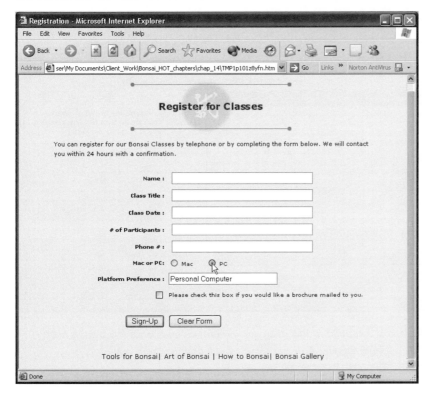

12. Press **F12** to preview this page in your primary browser. Click each of the radio buttons and watch the Platform Preference text field change automatically.

13. Return to Dreamweaver MX. **Save** and **close** this file. You will not need it for the remainder of the book.

Opening a New Browser Window

There are going to be times when you just can't cram everything onto a single Web page. An option that many Web developers use is to open additional yet related information in another window. In this next exercise, you will open a new browser window to display information that wouldn't fit comfortably on a single page.

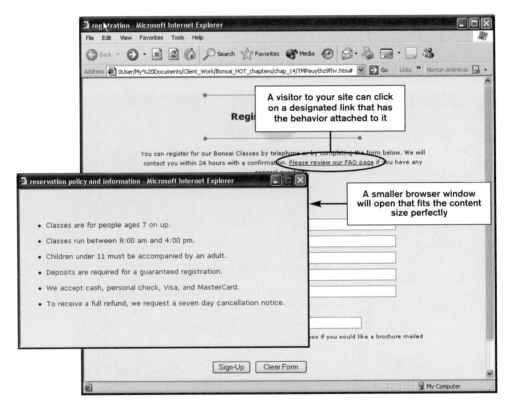

This is the example you will build in this exercise. When you click on a link on the main browser page, this second, smaller browser window will open without any of its own navigation bars.

1. Open **newwindow.html**, from the **chap_14** folder.

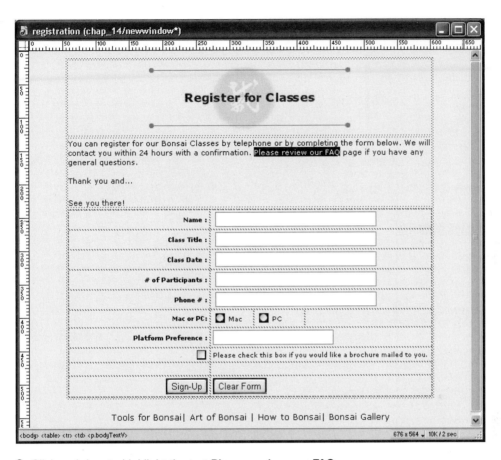

2. Click and drag to highlight the text **Please review our FAQ**.

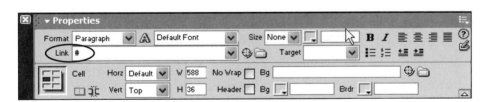

3. In the **Property Inspector**, enter a **#** in the **Link** field and press **Enter**. You remember why you should do this from Exercise 2, right?

4. From the **Behaviors** panel, click the **plus** sign and choose **Open Browser Window** from the pop-up menu. This opens the Open Browser Window dialog box.

5. Click **Browse** and browse to **FAQ.html**. Click **OK**. This is the HTML file that will be displayed in your new window. The link can be an internal or external link.

Next, you'll specify the size of your new browser window.

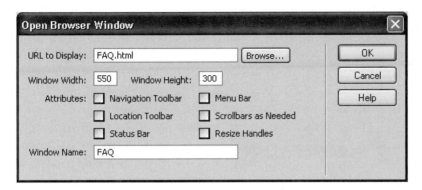

6. Back in the **Open Browser Window** dialog box, enter **Window Width: 550** and **Window Height: 300**. This specifies the pixel size of your window when it opens. At the bottom of the window, type **FAQ** in the **Window Name** field. Click **OK**.

We specified 550 x 300 pixels because those dimensions fit the contents of FAQ.html, the page you are going to display in the second browser window. On other projects, you could specify any size that's appropriate to the content of your second window.

This is what the Behaviors panel should look like now.

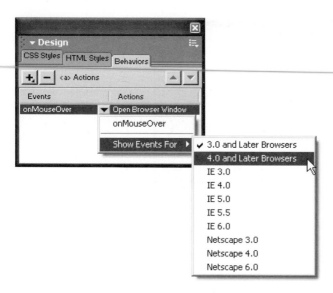

7. Click on the small arrow to the right of the **Events** column and make sure that **Show Events For** option is set to **4.0 and Later Browsers**. This displays the events that are allowed for 4.0 and later browsers. **Note:** JavaScript is supported differently by different browsers. You can see a detailed list of what behaviors work in the Macromedia Dreamweaver MX manual.

8. Click on the small arrow again and select **onClick** as the event. This option determines what the user must do before the new browser window will open. The **onClick** event means that the user must click on the link in order for the new window to open.

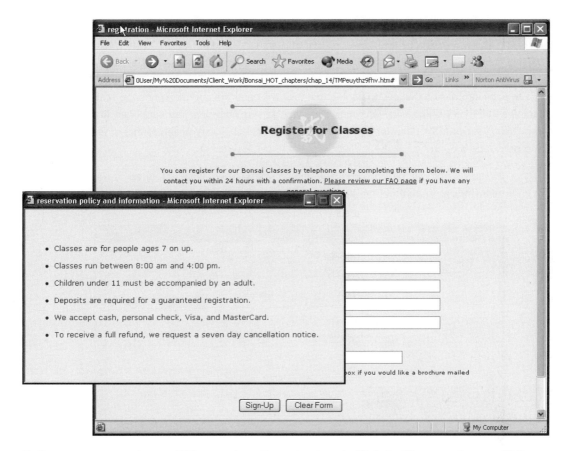

9. Save your page and press **F12** to preview all your hard work. Click the **Please review our FAQ page** link at the top of the page. Voila! A new browser window opens, displaying **FAQ.html** in a window set to 550 x 300 pixels.

10. Return to Dreamweaver MX and **save** the file. Leave it open for the next exercise.

5.————————**Validating Forms with Behaviors**

Now that you have learned how to create forms and lay them out with tables, it's a good time to show you how to validate the information being typed into the form. What does that mean? Giving users a place to enter information doesn't guarantee that they will enter the information correctly. It also doesn't guarantee that they will enter any information at all. What's a Web designer supposed to do? Well, by using Dreamweaver MX's behaviors, you can validate, or check, the type and format of the information being provided.

1. The file from the previous exercise should still be open. If it's not, open **newwindow_final.html** from the **chap_14** folder.

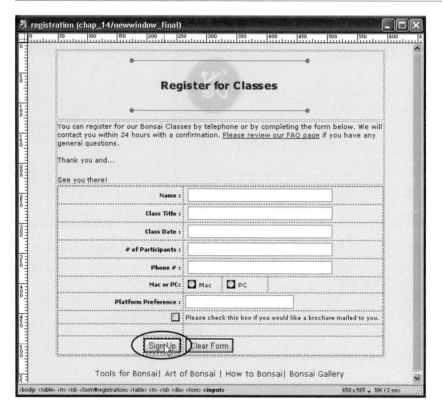

2. Click to select the **Sign-Up** button. By attaching the Validate Form behavior to this button, you can verify that the required information has been entered before a CGI script processes the form.

3. From the **Behaviors** panel, click the **plus** sign and select **Validate Form** from the pop-up menu. This opens the Validate Form dialog box.

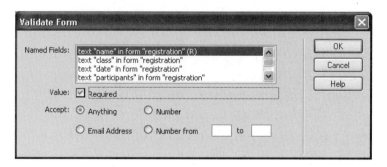

4. Make sure that the **"name" in form "registration"** option is highlighted. Click the **Required** check-box to make this field a required entry. A small (R) appears at the end when you do this. This is really important information, and you want to make sure that people don't forget to enter something. **Note:** Make sure the correct field is highlighted in the Validate Form dialog box before you click the Required checkbox. Don't click OK yet!

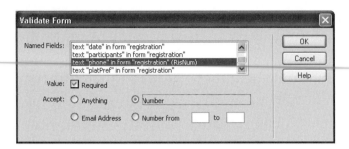

5. Highlight the **"phone" in form "registration"** option. Click the **Required** checkbox to make this a required entry. Click the **Number** radio button to set Number as the accepted entry. As you can see, this option can be set to Anything, Email Address, Number, or a range of numbers, depending on your forms requirement. Click **OK**.

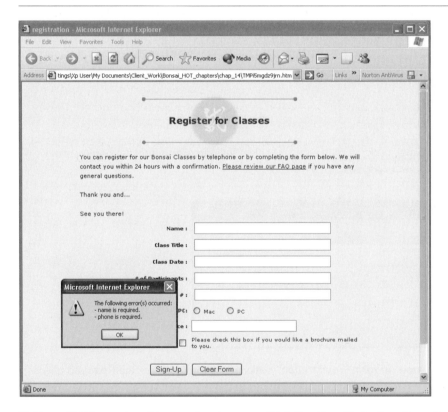

6. Press **F12** to preview this page in a browser. Click the **Sign-Up** button. You will get a JavaScript warning indicating that some fields are required. Click **OK**.

7. Return to Dreamweaver MX, and **save** and **close** this file.

The Macromedia Exchange for Dreamweaver

http://www.macromedia.com/exchange/dreamweaver/

Macromedia has set up a section of its Web site, designed to be a portal for Dreamweaver MX users, called the **Macromedia Exchange for Dreamweaver**. There you'll find hundreds of free extensions written by third-party users and developers for Dreamweaver MX (and previous versions of Dreamweaver) that can help you build new features into your Web site. Many of these are advanced features that normally would require the skills of a programmer to create. For example, some of these behaviors can give you the ability to perform complex browser detection, password-protect areas of your site, connect to back-end databases, etc.

The Macromedia site is not just for developers but for any Dreamweaver MX user who wants to take Dreamweaver MX to the next level. If you are a developer, this is a great place to learn how to write your own behaviors that take advantage of the Dreamweaver MX DOM (**D**ocument **O**bject **M**odel). The DOM for Dreamweaver MX is a specification that enables increased levels of extensibility not afforded by standard HTML and JavaScript.

The Macromedia Exchange for Dreamweaver MX is also where you can download a free copy of the **Macromedia Extension Manager**. This indispensable add-on for Dreamweaver MX lets you easily (and painlessly) download, install, and manage your extensions, which is a catch-all phrase for any behavior, command, or object. Installing the Extension Manager is recommended for any serious Dreamweaver MX user because it makes it easy for you to add new features to the program. Luckily, in Dreamweaver MX, the Extension Manager is preinstalled.

6. _____Downloading from Macromedia Exchange

Macromedia Exchange for Dreamweaver MX offers a gold mine of behaviors in the form of widgets and add-ons to help you add life to your Web pages. In this exercise, you will learn how to download one of these cool extensions from the Exchange and install it using the Extension Manager.

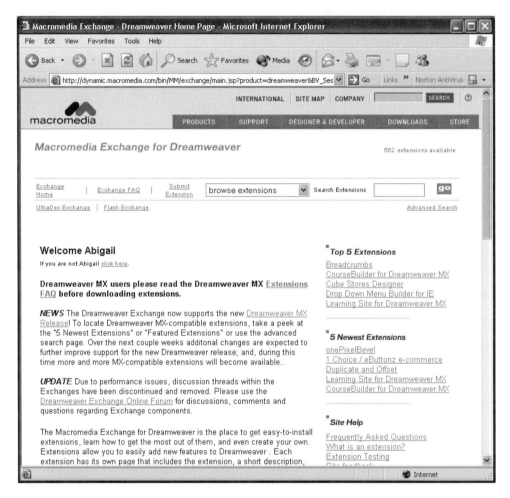

1. Open a Web browser and go to **http://www.macromedia.com/exchange/dreamweaver/**. This takes you to the Macromedia Exchange for Dreamweaver MX Web site. If you have not created an account yet (it's free), you will need to do so before downloading any of the extensions. If this is the case, click **Login** and follow the instructions for setting up an account before proceeding with the exercise.

NOTE | Behaviors, Commands, and Objects

As you start downloading extensions from the Exchange and other Web sites, you'll need to know more about where to find your installed behaviors, commands, and/or objects. These are accessed from different places in the Dreamweaver MX interface. Behaviors are accessed from the Behaviors panel, commands are accessed from the Commands menu, and Objects are accessed from the Insert panel.

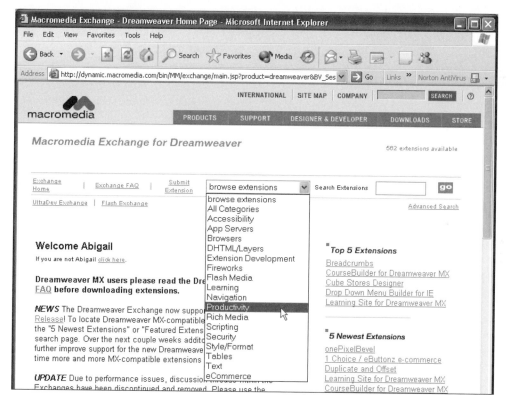

2. Once you have your own account, click on the pop-up menu at the top of the screen. As you can see, the extensions have been neatly organized into various groups for easy access. Select **Productivity**. This takes you to a page with extensions that relate directly to productivity.

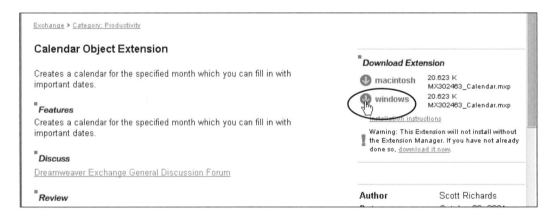

Auto Backup	Public Domain Ltd	Feb 7, 2001	1.0.5	No rating	ⓜ		9628
AutoResizable OpenWindow	Carlos Zumbado	Feb 7, 2001	1.2	1/5	ⓜ		28824
AutoTitle Untitled Documents	Paul Madar	Jul 3, 2000	1.0	4/5	ⓜ		23256
Borderless Frame	Massimo Foti	May 4, 2000	2.01	4/5	ⓜ		31272
CFML Form Insert Panel tab	Neil Clark	Jun 17, 2002	1.0.5	No rating	ⓜ		277
CN Show PopUp Window	Chris Acton	Dec 14, 2000	1.0.2	4/5	Basic	20037
Calculate Form	Jaro von Flocken	May 25, 2000	3.0.1	3/5	Basic	28991
Calendar Object	Scott Richards	Oct 22, 2001	2.0.1	3/5	ⓜ		36677
ChromelessWin	Public Domain Ltd	Feb 7, 2001	2.1.3	4/5	ⓜ		46404
Clean Up FrontPage HTML	Macromedia	Feb 9, 2001	1.0.5	3/5	ⓜ		48600
Cleanup FrontPage HTML Sitewide	Macromedia	Jun 7, 2001	2.0.2	2/5	ⓜ		21851

3. Notice that this page gives you a lot of useful information about each extension, such as author, date created, version, rating, approval, and number of downloads. Click on the **Calendar Object** link. This takes you to a page where you can download this extension.

Exchange > Category: Productivity

Calendar Object Extension

Creates a calendar for the specified month which you can fill in with important dates.

Download Extension

🔽 macintosh   20.623 K
MX302463_Calendar.mxp

🔽 windows   20.623 K
MX302463_Calendar.mxp

Installation instructions

Features

Creates a calendar for the specified month which you can fill in with important dates.

❗ Warning: This Extension will not install without the Extension Manager. If you have not already done so, download it now.

Discuss

Dreamweaver Exchange General Discussion Forum

Review

Author   Scott Richards

---

4. In the **Download Extension** section, click on the appropriate download link for the operating system you are using. For example, if you are using a PC, click on the **windows** link. This starts the download process.

5. When you are prompted to save the extension, choose a location on your hard drive and click **Save**. Remember where you saved this file, because you'll need to access it later. The best place to store it is in the Downloaded Extensions directory within the Dreamweaver MX application directory; this way, you'll know where it is in the future.

Note: Under OS X on the Macintosh, the Extension Manager will automatically launch once the extension has been downloaded. You can jump to step 10 if this occurs.

6. You're done with the Macromedia Exchange for Dreamweaver MX site for now, and you can log off before continuing with the exercise, if you wish.

7. Return to Dreamweaver MX. Select **Commands > Manage Extensions**. This launches the Extension Manager. Now, you will use the Extension Manager to install the extension you just downloaded.

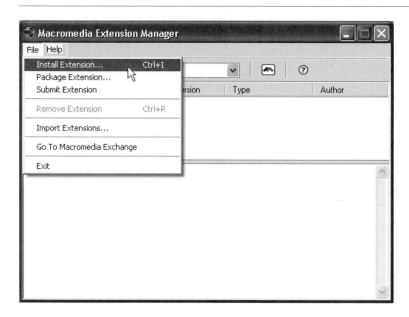

8. In the **Extension Manager**, select **File > Install Extension**. This opens a dialog box so you can browse to the extension file you just downloaded. **Note:** All extension files you download should have an extension of .mxp.

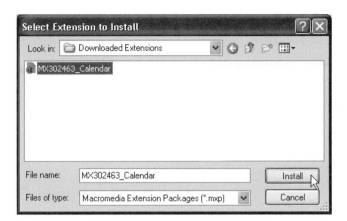

9. Locate the file on your hard drive and click **Install**.

10. The disclaimer that appears is the one you have seen before. Click **Accept**, and the installation will continue.

11. When the installation process is finished, the above dialog box is displayed. Click **OK**.

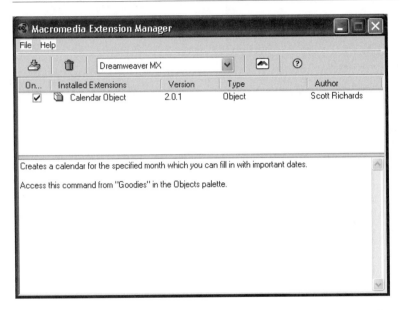

Once the installation is complete, your new extension appears in the Extension Manager window.

12. Select **File > Quit** (Mac) or **File > Exit** (Windows) to exit the Extension Manager.

13. Return to Dreamweaver MX. Quit, and then relaunch so you can check out your new extension.

14. From the **Site window** (**F8**), open the **calendar.html** file. This is nothing more than a blank file that we created for you.

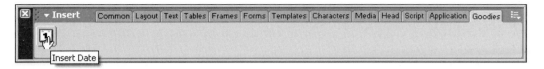

15. From the **Insert** panel, select **Goodies**. This is a new tab that was added when you installed the Calendar Object extension; it's not part of the normal installation. Aren't you glad we told you that?

16. Click on the **Insert Date** icon in the **Goodies** panel. This opens the **Insert Calendar** dialog box.

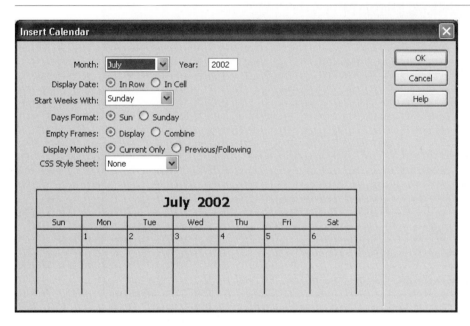

17. If you want to modify some of the options, you can. When you are finished, click **OK**. If you don't see an OK button, simply click the red X in the upper-right corner.

TIP | Extending Dreamweaver MX

If you're well versed in JavaScript, you can learn to write your own custom extensions, and you'll find plenty of great resources on the Macromedia Exchange for Dreamweaver MX. If you want, you can download a PDF version of the Extensibility Manual from the Macromedia Web site and/or subscribe to their Extensibility newsgroup. Both are great resources for extensibility authors.

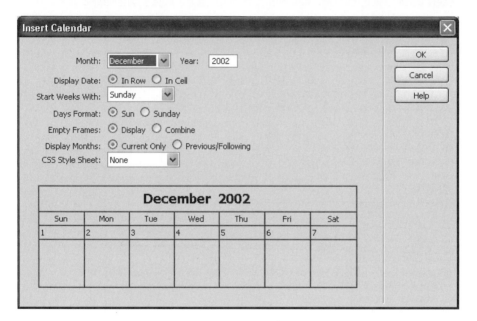

This extension, complete with the great interface, was designed by Scott Richards. Creating extensions requires a working knowledge of JavaScript and the Dreamweaver MX DOM.

This is what the calendar looks like within Dreamweaver MX. Pretty slick, huh? Can you imagine having to create that table and insert all the correct dates yourself? Now any time you want to add a calendar to a Web page, it's as simple as clicking a button object in the Insert panel. This is definitely a very handy and useful extension to Dreamweaver MX. **Note:** If you modified some of the options, your calendar may look different than this one.

18. Save and **close** this file.

This is just one example of the many cool extensions you can download from the Macromedia Exchange. It is definitely one of those sites you should bookmark and check back with on a daily or weekly basis, because new extensions are constantly being added.

If you have the energy, move on to the next chapter. If not, that's OK; it will be waiting when you are ready.

15.
Working with Fireworks

Integrated Workflow	Workflow Options
Understanding Design Notes	External Image Editor Preferences
Inserting Fireworks MX Images	Editing a Fireworks MX Image
Inserting a Fireworks MX Rollover	Updating Fireworks MX HTML
Fireworks MX Pop-Up	Show Pop-Up Menu Behavior

chap_15

Dreamweaver MX
H•O•T CD-ROM

Designing and developing Web pages cannot be done with Dreamweaver MX alone because you will need a graphics editor as well. Of course, you could hire a designer to do all of the graphics for your Web pages, but if you want to create graphics on your own, Macromedia has a graphics tool called Fireworks MX that integrates well with Dreamweaver MX. When you export images from Fireworks MX, the application places bits of comment code data into a separate HTML document as well as creating the graphic file. Fireworks MX's HTML code is easily understood by Dreamweaver MX, which makes these two tools work together very well.

In this chapter, you will learn how to insert graphics into your HTML pages that were created with Fireworks MX, how to edit images in Fireworks MX from within Dreamweaver MX, insert rollovers created in Fireworks MX, and much more. Dreamweaver MX and Fireworks MX have been designed to provide you with a smooth and integrated workflow for designing, generating, editing, optimizing, and placing Web graphics into your HTML pages. Like yin and yang, Dreamweaver MX and Fireworks MX were meant to be together.

The chart below outlines some of the ways that Dreamweaver MX and Fireworks MX can work together to accomplish many of your Web design tasks.

Dreamweaver MX to Fireworks MX Workflow	
Feature	**What It Does**
Launching Fireworks MX to optimize an image	Launches the Fireworks Optimize panel in Dreamweaver MX.
Inserting a Fireworks MX image in a Dreamweaver MX document	Inserts a .gif or a .jpg image that is linked by a .mno file or design note to a Fireworks MX .png image file
Inserting Fireworks MX HTML code in a Dreamweaver MX document	Inserts Fireworks MX HTML code into a Dreamweaver MX document with the push of a button. The HTML code is linked by a .mno file or design note to a Fireworks MX .png image file.
Pasting Fireworks MX HTML code into a Dreamweaver MX document	A method of placing Fireworks MX HTML code into a Dreamweaver MX document. The code can be pasted with or without the reference to the file design note or .mno file.
Editing a Fireworks MX image or table	Launches Fireworks MX through the design note, for the purpose of modifying images and tables. Revisions are then updated and sent back to Dreamweaver MX smoothly by the click of a button.
Inserting an image placeholder	Allows you to create a blank graphic of the right size to fit your design in Dreamweaver MX.
Updating a Dreamweaver MX image placeholder in Fireworks MX	Launches Fireworks MX and opens the Dreamweaver MX Placeholder Image for design. Then the image is saved and sent back to Dreamweaver MX.
Opening a Fireworks MX pop-up menu in Dreamweaver MX	Allows you to view Fireworks MX image pop-up and HTML-based pop-up menus in Dreamweaver MX.
Show pop-up menu	Allows you to set options to create and edit both image-based and HTML pop-up menus in Dreamweaver MX. Allows round-trip graphic editing with Fireworks MX through design notes.

The Importance of Design Notes

Design notes are a key component to Dreamweaver MX and Fireworks MX integration. When you export a .gif or a .jpg file from Fireworks MX to a Dreamweaver MX site folder, a folder is automatically created named _notes within your local root folder. This folder contains the Design Notes file, which uses the Macromedia note file extension (.mno). Design notes contain information about the graphic files that you exported from Fireworks MX, such as where the source .png file is located. This information is used when you launch and edit a Fireworks MX table or image from Dreamweaver MX. If design notes were enabled when the image was exported from Fireworks MX, the Property Inspector will display the Fireworks MX icon and the path to the source file.

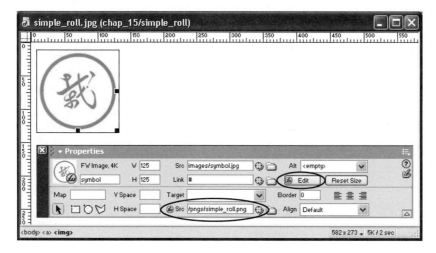

A Fireworks MX graphic selected in Dreamweaver MX with the Property Inspector displaying the path to the source file.

The best thing about design notes is there is really not much you have to do. All of the design notes' magic between Fireworks MX and Dreamweaver MX goes on behind the scenes, letting you focus on creating your Web pages.

External Image Editor and Launch and Edit Preferences

When you install the Macromedia Studio MX suite, external image editor preferences are set for you automatically. Fireworks MX is selected as the external image editor for Dreamweaver MX. This is what allows you to go between Dreamweaver MX and Fireworks MX smoothly and effortlessly. It is these preferences that launch Fireworks MX when you edit an image in a Dreamweaver MX document.

If your preferences aren't set properly, you can set them yourself by following these steps:

- Choose **Edit** > **Preferences** (Windows) or **Dreamweaver** > **Preferences** (Macintosh) and select **File Types/Editors** in the **Category** list on the left.

- In the **Editors** panel of the **Preferences** window, you should see Fireworks MX selected as your primary image editor.

- In the **Extensions** panel of the **Preferences** window, you can scroll through the extension types that Fireworks MX will edit upon selection. Click **OK** when you are done exploring.

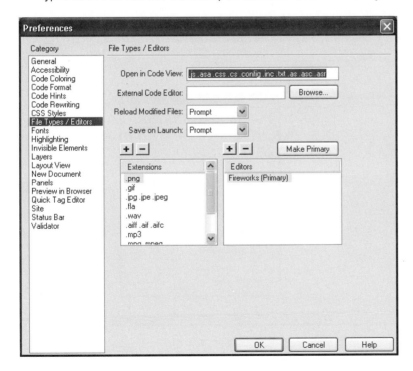

The preference settings for file types/editors in Dreamweaver MX.

I. ————————Inserting Fireworks MX Images

Now that you have a general understanding of what is going on behind the scenes, it is time to have some fun with Dreamweaver MX and Fireworks MX. In this first exercise, you will practice the simple technique of inserting a Fireworks MX image into a Dreamweaver MX document.

1. Copy **chap_15** to your hard drive. Define your site for Chapter 15, using the **chap_15** folder as the local root folder. If you need a refresher on this process, visit Exercise 1 in Chapter 3, "*Site Control.*"

2. Open the file **insert.html** from the **chap_05** folder. This file is a simple page containing a table, which is where you will be inserting the Fireworks MX graphic.

3. Make sure that the **Assets** panel is open; if it is not, select **Window > Assets**. Click on the **Image** radio button to display your image assets for this site.

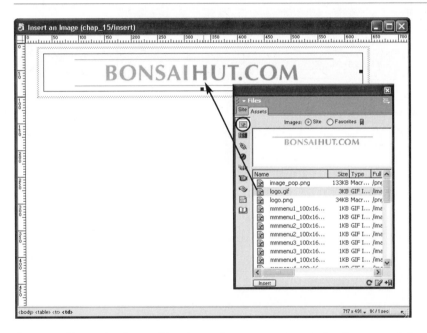

As you will see, the Assets Panel contains an assortment of .gif, .png, and .jpg images. The .png files are the original Fireworks graphics file for use for integrating updates between Dreamweaver MX and Fireworks MX.

4. Select **logo.gif** in the **Assets** panel and drag it into the table cell. The bonsaihut.com logo fills the cell, and your page should look like the image shown above.

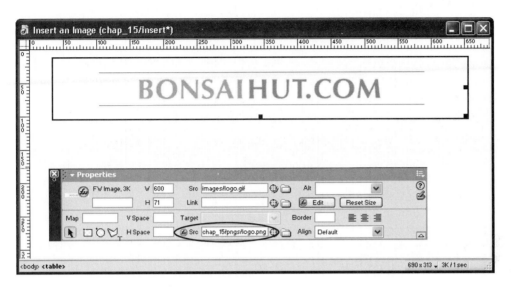

The Fireworks MX graphic inserted into the Dreamweaver MX document. You can tell that this is a graphic created in Fireworks MX because when you click it, the Src field in the Property Inspector tells you so! This means this graphic is linked to a .png file, and this is happening due to the design note.

5. Save this page and keep it open for the next exercise.

That was easy, huh? With this image inserted onto the page, you can continue learning more Fireworks MX and Dreamweaver MX integration magic.

Editing a Fireworks MX Image from Dreamweaver MX

In this next exercise, you will learn to edit an image that was created in Fireworks MX while you have Dreamweaver MX open and active. This exercise demonstrates that you can go between the two programs easily. **Note:** You must have Fireworks MX installed in order to complete this exercise. We have included a trial version of Fireworks MX on the CD-ROM for your convenience.

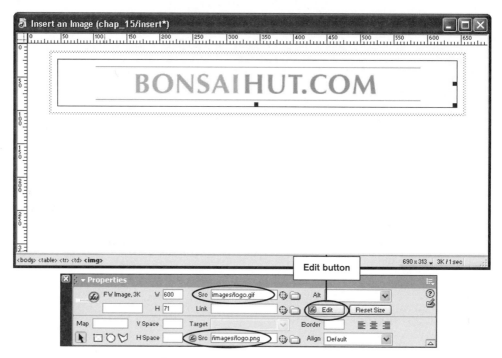

1. With **insert.html** still open from the previous exercise, select the **bonsaihut.com** (logo.gif) graphic. In the **Property Inspector**, notice the **Src** field beneath the **Target** option. The source text field is displaying the path to the source file for the selected image. In this case, it is pointing to the **logo.png** file. This option appears only when you have selected an image that has been exported from Fireworks MX.

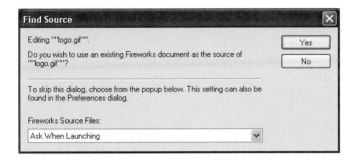

The Find Source dialog box in Fireworks MX.

2. Click the **Edit** button within the **Property Inspector**. This will launch Fireworks MX, and then you will be presented with the Find Source dialog box. This dialog box gives you a choice between two options: If you click **No**, Fireworks MX will open the .gif or .jpg file that you selected in Dreamweaver MX. If you click **Yes**, Fireworks MX will open the original .png file from which the .gif or .jpg file was initially created.

As a general rule of thumb, it is always best to work with the source file for an image, especially if you are going to resize and recompress the image, as will be the case in this exercise. Because the .png file that was saved from Fireworks MX is in the local root folder, you would click Yes. If you don't have the source file, your only option is to click No and work with a compressed graphic.

3. Click **Yes** in the **Find Source** dialog box, which will open the **Open** dialog box. Browse to the **chap_15/pngs/** file and click **Open**.

The Open dialog box will only open the first time you choose to launch and edit this image from Dreamweaver MX. After that, Dreamweaver MX will remember the path to find your .png source file. Nice!

You are now in Fireworks MX viewing the source document. At the top of the window, notice that it says Editing from Dreamweaver, *which indicates that you are editing this image while you have Dreamweaver MX open and active.*

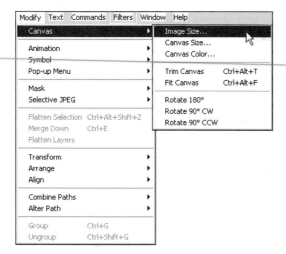

4. Choose **Modify > Canvas > Image Size**. This will open the **Image Size** dialog box.

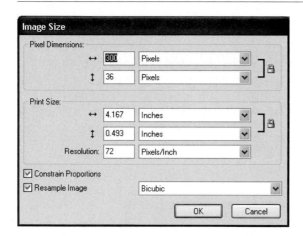

5. Make sure that both the **Constrain Proportions** and **Resample Image** checkboxes are checked. Change the pixel dimensions for **width** from **600 pixels** to **300 pixels**. You will see that the height attribute automatically updates to **35**.

6. Click **OK**. The graphic has now become much smaller. Because you edited the source file, the image will scale perfectly without distortion. This is one reason you want to work with the source file whenever possible because .gif or .jpg files do not always rescale without distortion.

7. Click the **Done** button. This will close Fireworks MX and return you to the document window in Dreamweaver MX. The image is resized and uses compression settings from the last time the file was exported.

8. In the **Property Inspector**, click the **Reset Size** button. This will refresh the display and display the resized image to appear in the document window if it does not refresh by itself.

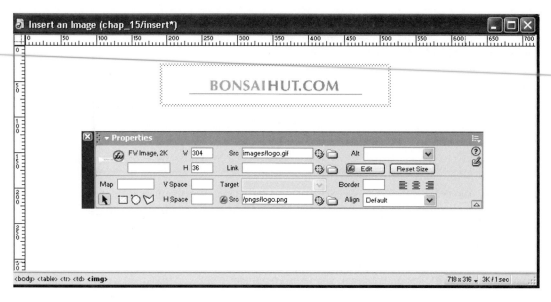

When you click in the empty area of your document, the table cell that the graphic is placed in will also resize to fit your new graphic.

Because there are so many different things that you can do to edit graphics between Dreamweaver MX and Fireworks MX, we have included a handy little chart at the beginning of this chapter to provide you some more possibilities.

9. Save and **close** this file now. You won't need it for the next exercise.

3. ——————————Inserting a Simple Rollover from Fireworks MX

Like peanut butter and jelly, Dreamweaver MX and Fireworks MX were made to go together. But once you've created your rollovers in Fireworks MX, how do you get them into Dreamweaver MX and still have them work? This exercise shows you how to import Fireworks MX HTML files that contain JavaScript rollovers into a page in Dreamweaver MX. You'll see that it's as easy as clicking a button.

Note: You need to have Fireworks MX installed to complete this exercise.

1. Open **fw_simple.html** from the **html** folder of **chap_15**. This is simply a blank file that we created for you.

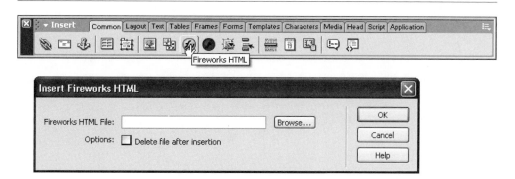

2. Click the **Fireworks HTML** object in the **Insert** panel. This will open the **Insert Fireworks HTML** dialog box.

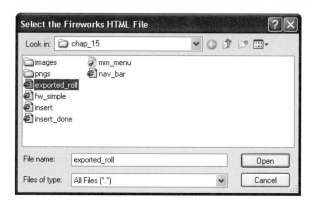

3. Click **Browse** and locate the **exported_roll.html** file inside the **chap_15** folder. This file was exported from Fireworks MX, and it contains the JavaScript rollover code. Click **Open**.

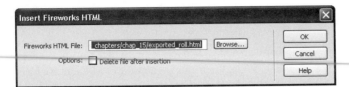

4. You'll be returned to the **Insert Fireworks HTML** dialog box. Click **OK**.

Note: If you check the Delete file after insertion *checkbox, the original HTML file that you selected will be deleted after it is inserted into your document. We recommend that you don't delete the file unless you are sure you don't want to import it into another page.*

NOTE | Import from Outside Your Local Root Folder

If you try to import an HTML file that is not within your local root folder, you will get the dialog box below. Click **OK** and choose a place inside your local root folder to save them.

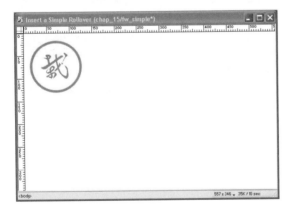

This is what your page should look like now.

---

5. Press **F12** to test the rollover in your browser. With the click of a few buttons, Dreamweaver MX imported the images and the necessary JavaScript to make this rollover work.

---

6. Save and **close** the file.

4. ———Updating Fireworks MX HTML Placed in Dreamweaver MX

Once you get deep into working with Dreamweaver MX and Fireworks MX in tandem, there will most likely be times when you will want to make changes to the original Fireworks MX HTML that you placed in your Dreamweaver MX document. This exercise steps you through the process of applying a simple modification to a Fireworks MX HTML file that has been placed in a Dreamweaver MX page.

In this example, you will modify a navigation bar that was created in Fireworks MX and then inserted into a Dreamweaver MX page. You will go back and forth between Dreamweaver MX and Fireworks MX accessing and modifying the original Fireworks .png file.

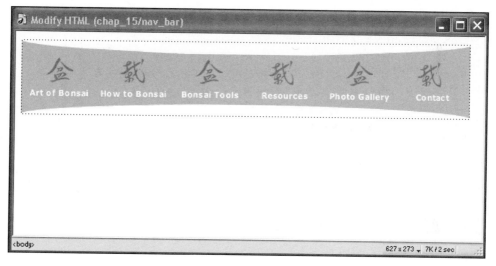

1. In Dreamweaver MX, open **nav_bar.html** from the **chap_15** folder.

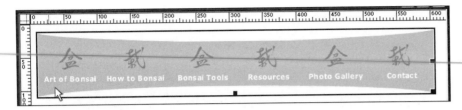

2. Click anywhere in the table to activate the **Tag Selector** at the lower left of the document window. You should see the word **<table>** appear in the Tag Selector. Click the **<table>** element in the **Tag Selector** to select the entire table.

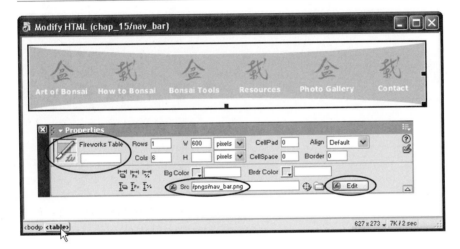

3. With the table tag selected, the **Property Inspector** indicates that you have a Fireworks MX table selected by displaying **Fireworks Table** in the upper-left corner of the Property Inspector. The source file for this table is **nav_bar.png**, as indicated at the bottom of the Property Inspector.

4. Click the **Edit** button at the bottom of the **Property Inspector**. This will launch Fireworks MX (if it is not already open) and open the file **nav_bar.png**.

Now that you are in Fireworks MX and the .png file is accessed, you will make some simple edits to it.

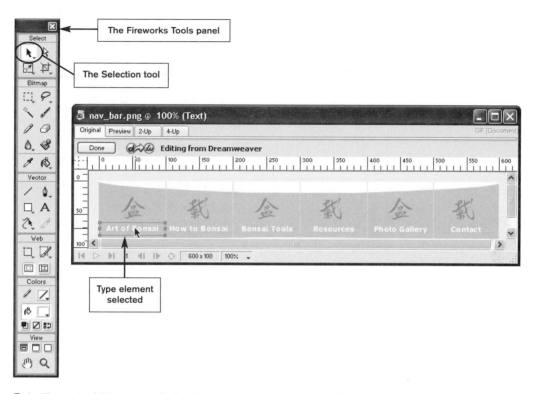

The Fireworks Tools panel

The Selection tool

Type element selected

5. In Fireworks MX, use the **Selection** tool to select the **Art of Bonsai** text block. (We have locked all the other layers in the document so you don't accidentally select something else) ;-).

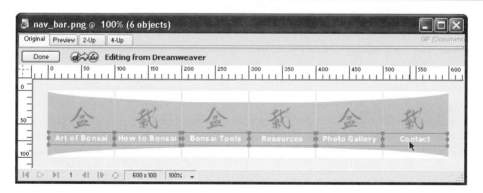

6. Hold down the **Shift** key and click to select the remaining text elements for **How to Bonsai**, **Bonsai Tools**, **Resources**, **Photo Gallery**, and **Contact**.

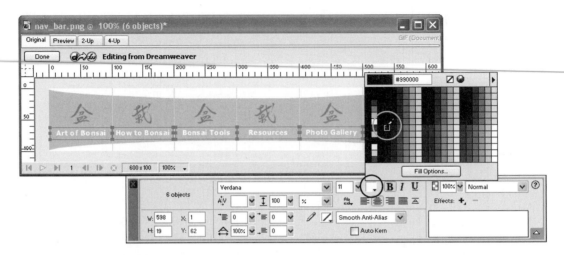

7. In the **Property Inspector**, click the **text color** box and change the color of the text elements from white to dark red **#990000**.

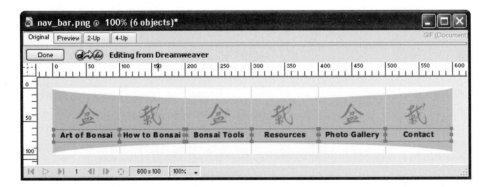

Your file should look like this now in Fireworks MX.

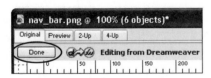

8. Click the **Done** button in the upper-left corner of the document window.

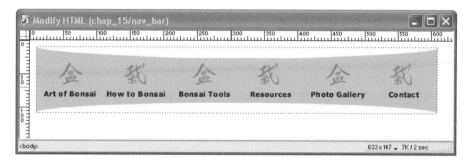

9. You are switched back to Dreamweaver MX, and your table has been updated automatically. **Save** and **close** this page.

Based on settings applied to the Web layer and within the export settings in Fireworks MX, the HTML has been updated. At the same time, it has exported the updated graphics and placed them in the correct folder. Additionally, the Fireworks MX .png file has been updated and saved. This is all going on behind the scenes with the help from the data comments in the Fireworks MX HTML, the .mno file (a.k.a the Design Notes file), and the HTML export preference settings in Fireworks MX.

About Fireworks MX Export Settings

Because Fireworks MX allows you to export both graphics and HTML, we thought it would be helpful for you to understand how Fireworks MX export settings are controlled.

In Fireworks MX, there are settings that control the type and amount of compression your graphics will receive, and there are separate settings for controlling various attributes of your Fireworks MX HTML.

There is a special layout layer in Fireworks MX called the Web layer that allows you to assign interactivity and HTML information to areas of your document that you assign as slices.

When preparing a document as a Web page in Fireworks MX, you use the Web layer to add interactivity and define page layout. On export, Fireworks MX uses this information to generate the HTML and JavaScript code that will display and animate your images according to your designs.

> ### NOTE | Fireworks MX Pop-Up Menus
>
> Fireworks MX lets you create both image-based pop-up menus and HTML-based pop-up menus. Dreamweaver MX lets you create HTML pop-up menus as well. If your pop-up menu is image-based and you want to make changes to it, you will need to edit the pop-up menu in Fireworks MX, rather than in Dreamweaver MX. But don't worry, you'll learn how to work with both types of pop-up menus next!

5. _____Editing an HTML-Based Pop-Up Menu

As you may have guessed from its title, this exercise gives you some experience making edits in Dreamweaver MX to a HTML-based pop-up menu originally created in Fireworks MX.

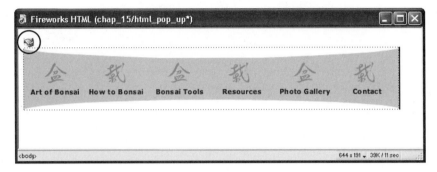

1. Open **html_pop_up.html** from the chap_15 folder. This file is an example of an HTML pop-up menu created in Fireworks MX. The little yellow icon indicates that there is JavaScript in this page.

2. Press **F12** to preview this page in a browser.

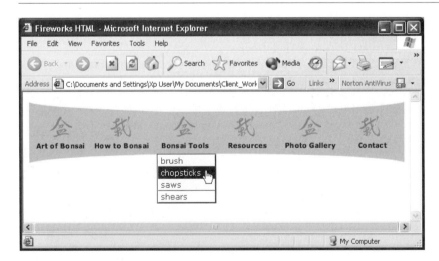

3. Move your cursor over one of the navigation images and you will see a pop-up menu appear. The menu items are not linked to anything yet, so if you click them they will not take you anywhere. Don't worry, you'll learn about this in a minute or two.

4. Switch back to Dreamweaver MX and click on the **Art of Bonsai** image to select it.

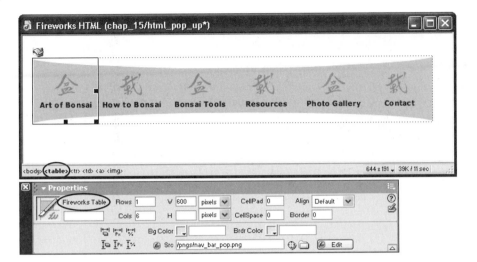

5. You should see the word **<table>** appear in the Tag Selector. Click the **<table>** element in the **Tag Selector** to select the entire table. Notice that this is a Fireworks MX table.

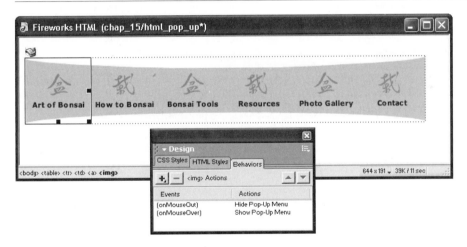

6. Click on the **Art of Bonsai** image to select it. Open the **Behaviors** panel by choosing **Window > Behaviors** (Shift+F3). Notice that some JavaScript behaviors are attached to this image.

Remember when you opened this page and saw the JavaScript element icon? Well, that was a hint about what you are looking at now. When this element is visible, it means there is some sort of script besides HTML in the code. These behaviors were written into the HTML when the file was exported from Fireworks MX. But guess what...? Now you are going to edit them in Dreamweaver MX.

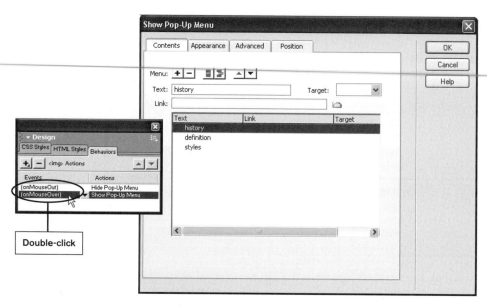

7. Double-click on the **(onMouseOver)** event in the **Behaviors** panel to open the **Show Pop-Up Menu** dialog box.

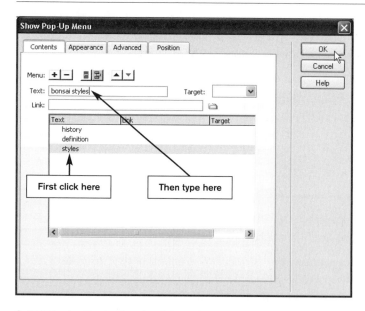

8. Within the **Contents** tab, click on the word **styles** in the text window to activate it in the **Text** field. Now, click before the word **styles** (which appears automatically in the **Text** field) and type the word **bonsai**. Click **OK**. (Don't worry, you will get a chance to work with more of these features in the next exercise).

9. When you look at the file, no change is evident. Press **F12** to preview the page in a browser.

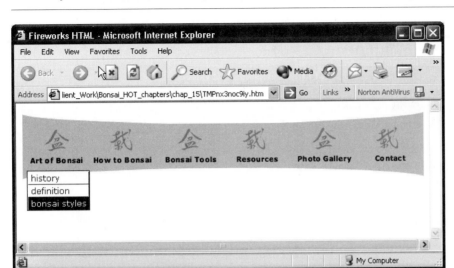

Your pop-up menu now looks like this in the browser. Notice that bonsai styles *now appears at the bottom of the pop-up menu instead of just the word* styles.

That was pretty easy to do, and you will be happy to know that editing the text in image-based pop-up menus works exactly the same way. Editing the images in image-based pop-ups, however, is a different story. In the next exercise, you will get a chance to modify an image-based pop-up menu. Woo-hoo!

10. Save and **close** this file.

6. ————Editing an Image-Based Pop-Up Menu

Now that you understand how to edit an HTML-based pop-up menu, you are ready to learn how to make changes to an image-based pop-up menu. In this next exercise, you will be working with a page in Dreamweaver MX that contains an image-based pop-up file. I have created this for you using the **Add Pop-Up Menu behavior** in Fireworks MX and selecting image-based for the button type.

When I exported the Fireworks MX file into the Dreamweaver MX site, I got the HTML and all the graphics required to "run" the menu. Plus, Fireworks MX exported the .mno (or Design Notes) file as well.

You can learn how to make your own original Fireworks MX pop-up menus from Abigail's book *Fireworks MX Fundamentals* (New Riders). In the meantime, you will get a pretty good feeling for the process by doing this exercise.

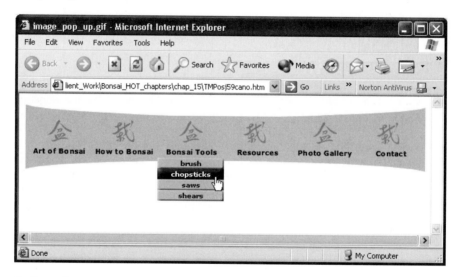

1. Open the **image_pop_up.html** from the **chap_15** folder. It looks just like the HTML version, but it isn't. Press **F12** to preview this page in a browser.

As you can see, the pop-up menu items look three-dimensional. That's because this is an image-based pop-up menu that I created in Fireworks MX. If you want to change the text on the buttons, you can follow the steps in Exercise 5. However, if you want to modify the backgrounds of the buttons, you must perform the steps that follow.

2. Switch back to Dreamweaver MX.

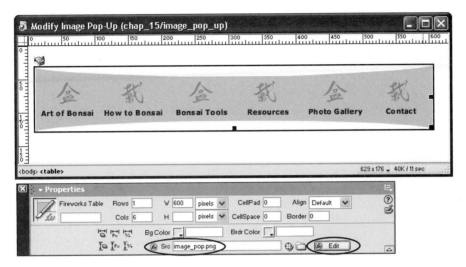

3. Click anywhere inside the table. Using the **Tag Selector**, select the table. The filename **image_pop.png** is displayed in the **Src** field. This path appears here because of the information stored in the design notes, which were automatically transferred when the Fireworks MX file was saved to the root directory. Click the **Edit** button.

4. Fireworks MX will launch, but may have trouble finding the source file because this is the first time it is locating the .png from within Dreamweaver MX. If so, you will need to show Dreamweaver MX where the source file is. Click **OK**.

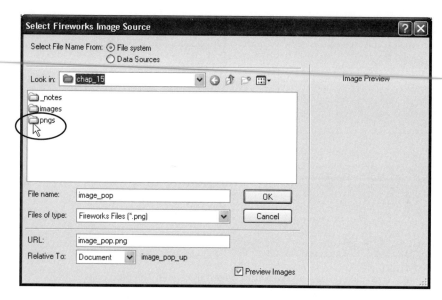

5. Browse to the **chap_15** folder and open the **pngs** folder.

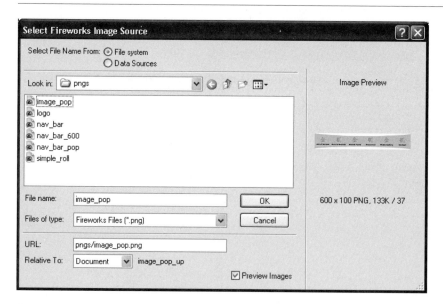

6. Select the **image_pop.png** file and click **OK**. This tells Dreamweaver MX where to find the source file for the selected image on the page.

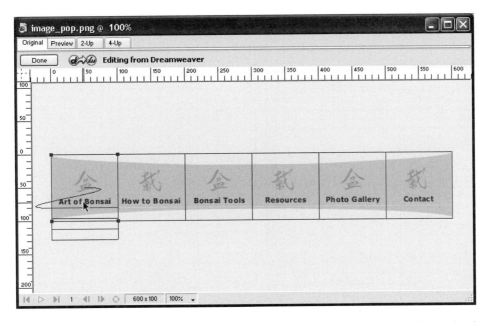

7. Expand the document window so you have some empty workspace around the navigation bar. Mouse over the **Art of Bonsai** image and you see red lines, which indicate that there is a pop-up menu attached to the Art of Bonsai image.

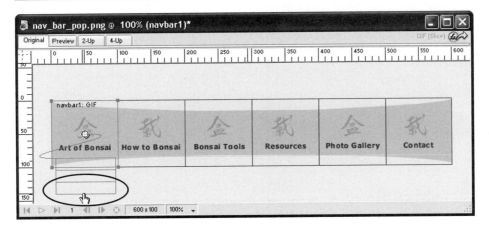

8. Click on the **Art of Bonsai** image. The lines turn blue indicating that the image is selected and the menu is now ready to select. Double-click on the blue lines of the pop-up menu to open the **Pop-Up Menu Editor**.

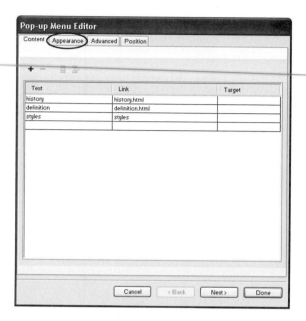

9. Click on the **Appearance** tab to modify the appearance, including the background graphics, of the pop-up menu.

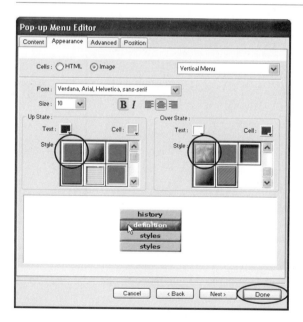

10. Use the image above to set the options in this window. When you are finished, click **Done**.

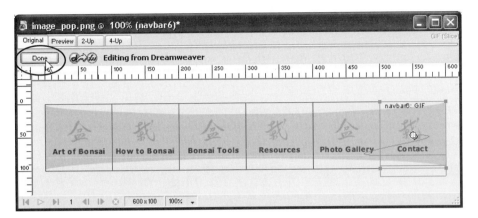

11. Repeat this process for the other five menus. When you are finished, click the **Done** button.

12. Back in Dreamweaver MX, there is no obvious change to see until you press **F12** to preview this page in a browser.

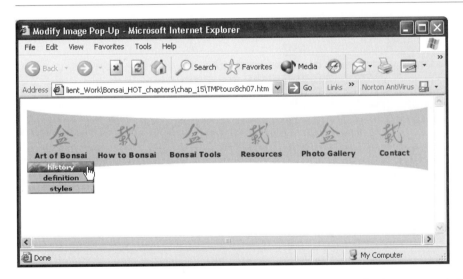

The image-based pop-up menu has been changed to reflect the modifications you made in Fireworks MX.

In the final exercise of this chapter, you will learn to create an HTML pop-up menu from Dreamweaver MX and attach it to an existing Fireworks MX navigation bar.

13. Save and **close** this file.

7. ——————Adding a Dreamweaver MX Pop-Up Menu Behavior

As you saw in a previous exercise, the Dreamweaver MX Show Pop-Up Menu behavior lets you edit and update the contents of your Fireworks MX HTML-based pop-up menus. You can use the Show Pop-Up Menu behavior in Dreamweaver MX to create, add to, delete, or change menu items, and rearrange and set menu items positioned within the page. In this exercise, you will attach an HTML-based pop-up menu to a navigation bar that I have already created for you using Fireworks MX. The pop-up menu is created using the Show behavior in Dreamweaver MX.

 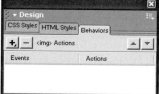

1. Make sure the **Behaviors** panel is showing. Open **dw_pop.html** from the **chap_15** folder and click on the **Art of Bonsai** graphic.

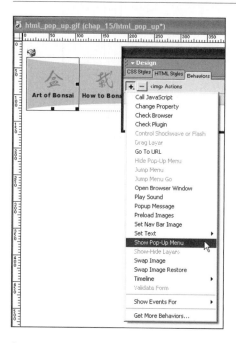

2. Click on the **plus** (+) sign on the **Behaviors** panel and scroll down to select **Show Pop-Up Menu** from the behaviors list.

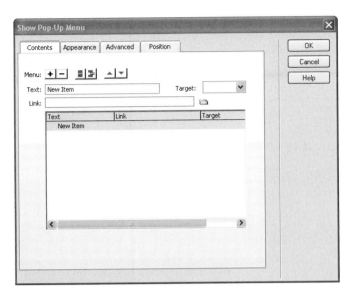

3. The Show Pop-Up Menu dialog box opens. You will create your pop-up menu by clicking on the tabs and entering your settings. The **Contents** tab is selected by default. This tab allows you to set the name, structure, URL, and target of the individual menu items.

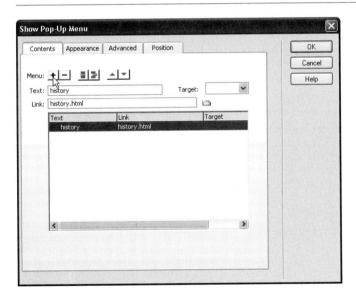

4. In the **Text** field, select the text that says **New Item** and change it to **history**. Click in the **Link** field and type **history.html**. When you are finished, click the **plus** (+) button to set this entry and begin the next menu item.

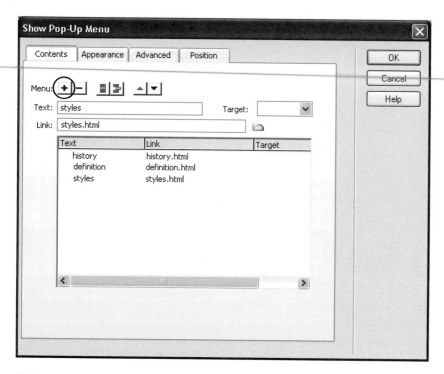

This is how the menu looks with all three menu items added.

---

5. Add the text **definition** in the **Text** field and enter **definition.html** for the **Link**. Click the **plus (+)** button and add the text **styles** in the **Text** field and enter **styles.html** for the **Link**.

---

6. Click the **Appearance** tab to see more options. This tab lets you set the look of the menu's up and over states. It also lets you specify the font for the menu's text.

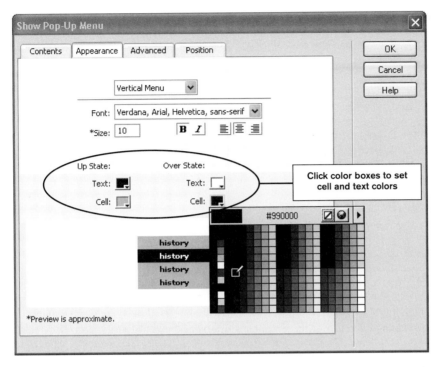

7. Make sure you have **Vertical Menu** selected at the top of the menu. For the **Font**, choose **Verdana, Arial, Helvetica, sans-serif**. Select **10** for the **Size** and click on the **B** to make the text bold.

8. Click on the color box to set the colors for the Up and Over State text. For the **Up State**, select dark red for the **Text** and select light green for the **Cell**. For the **Over State**, use light yellow for the **Text** and use dark red for the **Cell**.

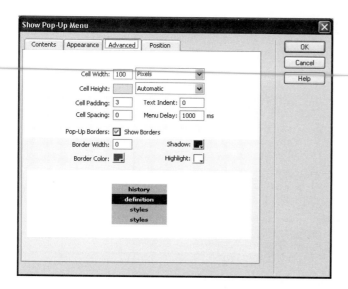

9. Click the **Advanced** tab. This tab allows you to set the properties of the menu cells. You can set cell width and height, cell color and border, text indentation, and the length of delay before the menu appears after the user moves the pointer over the trigger link or object.

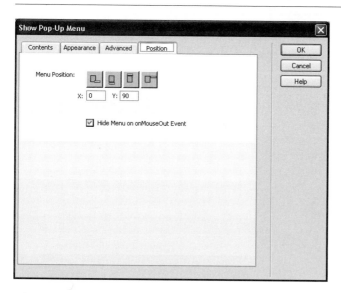

10. Click the **Position** tab. This tab lets you set where the menu is positioned relative to the triggering link or image. Leave the **X**, or horizontal, set at **0**. Set the **Y**, or vertical, position to **90**. Make sure the **Hide Menu onMouseOut Event** checkbox is checked. This will hide the menu when the user's mouse is no longer on it. Click **OK**.

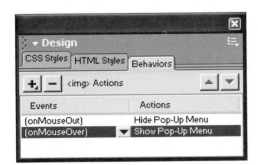

11. When the **Art of Bonsai** graphic is selected now, the **Behaviors** panel should look like this. Press **F12** to test your pop-up menu in the browser.

12. Save and **close** this page.

Great job! You have learned that there are a number of ways that Dreamweaver MX and Fireworks MX work together. If you have the energy, turn the page and move on to the next chapter.

16.

Automation

| Using the History Panel for Undo/Redo |

| Copying and Pasting History |

| Creating a Web Photo Album |

chap_16

Dreamweaver MX
H•O•T CD-ROM

If you design Web pages, you will quickly notice that an abundance of incredibly repetitive and boring tasks seem to be required. Fortunately, Dreamweaver MX has several features that can help you automate many of these boring tasks—such as the History panel and the use of custom objects and commands. In this chapter, you'll learn about the **History panel**, which memorizes and replays steps you've performed while you're creating a Dreamweaver MX document. This panel can be scripted to replay these steps, which is one great way to automate repetitive tasks. You will also work with one of the pre-existing commands that ships with Dreamweaver MX right out of the box: Create Web Photo Album.

What Is the History Panel?

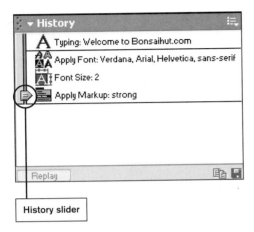

History slider

The History panel displays all of the steps that have been performed since you created or opened your file. This offers a nice visual overview of the different steps you've completed. You can use the slider to quickly undo and redo these steps. This visual approach to stepping backward and forward through your document gives you more feedback than pressing Ctrl+Z and Ctrl+Y or (Cmd+Z and Cmd+Y). The steps in the History panel can be copied from one document to another, which is helpful when you want to share information between documents. You can also copy steps from the History panel and save them as commands, which allows them to be replayed at a later time, in any document, with just a single click.

I. ————————Using the History Panel for Undo/Redo

This first exercise will get you comfortable working with the History panel. You will learn how to use this panel to repeat or delete operations you've performed. Working with the History panel can be much easier than choosing Undo and/or Redo multiple times.

1. Copy **chap_16** to your hard drive. Define your site for Chapter 16, using the **chap_16** folder as the local root folder. If you need a refresher on this process, visit Exercise 1 in Chapter 3, "*Site Control.*"

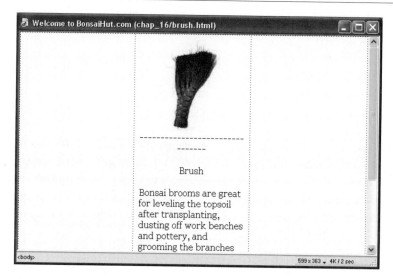

2. Open **brush.html**. For viewing text online, a sans-serif font, such as Verdana, can make the text easier to read. For this reason, you will learn to change the serif font used in the text in the middle of the screen (and learn about the History panel at the same time).

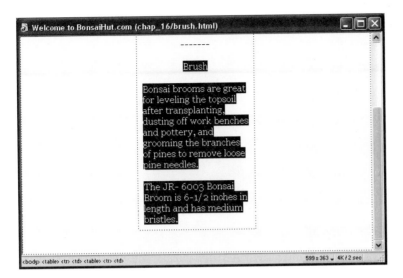

3. Click and drag so that all three paragraphs of text are highlighted.

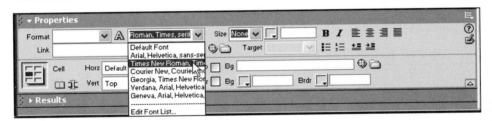

4. In the **Property Inspector**, click the **Font** pop-up menu and select **Times New Roman, Times, serif**. This changes the font used to display this text.

5. Make sure your **History** panel is open. If it is not, choose **Window > Others > History (Shift+F10)**.

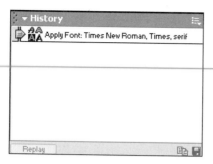

The History panel displays the change you made to the block of text in Step 4. As you continue to make additions and changes to your document, your steps will be displayed here.

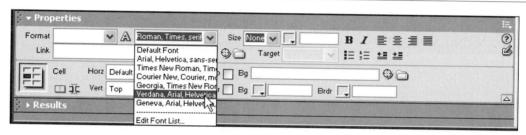

6. With the block of text still selected, change the font to **Verdana, Arial, Helvetica, sans-serif**. Notice that the History panel records this step as well.

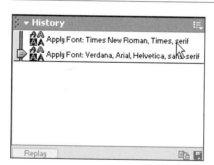

7. In the **History** panel, click and drag the **History** slider up so that the first step is highlighted. This will undo the last formatting you applied to the text, just as though you had used the **Undo** command. Click and drag the **History** slider down to the bottom of the list to reapply the text formatting.

This is a nice way to step through the changes you have made to your document. It beats having to press Cmd+Z (Mac) or Ctrl+Z (Windows) because it gives you feedback about what change you are undoing.

NOTE | The History Slider

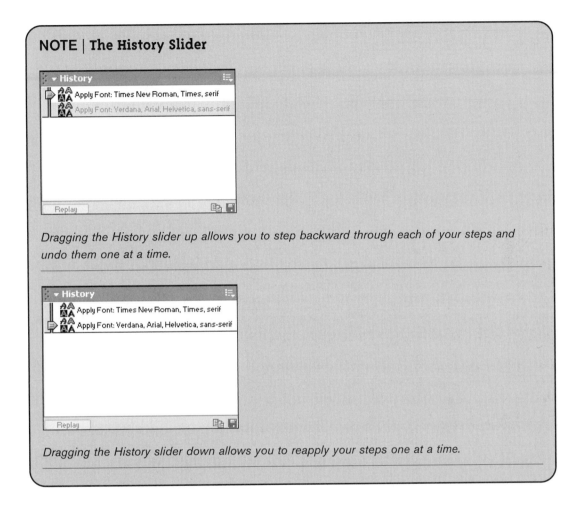

Dragging the History slider up allows you to step backward through each of your steps and undo them one at a time.

Dragging the History slider down allows you to reapply your steps one at a time.

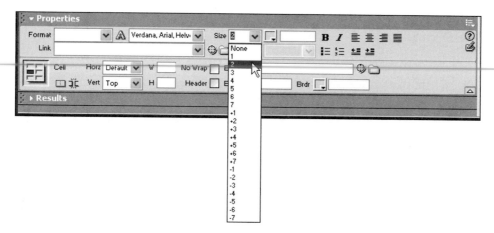

8. With the block of text still selected, reduce the **Size** to **2**. This too is recorded in the History panel.

9. Save the changes and leave this page open for the next exercise.

NOTE | Saving Files and Clearing the History Panel

The History panel is not cleared automatically when you save a file. This is great if you want to utilize it to make changes even after you have saved the document. However, if you close the file and reopen it, the history will be removed.

It is possible to clear the History panel at any time. Why would you want to clear the History? Because it uses a lot of RAM if you have made a lot of changes. Clear the history by clicking the **arrow** in the upper right of the **History** panel and choosing **Clear History** from the pop-up menu. This action cannot be undone, so be careful when using it.

2. _____Copying and Pasting History

Now that you have a grasp of the basic functions of the History panel, you will learn how to use it to automate some of your workflow. In this exercise, you will learn how to copy and paste information from the History panel into another document. This allows you to easily take what you have done in one document and replicate it inside another.

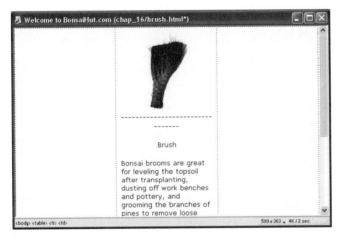

1. Make sure you have **brush.html** open from the previous exercise.

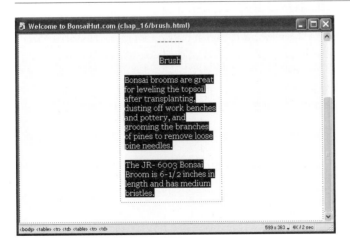

2. Open **chopsticks.html**. The text on this page can be quickly matched with the text on the **brush.html** page by copying and pasting the contents of the **History** panel.

3. Choose **Window > brush.html** to make it your current document.

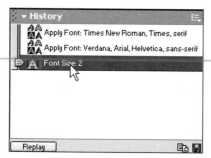

4. In the **History** panel, click the last entry. Next, **Shift+click** the top entry in the panel. This selects all of the steps in the History panel. You want to make sure that they are all selected before you copy them.

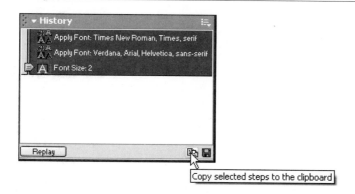

5. Click the **Copy selected steps to the clipboard** icon at the bottom of the **History** panel. This copies everything you have selected to the clipboard so that it can be pasted into the History panel of another document.

6. Choose **Window > chopsticks.html** to bring **chopsticks.html** forward and make it your current document.

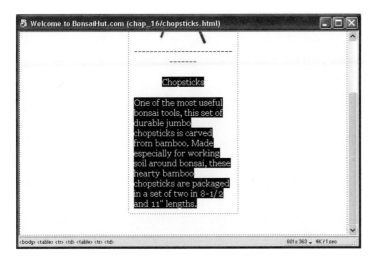

7. Select the text in the middle of the **chopsticks.html** page by clicking and dragging.

Make sure that the selection represents everything you want reformatted when you paste the steps from the other document into the History panel.

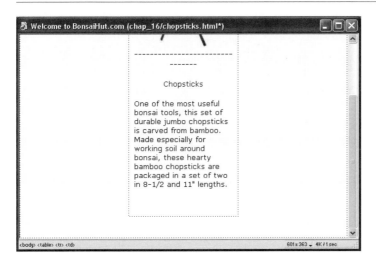

8. Choose **Edit > Paste**, or press **Cmd+V** (Mac) or **Ctrl+V** (Windows). This pastes the three steps you copied from the History panel of **brush.html** into this document. Notice that Dreamweaver MX has formatted the text you selected the same way it was formatted in **brush.html**. This is because it followed the steps you copied from the History panel of that file.

9. Save and **close** both documents. They will not be needed again for any exercises in this chapter.

NOTE | Paste Steps in the History Panel

Any time you paste steps from the History panel of one document into another, they will appear in the History panel as a single step, called **Paste Steps**. Regardless of how many steps you copied, they will always be pasted as one single entry in the History panel. In addition, pasted steps will have the Paste icon (a clipboard with a small piece of paper) next to them in the History panel.

NOTE | What Is a Command?

A command is a small JavaScript file that records specific functions performed in Dreamweaver MX. These files are stored inside the Commands folder within the Configuration folder. Some commands come with Dreamweaver MX, such as the Create Web Photo Album command, while others can be downloaded from a number of different Web sites, as we'll describe later. You can even create your own custom commands, using the History panel, or write them from scratch with JavaScript. For example, you can copy steps from the History panel and save them as a command. Dreamweaver MX will convert the selected steps into JavaScript so that they can be replayed again from any document. As you can see, commands can be very powerful and can save you a lot of time.

What Is a Web Photo Album?

The Create Web Photo Album command is a great feature in Dreamweaver MX that lets you quickly create a small Web site–based catalog of images. If you are a designer, photographer, or just someone who has a bunch of images to share with friends and family, you will really appreciate this feature. This command, which comes with Dreamweaver MX, works in conjunction with Macromedia Fireworks MX (or version 4) to batch-process a collection of images and create a set of Web pages that links them all together. You must have Fireworks 4 or MX installed to use this command. You simply tell Dreamweaver MX where your source images are located, and it will launch Fireworks MX to optimize them and create thumbnails (smaller versions of your images), then use Dreamweaver MX to create a page for each and link them all together. In the end, you have a great way to share your image collections with the rest of the world.

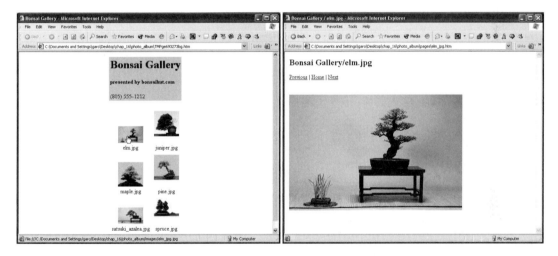

The Web photo album is created automatically from a folder of images. Dreamweaver MX will create a catalog page of thumbnail images (shown on the left) as well as individual pages for larger images. You'll learn to make this photo album yourself in the next exercise.

Getting More Commands

It is possible to create commands that are far more complicated than the ones this chapter describes, such as ones that script complex interactions between Dreamweaver MX and Fireworks. However, creating this type of command requires very strong JavaScript skills, which are way beyond the scope of this book.

The good news is that the JavaScript jocks who can create more complicated custom commands often distribute these from their own sites. There is actually a sizable third-party market for Dreamweaver MX commands. Below, you'll find information on the Macromedia Dreamweaver Exchange and a couple of the third-party sites we've found most useful. Make sure you also check out Appendix B, "*Online Resources*," for a listing of these sites. In addition, you can choose **Commands > Get More Commands** to access Dreamweaver Exchange, the online community for extensibility developers.

Dreamweaver Exchange

If you are proficient in HTML and/or JavaScript, the Macromedia site offers a great resource for developers who plan to create custom commands and other extensions for Dreamweaver MX. Macromedia has prepared a comprehensive document that gives detailed information on the extensive Dreamweaver MX API (**A**pplication **P**rogramming **I**nterface), which you can also download at the URL listed below. The API refers to the methods a programmer can use to make requests of the application.

`http://dynamic.macromedia.com/bin/MM/exchange/main.jsp?product=dreamweaver`

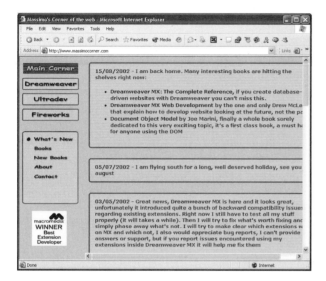

Massimo's Corner

Massimo's is a great site for getting some really useful commands.

http://www.massimocorner.com

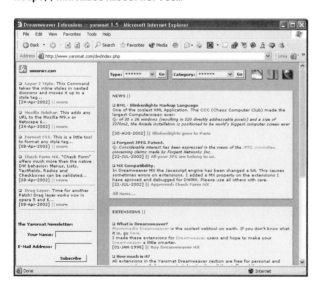

Yaromat

This is another great repository for Dreamweaver MX behaviors, commands, and objects.

http://www.yaromat.com/dw/index.php

3. ———————————Creating a Web Photo Album

The Create Web Photo Album command automatically creates a complex Web site that displays your images. An online photo album is great way for artists to display their work, for architects to show renderings to clients, for photographers to show proofs to clients, for families to share personal photos, and for other purposes too numerous to list here. All you need is a folder of images on your hard drive, and the Create Web Photo Album command will convert them into an elaborate Web site, complete with thumbnails and larger images and links to navigate between them. You'll be impressed by how easy it is to create this complex site with just a folder of images and the Dreamweaver MX Create Web Photo Album command.

Note: Before completing this exercise, you must have Fireworks 4 or MX installed on your computer. If you don't own a copy of Fireworks MX, don't worry. There is a free, 30-day trial demo copy in the **software** folder of the **H•O•T CD-ROM**.

1. Choose **File > New** to create a new blank document.

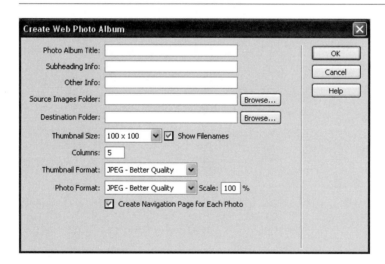

2. Choose **Commands > Create Web Photo Album**. This opens the **Create Web Photo Album** dialog box. If you don't have Fireworks installed yet, Dreamweaver MX will display a **Download Fireworks trial** button.

3. Enter **Photo Album Title: Bonsai Gallery**. This text, along with the other information you enter on this page, will appear at the top of the home page of your completed Web album site once you've completed this exercise.

4. Enter **Subheading Info: presented by bonsaihut.com**. This text will appear immediately below the **Photo Album Title** field on your Web album site.

5. Enter **Other Info: (805) 555-1212**. This text will appear immediately below the **Subheading Info** field.

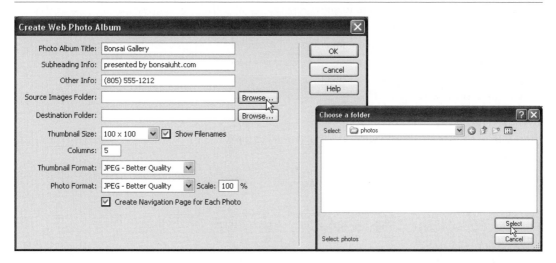

6. Click **Browse** to the right of the **Source Images Folder** field. Browse to the **photos** folder inside the **chap_16** folder.

• **Mac users:** Click **Choose**.

• **Windows users:** Highlight the folder, click **Open**, then click **Select**.

This option determines which folder contains the source files you want to use to create your Web photo album.

Tip: The Create Web Photo Album command can process only whole folders of images.

> **TIP | Web Photo Album Source Files**
>
> The source files for your Web photo album must be saved in the .gif, .jpg, .jpeg, .png, .psd, .tif, or .tiff file format. The files must have the proper extension in order to be included in the Web photo album. If they are in another file format, you will get an error message that says no files exist in your source folder.

7. Click **Browse** to the right of the **Destination Folder** field. Navigate inside the **chap_16** folder to select the **photo_album** folder. This is an empty folder we made for you that will be the destination folder for the Web photo album once Dreamweaver MX is finished executing this command.

• **Mac users:** Click **Choose**.

• **Windows users:** Highlight the folder, click **Open**, then click **Select**.

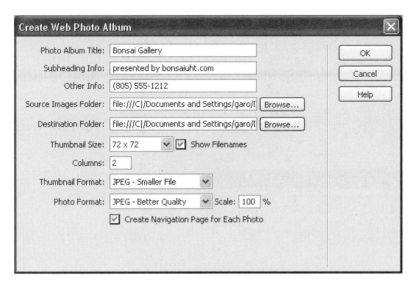

8. Make sure the rest of the **Thumbnail Size**, **Columns**, **Thumbnail Format**, and **Photo Format** settings match the image shown above.

9. Click **OK**. This causes Fireworks to launch and start processing the images.

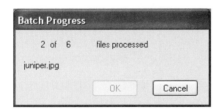

You will see a window like this while Fireworks is processing the images in your source folder.

10. When Fireworks is done processing the images, you are returned to Dreamweaver MX, and you see this dialog box. Click **OK**.

This is what your Dreamweaver MX page should look like after the photo album has been created.

11. Press **F12** to preview your page in a browser. Click any of the images to see the larger version. Dreamweaver MX and Fireworks worked together to modify your images, create several Web pages, insert the images, and create links to all of the pages. It all happened in just a few seconds! Sweet.

12. **Save** and **close** all open files.

> ### NOTE | Web Photo Album 2.1
>
> Macromedia has released the Web Photo Album 2.1 for Dreamweaver MX extension, a new (and improved) version of the Create Web Photo Album command that ships with Dreamweaver MX. The new version includes many more features and options for customizing a Web photo album in Dreamweaver MX. You can download the new version from the Macromedia Exchange for Dreamweaver.

Woo-hoo, another chapter under your belt. Congrats! If you feel up to it, keep on moving to the next chapter.

17.

Templates/Libraries

| Templates in Action |

| Creating and Modifying Templates |

| Library Items in Action |

| Creating and Modifying Library Items |

---
chap_17

Dreamweaver MX
H•O•T CD-ROM

Two of the biggest challenges that face Web designers are making pages look consistent and updating changes throughout a site. **Templates** and **Library items** can help you meet both challenges successfully, because they make it easy to create consistent pages and page elements and to automatically update multiple pages when changes are made.

Templates are useful for entire page designs. They can lock in colors, fonts, Cascading Style Sheets, tables, images and even behaviors while leaving other parts of the document editable. Once you have created a template, you use it by requesting a copy of it. Instead of creating a new untitled document, you request a new page based on a template that you have designed.

Library items are useful for page-design elements, such as a navigation bar or copyright notice. They are little pieces of HTML or text that can be dropped anywhere within a page. You will soon learn the differences between these two Dreamweaver MX features by following the hands-on exercises in this chapter.

I. ——————————**Templates in Action**

The best way to understand templates in Dreamweaver MX is to observe them in action. For this first exercise, you will modify an existing template, which will show you how quickly they can update across multiple pages in your site. You will also see how, with just a few clicks, you can use templates to change your color scheme across several pages.

1. Copy **chap_17** from the **H•O•T CD-ROM** to your hard drive. Define your site for Chapter 17 using the **chap_17** folder as the local root folder. If you need a refresher on this process, visit Exercise 1 in Chapter 3, "*Site Control*."

When you open a file that has a template applied to it, you will see a tab in the upper-right corner that identifies the name of the template file and a tab around each of the template's editable areas. The colors of these areas are set in the Highlighting category of the Preferences dialog box.

2. Open **zen_color_01.html** from the **chap_17** folder. This file, and several others inside the **chap_17** folder, including **zen_color_02.html**, **zen_color_03.html**, and **zen_color_04.html**, have a color scheme template called **zen_color** already applied to them. If you want, go ahead and open these other files and examine their page properties. You will notice that they all share the same color scheme.

TIP | Templates and Library Folders

You might have noticed that there are two folders inside the **chap_17** folder, called **Templates** and **Library**. Dreamweaver MX automatically creates these folders for you on any site that uses templates or Library items. If you do not use templates or Library items, Dreamweaver MX will not put these folders in your directory structure. These folders (Templates and Library) do not need to be uploaded to your Web site if you publish it to the Web. They are for internal purposes only. If Dreamweaver MX sees that these folders are present in your directory structure, it knows to insert any new Templates or Library items that you create into the appropriate folder (Templates or Library) without your having to do so.

---

3. When you are working with templates in Dreamweaver MX, you will typically want to have the **Assets** panel open and the **Templates** category button clicked so that you can see the templates you have within your site. By default, the Assets panel is part of the docked panels. If this panel has been closed, you can open it by choosing **Window > Assets**. Then click on the **Templates** category button to view the templates within your site.

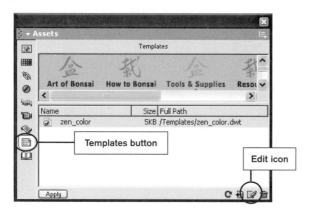

4. Highlight the template called **zen_color** in the **Assets** panel, and then click the **Edit** icon at the bottom of the panel. This opens the template so you can start editing it. **Tip:** As an alternative, you can switch to the Site panel to open **zen_color.dwt** from the Templates folder.

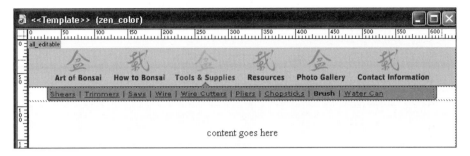

It's easy to tell when you are editing a template because the title bar displays <<Template>>, the template file name, and a .dwt extension. **Note:** *Windows users will not see the .dwt extension unless they are working with file extensions turned on.*

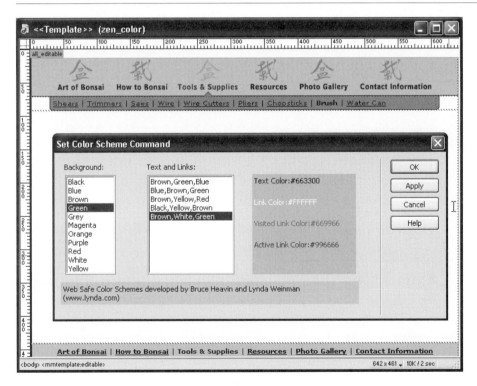

5. To change the color scheme of this template, you will use some of the preset color schemes that ship with Dreamweaver MX. Choose **Commands > Set Color Scheme**. This opens the **Set Color Scheme Command** dialog box. Select **Background: Green** and **Text and Links: Brown, White, Green**. Click **OK**.

6. Close the **zen_color.dwt** template and save your changes when prompted.

NOTE | Templates, Library Items, and HTML

The Dreamweaver MX template format (.dwt) and Library format (.lbi) are internal file-naming conventions only. These files do not mean anything to other HTML editors, nor are they meant to be viewed on the Web from a browser. Templates and Library items are used internally in Dreamweaver MX and function only in Dreamweaver MX. If you base an HTML page on a template or use Library items in it, it will appear as a normal page in the browser, the same as any other HTML page. It will be regarded differently in Dreamweaver MX only, in that it will be updated if the original template or Library items are changed.

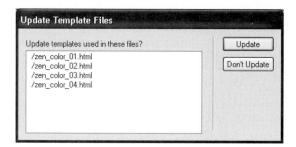

7. After you close and save the modified template, you are notified that you have modified a template and asked if you want to update all the files in your site that use this template. Because you want to apply the new color scheme to all four pages, click **Yes**. If you are presented with the Update Template Files dialog box, click **Update**.

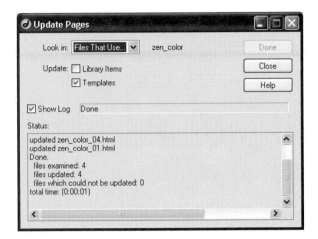

8. Dreamweaver MX will scan your site to determine whether any files are using this template. It will update any files that it finds during the scan. In this case, four files are updated, which are listed in Update Pages dialog box. Once you are finished reviewing this screen, click **Close**.

Note: If you have zen_color.html *open while performing this operation, the color scheme will be updated, but if you close the file without saving the changes, you'll lose them. Make sure you save your changes when you close any open files.*

TIP | Templates and Page Properties

Once a template has been applied to a page, you can no longer edit any of the Page Properties options, with the exception of the page title. Therefore, the only way to change the color scheme is by opening and editing the template itself, as you just did in this exercise.

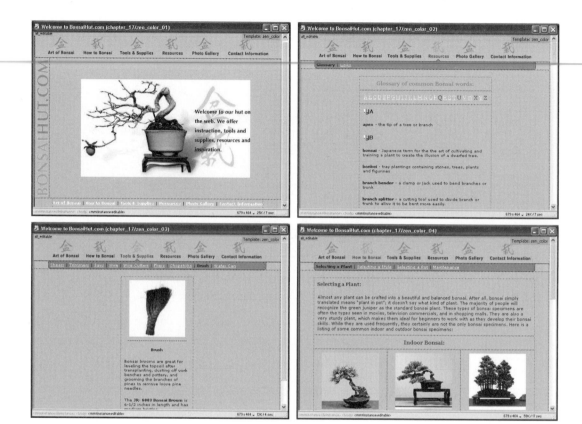

9. Open **zen_color_02.html**, **zen_color_03.html**, and **zen_color_04.html**, and you will see that each now has the new color scheme.

Imagine how much time this could save you if you had hundreds or thousands of pages that were created using a template and that share the same color scheme.

---

10. Close all the files. You will learn how to make a template from scratch in the next exercise.

Working with templates is an excellent technique to ensure design consistency. The only caveat is that you must work from a template file to begin with. How do you do that? Check out the next exercise to find out.

---

2. —————————————**Creating a New Template**

In this next exercise, you are going to create a new template from an existing document and then make parts of your template editable and other parts uneditable. Once you have this skill under your belt, you will understand the capabilities and limitations of templates much more clearly.

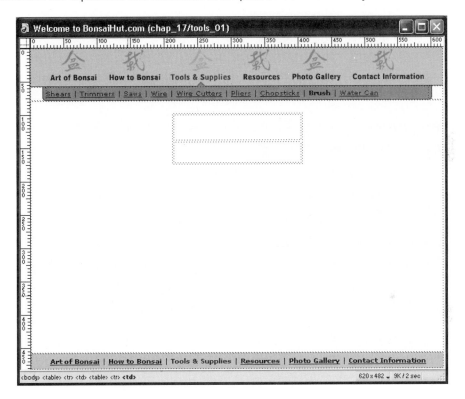

1. Open **tools_01.html** from the **chap_17** folder. This document was created for you, but the following steps would also work on a document of your own creation. Once you have created the basic layout of your document, the next step is to save it as a template.

2. Choose **File > Save As Template**.

3. When the **Save As Template** dialog box opens, make sure this template is named **tools_01**. Dreamweaver MX will automatically enter the name of the HTML file in the **Save As** field. You can see that your other template, zen_color, is already listed in this box. Click **Save**.

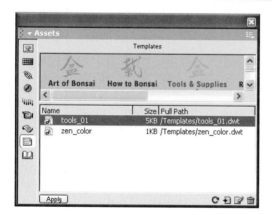

Your new template appears in the Templates category of the Assets panel. The top portion of the Assets panel displays a preview of the template.

Now that you have created your template, you need to decide which areas you want to be able to modify and which areas you want to lock. By default, the entire document is designated as uneditable. This means that if you were to close the file now, it would be impossible for anyone to modify it later. We walk you through this process in the next couple of steps.

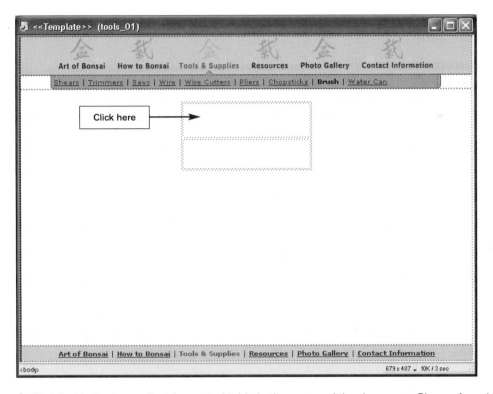

4. Click inside the **top cell** of the nested table in the center of the document. Choose **Insert >
Template Objects > Editable Region** to designate this area as an editable region so that you
or other members of your design team can place photos of the various bonsai tools here.

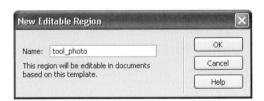

5. When the **New Editable Region** dialog box appears, type **tool_photo** in the **Name** field and
click **OK**.

Notice that the name you entered appears in that cell and as a label, surrounded by a highlighted box. This indicates that this area of the template is editable—you or other members of your team can enter information inside this cell. By naming this region tool_photo, *you can help others know what type of content should be entered there.*

---

6. Click inside the **bottom cell** of the nested table in the center of the document. Choose **Insert > Template Objects > Editable Region**. When the **New Editable Region** dialog box appears, type **tool_info** and click **OK**.

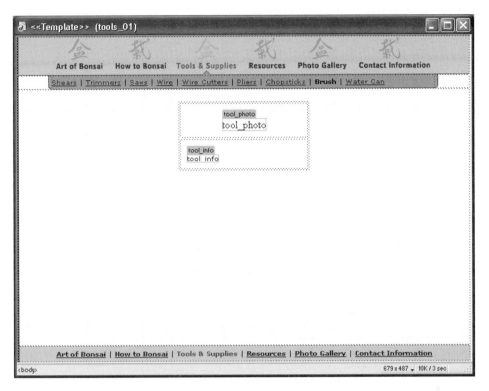

This is what your template should look like at this point. Notice that the two editable regions are aligned differently. You will learn how to adjust that later in this chapter.

7. Now that you have designated the necessary areas as editable, go ahead and **close** this file. When prompted, make sure that you **save** your changes.

Congratulations—you have just created a custom template. Next, you will create a new page based on your newly created template.

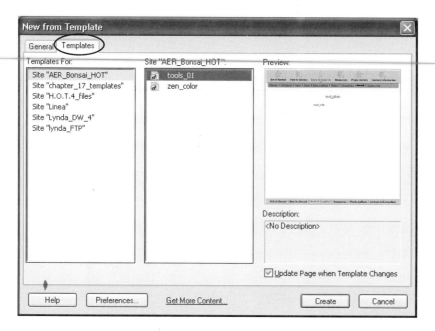

8. Choose **File > New from Template**. This will open the **New from Template** dialog box. Click the **Templates** tab to select it. **Note:** If you are using a Macintosh, you must select **File > New** and then select the Templates tab.

9. Highlight **tools_01** in the list and click **Create**. This creates a new document based on the **tools_01** template. Make sure the correct site it selected in the **Templates For:** column.

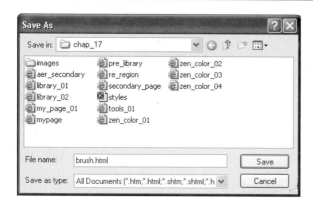

10. Choose **File > Save As** and save the file as **brush.html** inside the **chap_17** folder.

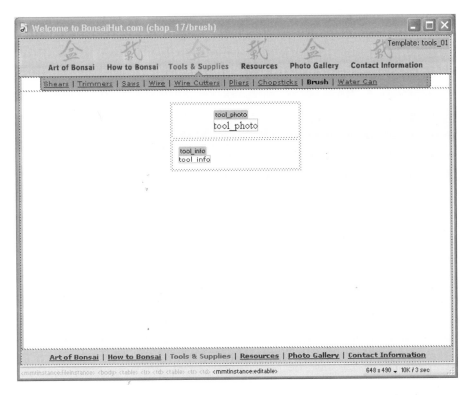

This is what the page looks like with a template applied to it. The highlighted areas are uneditable. The two areas you designated as editable are labeled and are ready to be edited.

TIP | I Don't See Any Highlighting!

If you don't see any highlighting on your screen, make sure that you have the **View > Visual Aids > Invisible Elements** option enabled. If you disable this feature, you will not see any highlighting. You can choose **View > Visual Aids > Invisible Elements** to disable/enable this feature.

You can modify your document's highlighting colors in Dreamweaver MX's Preferences dialog box. By choosing **Edit > Preferences** and then selecting **Highlighting** under **Category**, you can set the highlighting colors to any color you want.

11. Select the text **tool_photo** in the top cell, then press **Delete**. Click the **Insert Image** object in the **Insert** panel.

12. Browse to the **images** folder inside the **chap_17** folder to locate **brush.jpg**. Click **Open** (Windows) or **Choose** (Mac). This inserts the image into this editable region.

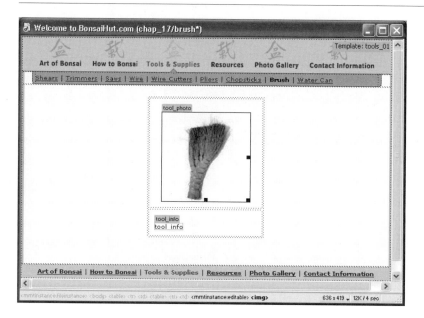

This is what the page looks like with the brush photo inserted.

13. Select the text **tool_info**, press **Delete**, and type:

Brush

Bonsai brooms are great for leveling the topsoil after transplanting, dusting off work benches and pottery, and grooming the branches of pines to remove loose pine needles.

The JR- 6003 Bonsai Broom is 6.5 inches in length and has medium bristles.

TIP | Formatting Table Regions

A great way to leverage the power of Dreamweaver MX templates is to format your editable regions. For example, you can set the editable region so that text entered will automatically be formatted using a specific font such as Verdana, a size such as 2, and cell alignment such as top or right. You can apply a color to specified tables and cells. Best of all, you can also apply styles from an attached style sheet and employ a number of attributes and controls. If you want some great information on Cascading Style Sheets, check out Chapter 11.

14. Save and keep this file open. You'll be using it in the next exercise.

TIP | Detaching a Template

You are not going to do this now, but for future reference it is good to know. There may come a time when you want to modify sections of a page that have a template applied to it. Because some areas are locked, you can't modify them with the template still applied to the page. By choosing **Modify > Templates > Detach from Template**, you can detach the template from the page and make the entire document editable.

3.————————**Modifying a Template**

Now that that you have created your first template, you are ready to learn how to update it. In this exercise, you will change the alignment of the text in your layout, causing the text to move to the center. Then, all you have to do is sit back and watch Dreamweaver MX update all the pages in your site that use this template!

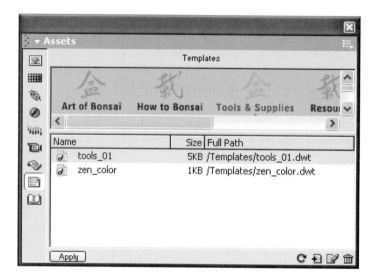

1. Make sure that **brush.html** from the previous exercise is open. Before you can modify a template, you must open it from the **Assets** panel. Double-click the **tools_01** template in the **Assets** panel to open that template.

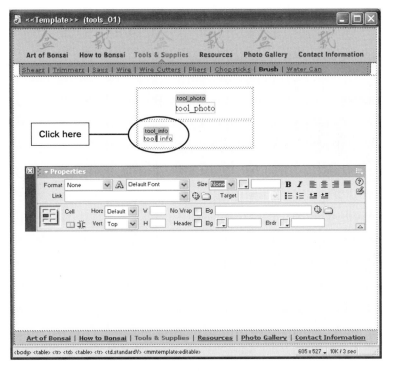

2. The actual template file opens for you to edit. Click inside the **tool_info** editable region.

3. In the **Property Inspector**, click the **Horz** (horizontal) pop-up menu and change it from Default to **Center**. This moves the text to the center of the cell.

4. Close this template file. When prompted, make sure that you save your changes. A dialog box appears, asking if you wish to update the files in your site that use this template.

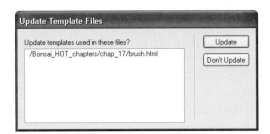

5. Click **Yes**. If you are presented with the **Update Template Files** dialog box, click **Update**. Any files using this template (in this case, the **brush.html** file) will be updated, and a dialog box will list which files were updated. Click **Close**.

This is what brush.html *looks like with the revised template applied to it.*

Note: Templates used in this fashion are helpful only if the pages share the same layout and the same editable region names.

6. Save and **close** all open files and move on to the next exercise.

WARNING | Template Beware!

Once you have applied a template to a page, you can no longer edit any information in the **<head>** tag. This means you can't add any JavaScript, styles, behaviors, or anything else that would be contained within a **<head>** tag. If you do need to add this type of code to a page that is based on a template, you need to break the template by choosing **Modify > Templates > Detach from Template**. This removes the page's link from the original template and allows you to edit anything within the **<head>** element. The downside to this, of course, is that if you make changes to the template, this unlinked copy will not be able to refer to it.

4. ——————————**Library Items in Action**

Library items and templates are somewhat similar in function. Both are used to apply changes to multiple pages with ease. The difference is that templates affect the entire page design, whereas Library items are used for individual page elements. You will start by working with an existing Library item. You'll quickly see how helpful these Library things are and how much time they can save you!

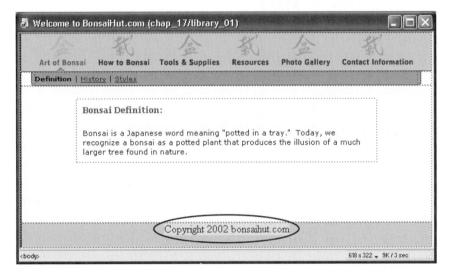

1. Open **library_01.html** from the **chap_17** folder. At the bottom of this page, you will see a copyright notice that is highlighted in yellow. The yellow highlight is an indication that this text is a Library item. You can change the highlight color in the Preferences.

2. In order to modify the Library item, you need to open the **Assets** panel. Choose **Window > Assets** if it's not already open and then click the **Library** button. You will see that one Library item already exists. This is what you will modify.

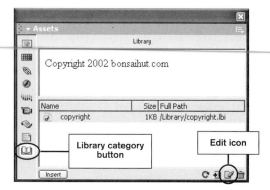

3. Highlight the **copyright** Library item and click the **Edit** icon at the bottom of the panel.

Just as with template, it's easy to tell when you are editing Library items. The title bar displays <<Library Item>> and the file name.

4. Highlight the text **2002** and type **2003**. Can you believe another year has gone by? Sheesh.

5. Close this file. If you are prompted, make sure to **save** your changes.

6. When you are asked to update the pages in your site that use this Library item, click **Yes**. If you see the Update Library Items dialog box, click **Update**.

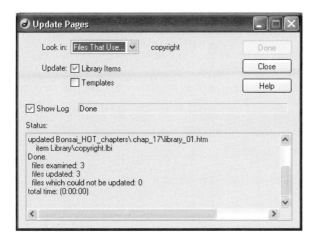

7. The **Update Pages** dialog box appears. Just as with templates, this dialog box gives you all the details of how many and which files were updated in your site. Click **Close** when you are finished reviewing this screen.

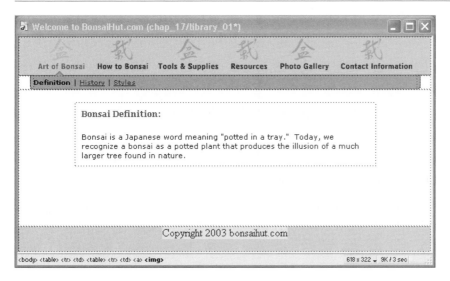

This is what your page should look like with the updated Library item. Can you imagine how long it would take to update this text on a hundred pages? Library items can offer incredible time savings.

8. Save your changes and **close** this file. You will not need it for the next exercise.

5. ————————**Creating a Library Item**

Now that you understand how efficient Library items can be, it's time to create your own. In this exercise, you will create a text navigation bar. You will then apply it to several pages by simply dragging it onto a page.

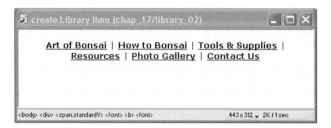

1. Open **library_02.html**. This is a just a simple file with text navigation already created.

2. The **Assets** panel should be open, and the **Library** category should be selected.

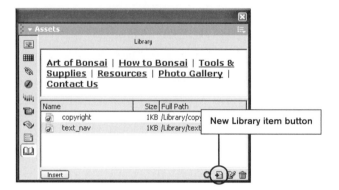

3. In the **library_02.html** file, highlight both lines of text. In the Library category of the **Assets** panel, click the **New Library Item** button. Your new Library item instantly appears in the category. It needs a name, so type **text_nav**.

4. Now that you have created your Library item, you can apply it to a page. Create a new blank document by choosing **File > New > General > HTML**. Save this file inside the **chap_17** folder as **my_page_01.html**.

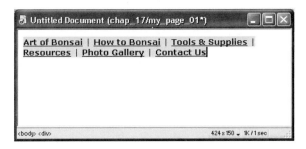

5. In the **Assets** panel, highlight **text_nav** and drag it into the page. As an alternative, you can also click **Insert** at the bottom of the **Assets** panel.

Pow! The Library item is applied to the page. Notice that it did not retain the center alignment you applied when creating it. You'll fix that next.

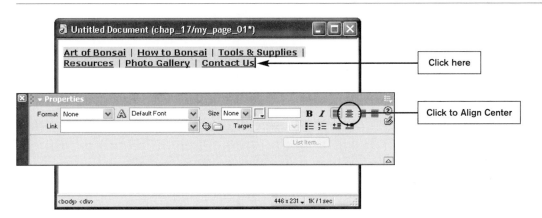

6. Click to the right of the **s** in **Us** and then, in the Property Inspector, click the **Center Align** button to center-align both lines of text.

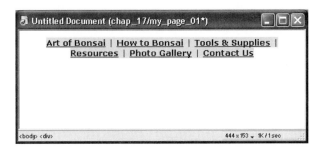

7. Save and **close** the **my_page_01**.html page. Leave **library_02.html** open; you will be working with it in the next exercise.

6. ————————Modifying a Library Item

Now that you know how to create Library items, you are going to modify the one you just created and then watch Dreamweaver MX quickly update your page. Can you imagine how overjoyed you would be if this were a change that needed to be made over hundreds or thousands of pages?

1. The **library_02.html** file should still be open from the previous exercise.

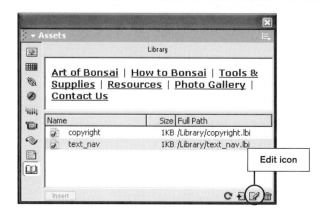

2. In the **Assets** panel, highlight the **text_nav** Library item and click the **Edit** icon. This opens the Library item for editing.

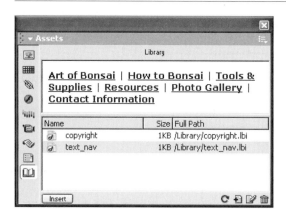

3. Select the word **Us**, and type **Information**. This will replace the word but maintain the link.

4. Close this file, and when you are prompted, make sure you save and update your changes. If you see the **Update Library Items** dialog box, click **Update**. Close the **Update Pages** dialog box when you are done reviewing it.

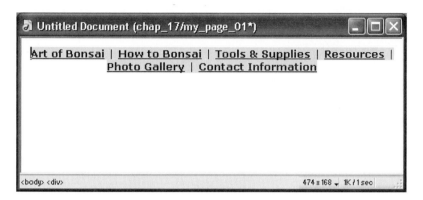

Check out what my_page_01.html *looks like now with the new Library item applied to it.*

5. Save your changes and **close** all documents.

You've just conquered making and modifying a Library item. It's all very simple, once you know how. If you are in the mood, move on to the next chapter. If not, don't worry; it will be there tomorrow. ;-)

18.

Accessibility

What Is Accessibility?	W3C Accessibility Guidelines
Accessibility Preferences	Accessible Images
Accessible Tables	Accessible Frames
Accessible Form Objects

chap_18

Dreamweaver MX
H•O•T CD-ROM

Accessibility is definitely one of the hottest buzzwords in the Web design industry today and rightfully so. This is not just the latest trend in Web development software; it is one of the most significant issues facing Web designers today. Accessibility means making your Web pages accessible to everyone, including those with disabilities. With the passing, and more recent enforcement, of Section 508 of The Rehabilitation Act, Web designers are now charged with not only making their sites visually appealing, but also "accessible." Dreamweaver MX has a suite of features that can aid you in creating accessible Web pages. It even has a great reporting feature that can help you identify accessibility problems in existing Web pages. In this chapter, we show you how to use the accessibility features in Dreamweaver MX to make the process of creating accessible Web pages within your grasp.

What is Accessibility?

Before you learn the nuances of Accessibility in Dreamweaver MX, it's important to first establish what the term "accessibility" means and also what it doesn't mean, specifically in the context of Web design. In a Web design arena, accessibility simply means "online content that can be used by someone with a disability." Although this definition is accurate, we suggest that you consider this as one part of the accessibility equation.

Making your Web sites accessible does not "only" mean you make them accessible to persons with disabilities, but rather you make them more accessible to "all" persons who visit you site, including those with disabilities and those without disabilities. For example, if you implement a technique that makes your site more accessible to a person who is blind and it now becomes less accessible to someone who has good vision, you have failed in making your site accessible.

W3C Accessibility Guidelines

Although Dreamweaver MX can help you create accessible Web pages, you should really understand what, how, and why things are going on behind the scenes. To help you with this task, the W3C (World Wide Web Consortium) has developed a collection of documents to help you understand accessibility and how to create accessible Web pages. Don't feel as if you have to memorize everything in these four documents, but taking the time to familiarize yourself with what's contained within each will be of great help when you have an accessibility question and there is no one around to ask.

There are four documents, published by the W3C, which are the de facto standard for understanding, creating, and developing accessible Web pages. Listed below are the document names, where each can be downloaded, and a brief explanation of each one:

Web Content Accessibility Guidelines 1.0
`http://www.w3.org/TR/WCAG10/`
This is one of the most important documents on Web accessibility. It identifies and explains the 14 guidelines and their checkpoints, and prioritizes each. This is the place to start learning more about Web accessibility.

Techniques for Web Content Accessibility Guidelines 1.0
`http://www.w3.org/TR/WCAG10-TECHS/`
This document gives you techniques and examples for making your Web sites accessible. Once you understand the 14 guidelines of Web accessibility, this document will help you create accessible pages by giving you sample code and different scenarios you might encounter. You will want to print and keep a copy of this one nearby.

CSS Techniques for Web Content Accessibility Guidelines 1.0
`http://www.w3.org/TR/WCAG10-CSS-TECHS/`
This document focuses on creating accessible Web pages using Cascading Style Sheets. You will find
examples using CSS in addition to deprecated code, which illustrates something developers should
not do! This is a really important document and should be read carefully.

HTML Techniques for Web Content Accessibility Guidelines 1.0
`http://www.w3.org/TR/WCAG10-HTML-TECHS/`
This document focuses on creating accessible Web pages using HyperText Markup Language (HTML).
You can probably imagine why this document is so important. ;-) Similar to the CSS Techniques document, this one also provides the reader with good code examples and bad examples, illustrating what
developers should not do.

I. ————————Accessibility Preferences

The first step to work with accessibility is to learn how to turn on the Accessibility preferences in Dreamweaver MX, which you will learn about in this exercise. These options let you create accessible pages as you add content to your pages, instead of adding them when the page is finished. This proactive approach can save you time and make sure you don't forget something later. If you learn to work with these options turned on, you will discover that creating accessible Web pages is no more difficult than creating non-accessible Web pages.

1. In Dreamweaver MX, choose **Edit > Preferences** (Windows) or **Dreamweaver > Preferences** (Macintosh) to open the **Preferences** dialog box.

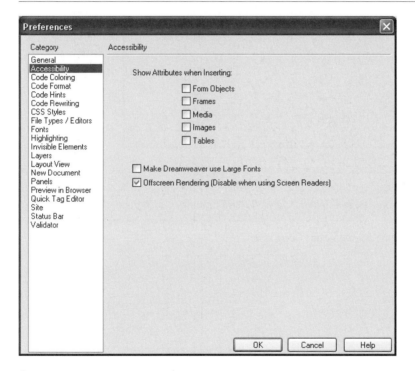

2. Select the **Accessibility** option in the category section to see what accessibility options are available in Dreamweaver MX. By default, the **Offscreen Rendering (Disable when using Screen Readers)** checkbox will be selected. **Note:** The two checkboxes at the bottom of this dialog box are available to Windows users only.

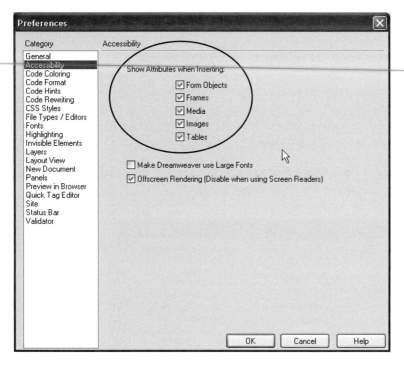

3. Check each of the checkboxes as shown in the image above. As you can see, you don't have to turn all of the accessibility options on; you can turn on only the options you want. At any time, you can return to this dialog box and uncheck any of these options to turn them off.

4. Click **OK** to close the Preferences dialog box.

You will get a chance to work with all of the accessibility features in the following exercises, so keep on reading!

IBM Home Page Reader

Throughout this chapter, you will see us refer to something called a "screen reader." We are using this term to refer to screen reading software collectively. One of the most popular screen reader programs is IBM Home Page Reader 3.0. This program will help blind and visually impaired users surf the Web by reading the contents of Web pages aloud.

We suggest that you download and install a trial version of the Home Page Reader, close your eyes, and experience firsthand what it is like surfing the Web as a blind or visually impaired person. You will be amazed at how much we all take for granted. Hopefully, this will convince you even more that making accessible Web pages is really the right thing to do! ;-)

You can download a trial version of the IBM Home Page Reader program at `http://www-3.ibm.com/able/hpr.html`. Currently, only a Windows version is available.

2. _____Inserting Accessible Images

There are millions of people in the world that have some type of visual impairment, such as color blindness and partial and/or total blindness. Because the Web is a visual-centric environment, making the images on your pages accessible should be a priority for every Web designer. In this exercise, you will learn how to add alternate text and a long description for images on a Web page.

1. Copy **chap_18** to your hard drive. Define your site for Chapter 18, using the **chap_18** folder as the local root folder. If you need a refresher on this process, visit Exercise 1 in Chapter 3, *"Site Control."*

2. Open the **images.html** page from the **chap_18** folder. Right now this is just a blank page, but it won't be for long. ;-)

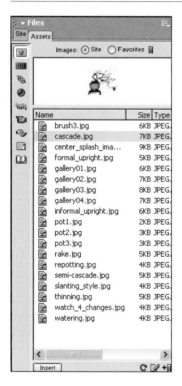

3. Make sure the **Assets** panel is open. If it's not, select **Window > Assets** (F11).

4. From the **Assets** panel, click and drag the **cascade.jpg** image onto the page. When you release the mouse button, the **Image Tag Accessibility Attributes** dialog box will open.

WARNING | Accessibility and the Site Panel

Throughout this book, we have instructed you to drag images from the Site panel onto your page. This technique ensures that your images are always selected from within the current local root folder, which in turn ensures that path to the image is correct. However, if you drag an image from the Site panel onto your page, you will not be prompted for the accessibility options, even if they have been turned on. This is just one of those gotchas that you need to be aware of when you are creating accessible conscientious Web pages.

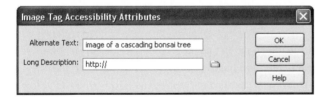

5. In the **Alternate Text** text field, enter the words **image of a cascading bonsai tree**. This will create an ALT tag for this image with whatever text is entered in this text field. The ALT attribute information is read out loud by a screen reader when it encounters an image on a Web page. You want to make sure that whatever text you enter here reflects the visual makeup of the image.

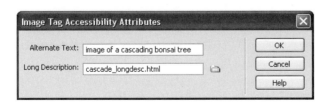

6. Click the **small folder** to the right of the **Long Description** text field. Browse to the **chap_18** folder and select **cascade_longdesc.html** and click **OK**. Click **OK** again to close the Image Tag Accessibility Attributes dialog box.

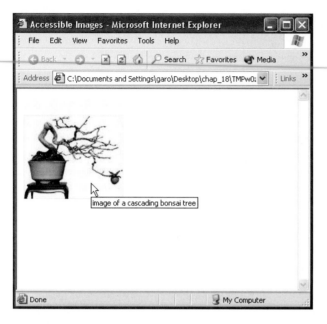

*The **alt** attribute is helpful to visually impaired people because that text is read out loud by the screen reader programs. In addition, in some browsers the text will appear in a small help tag (tooltip) when the mouse hovers over the image.*

7. Press **F12** to preview this page in a browser. Since you aren't using a screen reader to view this page, you won't notice anything visually different unless you hover your mouse over the image of the bonsai tree. For any image that contains an **alt** attribute, that text will appear as a tooltip (small yellow text box) when the mouse hovers over that image. **Note:** This feature is not supported by all browsers. Return to Dreamweaver MX.

NOTE | The longdesc Attribute

Adding the **alt** attribute to all of the images on your pages is a big part of making accessible Web pages. However, there may be times when you want to offer a more verbose explanation of an image. In these cases, you should use the **longdesc** attribute as well. The **longdesc** attribute lets you link to a text file that contains a longer description of the image. The link is no different than any other link, except it won't show up to people who aren't using a screen reader. If an image has a **longdesc** attribute applied, and a screen reader program encounters the image on the page, it will be read as a link so a visually impaired person knows there is a link to a longer description of that particular image.

8. Click the **Show Code View** button. This will change your document view so you can see the code being used to construct your page. Notice the **alt** and **longdesc** attributes that were added to the **<img>** tag. This is the code that Dreamweaver MX added when you entered information in the **Image Tag Accessibility Attributes** dialog box.

9. Click the **Show Design View** button. **Save** and **close** this file, you won't need it for the next exercise.

Adding the **alt** *and* **longdesc** *attributes to all of the images on your page is one of the easiest and most significant ways you can help make your Web pages accessible to everyone.*

3. —————————Inserting Accessible Tables

According to the Web Accessibility Initiative Guidelines, you should not use tables to control the layout of your pages. Instead, you should use layers and style sheets as we demonstrated in Chapter 8, *"Layout."* However, this does not mean that you cannot use tables at all. Tables are still very useful for displaying data in columns and rows. In this exercise, you will learn how to make a table more accessible.

1. Open the **table.html** file from the **chap_18** folder. Woo-hoo, another blank page! Hey, at least we didn't make you create and save it yourself. ;-)

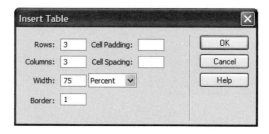

2. Click the **Insert Table** button in the **Common** panel. This will open the **Insert Table** dialog box. Make sure your options match the ones shown in the image above. Click **OK**.

This will close the Insert Table dialog box and open the Accessibility Options for Tables dialog box.

3. For the **Caption** option, enter **styles of bonsai trees**. The caption tag should be used to describe the purpose of the table. This text will appear in a row at the top of the table.

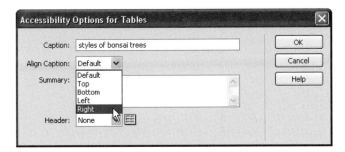

4. For the **Align Caption** option, choose **Right**. This will align the caption text along the top right of the table. This is purely a visual preference and has no impact on the accessibility of the table.

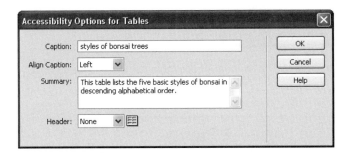

5. For the **Summary** option, enter **This table lists the five basic styles of bonsai trees in descending alphabetical order.** The summary should explain the structure of the table and the relationship of the information in the table cells and rows.

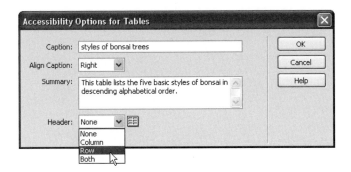

6. For the **Header** option, choose **Row**. This will specify the first row as headers for the table, using **<th>** tags. Screen readers read table headers with more importance than normal cells. The header is typically used to identify the types of data in a table.

7. Click **OK**.

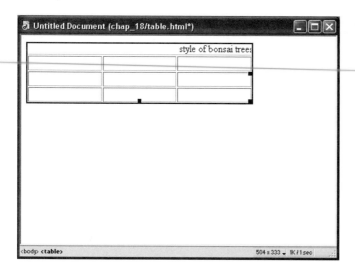

This is what the table should look like at this point. The caption for the table has been added to the top row.

NOTE | The Summary Attribute and Caption and TH Tags

The Web Content Accessibility Guidelines 1.0 dictates that you should not use HTML tables for layout purposes. However, there may be times when using a table makes sense, such as displaying a spreadsheet of numeric data online. In these cases, you want to make sure you use the proper supporting table attributes so your table is accessible to those with screen reading programs. There are a few tags and attributes you should know about:

`<caption>`: This tag is used to provide a brief description of the table's content. This is read first by the screen reading software and lets the user know that they have encountered a table and what is contained inside the table. For example, "A list of bonsai classes" would be an appropriate caption for an HTML table containing information on bonsai classes. The caption appears as the first row in the table and is visible on the page.

Summary: The **summary** attribute is used to provide a detailed explanation of the HTML table. For example, "This table lists the available bonsai classes, instructor, classroom number, and date of class in chronological order." would be a good table summary. The summary is not seen in the browser and is read only by screen reading programs.

`<th>`: The **`<th>`** tag is used to identify certains cells as a header. This lets the user know if the information in the table is organized horizontally or vertically and what the major groups of data are in the table. In most cases, the first row serves as the headers in a table.

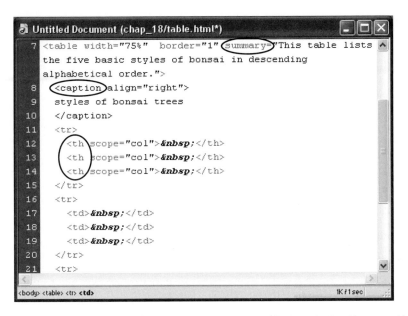

8. Click the **Show Code View** button to view the HTML code for this page. Here you can see the various tags that were added to make this table accessible.

9. Click the **Show Design View** button. **Save** and **close** this page.

_____**Inserting Accessible Frames**

Most accessibility experts recommend that you avoid using frames because of the problems they prevent for people using screen readers. Although we agree, we also recognize that there may be times when you just have to use frames. This exercise shows you how to add frames to a page and make them accessible by adding a title to each frame.

1. Create a new blank HTML document.

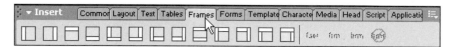

2. Click the **Frames** tab in the **Insert** panel.

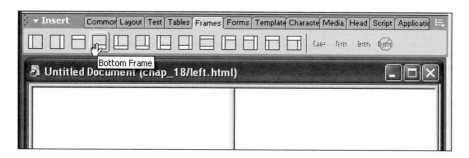

3. Click the **Bottom Frame** button. This will automatically create a frameset with a small frame at the bottom and a large frame at the top. The **Frame Tag Accessibility Attributes** dialog box will open as well.

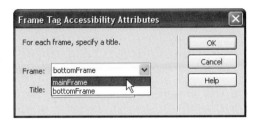

4. From the **Frame** drop-down menu, select **mainFrame**. This will let you specify the Title from the mainFrame (top) portion of this frameset.

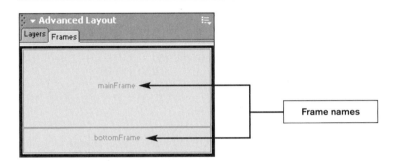

Normally, when you create frames you have to manually give each frame a name. This is usually done with the Name option in the Property Inspector. However, when you choose from one of the presets in the Frames panel, Dreamweaver MX will automatically assign names to each frame. You can see the names of each frame by opening the Advanced Layout panel. In this example, it assigned mainFrame to the top frame and bottomFrame to the bottom frame. That makes sense. ;-) If you were creating your own custom frameset, you would have to name each frame yourself. We show you how to name each frame in Chapter 9, "Frames."

5. In the **Title** text field, enter **content area**. This will add the `title` attribute to the `<frame>` tag so that when the page is read through a screen reader the title will be read out loud, offering the person viewing the page a better idea what type of content is on the page. In this case, the mainFrame area is where all the content from other pages will be loaded.

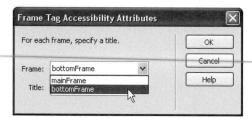

6. From the **Frame** drop-down menu, select **bottomFrame**. This will let you specify the Title from the bottomFrame (bottom) portion of this frameset.

7. In the **Title** text field, enter **navigation area**. This will add the `title` attribute to the **<frame>** tag, and when the page is read through a screen reader, the title will be read out loud so that the person viewing the page will have a better idea what type of content is on the page. In this example, the bottomFrame area is where the buttons and other navigation elements will be placed. Click OK.

8. Choose **File > Save Frameset As** and save it as **frameset.html** inside the **chap_18** folder.

9. Click inside the **top** frame and choose **File > Save Frame As** and save it as **top.html** inside the **chap_18** folder.

10. Click inside the **bottom** frame and choose **File > Save Frame As** and save it as **bottom.html** inside the **chap_18** folder.

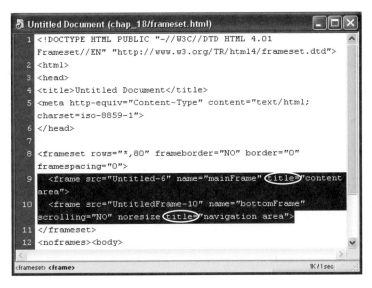

11. Select the **<frameset>** tag in the **Tag Selector**. Click the **Show Code View** button. Notice that the **title** attribute has been added to the **<frame>** tags.

NOTE | Title Attribute vs. Page Title

The **title** attribute is not the same as the page title. The page title appears at the top of the browser window and is set using the **<title>** tag for each HTML page. The **title** attribute is added to HTML tags to give an object a name. The **title** attribute is read aloud by screen readers to assist visually impaired users navigate around a Web page but is not visible to regular browsers.

---

12. Close all open files, you won't be using these files any more.

Inserting Accessible Form Objects

Form objects tend to be one of the most overlooked elements on an accessible Web page. For some reason, many people don't know that there are problems with forms and accessibility, as well as good ways to make form objects accessible. Fortunately, Dreamweaver MX has a feature that will help you make your form objects accessible, which is exactly what you are going to learn to do in this exercise.

1. Open the **forms.html** file from the **chap_18** folder. Yup, you guessed it—another blank page. Hey, we had to leave something for you to do. ;-)

2. Click the **Forms** tab in the **Insert** panel. This will display a collection of buttons that let you add various form objects to your page.

3. Click the **Text Field** button in the **Forms** panel to insert a text field on the page. This will open the **Input Tag Accessibility Attributes** dialog box. This occurs because you selected this option in the Accessibility preferences in Exercise 1.

Input Tag Accessibility Attributes

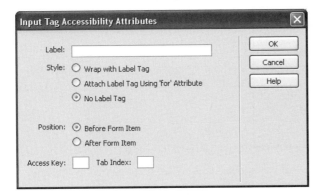

The chart below outlines the various options available in the Input Tag Accessibility Attributes dialog box.

Input Tag Accessibility Attributes	
Option	**Description**
Label	This text will appear next to the form object. Depending on which Position option you choose, the text will appear before or after the form object.
Style: Wrap with Label Tag	This option will place a **<label>** tag around the form object.
Style: Attach Label Tag Using 'for' Attribute	This option uses the **for** attribute to place a **<label>** tag around the form object. This causes a focus rectangle to appear around the form object and label. This is the recommended choice for accessibility. **Note:** Behavior will vary between browsers.
Style: No Label Tag	This option will not add a **<label>** tag around the form object.
Position: Before Form Item	This radio button will place the Label text before the form object.
Position: After Form Item	This radio button will place the Label text after the form object.
Access Key	Windows only—whatever key you enter here + the Ctrl key can be used to select this object in the browser window.
Tab Index	This option sets the tab order of the form object. This can help you specify how the form is navigated by someone using the Tab key to move from one form object to the next.

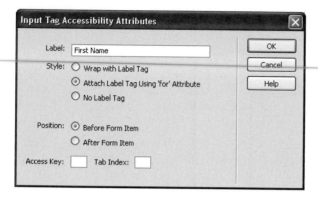

4. For the **Label** option, enter **First Name**. This text will appear on the Web page as normal text and lets the user know what information should be entered into this text field.

5. Make sure the **Style: Attach Label Tab Using 'for' Attribute** radio button is selected. This will cause a focus rectangle to appear around the form object and the label. This lets the user select the form object by clicking anywhere within the focus rectangle.

6. Make sure the **Position: Before Form Item** radio button is selected. This will place the label text before the form object. You probably already guessed that, huh? ;-) Click **OK**.

7. Click **Yes** when you are prompted to **Add form tag?** The form object will not work properly unless it is enclosed within the **<form>** tag. We discuss forms in greater detail in Chapter 13, "*Forms.*"

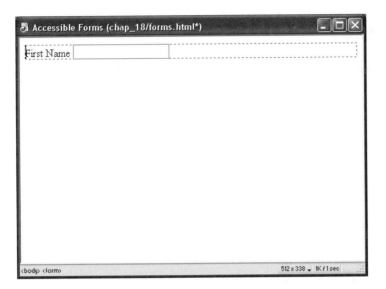

This is what the text field looks like on the page. How about that for excitement? ;-)

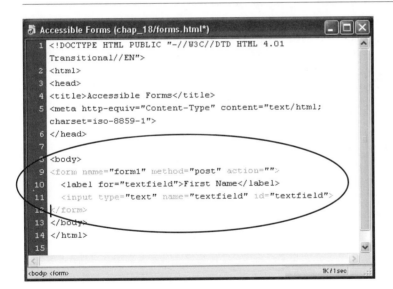

8. Click the **Show Code View** button. This is the code that was added to the form object to make it more accessible. Isn't it nice that you don't have to enter all of that code manually. Phew!

NOTE | Accessibility Testing

This chapter showed you how to create accessible Web pages as the page was created. What can you do if you already have a completed Web site and you want to make sure it is accessible? There is good news, folks! Dreamweaver MX has a feature that will analyze your Web pages and report back any accessibility errors it finds. Simply choose **File > Check Page > Check Accessibility** and Dreamweaver MX will analyze the page you have open and provide you with a list of errors.

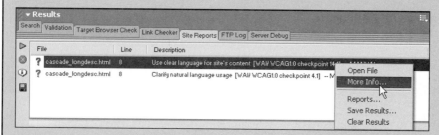

The **Results** panel is used to provide reports on the Web pages in your site, including the Check Accessibility report. If you right-click on one of the entries and choose **More Info**, you can access the UsableNet Accessibility Reference Guide to get more information.

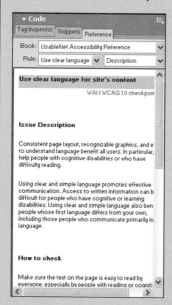

The UsableNet Accessibility Reference Guide will help you make sense of the accessibility errors in the Results panel. This is a fantastic resource that is built right into Dreamweaver MX. Sweet!

9. If you want, go ahead and try adding other form objects to your page. There is no harm in experimenting with these settings, and practice will definitely make you more comfortable.

10. Save and **close** this page.

Wow, another chapter under your belt—congratulations. If you have the energy, turn the page and move on to the next chapter.

19.
Plug-Ins

| Linking to Sounds | Embedding Sounds |
| Inserting Flash Content |
| Inserting Director (Shockwave) Content |
| Inserting QuickTime Content |

chap_19

Dreamweaver MX
H•O•T CD-ROM

Hey, you're almost through the book! There's still another important feature of Dreamweaver MX to learn about, though—how to work with **plug-in**-based content. What are plug-ins, you might ask? Plug-ins are special program extensions installed in your end user's browser that allow the user to view plug-in-based content, such as Flash, Shockwave, Real Audio, QuickTime, etc.

It's good to understand how to work with plug-ins in Dreamweaver MX because you may want to publish multimedia effects to your page that require plug-ins, such as sound, Flash content, Director content (Shockwave), or QuickTime content. In this chapter, you'll learn how to add this kind of content in Dreamweaver MX via a variety of objects, and you'll learn how to set parameters in the Property Inspector to control how and when your plug-in-based content will play.

Exciting as this sounds, it's also the area of Web development where compatibility issues between browsers really get intense. Not everyone has the same plug-ins loaded, and some of the plug-ins work differently on Macs than they do in Windows. Dreamweaver MX does a great job of letting you put this content on your site. It's the rest of the Web's limitations that you'll more likely have to struggle with!

NOTE | What Is a Plug-In?

In the early days of the Web, any file that wasn't an HTML file had to be downloaded and required a separate "player" for the content to be seen. This was a hassle for most Web surfers, because it meant that you had to break the flow of a good "surf" to view material in an external application. In response to this problem, Netscape introduced the idea of plug-ins, which extended the capability of HTML pages to display content that wasn't HTML-based. Today, a variety of plug-ins are pre-installed in most browsers. These can include QuickTime, Flash, and RealPlayer. This chapter focuses on techniques to insert plug-in-based content into HTML pages so it can be viewed as an "inline" element, without requiring the use of an outside player application.

Plug-Ins Require Viewer Participation

As you are working through these exercises, you might find yourself being directed to download plug-ins from the Internet or reassign them in your browser preferences. If this seems like a hassle, remember that you are asking your audience to do the same thing when you present plug-in-based content to them!

URLs for Downloading Plug-Ins	
Plug-Ins	**URL**
QuickTime	http://www.apple.com/quicktime
Flash	http://www.macromedia.com/software/flashplayer/
Shockwave	http://www.macromedia.com/software/shockwaveplayer/
Acrobat Reader	http://www.adobe.com/products/acrobat/readstep2.html
Real Player	http://www.real.com/player/

I. _____Linking to Sounds

There are multiple ways to add sound to your page. In this first exercise, you will learn to add sound to your page simply by creating a link to a sound file. As you will see, there are some nuances to consider when you are working with sound files. For example, there is no standard format for sounds on the Web. Sounds are handled differently between browsers and operating systems (as if designing Web pages was not difficult enough). But have no fear! By the time you finish the hands-on exercises in this chapter, you'll have a much better understanding of how to add sound to your site.

1. Define your site for Chapter 19. Copy the contents of **chap_19** to your hard drive and define the site using the **chap_19** folder. For a refresher on this process, revisit Exercise 1 in Chapter 3, "*Site Control.*"

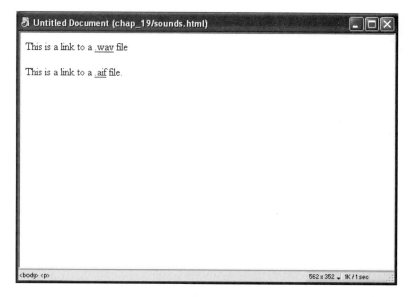

2. Open **sounds.html**. You will see two links at the top of the page. These two links point directly to two different sound files. The first link points to a .wav file, and the second link points to an .aif file.

3. Click on the **.wav** link at the top of the page. In the **Property Inspector**, notice that this links to the **tell-me-about.wav** file. That's all there is to it. When the user clicks on this link in a Web browser, the sound plays. You'll need to preview this file in a browser in order to play the sound.

4. Click on the **.aif** link. Notice that this link points to the **sound.aif** file. Nothing too complicated about this so far. You are simply creating a link, but instead of pointing to an HTML document, you are pointing to a sound file.

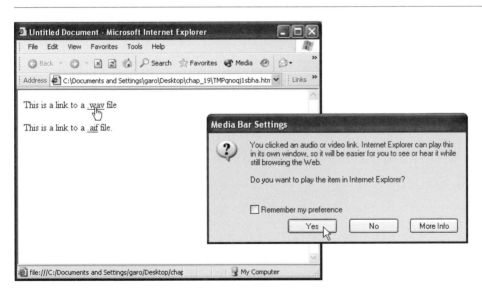

When the page is previewed in Internet Explorer 6.02 on the PC, clicking on the .wav link will open the Media Bar Settings dialog box. In the Windows version of Internet Explorer 6.02, you have the option of playing the sound through the Media Player in Internet Explorer by clicking Yes, or by saving the sound file to your hard drive by clicking No. As you will see shortly, clicking on the .aif link does not have the same effect.

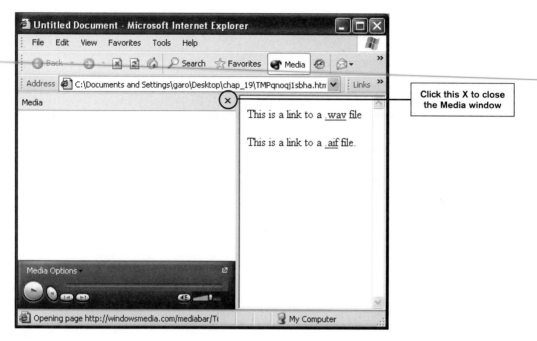

Here you can see the .wav file being played back through Internet Explorer 6.02 on the PC. You can close the Media Bar in Internet Explorer by clicking on the small black X in the upper-right corner of the Media window.

TIP | Different Sound Players

Both Netscape Navigator and Internet Explorer let you choose what application or plug-in will play audio files found on Web pages. In fact, you can set a different one for each type of audio format. For example, you might choose to have the QuickTime plug-in play .aif and .wav files and have the Flash plug-in play .swf files. You can control this by modifying your browser preferences. Check these settings if you experience any problems while trying to play sound files. For instructions on how to change these settings, refer to your browser's Help feature.

Clicking on the .aif link launches the QuickTime plug-in, if you have the QuickTime Player installed. **Note:** *This works identically on the Mac and Windows operating systems.*

---

5. Press **F12** to preview this page in a browser. Click on each of the links. Clicking on the **.wav** link plays the sound of a man saying, "Tell me about your childhood." Clicking on the **.aif** link plays a beeping sound. You will have to use the **Back** button in the browser after clicking on the first link. Depending on how your browser preferences are set up and what operating system you are using, clicking on the links might launch different audio players—or none at all!

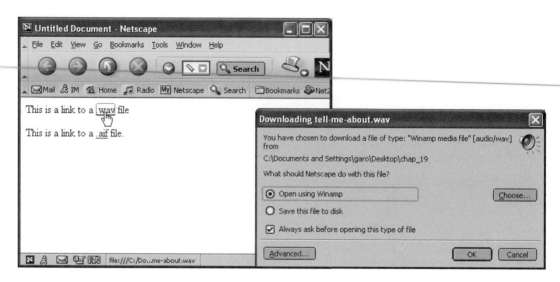

Clicking on the links in Netscape Navigator 7 on the PC is similar, but not identical, to Internet Explorer 6.02. This inconsistent behavior is just one of the problems with playing audio files in a Web browser. It has nothing to do with Dreamweaver MX, but everything to do with incompatibilities between browsers, file formats, and platforms.

6. Return to Dreamweaver MX and close the file.

Different Sound Formats

One of the problems in adding sound to your Web page is deciding which format to use. Most Web publishers use either .aif or .wav files—the two native sound formats for the Mac and Windows operating systems. It is a good idea, however, to be familiar with the other formats that you might run into on the Web. The chart below gives you an idea of what's out there:

Sound Formats	
Extension	**Description**
.au	This format was one of the first introduced on the Internet. It was designed for NeXT and Sun Unix systems.
.aiff/.aif	The .aif (**A**udio **I**nterchange **F**ormat) was developed by Apple and is also used on SGI machines. It is the main audio format for Macintosh computers.
.midi/.mid	The .midi (**M**usical **I**nstrument **D**igital **I**nterface) format was designed to translate how music is produced. MIDI files store just the sequencing information (notes, timing, and voicing) required to play back a musical composition, rather than a recording of the composition itself, so these files are usually small, but playback quality is unpredictable.
.MP3	The .MP3 (**M**PEG-1 Audio Layer-**3**) format is the hottest audio file format on the Web. It offers superior compression and great quality. This file format is widely used in Macromedia Flash content
.ra/.ram	The .ra (**R**eal **A**udio) format was designed to offer streaming audio on the Internet.
.rmf	The .rmf (**R**ich **M**usic **F**ormat) was designed by Headspace and is used in the Beatnik plug-in. This format offers good compression and quality.
.swa	The .swa (**S**hock**w**ave **A**udio) format was developed by Macromedia and is used in Flash.
.wav	The .wav audio format was developed by IBM and Microsoft. This is the main audio format for the Windows operating system, but .wav files play on Macs and other systems as well.

2. _____**Embedding Sounds**

In addition to linking to a sound file, there is another approach to adding sound to your Web pages. You can choose to embed the sound so that it plays from your page, instead of linking to it (as in the last exercise). This approach is good if you just want to play, not download, sounds within the Web browser. Embedding sounds gives you much more control over them, because they actually appear inside your HTML files, along with the other content. By modifying specific parameters, you can control when the sound plays and how it appears on the page, whether it loops (replays continuously) or not, and several other settings. So if you embed your sounds, you get more control, and hey, that's what most people want in life, right?

1. Open **embed.html** inside the **chap_19** folder. This is simply a blank file that we created for you.

2. Click on the **Plugin** object in the **Media** panel. Browse to the **chap_19 folder** and highlight **sound.aif**. Click **OK**. This inserts a small plug-in icon on your page.

In this example, it does not matter where the sound file is placed physically on the page. If you had a page where you wanted the sound controllers (Play, Stop, and Rewind buttons) to appear, you would simply position this element like any other image or text component of any page.

3. With the sound still selected, click on the **Parameters** button in the **Property Inspector**. This opens the **Parameters** dialog box, which is where you would insert any parameters and values you needed. We've listed some URLs at the end of this exercise that will give you more information about parameters and values; there are way too many to list in this book.

4. Under **Parameter** in the **Parameters** dialog box, type **autoplay**, then press **Tab**. Type **false**, and then click **OK**. This prevents the sound file from playing automatically and instead causes it to wait until the user clicks on the Play button. This is a very useful parameter! ;-)

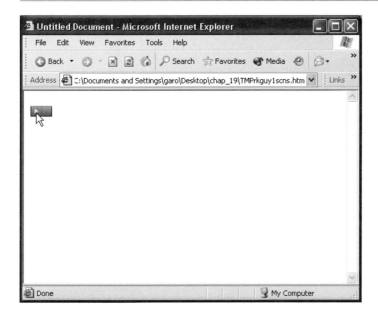

5. Press **F12** to preview your page in a browser. Click on the **Play** button to hear the sound. Here you can see that QuickTime is being used to play .aif files in Netscape Navigator 7 for the PC. **Note:** If you get a broken image icon, you might have to download the plug-in from **http://www.apple.com/quicktime**.

6. Return to Dreamweaver MX to save and close the file.

NOTE | What's a Parameter?

Most plug-in content is controlled by a variety of parameters (sometimes referred to as attributes), which are different for each kind of plug-in. A parameter is an option passed to the plug-in that tells it how to behave. In this exercise, you learned how to set the autoplay parameter to off. That parameter is part of the QuickTime specification.

This chapter covers sound, Flash, Shockwave, and QuickTime, but there are many other types of plug-ins on the Web as well. In order to learn what all the parameters are for a plug-in, it's best to visit the site from which it can be downloaded. Here's a list of sites with more information on plug-in parameters from a variety of vendors.

LiveAudio Plug-In
http://developer.netscape.com/docs/manuals/js/client/jsguide/liveaud.htm

Apple's QuickTime Plug-In
http://www.apple.com/quicktime/authoring/embed2.html

Macromedia's Flash Plug-In
http://www.macromedia.com/support/flash/ts/documents/tag_attributes.htm

Macromedia's Shockwave Plug-In
http://www.macromedia.com/support/director/how/shock/objembed.html

Netscape's Plug-In Registry
http://www.home.netscape.com/plugins

3. Inserting Flash Content

Because both Dreamweaver MX and Flash MX are Macromedia products, it is not entirely surprising that Dreamweaver MX's support for Flash MX is superb. Instead of the generic Insert plug-in object that you used in the last exercise, Dreamweaver MX has a Flash object all its own.

1. Create a new document and save it as **flash.html** inside the **chap_19** folder.

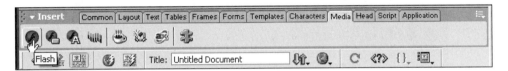

2. Click on the **Flash** object in the **Media** panel, and browse to insert **splash.swf**. Click **OK**. This Flash piece was donated courtesy of Greg Penny of Flower Records (**http://www.flowerrecords.com**) and was designed by Richard Joffray (**http://www.joffray.com**).

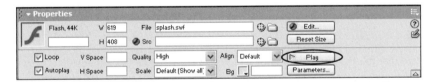

3. Notice that the **Property Inspector** has a **Play** button. You should be able to play the content right in Dreamweaver MX, unlike DHTML or generic plug-in content. Press **F12** to view the content in your browser, to check it again. It's that simple.

4. Return to Dreamweaver MX. Because Flash is vector-based, it can scale. Change both the **W** and **H** properties to **100%**, and press **F12** again. Now change the size of your browser. The content in your browser scales, too! This happens only if you set the width and height information to percentages.

5. Save and close the file.

The next exercise explains how to embed Shockwave content.

4. ———————————Inserting Director (Shockwave) Content

Next, you'll get a chance to work with some Director (Shockwave) content. Once again, because this is a Macromedia product, you'll have the advantage of using an Insert Shockwave object instead of the generic Plugin object.

1. Create a new document and save it as **director.html** inside the **chap_19** folder.

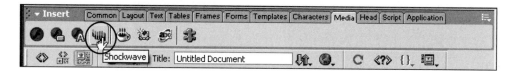

2. Click on the **Shockwave** object in the **Media** panel, and browse to **leroy.dcr**. Click **OK**.

3. Notice that the **Property Inspector** has **W 32** and **H 32** as the dimensions. These are the default dimensions that you'll see for Director or QuickTime content, because Dreamweaver MX can't detect the size of these two formats automatically. You'll need to type in the correct dimensions to get this object to work.

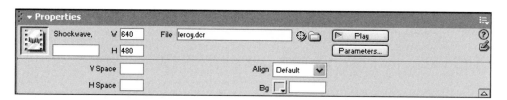

4. Enter the values **W 640** and **H 480**, and press **F12** to preview the content. How did we know that the width and height of the piece were 640 x 480? Because Bruce, Lynda's husband, created it! Sadly, you must know the dimensions of the Shockwave piece before you enter the values, because Dreamweaver MX doesn't detect them for you.

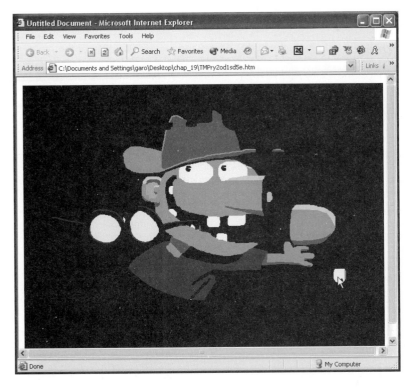

5. Try pulling Leroy's eyeglasses off. Lots of parts come off, so keep pulling on things. ;-)

6. Return to Dreamweaver MX. Save and close the file.

> **NOTE | What Is Shockwave?**
>
> **Shockwave** is a plug-in that allows a Web audience to view Macromedia Director content online. The plug-in is over 1MB in size, whereas the Flash plug-in is under 200K. Macromedia Director, like Flash, is an authoring tool that supports better animation, sound, and interactivity than HTML pages do. The differences between Flash and Director relate to how the authoring tool is structured, how the interactivity is programmed, and how images are formatted for the Web. Flash is installed in more browsers than Shockwave, and many more people know and use the authoring tool. Director is by far a more powerful authoring tool with much more sophisticated programming capabilities, but because of the larger download and smaller amount of Director content on the Web, it doesn't have the installed user base of Flash. For more information about the two, visit **http://www.macromedia.com** to read the specifications and features.

What Is QuickTime?

QuickTime is a both a file format and a plug-in that includes sound and movies. It is one of the most versatile file plug-ins on the Web, because it is able to play all of the formats listed in the chart below.

What QuickTime Supports		
3dMF	Image Sequence movie exporters	PLS
AIFF	JPEG/JFIF	PNG
AU	Karaoke	QuickTime image
AVI	MacPaint	QuickTime movie
BMP	Macromedia Flash	SGI
Cubic VR	MIDI	System 7
DLS	MPEG1	Sound
DV Stream	MP3	Targa
Flash Pix	Photoshop	Text
FLC	PICT	TIFF
GIF	Picture	WAV

5. ————————Inserting a QuickTime Movie

QuickTime content is inserted in Dreamweaver MX using the **Plugin** object. This exercise shows you how to embed the content and preview the results.

1. Create a new document and save it as **quicktime.html** inside the **chap_19** folder.

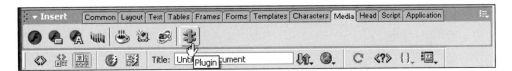

2. Click on the **Plugin** object in the **Media** panel, and browse to the file **bonsai.mov**. Click **OK**.

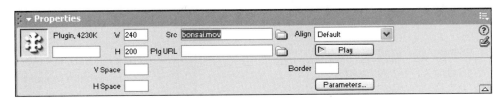

3. Change the width and height information to **W 240, H 200** in the **Property Inspector**. Note that Dreamweaver MX could detect the dimensions of a Flash movie but not the dimensions of QuickTime or Director content.

It's important that you know the dimensions of the file before you embed it into Dreamweaver MX, so you can insert the correct values into the Property Inspector. In this instance, the movie was 240 x 180, but we've added an extra 20 pixels to make room for the controller below the movie.

4. Press **F12** to preview the movie in your browser. **Note:** If you get a broken image icon, you might have to download the plug-in from **http://www.apple.com/quicktime**.

5. Return to Dreamweaver MX. Save and close the Dreamweaver file.

Phew; another chapter bites the dust. Good work! If you feel up to it, go ahead and move on to the next and final chapter.

20.

Getting It Online

| Setting Up a Tripod Account |
| Setting the FTP Preferences |
| Putting Files onto the Web Server |
| Getting Site Reports |

chap_20

Dreamweaver MX
H•O•T CD-ROM

It's one thing to design a Web page, and an entirely different thing to get what you've designed online so that everyone can see. One of the features we felt was missing from other books was concrete instructions covering how to access, upload, and update files to a Web server. Until now, you were forced to struggle through this process on your own, which could prove frustrating. Fortunately, this chapter walks you through the process of uploading your pages to a real live Web server. This means that you, your colleagues, your family, and your friends will be able to see the results of whatever you publish on the Web.

This chapter shows you how to create a free Web hosting account with Tripod and then use Dreamweaver MX to upload a Web site so that it can be viewed live on the Internet. You do not have to sign up for the Tripod account unless you want to follow along with the exercises. If you already have a Web hosting account, you can learn to use it by reading this chapter as well. Either way, this chapter shows you how to set up your FTP preferences and upload your site to a Web server using Dreamweaver MX.

Free Web Hosting with Tripod

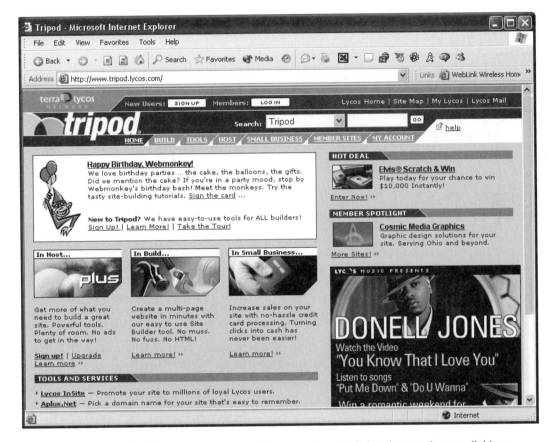

Tripod—http://www.tripod.lycos.com—is one of the many free Web hosting services available on the Internet.

Tripod is one of many Web services to offer free Web hosting to anyone who wants to sign up. Within just a few minutes, you can have a place to upload your files to on the Web.

You will be pleasantly surprised by how much you get for free. The Tripod free Web hosting package includes a lot of extras. All you need to complete the exercises in this chapter are the 20MB of free disk space and FTP access that are provided with the free Web hosting account.

If you already have a hosting service of your own, feel free to work with your own settings in the exercises, rather than those described for Tripod. For the FTP settings, just substitute your own settings instead of Tripod's. You can acquire your FTP settings by asking your own hosting service or the Web administrator for your company.

I. ——————————Signing Up with Tripod

The first step in getting your free Tripod Web site online involves filling out a form on their site. This exercise shows you what parts of the form need to be completed. If you plan to use your own Web server instead of Tripod's, you can skip this exercise.

1. Launch your preferred Web browser and browse to the Tripod home page at **http://www.tripod.lycos.com**. Here you'll find a complete rundown on their services.

2. Click on the **Sign Up** button at the top of the page. This takes you to another Web page where you can create your own Tripod account.

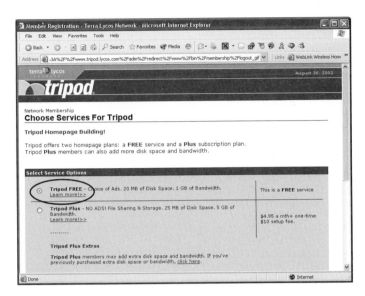

3. Make sure the **Tripod FREE** radio button is selected. This option lets you create a free Web hosting account with Tripod. Scroll down to the bottom of the page and click **Continue**.

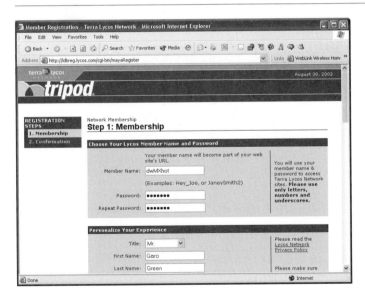

4. Complete all of the information requested on the form. Your **Member Name** will appear as part of your Tripod URL. For our ID, we used **dwMXhot**; therefore, when the account is set up, our URL will be: **http://www.tripod.lycos.com/dwmxhot/**. **Note:** Do not use dwMXhot as your ID; be sure to use your own unique ID.

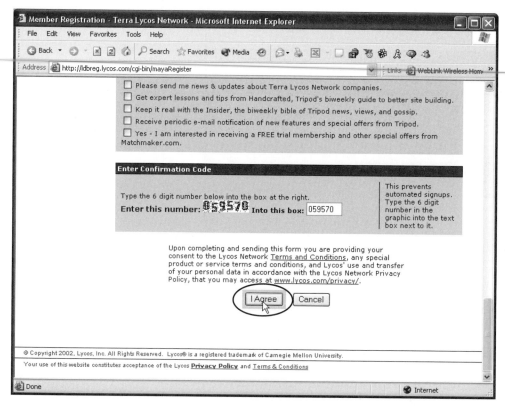

5. When you are finished entering your information, click the **I Agree** button at the bottom of the page. This submits your information for processing.

NOTE | Privacy Policies

Any time you provide personal information about yourself on a Web site, you should be familiar with the recipient's privacy policy. Some sites gather personal information and then sell it to marketing companies. This can result in some extra and unsolicited emails in your inbox. If this is of serious concern to you, make sure you review Tripod's privacy policy before you provide them with information. You can review their privacy policy at **http://www.lycos.com/privacy/**.

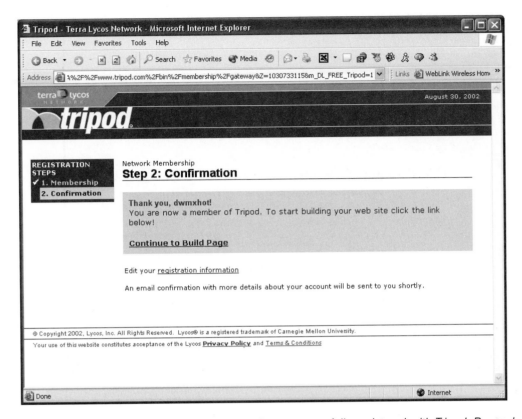

This is what your page should like when you have successfully registered with Tripod. Remember, you are supposed to use your own ID, so your screen won't display "Thank you, dwmxhot!"; instead it will display whatever ID you selected.

6. The next page confirms that your account has been set up properly. Click the **Continue to Build Page** link to learn about some of the resources available for creating your Web page.

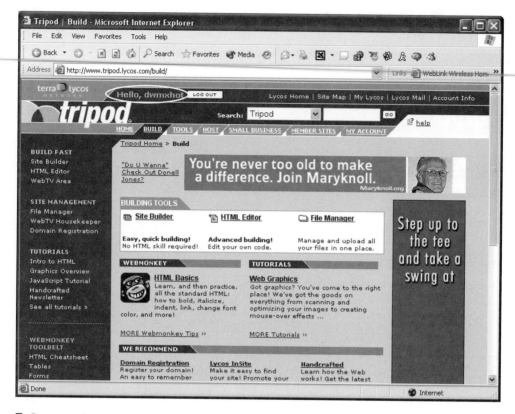

7. Once you have set up this Tripod account, you will be ready to set up your FTP preferences in Dreamweaver MX and begin uploading your site. Quit the browser; you will come back to it later after you have uploaded your site from Dreamweaver MX.

2. —————————**Setting the FTP Preferences**

In order for your site to be seen on the World Wide Web, your files need to be uploaded to a live Web server. Most Web developers and designers build pages on their hard drives (as you have done in this book) before transferring their files to a live Web server. In Dreamweaver MX terminology, the files on your hard drive are referred to as **local** files, and the files on a live Web server are referred to as **remote** files. You can upload your files from Dreamweaver MX by using the **Site Definitions** FTP settings.

In order to complete this exercise, you need to know the member name and password you selected when you created your Tripod account, or have the information handy from your own account. If you forgot that information or have not signed up for a Tripod account yet, you need to go to **http://www.tripod.lycos.com** and complete Exercise 1 before completing this exercise.

> **1.** Copy **chap_20** to your hard drive. Define your site for Chapter 20, using the **chap_20** folder as the local root folder. If you need a refresher on this process, visit Exercise 1 in Chapter 3, "*Site Control*."

> **2.** Select **Site > Edit Sites**. In the dialog box, choose **Chapter 20** and click **Edit**.

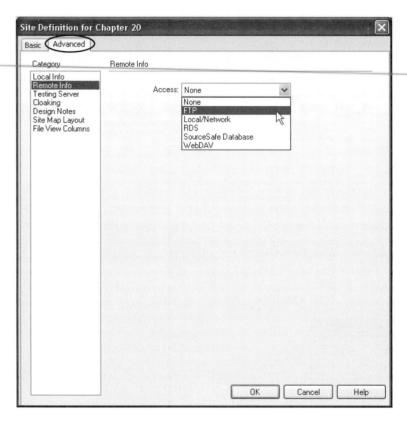

3. Make sure the **Advanced** tab is selected. Click on **Remote Info** in the **Category** list, and then choose **FTP** from the **Access** pop-up menu. This will give you access to the various FTP settings you will need to modify before you upload files to your site.

FTP Information for Tripod	
(Note: This information will be different if you have another account.)	
FTP Host	ftp.tripod.com
Host Directory	(Leave this blank)
Login	(Your Tripod ID)
Password	(Your password)

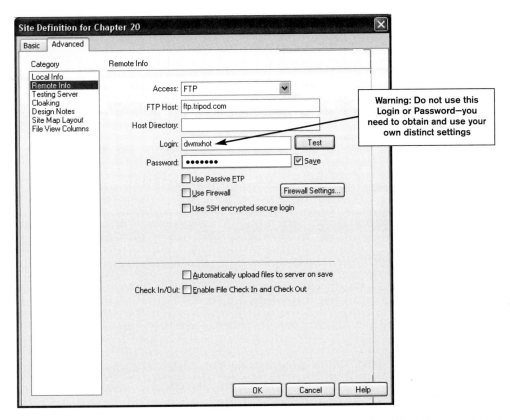

If you signed up for the free Tripod account, your FTP information should be similar to the information shown above, except that you would enter your own ID, not the one shown here. However, if you are using your own Web hosting service, you would enter that information instead.

4. Enter the information for the **Remote Info** options, as shown above.

5. Click **OK**. This returns you to the **Define Sites** dialog box. Click **Done**.

What Is FTP?

FTP stands for **F**ile **T**ransfer **P**rotocol. This term is usually associated with the process of uploading Web files to a live Web server. You will hear this term used as a noun ("I used an FTP program to upload my files") and as a verb ("I am going to FTP all of my files now!").

It is important to note that you do not have to use Dreamweaver MX to exchange files with the remote server. You can use other FTP applications as well, such as Fetch (Mac) or WS_FTP (Windows). There are advantages to using Dreamweaver MX over these applications, however, such as file synchronization and site management. You'll learn about these advantages shortly.

Here is a handy chart that describes the FTP settings in Dreamweaver MX.

FTP Settings in Dreamweaver MX	
Setting	**Description**
FTP Host	This will typically be an address similar to the URL of your Web site. In some cases, it may begin with the prefix "FTP".
Host Directory	If you have a specific directory on the server where you are supposed to place your files, you would enter it here. This option is not always used.
Login	You will be given a user name or ID to use to access the remote server. It is important that you enter this information exactly as it is given to you; otherwise you will have problems connecting.
Password	In addition to a user name or ID, you will also be given a password to use when accessing the remote server. If you don't want to enter the password every time you connect to the remote server, select the **Save** checkbox, and then Dreamweaver MX will remember your password! **Note:** The password you enter here is just stored in a text file on your hard drive, so anyone can read it. Don't check the Save checkbox if security is a concern at your location.
Use Passive FTP	The Passive FTP option enables your local software to set up the FTP connection rather than the remote server. Leave this option unchecked unless directed by your system administrator
Use Firewall	Check this box if you are connecting to the FTP server from behind a firewall.
Use SSH encrypted secure login	(Windows only); Check this option if your FTP server requires that you log in using SSH authentication.

3. ————————Putting Files onto the Web Server

Now that you have set up your FTP preferences, you are ready to use Dreamweaver MX to connect to a Web server and upload your files. Once you have completed this exercise, you will be able to see your Web site live on the Internet. Woo-hoo!

1. Before you try to upload your files to the Web server, make sure you have established a connection to the Internet. You should be able to browse the Web and look at other sites as a test to see that your Web connection is working.

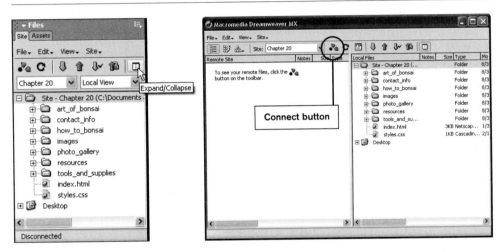

The Windows Site panel collapsed.

The Windows Site panel expanded.

2. Make sure your **Site** panel is open; if it is not, press **F8**. Notice that the **Connect** button, at the top of the panel, is no longer dimmed. Once you enter your FTP preferences, you will have access to the Connect feature.

• **Windows users only:** Click the **Expand/Collapse** button in the **Site** panel to expand the Site panel so you can see both the local files and remote site at the same time. Macintosh users won't have to do this because their Site panel is already displaying both Local Files and Remote Site views.

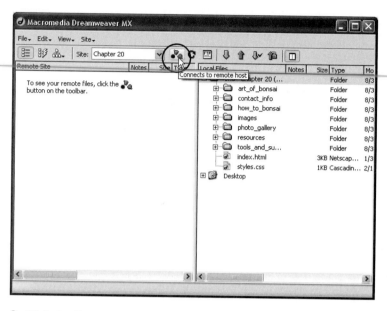

3. Click the **Connect** button. This will connect Dreamweaver MX to your Web server. If you have not established a connection to the Internet with your modem or network, you will get an error message.

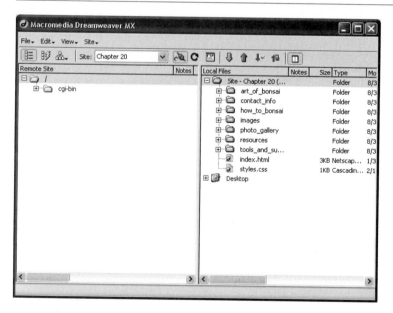

After making a successful connection to the Web server, the contents of the Web server are displayed in the left side of the window.

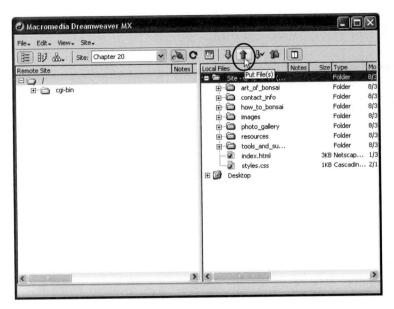

4. With the local root folder selected, you are ready to upload your site. Click the **Put Files** button. **Note:** If you wanted to upload a single file; you wouldn't select the local root folder, instead you would select the particular file and then click the **Put Files** button.

5. You are asked whether you want to upload your entire Web site. Because this is the first time you are uploading your site, click **OK**.

NOTE | The Difference Between Getting and Putting

There are two different ways to transfer files between the local site and the remote site (the Web server). The Get command copies the selected files from the remote site to your local site. This process is referred to as **downloading**. In addition, if you are using the Check In and Check Out options, the Get command copies the file to the local site as a read-only file, leaving the original on the Web server for others to download. The Put command copies the selected files from the local site to the remote site. This process is referred to as **uploading**.

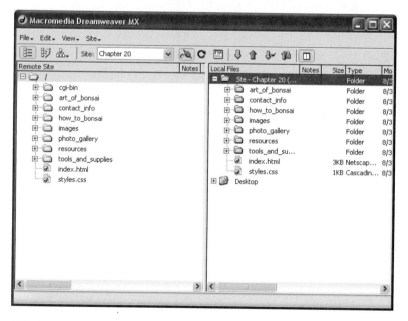

This is what the Site panel should look like after the Web site has been uploaded. Note: If an error occurs during the transfer process, Dreamweaver MX maintains a log of FTP errors that you can review to help troubleshoot the problem. You can access this log by selecting Window > Results > FTP Log (Windows) or Site > FTP Log (Mac).

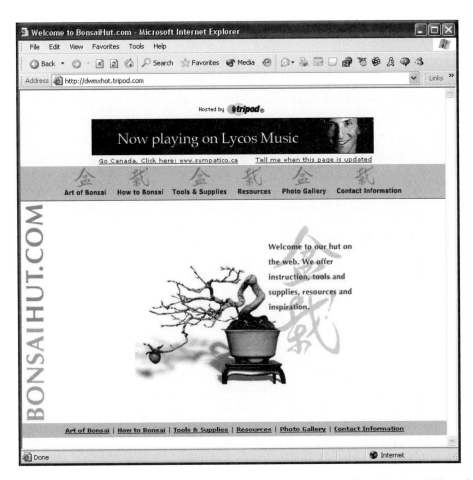

6. Open a browser. Because we are using Garo's account, the URL will be **http://dwmxhot.tripod.com**. Of course, your URL will be different. Just replace **dwmxhot** with your own Tripod ID and voila—your Web site is live on the Web! Congratulations! Make sure you show all your friends. ;-)

4. ——————Getting Site Reports

As your sites get larger, you will find it increasingly difficult to manage all of the files. Trying to locate files with missing **<alt>** tags, untitled documents, redundant nested tags, etc. can prove to be a very time-consuming task. Dreamweaver MX has a feature that lets you identify and locate files that meet specific criteria. This feature can save you time hunting for the files manually, and will make sure your files are in good shape.

This exercise has you run a report on a finished site and fix some of the problems identified in the report.

1. Select **Site > Reports**. This opens the Reports dialog box, where you can specify the type of report you would like to generate.

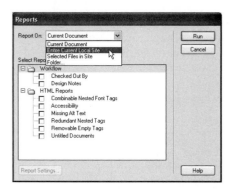

2. From the **Report On** drop-down menu, select **Entire Current Local Site**. This ensures that all of the files within the local root folder are processed.

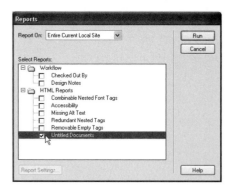

3. Click the **Untitled Documents** checkbox. This option causes all of the page titles of the documents within your site to be examined to make sure each has a unique name. This is a good thing because some search engines use the page title as part of their listings.

4. Click **Run**. Dreamweaver will begin to scan all of the files in your site, looking for ones that have **Untitled Document** as their page title.

When Dreamweaver MX is finished scanning your site, it will produce a Results dialog box that displays the files that meet the criteria you specified. In this case, you are looking for files that have Untitled Document as their page title.

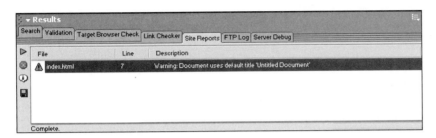

5. Double-click **index.html** to open that file so you can correct the problem. It's really nice that you can open the files directly from this dialog box.

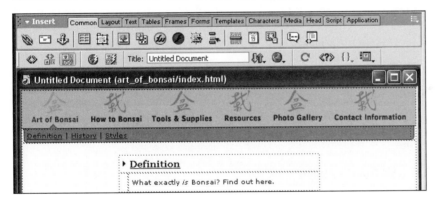

6. Notice that the **Title** option is set to **Untitled Document**. Change the **Title** option to **Welcome to Bonsaihut.com**.

7. Save and **close** this file.

The Reports Dialog Box

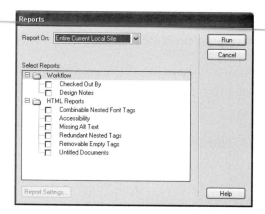

The Reports dialog box has several features that offer you a wide range of options and flexibility. The table below outlines these options and offers a brief description of each.

Reports Dialog Box Options	
Option	Description
Report On	
Current Document	Checks only the active document.
Entire Local Site	Checks every file within the local root folder.
Selected Files in Site	Checks only the files that are selected within the Site window. You must have the files selected before choosing this option.
Folder	Checks a specific folder. When you choose this option, you can browse to the specific folder you want to process.
Workflow	
Checked Out By	Identifies files that have been checked out by a specific user. When this option is selected, you can specify the name by clicking on the Report Settings button.
Design Notes	Searches all of the Design Notes in your documents. The Report Settings button will give you access to specific search criteria.

continues on next page

Reports Dialog Box Options *continued*	
Option	**Description**
HTML Reports	
Combinable Nested Font Tags	Combines all possible nested font tags. For example, **`<font color="#CC3366"><font size="1">Hello</font></font>`** would be reported.
Accessibility	Analyzes the Web pages against the Section 508 Guidelines to determine if your pages meet these accessibility requirements. This is a very useful feature and can even help you make existing Web pages accessible. This feature is covered in detail in Chapter 19, "*Accessibility*."
Missing ALT Text	Identifies all images that do not have an **`<alt>`** tag applied to them. This is good option to run to make sure your site has good accessibility.
Redundant Nested Tags	Reports nested tags that can be cleaned up. For example, **`Welcome to Bonsaihut.com <i> is</i> a great place to learn about bonsai</i>`** would be reported. This option helps clean up your HTML.
Removable Empty Tags	Removes any empty tags, which can help clean up your HTML. This is another option that will help clean up unnecessary HTML code.
Untitled Documents	Searches the document to see if it has a page tile of Untitled Document. It's always best to give your documents page titles that reflect their content.

Congratulations! You certainly deserve it! You've made it through all the chapters!! We hope that this book helped you get up to speed with Dreamweaver MX quickly, and that you now feel ready to use your skills to create just about any Web site project. We wish you the best of luck with all of your future projects. Rock on!

A.

Troubleshooting FAQ
and Technical Support

| Appendix A |

H•O•T

Dreamweaver MX

If you run into any problems while following the exercises in this book, this F.A.Q. is intended to help. This document will be maintained and expanded upon at this book's companion Web site: **http://www.lynda.com/ products/books/dwmxhot**.

Macromedia Technical Support

http://www.macromedia.com/support/

415.252.9080

If you are having problems with Dreamweaver, please contact Macromedia Technical Support at the number listed above. Macromedia staff will be able to help you with such typical problems as: the trial version has expired on your computer; your computer crashes when you try to launch the application; etc. Please note that lynda.com cannot help troubleshoot technical problems with Dreamweaver.

Peachpit Press

customer_service@peachpit.com

If your book has a defective CD-ROM, please contact the customer service department at the above email address. We do not have extra CDs at lynda.com, so they must be requested directly from the publisher.

lynda.com

http://www.lynda.com/products/books/dmx4hot/

dwmxfaq@lynda.com

We have created a companion Web site for this book, which can be found at **http://www.lynda.com/books/dwmxhot/**. Any errors in the book will be posted to the Web site, and it's always a good idea to check there for up-to-date information. We encourage and welcome your comments and error reports to dwmxfaq@lynda.com. Both Garo and Abigail receive each of these emails.

If you don't find what you're looking for here or there, please send an email to dwmxfaq@lynda.com.

Frequently Asked Questions

Q: How do I call up the Property Inspector?

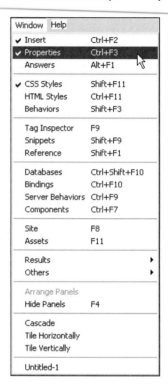

A: If you can't see the Property Inspector or, for that matter, any of Dreamweaver's panels, pull down the **Window** menu and click on the one you want to open. A list of shortcut keys that will help you quickly access all of Dreamweaver's panels can be found at the end of Chapter 2, "*Interface.*"

Q: I defined my site for a chapter, but files that are listed in the exercises aren't there. What happened?

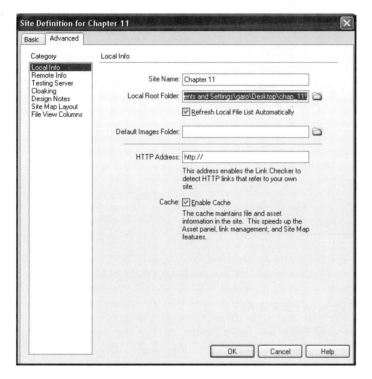

A: This could be because when you were defining the site you specified a folder that was inside the chapter folder, instead of the chapter folder itself. Go ahead and redefine the site. (If you need to revisit these steps, visit Exercise 1 in Chapter 3, "*Site Control*"). **Note:** Selecting the correct folder is done differently on Mac and Windows, as shown below.

- **Mac:** When you're browsing to define the chapter folder and the **Choose Local Folder** dialog box pops up, notice how there's both an **Open** and a **Choose** option. Highlight the chapter folder, and click **Choose**. Don't click **Open**, because you would then define your site as an interior folder, instead of the main folder. This is opposite to the way Windows users define their sites.

- **Windows:** When you're browsing to define the chapter folder and the **Choose Local Folder** dialog box pops up, select the chapter folder. First click **Open**. After the folder is opened, click **Select**. This is opposite to the way Macintosh users define their sites.

Q: Where's the Color panel?

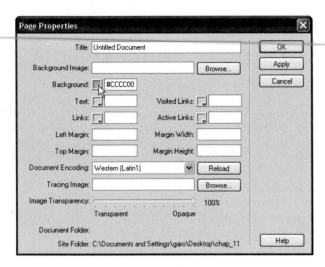

A: Because it's context-sensitive, the Color panel appears only when you click in one of Dreamweaver's color wells. Color wells appear inside the Property Inspector and the **Page Properties** dialog box.

Q: I put one layer on top of another! How do I delete it?

A: To delete a layer, select it by the handle at its top and press **Delete**. You can also use the Layers panel to select the layer, which might be easier in some cases where they overlap. Of course, there's always the universal undo command, **Cmd+Z** (Mac) or **Ctrl+Z** (Windows).

Q: When I convert layers to tables, I get an error message stating that one of the layers is off-screen. How did this happen, and how do I fix it?

A: It is possible to create a layer and move it, using the arrow keys, so that it is partially or fully off-screen. This is actually handy for images that you want to have bleed off the edge, or animations that begin outside the document window. When converting layers to tables, however, it won't work! If you can locate the offending layer, click on its edge and use the arrow keys to move it back into the screen area. If you can't find the layer, try opening the **Layers** window (**Window > Layers**) and selecting each layer name that appears inside the window. Eventually, you'll be able to figure out which layer is on or off the screen by process of elimination.

Q: I just specified a Tracing Image in my Page Properties window, but I can't see it when I pre-view the page in my browser. Panic is starting to set in!

A: The **Tracing Image** is a template to be used for layout in Dreamweaver. It is invisible in the browser window, so if you don't see it, that's the whole point! It's there for your reference only, and your end users will never see it.

Q: Why do I get the message, "To make a document-relative path, your document should be saved first"? I can't figure out what this gibberish means!

A: Hey, we're with you. It would be nice if the dialog box simply stated, "Save your file now, or Dreamweaver can't keep track of your files," because that's all it's asking you to do. Sigh. If only developers knew how to speak in nontechnical terms at times, eh? All you need to do is click **OK** and save your file (inside the defined site), and Dreamweaver won't bark any more.

Q: Why do I get the message that my file is located outside of the root folder?

A: Dreamweaver is asking you to move the file into the root folder that you've defined as your site. If you work with files outside your defined root folder, Dreamweaver cannot keep track of your links or manage your site, which is counterproductive to the way the program is structured and to your work-flow. Though this message is annoying, it is actually helping you maintain a healthy site without experiencing broken links and problems uploading your files when you publish it. **Note:** There are different ways to handle this message, depending on the system you are running.

- **Macintosh:** You should click **Yes**, and then browse to the correct folder. At that point you will be prompted to save, which you should do.

- **Windows:** You should click **Yes**, and Dreamweaver will automatically pop you into the correct folder. Click save, and the file will be moved.

Q: Why aren't my templates working?

A: If you leave a template file open and work on another site (such as another chapter in this book that you've defined as a different site), Dreamweaver can't keep track of your templates. It's best to work on a single site at a time, and not flip between sites while leaving files open from another defined site. This is true with all Dreamweaver documents, although templates and libraries are particularly sensitive to site-definition confusion.

Q: When I try to locate class files, why can't I see the file extensions at the end of file names, such as *.gif*, *.jpg*, and *.html*?

A: On Windows, you will need to change your Preferences to view file name extensions. Instructions to do this are inside the "*Introduction*."

B.

Online Resources

| Appendix B |

H•O•T
_____
Dreamweaver MX

The Web is full of great resources for Dreamweaver users. You have ample choices among a variety of newsgroups, listservs, and third-party Web sites that can really help you get the most out of the new skills you've developed by following the exercises in this book. This appendix lists some of the best resources for learning and extending Dreamweaver MX.

Discussion Groups

Macromedia has set up several discussion boards (newsgroups) for Dreamweaver. This is a great place to ask questions and get help from thousands of Dreamweaver users. The newsgroup is composed of beginning to advanced users, so you should have no problem finding the type of help you need, regardless of your experience with the program. In order to access these newsgroups, you will need a newsgroup reader, such as Microsoft Outlook or Free Agent.

Dreamweaver
`news://forums.macromedia.com/macromedia.dreamweaver`

Course Builder for Dreamweaver
`news://forums.macromedia.com/macromedia.dreamweaver.coursebuilder`

Dynamic HTML
`news://forums.macromedia.com/macromedia.dynamic.html`

Listservs

A listserv is different from a newsgroup, and offers another way people can ask questions and get help with Dreamweaver. Questions and answers are exchanged through the email application of your choice. Blueworld, the developers of Lasso for Dreamweaver, for example, maintains an active and very useful listserv for Dreamweaver.

Blueworld Listserv:
`http://www.blueworld.com/blueworld/lists/dreamweaver.html`

A Few Third-Party Dreamweaver Web Sites

Massimo's Corner

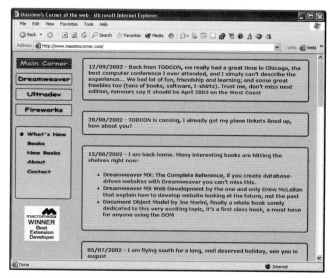

http://www.massimocorner.com/

Yaromat

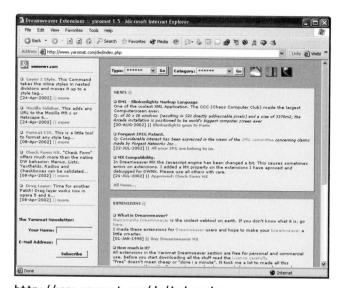

http://www.yaromat.com/dw/index.php

Project VII

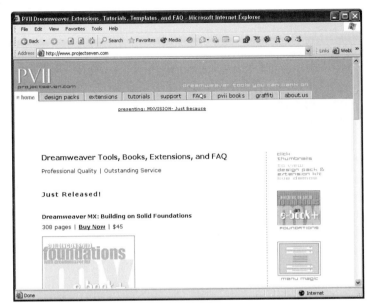

http://www.projectseven.com

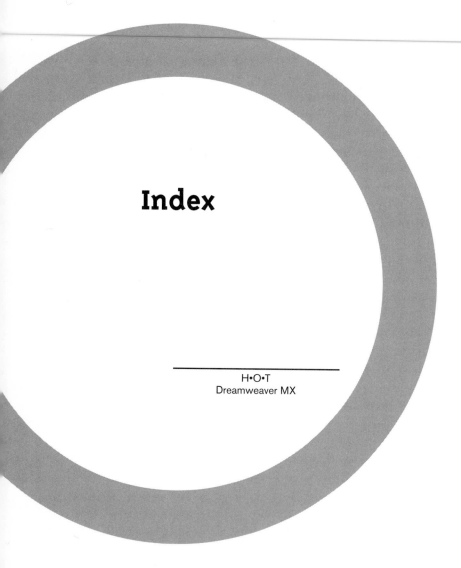

Index

H•O•T
Dreamweaver MX

Merge Cells button/command, 216, 217
META tags, 119–121
    entering, 119–120
    purpose of, 7, 119
    resources, 121
Microsoft
    FrontPage, 3
    Internet Explorer (*See* Internet Explorer)
    Outlook, 653
    Word, 434–437
Middle alignment, 178
.midi/.mid extension, 617
.mno extension, 508, 523
monitors, xxix
.mov extension, 9
movies
    on H•O•T CD-ROM (*See* movies folder)
    QuickTime, 9, 625
movies folder
    custom-classes movie, 391
    external-CSS movie, 409
    external-style-sheets movie, 391
    frames-settings movie, 320
    layers movie, 272
    Layout-view movie, 297
    named-anchor movie, 147
    saving-frames movie, 303
.MP3 extension, 617
MPEG-1 Audio Layer-3, 617
multiple-event rollovers, 352–359
Musical Instrument Digital Interface, 617
.mxp extension, 500

N

Named Anchor dialog box, 145, 146, 150
Named Anchor icon, 145
named anchors
    components of, 144
    creating, 144–150
    keyboard shortcut for, 147
    movie on, 147
    purpose of, 144, 149
    renaming, 145
Namespace, XHTML, 11

naming
    files, xxi, 8, 97–98
    folders, 62
    frames, 312–313, 325, 601
    HTML styles, 188
    Library items, 564
    named anchors, 145
    panel groups, 39
    rollover images, 370, 373
    targets, 315
    templates, 564
    Text Field objects, 444
    Web sites, 53, 84, 90
navigation bars
    adding elements to, 374
    adding pop-up menu to, 534–539
    creating
        with image maps, 151–153
        with layout cells/tables, 284–297
        with Library items, 582–583
        with reassembled images, 236–238
    naming elements in, 370, 373
    setting rollover states for, 368–375
navigation icons, 116
NCDesign, 5
nested files, 68
nested tables, 229, 240, 244–250
nested tags, 433, 645
Netscape Navigator. *See also* Web browser
    and CSS, 377
    detecting installed version of, 469
    email settings, 143
    font considerations, 384
    and H•O•T CD-ROM, xxix
    installing, 469
    and sound files, 615–616
    trial version, xxix
Netscape Plug-In Registry, 620
New CSS Style dialog box, 383, 388, 393, 398, 402, 404
New Document dialog box, 94–96
New Editable Region dialog box, 569
New File command, 85
New Folder command, 62
New Site command, 83, 89
New Style icon, 188

Notes

CD-ROM LICENSE AGREEMENT

THIS SOFTWARE LICENSE AGREEMENT CONSTITUTES AN AGREEMENT BETWEEN YOU AND, LYNDA.COM, LLC. . YOU SHOULD CAREFULLY READ THE FOLLOWING TERMS AND CONDITIONS BEFORE OPENING THIS ENVELOPE. COPYING THIS SOFTWARE TO YOUR MACHINE, BREAKING THE SEAL, OR OTHERWISE RE-MOVING OR USING THE SOFTWARE INDICATES YOUR ACCEPTANCE OF THESE TERMS AND CONDITIONS. IF YOU DO NOT AGREE TO BE BOUND BY THE PROVISIONS OF THIS LICENSE AGREEMENT, YOU SHOULD PROMPTLY DELETE THE SOFTWARE FROM YOUR MACHINE.

TERMS AND CONDITIONS:

1. GRANT OF LICENSE. In consideration of payment of the License Fee, which was a part of the price you paid for this product, LICENSOR grants to you (the "Licensee") a non-exclusive right to use and display this copy of a Software program, along with any updates or upgrade releases of the Software for which you have paid (all parts and elements of the Software as well as the Software as a whole are hereinafter referred to as the "Software") on a single computer only (i.e., with a single CPU) at a single location, all as more particularly set forth and limited below. LICENSOR reserves all rights not expressly granted to you as Licensee in this License Agreement.

2. OWNERSHIP OF SOFTWARE. The license granted herein is not a sale of the original Software or of any copy of the Software. As Licensee, you own only the rights to use the Software as described herein and the magnetic or other physical media on which the Software is originally or subsequently recorded or fixed. LICENSOR retains title and ownership of the Software recorded on the original disk(s), as well as title and ownership of any subsequent copies of the Software irrespective of the form of media on or in which the Software is recorded or fixed. This license does not grant you any intellectual or other proprietary or other rights of any nature what-soever in the Software.

3. USE RESTRICTIONS. As Licensee, you may use the Software only as expressly authorized in this License Agreement under the terms of paragraph 4. You may phy-sically transfer the Software from one computer to another provided that the Software is used on only a single computer at any one time. You may not: (i) electronically transfer the Software from one computer to another over a network; (ii) make the Software available through a time-sharing service, network of computers, or other multiple user arrangement; (iii) distribute copies of the Software or related written materials to any third party, whether for sale or otherwise; (iv) modify, adapt, translate, reverse engineer, decompile, disassemble, or prepare any derivative work based on the Software or any element thereof; (v) make or distribute, whether for sale or otherwise, any hard copy or printed version of any of the Software nor any portion thereof nor any work of yours containing the Software or any component thereof; (vi) use any of the Software nor any of its components in any other work.

8. THIS IS WHAT YOU CAN AND CANNOT DO WITH THE SOFTWARE. Even though in the preceding paragraph and elsewhere LICENSOR has restricted your use of the Software, the following is the only thing you can do with the Software and the various elements of the Software:DUCKS IN A ROW ARTWORK: THE ARTWORK CONTAINED ON THIS CD-ROM MAY NOT BE USED IN ANY MANNER WHATSOEVER OTHER THAN TO VIEW THE SAME ON YOUR COMPUTER, OR POST TO YOUR PERSONAL, NON-COMMER-CIAL WEB SITE FOR EDUCATIONAL PURPOSES ONLY. THIS MATERIAL IS SUBJECT TO ALL OF THE RESTRICTION PROVISIONS OF THIS SOFTWARE LICENSE. SPECIFI-CALLY BUT NOT IN LIMITATION OF THESE RESTRICTIONS, YOU MAY NOT DISTRIB-UTE, RESELL OR TRANSFER THIS PART OF THE SOFTWARE DESIGNATED AS "CLUTS" NOR ANY OF YOUR DESIGN OR OTHER WORK CONTAINING ANY OF THE SOFTWARE DESIGNATED AS "DUCKS IN A ROW ARTWORK" NOR ANY OF YOUR DESIGN OR OTHER WORK CONTAINING ANY SUCH "DUCKS IN A ROW ARTWORK," ALL AS MORE PARTICULARLY RESTRICTED IN THE WITHIN SOFTWARE LICENSE.

5. COPY RESTRICTIONS. The Software and accompanying written materials are protected under United States copyright laws. Unauthorized copying and/or distribution of the Software and/or the related written materials is expressly forbidden. You may be held legally responsible for any copyright infringement that is caused, directly or indirectly, by your failure to abide by the terms of this License Agreement. Subject to the terms of this License Agreement and if the software is not otherwise copy protected, you may make one copy of the Software for backup purposes only. The copyright notice and any other proprietary notices which were included in the original Software must be reproduced and included on any such backup copy.

6. TRANSFER RESTRICTIONS. The license herein granted is personal to you, the Licensee. You may not transfer the Software nor any of its components or elements to anyone else, nor may you sell, lease, loan, sublicense, assign, or otherwise dispose of the Software nor any of its components or elements without the express written consent of LICENSOR, which consent may be granted or withheld at LICENSOR's sole discretion.

7. TERMINATION. The license herein granted hereby will remain in effect until terminated. This license will terminate automatically without further notice from LICENSOR in the event of the violation of any of the provisions hereof. As Licensee, you agree that upon such termination you will promptly destroy any and all copies of the Software which remain in your possession and, upon request, will certify to such destruction in writing to LICENSOR.

8. LIMITATION AND DISCLAIMER OF WARRANTIES. a) THE SOFTWARE AND RELATED WRITTEN MATERIALS, INCLUDING ANY INSTRUCTIONS FOR USE, ARE PROVIDED ON AN "AS IS" BASIS, WITHOUT WARRANTY OF ANY KIND, EXPRESS OR IMPLIED. THIS DISCLAIMER OF WARRANTY EXPRESSLY IN-CLUDES, BUT IS NOT LIMITED TO, ANY IMPLIED WARRANTIES OF MERCHANTABILITY AND/OR OF FIT-NESS FOR A PARTICULAR PURPOSE. NO WARRANTY OF ANY KIND IS MADE AS TO WHETHER OR NOT THIS SOFT-WARE INFRINGES UPON ANY RIGHTS OF ANY OTHER THIRD PARTIES. NO ORAL OR WRITTEN INFORMATION GIVEN BY LICEN-SOR, ITS SUPPLIERS, DISTRIBUTORS, DEALERS, EMPLOYEES, OR AGENTS, SHALL CREATE OR OTHERWISE ENLARGE THE SCOPE OF ANY WARRANTY HEREUNDER. LICENSEE ASSUMES THE ENTIRE RISK AS TO THE QUALITY AND THE PERFOR-

MANCE OF SUCH SOFTWARE. SHOULD THE SOFTWARE PROVE DEFECTIVE, YOU, AS LICENSEE (AND NOT LICENSOR, ITS SUPPLIERS, DISTRIBU-TORS, DEALERS OR AGENTS), ASSUME THE ENTIRE COST OF ALL NECESSARY CORRECTION, SERVIC-ING, OR REPAIR. b) LICENSOR warrants the disk(s) on which this copy of the Software is recorded or fixed to be free from defects in materials and workmanship, under normal use and service, for a period of ninety (90) days from the date of delivery as evidenced by a copy of the applicable receipt. LICENSOR hereby limits the duration of any implied warranties with respect to the disk(s) to the duration of the express warranty. This limited warranty shall not apply if the disk(s) have been damaged by unreasonable use, accident, negligence, or by any other causes unrelated to defective materials or workmanship. c) LICENSOR does not war-rant that the functions contained in the Software will be uninterrupted or error free and Licensee is encouraged to test the Software for Licensee's intended use prior to placing any reliance thereon. All risk of the use of the Software will be on you, as Licensee. d) THE LIM-ITED WARRANTY SET FORTH ABOVE GIVES YOU SPECIFIC LEGAL RIGHTS AND YOU MAY ALSO HAVE OTHER RIGHTS WHICH VARY FROM STATE TO STATE. SOME STATES DO NOT ALLOW THE LIMITATION OR EXCLUSION OF IMPLIED WARRANTIES OR OF INCIDENTAL OR CONSEQUENTIAL DAMAGES, SO THE LIMITATIONS AND EXCLUSIONS CONCERNING THE SOFTWARE AND RELATED WRITTEN MATERIALS SET FORTH ABOVE MAY NOT APPLY TO YOU.

9. LIMITATION OF REMEDIES. LICENSOR's entire liability and Licensee's exclusive remedy shall be the replacement of any disk(s) not meeting the limited warranty set forth in Section 8 above which is returned to LICENSOR with a copy of the applic-able receipt within the warranty period. Any replacement disk(s)will be warranted for the remainder of the original warranty period or thirty (30) days, whichever is longer.

10. LIMITATION OF LIABILITY. IN NO EVENT WILL LICENSOR, OR ANYONE ELSE INVOLVED IN THE CREATION, PRODUCTION, AND/OR DELIVERY OF THIS SOFTWARE PRODUCT BE LIABLE TO LICENSEE OR ANY OTHER PER-SON OR ENTITY FOR ANY DIRECT, INDIRECT, OR OTHER DAMAGES, INCLUDING, WITHOUT LIMITATION, ANY INTERRUPTION OF SERVICES, LOST PROFITS, LOST SAVINGS, LOSS OF DATA, OR ANY OTHER CONSEQUENTIAL, INCIDEN-TAL, SPECIAL, OR PUNITIVE DAMAGES, ARISING OUT OF THE PURCHASE, USE, INABILITY TO USE, OR OPERATION OF THE SOFTWARE, EVEN IF LICENSOR OR ANY AUTHORIZED LICENSOR DEALER HAS BEEN ADVISED OF THE POSSIBILITY OF SUCH DAMAGES. BY YOUR USE OF THE SOFTWARE, YOU ACKNOWLEDGE THAT THE LIMITATION OF LIABILITY SET FORTH IN THIS LICENSE WAS THE BASIS UPON WHICH THE SOFTWARE WAS OFFERED BY LICENSOR AND YOU ACKNOWLEDGE THAT THE PRICE OF THE SOFTWARE LICENSE WOULD BE HIGHER IN THE ABSENCE OF SUCH LIMITATION. SOME STATES DO NOT ALLOW THE LIMITATION OR EXCLUSION OF LIABILITY FOR INCIDENTAL OR CONSEQUENTIAL DAMAGES SO THE ABOVE LIMITATIONS AND EXCLUSIONS MAY NOT APPLY TO YOU.

11. UPDATES. LICENSOR, at its sole discretion, may periodically issue updates of the Software which you may receive upon request and payment of the applicable update fee in effect from time to time and in such event, all of the provisions of the within License Agreement shall apply to such updates.

12. EXPORT RESTRICTIONS. Licensee agrees not to export or re-export the Soft-ware and accompanying documentation (or any copies thereof) in violation of any applicable U.S. laws or regulations.

13. ENTIRE AGREEMENT. YOU, AS LICENSEE, ACKNOWLEDGE THAT: (i) YOU HAVE READ THIS ENTIRE AGREEMENT AND AGREE TO BE BOUND BY ITS TERMS AND CONDITIONS; (ii) THIS AGREEMENT IS THE COMPLETE AND EXCLUSIVE STATEMENT OF THE UNDERSTANDING BETWEEN THE PARTIES AND SUPERSEDES ANY AND ALL PRIOR ORAL OR WRITTEN COMMUNICATIONS RELATING TO THE SUBJECT MATTER HEREOF; AND (iii) THIS AGREEMENT MAY NOT BE MODIFIED, AMENDED, OR IN ANY WAY ALTERED EXCEPT BY A WRITING SIGNED BY BOTH YOURSELF AND AN OFFICER OR AUTHORIZED REPRESENTATIVE OF LICENSOR.

14. SEVERABILITY. In the event that any provision of this License Agreement is held to be illegal or otherwise unenforceable, such provision shall be deemed to have been deleted from this License Agreement while the remaining provisions of this License Agreement shall be unaffected and shall continue in full force and effect.

15. GOVERNING LAW. This License Agreement shall be governed by the laws of the State of California applicable to agreements wholly to be performed therein and of the United States of America, excluding that body of the law related to conflicts of law. This License Agreement shall not be governed by the United Nations Convention on Contracts for the International Sale of Goods, the application of which is expressly excluded. No waiver of any breach of the provisions of this License Agreement shall be deemed a waiver of any other breach of this License Agreement.

16. RESTRICTED RIGHTS LEGEND. Use, duplication, or disclosure by the Government is subject to restrictions as set forth in subparagraph (c)(1)(ii) of the Rights in Technical Data and Computer Software clause at 48 CFR § 252.227-7013 and DFARS § 252.227-7013 or subparagraphs (c) (1) and (c)(2) of the Commercial Computer Software-Restricted Rights at 48 CFR § 52.227.19, as applicable. Contractor/manufacturer: LICENSOR: LYNDA.COM, LLC, c/o PEACHPIT PRESS, 1249 Eighth Street, Berkeley, CA 94710.